NetSuite®
FOR
DUMMIES®

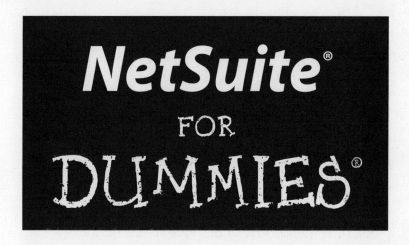

NetSuite® FOR DUMMIES®

by Julie Kelly, Luke Braud, and Malin Huffman

WILEY

Wiley Publishing, Inc.

NetSuite® For Dummies®

Published by
Wiley Publishing, Inc.
111 River Street
Hoboken, NJ 07030-5774

www.wiley.com

Copyright © 2011 by Wiley Publishing, Inc., Indianapolis, Indiana

Published by Wiley Publishing, Inc., Indianapolis, Indiana

Published simultaneously in Canada

For general information on our other products and services, please contact our Customer Care Department within the U.S. at 877-762-2974, outside the U.S. at 317-572-3993, or fax 317-572-4002.

For technical support, please visit www.wiley.com/techsupport.

Wiley also publishes its books in a variety of electronic formats. Some content that appears in print may not be available in electronic books.

Library of Congress Control Number: 2010937822

ISBN: 978-0-470-19107-1

Manufactured in the United States of America

10 9 8 7 6 5 4 3 2 1

WILEY

About the Authors

Julie Kelly worked as a technical writer with NetSuite writing help documentation for CRM, Shipping, and Web features for over five years. She now lives with her family in the Charlotte, NC, area and works as a consultant and technical support manager with Ncompass Solutions, a NetSuite Solution Provider. She would like to thank the NetSuite Technical Publications Team for their input, Valerie Steele for managing the project tirelessly, and her family for their endless patience.

Luke Braud has 12+ years of software-as-a-service experience and B.S. in Computer Science (Mathematics) from Santa Clara University. They have served him well in writing this book. Luke is currently focused on defining and building the most advanced SaaS application available on the Web. He holds multiple U.S. patents in SaaS delivery and has helped push the limits of browser technology using AJAX. In addition, Luke serves as an evangelist for excellence in user experience.

Malin Huffman has been creating software-as-a-service business applications for over nine years. As a product manager at NetSuite, he has represented the voice of the customer and helped define many of the features described in this book, particularly in the areas of accounting and reporting. Malin is passionate about both technology and music, and likes to spend his free time performing orchestral and choral repertoire. He holds a B.M. degree in Violin Performance.

Authors' Acknowledgments

This book could not have been written without the team effort of a number of wonderful people. We would like to thank Graham Walker for knocking on Wiley's door; Brian Taylor, who provided his expertise on customization; Chris Blum, for his superior knowledge of NetSuite security; and Sean Kennedy, for lending his understanding of projects and services. John Browne and Elham Ghassemzadeh offered their insight and input on SuiteFlex. Jason Flanagan, Cynthia Sloan, Kate Rodrigues, Tracy Adkins, and Sabina Letang from the NetSuite Technical Publications team contributed content and reviewed material. Deb Cameron, Dan Woods, and their team at Evolved Media helped us finish up and round out the content when the going got tough. Valerie Steele pushed this project through to completion, and Evan Goldberg's sponsorship and thorough review of this book was an invaluable asset. Finally, we would like to thank our NetSuite customers, who clamored for this book and provided the spark that made it happen.

—J.K.
—L.B.
—M.H.

Publisher's Acknowledgments

We're proud of this book; please send us your comments at http://dummies.custhelp.com. For other comments, please contact our Customer Care Department within the U.S. at 877-762-2974, outside the U.S. at 317-572-3993, or fax 317-572-4002.

Some of the people who helped bring this book to market include the following:

Acquisitions, Editorial, and Media Development

Project Editor: Tonya Maddox Cupp

Acquisitions Editor: Katie Feltman

Editorial Manager: Jodi Jensen

Media Development Project Manager: Laura Moss-Hollister

Media Development Assistant Project Manager: Jenny Swisher

Media Development Associate Producers: Josh Frank, Marilyn Hummel, Douglas Kuhn, and Shawn Patrick

Editorial Assistant: Amanda Graham

Sr. Editorial Assistant: Cherie Case

Cartoons: Rich Tennant (www.the5thwave.com)

Composition Services

Project Coordinator: Katie Crocker

Layout and Graphics: Carl Byers, Joyce Haughey, Christin Swinford

Proofreader: Toni Settle

Indexer: Potomac Indexing, LLC

Publishing and Editorial for Technology Dummies

    Richard Swadley, Vice President and Executive Group Publisher

    Andy Cummings, Vice President and Publisher

    Mary Bednarek, Executive Acquisitions Director

    Mary C. Corder, Editorial Director

Publishing for Consumer Dummies

    Diane Graves Steele, Vice President and Publisher

Composition Services

    Debbie Stailey, Director of Composition Services

Contents at a Glance

Table of Contents

Introduction

This book provides a friendly introduction to NetSuite. If you've picked up this book, chances are you already know something about the product, but here's a quick summary: NetSuite is the number one, Web-based business software suite available as of early 2010. NetSuite offers an integrated application that wraps all the essential information technology needs — ERP, CRM, HR, customer service, ecommerce, warehouse and inventory management, and project management — into one tidy application.

Why should you consider NetSuite? Chances are you're drawn to some of the benefits commonly enjoyed by NetSuite customers:

- Reduced IT costs
- End-to-end integration of information systems into one comprehensive platform
- Ability to redeploy budgets and personnel to more strategic parts of the business
- Flexibility to add new business partners and divisions anywhere in the world and allow employees to work remotely
- Real-time operational intelligence, easily personalized to individual users who can customize their own pages and reports with minimal training and without IT staff
- The expertise of a vendor who takes care of upgrades and maintenance and can provide iron-clad security to protect essential customer and business data

NetSuite is part of the larger trend of Software as a Service (SaaS). In the SaaS model, users no longer have to buy on-premise software like ERP packages. Nor do they have to host their own servers in those all-too-familiar air-conditioned, glassed-in computer rooms. Instead, they can simply purchase a subscription to a software service and access it online. They don't have to maintain their own server rooms, pay huge up-front infrastructure costs, or worry about upgrades. A SaaS customer only needs some computers and an Internet connection. In short, the IT burden shifts from customer to vendor. The SaaS model is growing increasingly popular. One recent study by the research and intelligence firm IDC predicted that nearly 45 percent of U.S. firms will devote at least a quarter of their IT budgets to SaaS applications by 2010. This percentage has doubled in only two years and is projected to accelerate even more. Many companies are migrating to SaaS because this model allows them to pay as they go, buy only what they need, easily scale up or down based on current business needs, and outsource their computing needs to experts. Often, they can reap substantial savings, especially in infrastructure costs.NetSuite is flexible enough to meet the needs of many types of companies. Small businesses can use NetSuite to replace QuickBooks or Peachtree. Large multinational businesses can use NetSuite to replace on-premise ERP systems from vendors like Oracle or SAP and have one system that rolls up data from subsidiaries, automatically converts currency, and calculates local taxes.Throughout this book, you see how NetSuite can be customized to be:

- ✔ **Adaptable:** You can adjust your account to fit your habits of doing business. You can customize your business records, forms, and fields — or create new ones from scratch. You also can fine-tune your business flows to harmonize with your company's operations.

- ✔ **Easy to use:** NetSuite emphasizes "click, not code" and drag-and-drop customization. Business employees can easily create their own reports and dashboards — no programmers or analysts required.

- ✔ **Personalized to individual users:** NetSuite lets users customize their own dashboard, reminders, and pages.

- ✔ **Durable:** All customizations are carried forward during upgrades. Unlike some on-premise enterprise packages, you don't have to junk or overhaul all your existing customizations.

- ✔ **Verticalized:** You can share your customizations with partners. You can reproduce templates and share them with business partners. NetSuite account cloning allows replication and instant access to your specific solution . . . and further customization by partners.

About This Book

This book provides both a comprehensive overview of NetSuite and, in some sections, detailed instructions on specific topics.

NetSuite offers extensive online help. But because the system is so comprehensive, the Help section is necessarily voluminous as well. This book seeks to provide a more succinct, and sometimes lighthearted, summary of NetSuite and share a few tricks and tips along the way. This book takes a layperson's approach. We've tried to make this book accessible and provide examples, not just bore you with dry technical jargon and code. After reading this book, you should have a better handle on how the system works and its unique capabilities, and you will be able to reap more from the NetSuite user guides and help materials.

Custom forms can change your ability to follow the instructions given in this book. The good news is that the help is dynamic, so it tells you how to get to stuff.

This book is suitable for different types of people:

- Maybe you're just thinking about becoming a NetSuite customer. Perhaps your company currently has an on-premise ERP system, but you've grown tired of maintaining this system, paying for expensive upgrades, maintenance, and patches, and hosting your own servers. Maybe you're enticed by the promise of cloud computing, which allows you to outsource your computing needs so you can focus your energies on the core products or services that actually distinguish your business. Or maybe you use other cloud-based software (we politely won't mention any names) but are drawn to NetSuite because it lets you do everything in one comprehensive package instead of cobbling together solutions from multiple vendors.

- Maybe you have a NetSuite test account. Even if you've started playing with a demo account, this book will give you more ideas and new tricks and help you make a more informed decision.

- Maybe you're an existing NetSuite customer who wants to extend your company's use of the product. In this book, you find sections on the important facets of NetSuite, including those you may not fully understand or haven't even tried. Even if you already use NetSuite, this book will help you wring greater value from your IT investment.We wrote this book to be accessible to many levels of people, from technophobes with English degrees to eggheads who dream in code. We hope this guide can be passed around and become the most dog-eared book in your business. Actually, we hope you buy a copy for *everybody* in your company.

Foolish Assumptions

When writing this book we made a few assumptions. If you fit these assumptions, this book is for you:

- You either use NetSuite or you're thinking about using it.

- You have some background in common business terms like *profit* and *loss* and common accounting terms such as *general ledger* and *purchase order*. What you don't need is the ability to speak fluent accounting (though we're happy to point out the accounting implications in debit and credit speak at relevant points along the way).

How This Book Is Organized

This book is organized by topics. Everybody should read, or at least skim, Part I, which covers the basics of NetSuite. The rest of the book delves in to more specific topics that may or may not interest you.

You shouldn't feel compelled to read this book in the exact order in which the chapters are numbered. *For Dummies* books are so chapters can stand alone. Skip around, read the chapters relevant to you, and skim or ignore the rest. For example, if you don't ship physical product, you don't need to waste time reading the shipping and fulfillment chapters. Similarly, if you're certain you will never, ever — so help you God — try your hand at coding, you can probably skip the sections on scripting.

Part I: NetSuite Basics

You need a solid foundation in the fundamentals of NetSuite to understand how it can help your company. Part I covers basics such as setup, customization, forms and records, terminology, and personalizing your screens, portlets, and dashboards.

Part II: Tracking Money and Resources

We're going out on a limb and assuming your company handles money. Part II shows you how NetSuite can help you track the moola. This section explores bookkeeping, accounting, invoicing, paying bills, and managing inventory.

Part III: Marketing and Driving Sales

This section explores how to attract potential customers. Read this part to know how NetSuite serves as an engine for marketing as well as helping you establish a disciplined and well-organized sales team. This section shows how you can use NetSuite for sales force automation and developing leads into satisfied customers.

Part IV: Taking Care of Your Partners and Customers

Sales comes to its logical conclusion with fulfillment and shipping (if you sell physical products) and project management (if you deliver services).

Partners also often play a role with customers, so this section describes partners as well as how NetSuite can help you provide excellent customer care and help customers help themselves.

Part V: Selling Online

NetSuite can help you set up and host your virtual storefront. This section explains the basics of planning your Web site; creating content; making your pages look sharp; taking online orders; and fine-tuning.

Part VI: Dashboards, Searches, and Analytics

One of the most powerful aspects of NetSuite is its ability to produce real-time business intelligence, from simple at-a-glance dashboards to comprehensive reports that roll up whatever data you desire. This section introduces you to analytics features such as saved searches, key performance indicators for your dashboard, and reporting.

Part VII: The Part of Tens

No *For Dummies* book would be complete without The Part of Tens. In this section, we distill the wisdom of this book into lists of take-home essentials. You find lists of key differentiators, keys for successful implementation, and frequently asked questions.

Bonus Chapters on the Companion Web Site

Meeting the specific needs of *your* business requires that NetSuite be flexible, extensible, and secure. This book's companion Web site, at **www. dummies.com/go/netsuitefd**, provides seven jam-packed chapters that address topics ranging from partner relationships (and how to manage them best) to SuiteScript (a JavaScript-based API that extends NetSuite with programming). Other bonus content includes field, tab, and table customization; checkout options; knowledge base setup; and security.

Icons Used in This Book

To help you get the most out of this book, we use icons that tell you, at a glance, if a paragraph has important information of a particular kind.

Look out! This is something tricky or unusual or risky to watch for.

This icon marks important NetSuite stuff you should file away in your brain, so don't forget it.

There's more to know about the topics associated with this icon. Check out the book's companion Web site at **www.dummies.com/go/netsuitefd**.

When you see this icon, you know we're offering advice or shortcuts to quickly improve your understanding of NetSuite and teach you the tricks of the trade.

This icon indicates information that's more technical in nature, and not strictly necessary to read. If technical jargon gives you a headache, feel free to skip these.

Where to Go from Here

Start by reading Part I. Then ask yourself how you may use NetSuite and read the relevant sections.

If you're completely new to NetSuite, head straight to Chapter 1, which will give you an overview of the platform.

If you're a professional in a particular area — such as accounting, sales, marketing, or warehouse management — you can decide to visit chapters in no particular order. But (and we're probably biased) we think the best way forward is by reading Part I. After that, feel free to jump straight to the chapters that call your (professional) name.

Part I
NetSuite Basics

The 5th Wave
By Rich Tennant

"We monitor our entire operation from one central location. We know what the 'Wax Lips' people are doing, we know what the 'Whoopee Cushion' people are doing, we know what the 'Fly-in-the-Ice Cube' people are doing. But we don't know what the 'Plastic Vomit' people are doing. We don't want to know what the 'Plastic Vomit' people are doing."

In this part . . .

NetSuite is the industry's first and only online application that supports every aspect of your business, including customer relationship management (CRM), Enterprise Resource Management (ERP), accounting, e-commerce, customer support, partner/vendor portals, and much more.

In Part I we discuss high-level features and concepts about NetSuite to get you up and running quickly. Chapter 1 provides an overview of NetSuite's fundamental record types, how they're used in your business flows, and how to use them to monitor and analyze your business. But your business isn't like anyone else's exactly, so Chapter 2 explains how you can customize NetSuite to meet your company's needs. We then take a quick tour of NetSuite so you can understand system navigation (Chapter 3) and personalize your workspace to maximize efficiency (Chapter 4). Onward and upward!

Chapter 1

Peeking Under the NetSuite Hood

hy NetSuite?

The simple answer is that it's a one-stop solution that combines most of your business needs into one application. NetSuite tracks the core operations of your business in real time. You don't have to worry about piecing together different productivity programs for customer relationship management, accounting, e-commerce, and so on. NetSuite wraps all these functions into a single integrated application with an integrated database. It all works together right out of the box, with a customizable interface that is accessible from anywhere with an Internet connection.

NetSuite provides all the tools you need to do the following:

✔ Market goods or services to your customers/clients

✔ Deliver goods or services

✔ Bill customers and get paid

✔ Help customers or clients

✔ Buy the goods or services you need to run your business

✔ Account financially for all of the above

How can it do all these things? NetSuite stores information about these operations in a database that's shared across your business. It runs in an online data center (instead of in your own data center), which is referred to as running in the *cloud*. This means that all users work on the latest version of software. This translates into instant, real-time access for all users, including employees, contractors, Web store shoppers, and partners.

Speaking NetSuite Lingo

This basic terminology shows up throughout the book, and knowing it before-hand can help. Basic NetSuite categories follow:

- ✓ **Record:** Entry of information related to a single business concept.

- ✓ **Form:** Page through which you enter records and transactions. Forms contain fields and usually have tabs.

- ✓ **Field:** Place on a record or transaction where you enter information.

- ✓ **Subtab:** Section of a record or transaction that clusters fields by subcategory. This book uses *tab* versus *subtab*.

- ✓ **List:** Menu of values that you can select in a field.

- ✓ **Script:** SuiteScript JavaScript file that runs against a specific form or record type or that creates a custom portlet.

- ✓ **Role:** Set of permissions assigned to a NetSuite user.

- ✓ **Center:** Configuration of NetSuite created for a specific group of roles with similar tasks.

- ✓ **Center tab:** Grouping of similar links and information. These may include Home, Reports, Documents, Activities, and Setup. You also can create custom center tabs.

Naming Your Most Important Data

NetSuite stores your data in three major categories: entities, items, and transactions.

Entity

Entity is a generic category that includes individual people or companies. Everything about a person or business can be found in a single place. A single place can be thought of like a file folder of information. In database parlance, that single place is called a *record,* like a row in a spreadsheet where the columns are things like name, address, and phone number.

Entities can be a lead/prospect/customer, a contact, a vendor, a partner, or an employee.

Leads, prospects, and customers

The same entity represents an individual or company from the moment they become a lead all the way through to when they pay you for goods or services.

Depending on what stage of the lifecycle it's in, an entity may be called:

- ✔ **A lead:** When you first make contact with a potential customer.
- ✔ **A prospect:** After your sales team contacts him and verifies his interest in purchasing.
- ✔ **A customer:** When he buys something.

Contacts

Contacts are individuals who you have business relationships with, including colleagues, friends, and other acquaintances who you would keep in an address book. You can associate contacts with leads, prospects, customers, vendors, and partners, and you can enter private contacts that only you can access.

Vendors

Vendors supply you with the goods or services you need to run your business. Vendor records allow you to keep track of the vendor's location and contact information, track the items you purchase from them, and report on financial data based on your purchases. You can also give vendors access to your account to view the orders that have been made.

Partners

A *partner* is a company with whom you have a business agreement, typically to allow it to sell your products or services. Partner records allow you to keep track of your partner sales and activity. Partners can also be given access to your account to view reports and transaction data.

Employees

In NetSuite, the employee record contains employee information for contact, login, payroll, and human resources purposes.

Items

Items are the goods or services you're buying or selling. Items are used for anything you buy or sell while running your business.

   ✓ For product companies, items can be hard goods in your inventory, such as washers and dryers.

   ✓ For service companies, items can be services you perform for your clients, such as consulting, lead generation, or technical writing.

Transactions

Transactions represent the day-to-day business activities that occur between entities and items. Examples may include customers making purchases or employees being paid. Several dozen types of transactions exist, each representing a distinct type of business activity.

Transactions include the following:

   ✓ Invoices to track money owed

   ✓ Sales orders to track a closed deal

   ✓ Opportunities to track a deal in the negotiation process

Of course, behind the scenes, all these transactions have an accounting impact. Naturally you can do all your bookkeeping within NetSuite, from managing general ledger accounts to having sales placed through your Web site entered directly into the books like any other sale. (Part II explains bookkeeping and its details.) Aaah! Integration, sweet integration!

Leading to Profits

To understand how NetSuite tracks your operations, it's useful to think in terms of a business flow. A *business flow* is any particular process that you undertake in your business. For example, the customer flow in Figure 1-1 represents the entire series of activities undertaken for a particular customer, from the moment that customer contacts you until a payment has been made and accounted for. In many cases, a customer flow also includes post-sales support and customer feedback.

To illustrate how the different parts of a company can interact with a particular business flow, check out the customer flow in a bit more detail. (Of course, not all elements of this flow are applicable to every business; even so, this example shows the breadth of activities that NetSuite tracks and the variety of departments involved.)

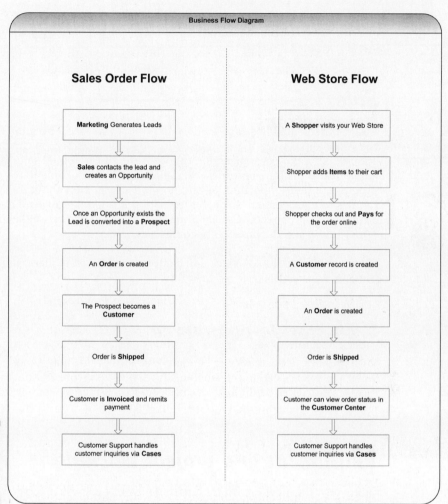

Figure 1-1: Customer flow looks this way.

Marketing

The key to any successful business is generating leads. Your business may use a variety of vehicles to generate leads, such as online or offline advertising, public relations (PR), or referrals. NetSuite allows your marketing department to track its efforts and determine which lead-generation method is most effective. Your marketing department records campaigns in your account to represent marketing activities.

These marketing activities, if successful, should create new leads. Each new lead is then recorded in NetSuite and sent to sales. For more information on marketing, see Chapter 11.

Sales

A salesperson qualifies each lead to determine whether it's a good fit for the goods or services that you provide. Next, the salesperson can create an *opportunity,* a type of transaction that represents a potential sale. The *lead* entity now turns into a *prospect.* NetSuite allows salespeople to track the progress of their opportunities and provide information about those opportunities to management through forecasts. Salespeople can send *quotes,* or *estimates,* to prospects. If a sale is made, a *sales order* is created from the opportunity, and the *prospect* becomes a *customer.*

For more information on sales and customer relationship management, see Chapter 9.

Web store/e-commerce

With NetSuite, a business can set up a Web store to display goods or services. Customers can purchase items from the Web store 24 hours a day, 7 days a week. After a purchase, a sales order is created in NetSuite. For more information on using NetSuite to set up and run your Web store, see Part V.

Fulfillment and project tracking

Ultimately, the most important function in your business is the delivery of goods or services. Delivering a sales order completely and efficiently is the most central element of the customer flow. It determines whether your customers buy again and whether they recommend you to others.

The process of packaging and shipping the goods the customer has purchased is called *fulfillment.*

✔ For product companies, delivery generally consists of packaging goods and delivering them to the customer, often using a shipper. NetSuite partners with UPS and FedEx, which allows you to generate real-time rates and track your shipments with detailed information about fulfillment, such as:

- Current inventory levels
- Goods committed to customers
- Addresses of shipments

See Chapter 10 for a more detailed discussion of fulfillment.

- For service companies, "delivery" often consists of tracking a project for services a customer has requested. As with physical deliverables, NetSuite tracks detailed information about the service fulfillment process:
  - Tasks required from internal employees
  - How much time each employee has spent on the project
  - Milestones required to receive customer payment

For more information on project tracking, see Bonus Chapter 1 at **www.dummies.com/go/netsuitefd**.

Invoicing and collections

When the goods or services are delivered, it's time to *invoice* the customer. NetSuite builds invoices from the sales order and allows you to print them, e-mail them, and see them online. When the customer remits payment, a *payment* is recorded, and the invoice is closed . . . and maybe a pizza party is thrown.

For more information on invoicing, see Chapter 6.

Customer support

After you deliver the goods, your work isn't done; customers will always have questions, problems, or suggestions for your business. NetSuite tracks these types of requests in *cases* and lets you assign them to an appropriate employee (usually a support representative) for resolution. Because the support rep uses the same system that tracked the customer from day one, she has the low-down on that customer, making it much easier to understand and resolve the case.

For more information on customer support, see Chapter 13.

Financials

Besides collecting money, finance employees track customer information (such as profitability) and expenses to help ensure the business is running efficiently and maximizing opportunities. Again, because NetSuite is a single system, financial employees have access to information from the entire customer lifecycle to perform their analysis. For more information on financials, see Chapter 5.

Workflows

NetSuite's Workflow Manager, described briefly in Bonus Chapter 5 (at **www. dummies.com/go/netsuitefd**), lets you tailor the flow of work in NetSuite to follow your business processes. So whether it's getting a purchase order approved or moving a lead through the sales cycle, setting up workflows is another easy way to customize NetSuite to meet your needs. Read more on that in Chapter 2.

Leveraging Key Data to Make Excellent Decisions

With all of your data in one system, you have everything you need to run your business, manage your employees, serve your customers, make smart decisions, improve efficiency and boost profits. NetSuite offers several ways to access your key business metrics and present them in a way that makes it easy to see the big picture in real time.

Dashboards

Dashboards, one of which appears in Figure 1-2, are the heart of NetSuite's approach. The Home dashboard is the first page you see when you log in to NetSuite.

Dashboards display snapshots of your critical data in many ways:

- ✔ Graphs
- ✔ Trending
- ✔ Key performance indicators (KPIs)

NetSuite makes it easy to personalize your dashboard specifically for your needs. For more information, see Chapter 4.

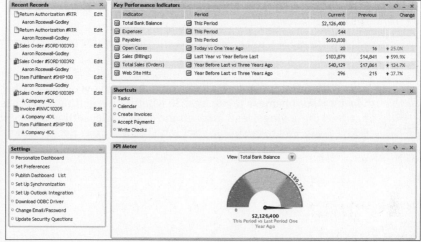

Figure 1-2:
Portlets
show key
business
metrics on
the home
dashboard.

Lists and saved searches

You can access virtually all your data via lists or saved searches, as shown in Figure 1-3. NetSuite provides lists for basic record types such as customers, transactions, and employees.

If you need more flexibility, you can modify an existing list or create a saved search. Saved searches can answer many types of pressing questions about your business and can be private or shared across a group of users. For more information and steps for creating your own saved searches, see Chapter 19.

Figure 1-3:
A quick
saved
search
brings up
a list of all
customers.

Reporting and analytics

NetSuite includes a long list of extremely powerful reports, including financials and analytics. Figure 1-4 shows the Sales by Customer report. If one of NetSuite's built-in reports doesn't meet all your needs, you can modify an existing report or create a new one from scratch. See Chapter 21 for more information on reporting and analytics.

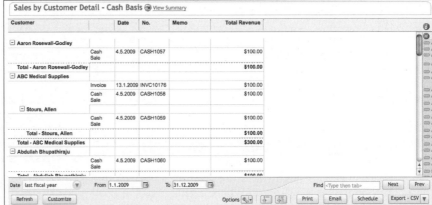

Figure 1-4: Analyze customer profitability with the sales by customer report.

NetSuite also offers a fully customizable key performance indicator (KPI) scorecard portlet on your dashboard. KPIs provide a way to keep "score" of how well you (or your employees) are doing in particular areas. The KPI scorecard portlet, shown in Figure 1-5, lets you display KPIs that are important to your job. KPI scorecards can provide complex comparisons among multiple KPIs over multiple date ranges or accounting periods. KPI scorecards also can include Excel-like formulas with KPIs and functions in their expressions. KPIs and KPI scorecards are discussed in detail in Chapter 20.

Going Global with NetSuite OneWorld

NetSuite OneWorld makes the world feel a little smaller — at least from the perspective of managing your business. The product, which is a particular flavor of NetSuite that larger companies with multiple subsidiaries often purchase, is custom-made for companies that do business internationally. It allows companies to quickly and efficiently expand their operations across international borders — often at a fraction of the cost and time of traditional on-premise enterprise resource planning (ERP) systems.

NetSuite OneWorld supports multiple subsidiaries and multiple currencies, but in other respects is the same as the simpler single-currency version of NetSuite.

Except where specifically noted, everything in this book also applies to NetSuite OneWorld.

OneWorld abilities

Like NetSuite in general, OneWorld lets you see into all facets of your business in real time. In addition, NetSuite OneWorld handles currencies as well as tax rules and regulations for your base country as well as for countries where you have subsidiaries, vendors, and customers.

Say you're a U.S. company with a subsidiary in Tokyo, Japan. Your Japanese subsidiary would see its Web pages written in Japanese, with currency in Yen, and roles and permissions set to reflect its business' needs. Meanwhile, a manager at the U.S. headquarters can get real-time information about sales in Japan and even drill down for details on specific projects or warehouse inventories — all translated into English and U.S. dollars.

With OneWorld, you can do one of the following:

- ✔ Populate single charts-of-accounts across subsidiaries
- ✔ Use separate charts-of-accounts for each company with postings between subsidiaries.

OneWorld features

OneWorld features a built-in tax engine that calculates local taxes and generates multiple tax schedules. And it allows you to manage inventory and fulfillment over multiple locations across the world and represent items either globally or by subsidiary.

Key features of NetSuite OneWorld include the following:

- ✔ **Global Accounting/ERP:** Multi-currency and real-time financial consolidation.
- ✔ **Global CRM:** Tools to manage a multi-national sales organization in multiple languages and currencies and gain visibility into every aspect of CRM, including quotas, forecasts, sales, customers, partners, support cases, issues, leads and campaigns.

✔ **Global Ecommerce:** Multi-brand Web stores that all can be run and managed from a single NetSuite system in multiple languages, currencies, and countries.

✔ **Global Services Resource Planning (SRP):** End-to-end, real-time visibility across all levels of organization, including corporate, subsidiaries, geographies, and even individual projects.

✔ **Global Business Intelligence:** Multiple levels of consolidated, real-time reporting and key performance indicators.

The biggest selling point of OneWorld is that it lets you roll up your financials into your base currency. Also, you can rebrand your company pages by assigning different company names and logos to each local subsidiary.

Chapter 2

Tailoring NetSuite to Your Company

In This Chapter

▶ Using the Setup Manager

▶ Enabling features

▶ Renaming records and transactions

▶ Programming on top of NetSuite

*O*ne of NetSuite's key selling points is its adaptability. You can give it your own look and feel by adding logos, selecting fonts, and specifying terminology. You can adapt it to your business processes by selecting options, designing workflows, customizing forms, and even adding your own programming.

Even though NetSuite is a software-as-a-service offering in which customers share the same data center and code, it's not one-size-fits-all. Rather, it's one comprehensive package *adaptable* to all.

NetSuite offers several levels of customization, and they're listed here from easiest to most advanced:

✔ Configuring options with NetSuite's point-and-click and drag-and-drop tools. This may involve moving fields around, creating new fields, and tailoring your forms and records to your business processes.

✔ Creating new forms, records, and business flows from scratch. One example of a custom record may be a vacation approval form. Other examples include travel records or warranties.

✔ Adding your own scripting, which can range from basic programming to advanced programming.

Later chapters explore customization in greater depth, including dashboard personalization for the individual user (Chapter 4), customization using options (Bonus Chapter 4), and scripting (Bonus Chapter 5). Bonus chapters are available at **www.dummies.com/go/netsuitefd**.

Starting with the Basics

NetSuite works right out of the box, but you should make some basic tweaks to tailor it to your organization. At a minimum, do this basic customization:

✔ Enter your company's name, address, and phone number.

✔ Activate the features you need.

✔ Turn off the features you *don't* need (to avoid cluttering your interfaces). You run a manufacturing plant in Peoria: Do you really want to present your employees with options for sales orders in Chinese and currency in Euros?

Before plunging into customization, you should know the basic terminology provided in Chapter 1.

Customizing from the Get Go: Setting Up NetSuite

It helps to have an idea of all the possibilities before customizing. What features will your company actually use? Which ones are unnecessary? For example, if your business doesn't ship any products or manage a warehouse, you may disable the features related to shipping and fulfillment. You don't want employees trying to manage inventory in a warehouse that doesn't exist.

The Setup Manager is an area of NetSuite that allows administrators to handle numerous setup tasks. You get to the Setup Manager by clicking the Setup tab. The Setup Manager allows you to:

✔ Enable features

✔ Enter company information

✔ Set company preferences

✔ Rename records and transactions

✔ Set accounting preferences

- ✔ Set up subsidiaries (OneWorld users only)
- ✔ Set up departments, classes, and locations
- ✔ Set up payroll preferences (if using NetSuite for payroll)
- ✔ Set up employees and assign roles to give them access to NetSuite
- ✔ Import existing data into NetSuite

From the Setup Manager's welcome page (see Figure 2-1), you can click the image for the area you want to set up. You'll see an overview of how to activate features in that area and where to find specific information for each feature.

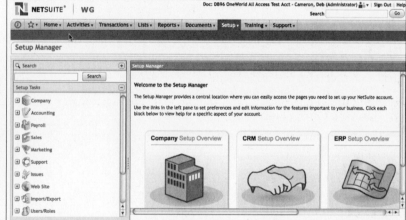

Figure 2-1:
The Setup Manager welcome page is ready for your customization.

The following sections explain some of the most important customization features you encounter when setting up NetSuite. You can reach all of these features using the Setup Manager.

Company Information

This page acts as your account profile, and filling it in should be one of the first tasks you complete. Enter your company name, phone number, address, tax ID numbers, time zone, currency, and other important information.

The information you enter on the Company Information page is used throughout your account for forms for tax purposes and basic financial preferences.

Another simple but very important customization step is to upload your company logo into NetSuite so your logo appears on forms and communications:

1. **From the Setup tab menu choose Setup⇨Company⇨Company Information.**

2. **To the right of the Company Logo (Pages) field, click the New button (+).**

   The File window appears.

3. **Click the Browse button and select a file to upload.**

4. **Click the Save button to upload the file to NetSuite.**

   The Company Information window appears.

5. **Click Save to update the logo.**

Enable Features

This section allows you to select important preferences that apply across your company. You see eight tabs:

- ✔ Company
- ✔ Accounting
- ✔ Transactions
- ✔ Items & Inventory
- ✔ Employees
- ✔ CRM
- ✔ Web Presence
- ✔ SuiteFlex

These options touch virtually every facet of NetSuite and are discussed in greater detail elsewhere in this book. Since NetSuite is so customizable, the steps for enabling the features you will need are discussed in context in relevant chapters.

Rename Records and Transactions

Do you speak your own lingo? These fields allow you to choose names for basic elements of your business. Setting this preference renames these entities on all your records and allows you to customize NetSuite with your own terminology.

Do you use the term *vendor* or *supplier?* Do you want to call your customers clients, guests, or parrotheads (because you sell Jimmy Buffet fan items)? Similarly, you can decide whether you want to use the term *projects* or rename it *jobs, assignments,* or *missions.* The same goes for department, class, lead prospect, partner, case, event, task, and even phone call.

To rename records or transactions:

1. **From the Setup tab menu choose Setup⇨Company⇨Rename Records/Transactions.**

   The Rename Records/Transactions window appears, where you can change the default names for customers, phone calls, vendors, and more.

2. **Make any terminology changes you want.**

3. **Click the Save button.**

What if you make a mistake? Just come back to the Rename Records/Transactions page and update it. But we don't recommend changing the terminology over and over again, mainly because you don't want to keep changing the screens that appear for your users.

Auto-Generated Numbers

By default, NetSuite uses names for ID fields rather than numbers. This means that the employee ID for Liza Minnelli would be Liza Minnelli rather than EMPLOYEE-0053. Using the auto-generated numbers feature, you can make NetSuite automatically generate ID numbers.

You can set up auto-generated numbers for three classes of things:

✔ Entities (such as customers, jobs, employees, partners, or vendors)

✔ Transactions

✔ Customer Relationship Management (CRM) relevant items, like support cases or marketing campaigns

You can define your own prefixes and numbers, specifying the number of digits and the starting number. For example, you may designate that your customers be defined by the prefix GUEST followed by a four-digit number: GUEST-0001, GUEST-0002, and so on.

You can turn numbering on and off at any time. Say you use names for ID fields and then decide that you want numbers instead. When you click the

Save button on the Set Up Auto-Generated Numbers screen, NetSuite goes through and numbers all existing records.

Be forewarned: Existing record numbers can't revert back to names. If you later decide you don't want numbers any more, NetSuite won't revert existing records with numbers back to names. In other words, Liza Minnelli will be EMPLOYEE-0053, but new hire Sal Mineo will have an ID of Sal Mineo. It's best to decide whether to use names or numbers at the outset so that all your records have consistent IDs.

General Preferences

The General Preferences page establishes some basic but very important options for your entire company. You can:

✓ Designate the format for displaying time and date.

✓ Set minimum password lengths and how long these passwords can be used before they expire.

✓ Determine the font for your pages.

✓ Specify which options individual users can override and which remain no matter what. (For example, maybe allowing employees to change the date format causes too much confusion because half of your employees put the month first and other half put the day first? Does 11-12 mean November 12 or December 11? To avoid such confusion, you can go to date format and uncheck Allow Override.)

✓ Specify the languages available to your employees. Say your company has offices in Estonia, Tokyo, Qatar, London, Paris, and Buenos Aires. You can add Estonian, Japanese, Arabic, English, French, and Spanish so all six tongues appear as options for employees. Individuals can specify the language they prefer on their personal accounts. This ensures that your workers can access your records in any of these languages . . . but not Icelandic.

The steps for doing each of these are intuitive, so we won't go into detail here.

Printing, Fax, and E-mail Preferences

You can customize templates for faxes, e-mails, and other forms. For example, you may want to include some boilerplate disclaimers in some of your standard forms like receipts, packing slips, or sales forms.

To set preferences like these, from the Setup tab menu, choose Company➪Printing, Fax, and E-mail Preferences.

For example, your return forms and receipts may have a disclaimer that states that returns must be made within 30 days in original packaging. If you're a reptile distributorship, you may add a disclaimer at the bottom of sales forms that declares "Not liable for snakes let loose in aircraft." Important disclaimer text such as this can be added in the Sales Form Disclaimer entry box on the Printing tab. The Fax tab allows you to set preferences regarding how to e-mail faxes to recipients from NetSuite. The E-mail tab allows you to enter information so that e-mail from your company is not accidentally marked as spam. (See Chapter 11 for details on e-mail marketing.)

Getting picky about Set Preferences

Personal preferences allow you to tailor your account to meet your individual needs. To access the Set Preferences page shown in Figure 2-2, choose Set Preferences from the Home tab menu.

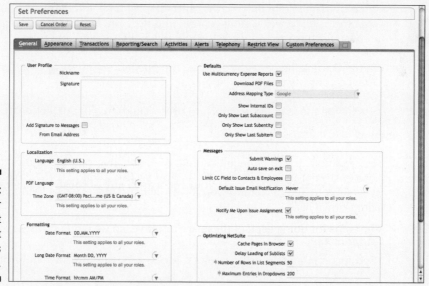

Figure 2-2:
Tailor your account on the Set Preferences page.

Most preferences only allow you to make changes to the role you're currently logged in as. Choosing a color theme in your Sales Person role, for example, doesn't affect the color theme in your Administrator role. Other preferences, such as your language and time zone, apply to all of your roles. On the Set Preferences page, the label This Setting Applies to All Your Roles identifies preferences that apply to all roles.

The following list describes the tabs you see on the Set Preferences page, and what settings you can change on each tab. We also tell you the most important settings to make on each tab.

These preferences are a small subset of what NetSuite offers. As you become familiar with your account and your preference options, you will discover many settings that can help you speed up data entry, locate records, and improve your overall experience. Also, some preferences described in the following sections may not be available. The preferences you see depend on the features enabled in your account. Additionally, some preferences may be set at the company level by an administrator, and individual users can't change those.

General

Settings on this tab include e-mail signature, time zone, and date, time, and phone-number formats.

Make sure the time zone is set correctly. Select the time zone you want to use from the Time Zone drop-down list to display time and dates on phone calls, events, tasks, cases, system-generated notes, and audit trails. The setting you choose for this preference will apply to all of your NetSuite roles.

In the Optimizing NetSuite section, the Maximum Entries in Dropdowns preference controls whether you do one of these two:

- ✔ Type the first few letters and press Tab to make a selection on a form
- ✔ Use a drop-down list

For example, if you change this field to 0, you always type the first few letters of a customer name on an order and press Tab to choose the correct name. If you set it to 500 (assuming you have <500 customers), this field appears as a drop-down list.

Appearance

Settings on this tab include colors, fonts, and user interface behavior.

If you want to change the default colors, select a new theme from the Color Theme drop-down list. Your chosen color theme applies to every page in your account. Choose from basic color themes such as Blue and Silver, or select a college theme such as Pac-10: UCLA. Administrators and users with the appropriate permission can create custom color themes from scratch for everyone in the company to use.

Two other fields affect your user experience:

> ✔ **Limit Entry Forms to Two Columns.** Limiting entry forms to two columns creates a cleaner page than the default of three columns, so you may like that setting.
>
> ✔ **Expand Tabs on Entry Forms.** This preference does away with NetSuite's tabs and makes it into one long, scrolling page. The small double arrow button on the right side of each page lets you try this on for size before committing to it across the product.

Transactions

Settings on this tab include whether transactions should autofill, as well as options for various warnings, such as inventory-level warnings, customer credit warnings, or duplicate number warnings.

To enable the duplicate number warning (as in, "Hey, that's the second Check 2005 you've entered today"), select the Duplicate Number Warnings check box. You select the other warnings in similar fashion. Of course, clearing the check box eliminates the warnings if you don't need the safety net they provide.

Reporting/Search

Settings on this tab include report formats, the default bank account for reports, and the behavior of search options (such as Global Search).

We recommend making two settings on this tab:

> ✔ **Select the Global Search Auto Suggest check box.** When this option is enabled, NetSuite automatically suggests matches for the text you enter in the Global Search field as you type. Records that display in the suggestion box are accessible by a single click, or by navigating with the arrow keys and pressing the Enter or Tab key.
>
> ✔ **Select All Reports from the Report by Period drop-down list (if you use accounting periods).** You can change this setting as needed, but it should be the first thing you investigate if you're seeing differing balances on reports.

Activities

Settings on this tab include calendar and task options.

TIP

If your company has many external contacts, partners, and vendors, the drop-down list you use when adding invitees to events can get very long. That can make it tough to find employees. Select the Restrict Invitees to Employees check box to restrict the Invitee drop-down list to only include employees.

Alerts

Settings on this tab include your e-mail address and times at which you'd like to receive e-mail alerts that contain your Home tab KPIs (such as Actual vs. Quota, if you're a sales rep), as well as other information on your dashboard.

Alerts enable you to get your Home dashboard by e-mail three times a day. Choose from First Selection, Second Selection, and Third Selection drop-down lists, as shown in Figure 2-3.

Figure 2-3:
Set up
your e-mail
alerts.

Set Preferences

Save Cancel Order Reset

General | Appearance | Transactions | Reporting/Search | Activities | **Alerts** | Telephony | Restrict View | Custom Preferences

Alert Email can be sent to you up to three times a day.
Please select the time(s) at which you want to receive alert email.

First Selection ▼

Second Selection ▼

Third Selection ▼

Include links in HTML alerts ☑

Respect Quick Date Portlet Settings ☑

E-Mail Primary (dcamero...olvedmedia.com) ▼

Send an On-Demand Alert from this Role ☐

Click Here to send a test email message to dcameron@evolvedmedia.com.

You can receive email alerts when records that fit your saved search criteria are added or updated. To appear in this list, saved searches must be marked "Allow Users to Subscribe" by an administrator.

Record Type	Search	Send on Update	Show Recent Changes
▼			

Add Invert Remove Cancel Order

Save Cancel Order Reset

Restrict View

Settings on this tab include ways to filter the information you see in NetSuite. For example, you can use the Location drop-down list to restrict your view of items related to a particular corporate location. Use the Class drop-down list to restrict your view in NetSuite to include a particular class of customers or opportunities (such as those from the Web site, repeat customers, or seasonal sales).

Customizing Fields, Records, Forms, and Lists

After you set basic companywide preferences, think about how you want to customize NetSuite to your business processes.

NetSuite is a bit like clay. Don't like the screens? Mold them into what you want. Don't see the field you want on a given screen? Take a bit off the hunk and put it on there where the field should go. But seriously, you can add fields, records, forms, and lists.

You explore how to create custom fields, forms, records, and lists in more detail in Bonus Chapter 4 at **www.dummies.com/go/netsuitefd**.

Fields

Fields represent a single item of information. Custom fields extend the data for built-in records. This is where you can add the customer's Twitter handle or her Facebook page or her blog as extra fields on the customer record.

Records

Records are a group of fields; in NetSuite you can think of the customer record in this category. (Chapter 3 describes records in more depth.) You may add a record for social networking information and include customer accounts on a variety of social networking sites.

With custom records you can:

✔ Create a new custom record type.

✔ Edit an existing custom record.

✔ View a list of records that have been created using each custom record type.

✔ Create a new record for a selected custom record type.

✔ Create a new search for a selected custom record type.

Forms

Forms are the way you get information into a record. You may normally think of them as screens. You can add a field to an existing form or screen, or you can create a new form just to suit your information capture needs. You can reorganize these forms to better fit your business practices. You can take an existing template and rearrange or rename fields and tabs. You can conceal or disable fields, make some fields mandatory, or add custom fields, drop-down lists, and custom code.

You can customize forms (think "screens") in NetSuite two ways:

✔ Take standard options and configure them to suit your business processes.
✔ Create entirely new forms from scratch.

NetSuite contains an array of standard forms such as customer records, sales orders, or estimates, to name a few.

Lists

Lists are simple screens that show information from a particular record type or types. The chart of accounts, the employee list, and the items list are examples of lists in NetSuite.

The simplest type of screen in NetSuite are lists. The customer list lists (you guessed it) customers. The employee list lists (that's right) employees. You can add custom lists to create lists of star salespeople, exceptionally good customers, or even items frequently returned.

Bringing in Data

Happily, NetSuite has an excellent tool that brings in all types of data, whether employee data, customer data, or transactions. The CSV Import tool offers wizard-like functionality for bringing in text data that is in *comma-separated variable (CSV)* format.

CSV files don't look beautiful in Notepad (all those commas can make your head spin as you track fields); Microsoft Excel is a much better tool for viewing these files. In fact, any Excel file can be saved as a CSV file. If you can get data either in CSV format or in Excel format (and then save it as a CSV file using the File⇨Save As option in Excel), importing it into NetSuite is a piece of cake. See Figures 2-4 and 2-5.

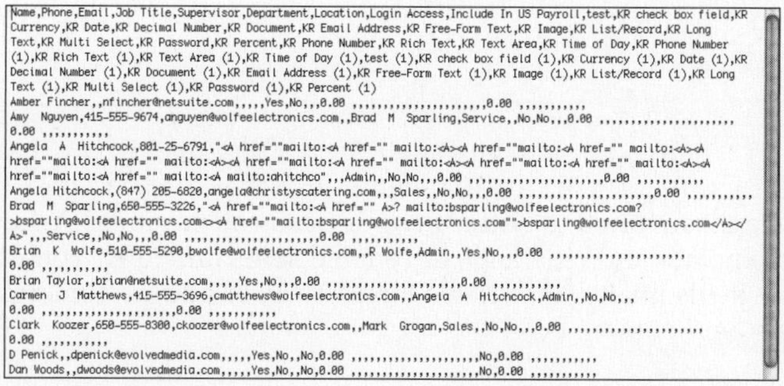

Figure 2-4:
This is a
CSV file in
Notepad:
pretty ugly!

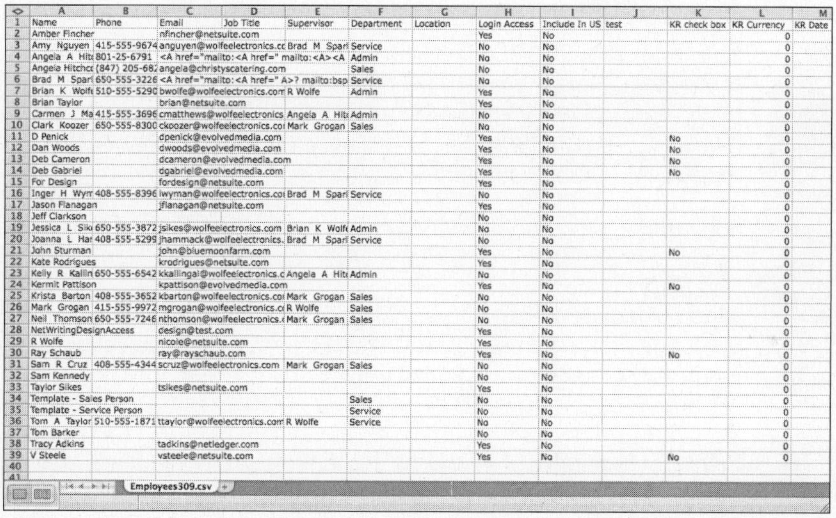

Figure 2-5:
This is a
CSV file
in Excel:
pretty!

Saving an Excel spreadsheet as a CSV file

Save an Excel worksheet as a CSV file:

1. **Open the worksheet whose data you want to save as a CSV file.**

2. **Choose File⇨Save As.**

3. **Choose Comma Separated Values (.csv) as the file format.**

4. **Click the Save button.**

Thinking about data import

Once data is in CSV format, consider what the corresponding record is in
NetSuite:

- Employees
- Customers
- Contacts
- Leads
- Partners
- Projects (if Advanced Projects is enabled)
- Prospects
- Vendors
- Competitors

You will want to match the records in your CSV file with the corresponding records in NetSuite so each piece of information about employees (such as name, address, social security number, holiday fruitcake preference) can go into the corresponding field in NetSuite's customer record. Don't worry; the wizard will help you match things up.

Sometimes it's obvious. Sometimes it isn't. How can you look at NetSuite to find out what fields are stored in each record?

NetSuite makes it easy for you. The data in any one record is on the corresponding screen (employee data on the Employee screen, for instance). By going to that screen, you can see the fields in the record.

Variability comes in if you have created a custom form that shows only certain fields, for example. Of course, if you've added custom fields to a record, as outlined in Bonus Chapter 4, visit **www.dummies.com/go/netsuitefd**), you can also import data into those. You can import data into custom records as well.

Have a look at the standard form so you know what all the fields are. What if you don't know what those fields mean? NetSuite field-level help to the rescue! Just click a field name on the Employee screen to see what a field refers to.

Using the CSV Import Assistant

The CSV Import Assistant is a wizard that helps you bring data into NetSuite. Its main use is to bring data into NetSuite when you start using NetSuite. But there are other uses, including bringing in:

- Leads from lists sent by external firms or from tools used at trade shows
- Payments from banks
- Item price lists from vendors

Administrators can start the CSV Import Assistant this way: Choose Import/Export⇨Import CSV Records from the Setup tab menu. You see the initial screen of the Import Assistant, as shown in Figure 2-6.

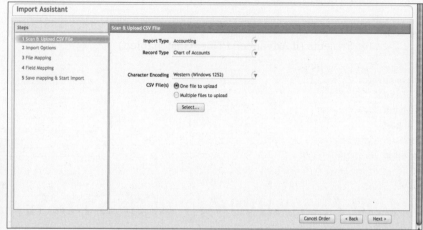

Figure 2-6: Start the CSV Import Assistant.

The CSV Import Assistant walks you through the process:

✔ Scanning and uploading CSV file or files (yes, you can import more than one at a time).

✔ Specifying the nature of the imported data (new records that should be added, updates to existing records, or a mixture of the two, which as you may guess can get a little tricky).

✔ Mapping files is optional. You only do this step if you're importing multiple CSV files at the same time.

✔ Mapping fields. This is where the beauty of the CSV Import Assistant really shines. You know what the data is called in your old system. If you called something "green cruciferous vegetable" and NetSuite calls the same thing "broccoli," here is where you establish that mapping. Furthermore, if this is something you may do again, you can save the mapping and reuse it. See Figure 2-7.

The CSV Import Assistant is very straightforward and easy to use, but it includes advanced features that require deeper discussion. After all, we're talking about your data here — a serious subject indeed. This book provides an overview. For detailed documentation, see the NetSuite Help Center (available by clicking the Help link in the upper-right corner of the screen).

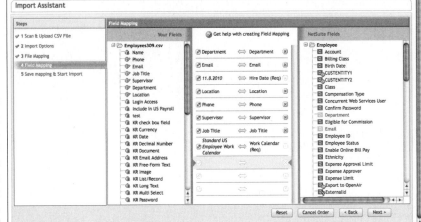

Figure 2-7:
Field map-
ping is easy
if you're
using the
CSV Import
Assistant.

Custom Programming with SuiteScript

You can do your own programming on top of the NetSuite platform. SuiteScript is a JavaScript-based API that gives developers the ability to extend NetSuite beyond the point-and-click customization described in Bonus Chapter 4. This kind of advanced customization often requires a programmer. You delve into these capabilities in greater depth in Bonus Chapter 5 at **www. dummies.com/go/netsuitefd**.

Briefly, here are some of the things you can do with SuiteScript:

✔ Custom business processing

✔ Custom validations and calculations in the browser client

✔ Create custom user interfaces

✔ Run batch processes

✔ Execute NetSuite searches

✔ Utility processing such as sending e-mail and faxes, creating and uploading files, or working with XML documents (using script types such as
User Event Scripts or Suitelets)

✔ Create custom dashboard portlets

A related capability is the creation of workflows. Part of SuiteScript, the NetSuite Workflow Manager can use scripts, but is so easy that even nonpro-grammers can use it. Workflow Manager can help set up approval processes and other workflows that match your company's business processes and ensure that best practices are followed consistently.

Chapter 3

Personalizing Your Suite

. . . .

. . . .

Although users' needs may be highly specialized, everyone gets around NetSuite and performs tasks the same way. This chapter describes basic NetSuite use, key terms, and the built-in tools that access your data. In this chapter, you also discover best practices to help you find what you're looking for.

Getting into NetSuite

One of the ways that NetSuite achieves its famed adaptability is through roles. NetSuite understands that each user has different needs and expectations. An accountant, for example, doesn't need to know about hot leads in the sales department, and a warehouse manager doesn't want to be bothered with information about past due accounts.

To address each set of needs, NetSuite provides a role-based system for accessing your business's data. Roles are based on the myriad business functions that different users may have, from CFO to sales representative to store clerk to engineer. NetSuite provides a set of predefined roles so that you can get up and running quickly.

One or more roles are granted to each business user based on the function (or position) that user serves in the business and the level of access the user needs. For example, a sales representative needs to be able to modify leads and create opportunities but should not have access to other sales reps' employee data. A sales *manager,* however, needs access to quotas and commissions.

Roles are set on the Access tab of the Employee screen. (Admins, see Chapter 27 for more about roles.)

Mother, may I?

Roles aren't set in stone. Each role has certain permissions and can be given additional permissions where needed.

Permissions specify two things:

- ✔ Which pages users can access
- ✔ Actions the users can take

At any time, your account administrator can modify existing roles or create new roles with any combination of permissions. So if you really are both the chief cook and the bottle washer, your administrator can help define those roles for you (though we admit that NetSuite doesn't have much to offer in the cooking and bottle-washing departments). To read more about roles, see Chapter 27.

Logging in to NetSuite

To sign in to NetSuite, you go to the home page at www.netsuite.com and choose the Customer Login link in the upper-right corner of the page. If you (or someone else) has logged in before, you'll see a place to enter your e-mail address (your username) and password right on the home page.

Enter the username and password your administrator gave you.

Who am I?

When you log in to NetSuite, you'll be logged in to your default role, displayed below the Global Search box in the upper-right corner of the screen, right above the link that says, "Customize this page."

Users with multiple roles have a Change Roles link in the upper-right corner of the screen. Click the link for a full list of your available roles or hover the cursor over the link to see a drop-down list that allows single-click role switching. Select another role from that list to change roles and watch in amazement as NetSuite changes your home page to suit that role.

Keeping Tabs and Checking Your Dashboard

NetSuite's intuitive user interface can be explained in just a few paragraphs. Tabs help you find your way around and the dashboard tells you what you need to know (once they're properly set up).

Tabs

Across the top of every page in NetSuite is a navigation bar made up of tabs, as shown in Figure 3-1. The tabs at the top of every page provide access to all the functions you need in a given area, such as Reports. Further, the tabs you see are tailored for your role. (For example, when logged in as a sales person, you see tabs for Leads, Opportunities, and Customers. As an accountant, you see tabs for Vendors, Payroll & HR, and Financial.) Menus on each tab provide instant access to all available options for that area.

Figure 3-1:
The navigation bar shows all the tabs you have access to.

To view a tab menu, simply hover the cursor over a tab, as shown in Figure 3-2. Tab menus often have multiple levels. Click a menu option or hover over a menu to display submenus.

For example, hovering over the Activities tab displays the Activities menu, and sliding the mouse over to Scheduling displays the Scheduling submenu. As you read this book, instructions are described like this: "From the Activities tab menu, choose Scheduling ➪ Events ➪ New."

Figure 3-2:
Hovering the
mouse over
a tab name
displays
tab menus
(the main
way you
navigate in
NetSuite).

The Home dashboard and overviews

NetSuite's home dashboard (see Figure 3-3) provides a visual workspace that allows instant access to all of your real-time account information. Each tab has an overview of functions related to that tab.

To view an overview, click the tab name. Both your dashboard and your tab overviews are broken up into small, customizable windows called *portlets*. For detailed information on how to personalize your home dashboard and overviews for each tab, see Chapter 4.

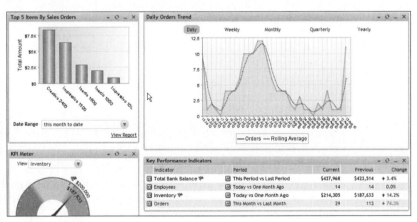

Figure 3-3:
Your home
dashboard
provides
instant
access and
can be per-
sonalized.

Show Me the Records

NetSuite stores all the data in your account as records (but not the old vinyl kind). When you need to add data, such as a new customer, you enter that information into a record. When you need to view customer information, you display a customer record. When you need to edit information about the customer, you edit the customer record, assuming you have permission to do so.

Record types in NetSuite include:

- ✔ Employees
- ✔ Customers
- ✔ Contacts
- ✔ Leads
- ✔ Partners
- ✔ Projects
- ✔ Prospects
- ✔ Vendors
- ✔ Competitors
- ✔ Transactions

Creating new records

You need to create a new record whenever you have a new lead or product or vendor, or when you hire a new employee. For example, adding a new product means you'll need to create a new item record to describe all the information about that product. Or, when you go to a trade show and return with a fishbowl filled with business cards, you will want to create lead records for each of those potential customers.

You can create records in the following ways:

- ✔ **Tab menus:** Hover the cursor over the Lists menu, navigate to the record type, and then click New. For example, to create a new customer record, choose Lists⇨Relationships⇨Customers⇨New. (For some users it's at Customers⇨Lists⇨Customers⇨New.)

  Tab menus change for your role. What if the instructions in this book are different from what you see on your screen? NetSuite adjusts its tab menus to suit your role as your company has defined it. The good news is that it also adjusts its help text and does other tricks (like letting you search for a given screen). See "The NetSuite Help Center" later in this chapter for more information on using help.

- ✔ **The dashboard Links portlet:** The Links portlet has the same options that are available in the tab menu, as shown in Figure 3-4. The Links portlet may not display by default, but you can add it by clicking Customize This Page in the upper right of the dashboard.

Figure 3-4:
The Links
portlet
shows all
the options
available
in the
Activities
tab menu.

TIP

The Links portlets shrink to show only the most important links when positioned in the far-left or far-right columns on your dashboard. If you drag and drop the Links portlet into the wider center column, it will redraw with the full set of available links.

✔ **The Create New toolbar on your dashboard:** Your dashboard has a Create New toolbar at the top of the page, just below the tabs. The Create New toolbar on a dashboard provides instant one-click access to the records that are most relevant to your role. Just click the button that corresponds to the type of record you'd like to create, and a new blank record for that type appears. For example, click the Phone Call button to create a new record for a phone conversation with a sales lead.

TIP

✔ **The Create New toolbar on records:** Records also display a Create New toolbar (see Figure 3-5), but it works differently than the Create New toolbar on a dashboard. When you're viewing an existing record, any record you create with the Create New toolbar is automatically linked to the current record you're viewing. For example, if you click the Contact button on the Create New toolbar on a customer record, a new window allows you to create a contact linked specifically to that customer.

Figure 3-5:
Select an
option from
the Create
New drop-
down list to
link the new
record to the
customer.

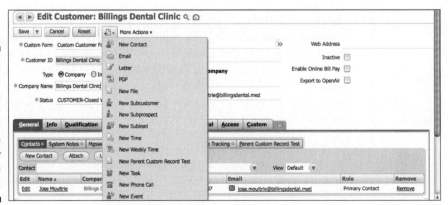

Accessing information in records

You can access information in records to update fields, manage and track activities, and view related data on tabs. Tabs on each record provide detailed data and activities related to a given record, including transactions, phone calls, message history, and more. In a customer record, for example, the Transactions tab shows all transactions associated with the current customer.

Field-level help is available. Just click the label beside a field; a window opens and describes the field's purpose and how it functions in NetSuite. Clicking these labels is an easy way to learn more while you're working.

Locating records using lists

NetSuite provides lists for all of the major record types, including customers, transactions, opportunities, and events. Lists display spreadsheet-like results that allow you to locate any record type in the system, as shown in Figure 3-6.

You can get to lists using the tab menus or from the Links portlet on your dashboard. To view a list of customers, choose Lists⇨Relationships⇨Customers. (Additional menu options pop up for New and Search, but if you want to simply view a list, ignore these options until you need them to create a new customer or search for customers, respectively.)

List shortcuts

Lists have the following shortcuts that help you locate records quickly:

- ✔ **To sort a list by a particular column, click the column header.** An arrow image appears in the header to show whether the sort order is ascending or descending. Click the header again to reverse the sort order.

- ✔ **Lists always display a footer section at the very bottom of the page.** The footer section contains footer filters that allow you to change the results of your list. For example, many lists contain a Quick Sort drop-down list that allows you to limit results to recently created, recently viewed, or recently modified records.

- ✔ **The footer contains a View drop-down list.** Views allow you to instantly change the columns of data in the list, or to filter the results. For example, on the customer list, you may create a view named Customers in California that only shows customers with a billing address in California and displays the customer name, billing address, and phone number columns. You can create as many personal views as you want simply by clicking the Customize View button in the footer area.

Inline Editing switch

Customers	Inline Editing	OFF	

Edit | View		Name ▲	Duplicate	Primary Contact	Category	Subsidiary	Sales Rep	Partner	Status	Phone	Email
Edit | View	☑	Barry Springsteen			Web Search	Parent Company	Jon Baker		CUSTOMER- Closed Won	504-888-9632	info@
Edit | View	☑	Battery Technologies				Parent Company			CUSTOMER- Closed Won		
Edit | View	☑	Beverly Linden				Parent Company	Theodore Hosch		CUSTOMER- Closed Won	801-218-3753	
Edit | View	☑	Billings Dental Clinic		Jose Moultrie		Parent Company	Theodore Hosch		CUSTOMER- Closed Won		jose.
Edit | View	☑	Bobby Plant			From advertisement	Parent Company	Jon Baker	X-Rays For Less	CUSTOMER- Closed Won	504-231-9984	info@
Edit | View	☑	Boulder Chiropractic Center		Shawn Warren		Parent Company	Jessie Barto		CUSTOMER- Closed Won	406-782-8016	shaw
Edit | View	☑	Brandon Sommerville (bsommerville@neolamed.med)				Parent Company	Theodore Hosch		CUSTOMER- Closed Won	435-950-0598	bsom
Edit | View	☑	Burt Sparling			From advertisement	Parent Company	Jon Baker		CUSTOMER- Closed Won	504-995-7743	jbush

Sales Rep	- All -	▼	Stage	Customer	▼	From-To	A — Craig Erickson	▼	Total Found: 122			
Show Inactives ☐	Style	Normal	▼	View	General	▼	Quick Sort		▼	New | Print | Customize View	Export - CSV ▼	

Figure 3-6:
Use the footer filters to refine and sort the presentation of data.

Footer filters

Changing or adding records from the list page

What if you're looking at a list and want to quickly make a change? What if you want to add a record quickly?

To change an entry in the list, click Enable Editing (just to the right of the page name). If the link says Disable Editing instead, then Enable Editing has already been turned on for you; just go ahead and fix whatever problems you see.

After you click the Enable Editing link, adding a bare-bones record is just as easy. The required fields for the record appear near the very bottom of the screen. Enter the information and click the Save button to the left of the fields. Who knew that a list could improve your productivity this much?

Saving Searches (and Time)

If you can't get the information you need using a list included in your account, NetSuite also provides powerful saved search options. You can get to them through the Reports tab menu (shown in Figure 3-7) and on your dashboard.

Saved searches are an important concept in NetSuite, and if you created a list view (described under "List shortcuts"), you've already created a simple saved search.

Click Search to create a personalized search where you define the result columns you want to see and the type of records you want to see. You can then save the search for future use. For more information on creating saved searches, see Chapter 22. You can also create a saved search from scratch by selecting New Search from the Reports tab menu.

The NetSuite Help Center

The NetSuite Help Center is complete help documentation that's always at your disposal. Simply click the Help option in the upper-right corner of the page (just to the left of the Global Search field) to open the NetSuite Help Center in a second browser window. In most cases, the document that opens applies to the page you're viewing, but often other topics exist on the subject. To find more, you can also search the entire Help Center or browse the table of contents.

Figure 3-7:
You can create a saved search by selecting New Search from the Reports tab menu.

New Saved Search
Search Type
2008 Customer Survey
2008 Documentation Survey
Account
Activity
Amortization Schedules
Another Test Custom Record
Budget
Campaign

Going Global Search

Every page in NetSuite contains a Global Search field in the upper-right corner. Among other options, you can look for the following:

- ✔ Records by name
- ✔ Customers by e-mail address
- ✔ Transactions by number

Global search is typically the quickest way to get information in NetSuite.

Global Search offers great shortcuts, such as auto suggest, prefixes, capitalization, and wildcards. These shortcuts are described in the following sections.

Auto suggest

Wouldn't it be great if a search engine could read your mind? The Auto Suggest function on Global Search is about as close as you can get to mind reading without getting spooky. As you type in the Global Search field, a box drops down and displays matches for your current search term, as shown in

Figure 3-8. You can select a suggestion to go straight to the page, or click the Go button to view a complete list of results.

Figure 3-8:
Type a
search term
in the Global
Search field
and get a
suggestion.
Or lots of
them.

Often, when you're searching for a record, you want to find and immediately modify it. Doing so is simple with the Auto Suggest Edit function. To open any Auto Suggest match for editing, click the Edit link that appears on the right side of the suggestion as you hover over the match. For record types that provide a dashboard, click the Dashboard icon that appears when you hover over the suggested match.

When the Auto Suggest box opens as you type in the Global Search field, you can click the record names or the Edit links to be taken directly to the record.

Using prefixes to search

If you know the record type that you're looking for, just prefix your search term with the first few letters of that record type, followed by a colon. Prefixes speed up the search process by limiting the results.

If you type c:, you get contacts and customers, but if you type cu:, you limit the search to customers.

For example, type cu:max in the Global Search field to search only for customers with records containing max. Type e:Jones to search for employees with records containing Jones.

Using a wildcard in numeric searches

Global Search returns exact matches on purely numeric search terms, such as case numbers or warehouse part numbers, in order to avoid returning extremely large result sets. For example, by default, when you type inv:115, only invoice number 115 is returned.

Use the percent sign (%) as a wildcard to get around the default behavior. For example, if you add the % sign to the previous entry (type in inv:115%), all invoices with numbers starting with 115 are returned.

Editing global search results

Prefixes in Global Search not only limit your search results, they can take you directly into a record in edit mode. Simply capitalize the first letter of the prefix to open the record in edit mode.

Say you're looking for an employee named Augustus and you know you only have one Augustus. Type in E:Augustus and snap — you're editing Augustus's employee record. (If you have more than one Augustus, of course you'll see a list instead. Then you'd click the Edit link, as before, to edit the record.)

If you can't find the page you're looking for in NetSuite, use Global Search and type page:*page name*. For example, type page:Payment to list pages with the word Payment in the title. Remember that the path to the page is displayed just below the Home tab. If it's a page you use frequently, click the Add to Shortcuts link in the upper-right corner of the page, under your name. You can give the shortcut a name, and your new shortcut will appear on your dashboard in your Shortcuts portlet and on your Home menu.

Clocking in on the Calendar

NetSuite's powerful group calendaring capabilities allow you to effectively manage your time, share your calendar with others, and link events to records in the system. Figure 3-9 shows how the interactive calendar is available on the Activities dashboard.

Microsoft Outlook users should know about NetSuite for Outlook, a no-cost feature that offers bidirectional synchronization of calendars, tasks, events, and contacts between NetSuite and Outlook. To read more, click Help in the upper right on the dashboard and search for **NetSuite for Outlook**.

Figure 3-9:
Schedule
meetings
and view
upcom-
ing events
on the
Activities
dashboard.

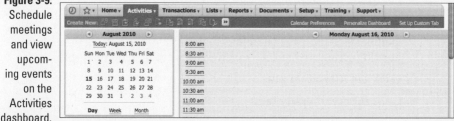

Setting up calendar preferences

Before you start working with your calendar, we recommend setting up these basic calendar preferences:

- ✔ **Set time zone:** Choose Home➪Set Preferences. On the General tab, choose from the Time Zone drop-down list, and click the Save button.

- ✔ **Name your calendar:** Click the Activities tab. In the upper right, click the Calendar Preferences link. In the Title field, enter a name for your calendar. You're the only person who can see this title. However, if you give other employees access to your calendar, those employees see the name when viewing your availability.

- ✔ **Share your calendar (or keep it private):** Choose Activities➪Calendar Preferences. The Sharing drop-down list allows you to decide who has access to your calendar. If you don't want anyone else to see events on your calendar, choose Private. If you want everyone to see events on your calendar, choose Public. If you want more control over who can see events on your calendar, use the Calendar Access tab to select specific people to view your calendar.

Scheduling events

You can display the calendar in Day, Week, or Month view by default. Choose a link below the small calendar on the left side to change to a different view.

Scheduling an event the traditional way

To schedule an event (such as a meeting), follow along:

1. **Click the Today link near your calendar.**

   The Calendar page displays.

2. **Click a time for the event (if it's today).**

   Or, if it's not today, click a date on the small calendar on the left side of the page, and then click a time.

   The Event screen appears.

3. **Fill in the Event and Location fields.**

4. **Enter information in the Message field.**

   Include data such as dial-in information (if you're setting up a phone meeting) or any other information you want to send to attendees.

5. **Click the Attendees tab.**

6. **Click the Availability tab.**

7. **(Optional) Click the Recurrence tab.**

   Now you can set up patterns if this event repeats, such as a weekly meeting.

8. **Click the Resources tab.**

   From here, book conference rooms and equipment.

9. **(Optional) Click the Related Info tab.**

   Do this if you want to specify that this meeting is about a particular customer or support case.

10. **(Optional) Click the Files tab.**

    Do this if you want to attach any files to the invitation, such as an agenda or a proposal.

11. **Click the Save button.**

    You can also create events from the Activities tab menu by choosing Scheduling ⇨ Events ⇨ New.

Scheduling via the Scheduler portlet

For quick event scheduling based on invitee availability, the Scheduler portlet on the Activities Overview page lets you quickly determine the best time for a meeting and schedule it speedy quick.

1. **Click the Activities tab and scroll down to see the Scheduler portlet.**

   If you don't see the Scheduler portlet, click the Activities tab to view the Activities Overview, and then click the Customize This Page link in the upper right.

2. **Select multiple invitees and determine free time.**

3. **Click the Create New Event button.**

   You end up at the event entry form with date, time, and invitee data pre-populated.

4. **Make any additions to this information.**

5. **Click the Save button.**

The Scheduler portlet provides a visual indicator for what time of the day all of your attendees are available. The thin colored line below the time bar is green if everyone is available and orange if one or more invitees is busy.

Attaching events to records

NetSuite lets you attach events to records to track meetings, phone calls, and tasks.

1. **Open a record.**

2. **Click the General tab, then the Activities tab.**

   The tab is shown in Figure 3-10.

3. **Notice the list of all activities associated with the customer:**

   • **New Task**

   • **Log Task**

   • **New Phone Call**

   • **Log Phone Call**

   • **New Event**

   • **Log Event**

   The buttons allow you to create new activities and automatically associate them with the current record.

   The New buttons indicate that you haven't done whatever it is yet, but plan to do it. The Log buttons indicate that you already did it but are noting it in the customer record, ensuring that all touchpoints with the customer are recorded.

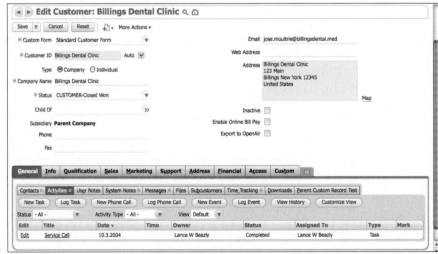

Figure 3-10: View activities associated with a customer on the customer record's Activities tab.

Chapter 4

Grabbing Hold of the Dashboard

In This Chapter
- ▶ Choosing your personal preferences
- ▶ Adding portlets to your dashboard
- ▶ Setting up your portlets

*I*t's time to make NetSuite your own. Personalizing your suite can make your workday more productive and more enjoyable. You can organize your dashboard and put your most important data right at your fingertips.

Your home dashboard and overview screens are broken up into small, customizable windows called *portlets*. Portlets summarize critical business metrics and are specific to your role. For example, if you're logged in as a Sales Person, the Leads Dashboard displays a list of leads that belong to you and a set of links to common tasks.

You can add and remove portlets, drag and drop portlets to move them to new locations, and alter the content each portlet displays. Put your most important data right at your fingertips, whether you're a sales person who wants a list of leads or a billing manager who wants a list of overdue accounts.

There is much more to know about customization, of course; see Bonus Chapter 4 (at **www.dummies.com/go/netsuitefd**) for more information on customization and Chapter 20 for a deeper dive on dashboards.

Being Privy to Different Portlets

Not all users are created equal. Even if you're a sales person surrounded by 100 other sales people, you may have different needs and expectations than the rest of the team. You may only want the list of your hottest leads on your Home tab, while your coworker wants to load his Home tab with every possible option, including KPIs, report snapshots, and daily phone calls.

NetSuite dashboards provide ultimate flexibility in organizing your workspace. Setting up your dashboard to meet your individual needs is one of the most important and effective ways to ensure success in NetSuite and to give you an edge over your competition.

NetSuite offers many kinds of portlets so you can display the data you need:

- ✔ **Activities:** Shows daily and upcoming activities, with links to detailed activity records.

- ✔ **Custom Search:** Shows the results of a saved search. Custom search portlets display three columns of data when placed in the right or left (skinny) columns of a dashboard, and eight columns when placed in the center (wide) column of your dashboard. See Chapter 3 for more on saved searches.

- ✔ **Lists:** Shows the type of records you choose with links to view (and edit, if you have permission) individual records.

- ✔ **Key Performance Indicators:** Shows summary data and key business metrics, with options to highlight results that don't meet defined thresholds, and to show comparisons between date ranges. As shown in Figure 4-1, the KPI portlet brings your critical business data to the forefront of the dashboard.

No matter what role you use or what job function you serve, you'll want at least one KPI on your dashboard. If none of the standard KPIs meet your needs, you can create custom KPIs using saved searches. (Creating custom KPIs is covered in Chapter 20.)

- ✔ **KPI Meters:** Shows a graphical meter of KPI data, with options to flag metrics that meet a specific threshold and to compare across date ranges.

- ✔ **KPI Scorecard:** KPI scorecards can provide complex comparisons among multiple KPIs over multiple date ranges or accounting periods. Scorecards also can include Excel-like formulas with KPIs and functions in their expressions.

Figure 4-1:
Find critical business data in the Key Performance Indicators portlet.

Key Performance Indicators				▼ ⊙ _ ×
Indicator	Period	Current	Previous	Change
Total Bank Balance	This Period	$2,126,400		
Expenses	This Period	$44		
Payables	This Period	$653,838		
Open Cases	Today vs One Year Ago	20	16	↑ 25.0%
Sales (Billings)	Last Year vs Year Before Last	$103,879	$14,841	↑ 599.9%
Total Sales (Orders)	Year Before Last vs Three Years Ago	$40,129	$17,861	↑ 124.7%
Web Site Hits	Year Before Last vs Three Years Ago	296	215	↑ 37.7%

What's the difference between KPIs, KPI meters, and KPI scorecards?

- **KPIs** show a quick table of key performance indicators that you select. The table includes the KPI name, the period being compared (this month versus last month, for example), the current value, the previous value, and the percentage change. This portlet provides a quick overview of a number of KPIs.

- A **KPI meter** shows how you're doing on a particular KPI. Maybe you're a customer support representative who shouldn't have more than ten cases open at any one time.

- **KPI scorecards** are powerful analytical tools that are mainly used by managers to monitor the relationships among KPIs. They can watch the company's fiscal health, for example. This isn't your average Joe's "How am I doing this week?" kind of a KPI tool, in other words.

✓ **Quick Date Selector:** Shows a drop-down list of time period comparisons. Your selection from this drop-down list resets the date ranges for all dashboard portlet content. Does your dashboard show results for the last month? Change the dates in this drop-down list and you can change all the dashboard portlets to year-to-date values, for example. Choices include comparisons like This Week versus Last Week.

✓ **Reminders:** Shows reminders of upcoming and overdue tasks such as outstanding bills, overdue calls, and items that need to be ordered.

✓ **Report Snapshots:** Shows a graphical summary of a report's data, with a link to view the underlying report. The summary can be displayed as a bar graph, pie chart, or list. If none of the standard report snapshots meet your needs, you can create a custom report snapshot and display it in this portlet. (Creating custom report snapshots is covered in Chapter 20.)

✓ **RSS/Atom Feed:** You can publish information from news sources on your dashboard. By default NetSuite offers feeds from CNN, Reuters, Yahoo!, CBS Market Watch, and more. In addition to the predefined feeds, you can display custom RSS feeds from other sites or create a custom feed to publish messages to users of your NetSuite account. To stop a feed, click the X in the upper-right corner of the portlet.

✓ **Shortcuts:** Shows links to selected pages so you can navigate quickly to frequently used pages. You can edit the default shortcuts or create your own from scratch.

✓ **Trend Graphs:** Shows a line graph of KPI data trended over a time-based X-axis. Custom KPIs based on a saved search can also be displayed.

Figure 4-2 shows a dashboard with several portlets enabled.

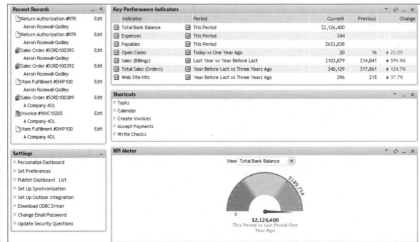

Figure 4-2:
This dash-
board
shows busi-
ness data.

Adding, Subtracting, and Moving Portlets

Dashboards in NetSuite are a lot more malleable than the dashboard in your car. You can customize the page by adding, hiding, or repositioning portlets. Don't try this at home with your speedometer.

Adding and removing portlets

To expose the Add Content pane, click the Personalize Dashboard link in the upper-right corner of your dashboard. For a description of what a portlet looks like and the data it displays, roll your cursor over its label in the Add Content pane. An enhanced tooltip box appears with a graphical representation and a brief description, as shown in Figure 4-3.

The Add Content pane shows the portlets available to you, organized in folders. All roles will see a Standard Portlets folder; only roles with the appropriate permissions will see the Report Snapshots and Trend Graphs folders.

1. **Click Personalize Dashboard.**

   The option is available on every dashboard.

2. **Drag the portlet you want from the Add Content pane to the dashboard location where you want it to live.**

   You can also click the portlet in the Add Content pane to add that portlet to the top row of your dashboard.

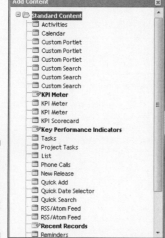

Figure 4-3:
Add portlets
via the Add
Content
pane.

Your administrator can create and publish specific content to a dashboard. If your administrator has published a specific dashboard for you and locked down the content, you can't add, remove, or set up your portlets. Published dashboards are covered in Chapter 21.

Removing a portlet really means hiding it: Click the X in the upper-right corner of the portlet.

Positioning portlets

Repositioning, removing, and minimizing portlets are as easy as clicks of a mouse. All portlets allow you to these basic actions, as shown by the crossed arrows when you hover over the portlet. Figure 4-4 shows the Shortcuts portlet being dragged to a new location.

- ✓ **Reposition by drag and drop:** To move a portlet into a new position, simply click and drag its title bar. Some portlets, such as Report Snapshots and Custom Searches, expand to show more data when they're in the wide center column.

- ✓ **Minimize/maximize a portlet:** You can minimize portlets so they're easily accessible but don't take up space on your dashboard. Minimizing also reduces the time your dashboard takes to load. When a portlet is minimized, you only see the title bar that displays the portlet name.

  Maximize and minimize via the icon in the upper-right corner of the portlet. When you want to minimize, click the minus sign (–) icon. When you want to maximize, click the plus sign (+).

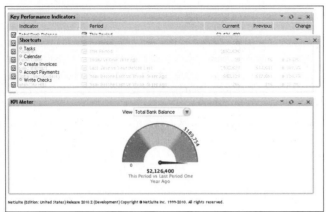

NetSuite (Edition: United States) Release 2010.2 (Development) Copyright © NetSuite Inc. 1999-2010. All rights reserved.

Figure 4-4:
You can
drag and
drop a port-
let when
you want to
reorganize.

Customizing Portlets

Most portlets allow you to control the displayed data and how it's formatted.
Click Set Up (shown in Figure 4-5) at the bottom of a portlet to expose a setup
window with all of the available options.

Report Snapshot, Trend Graph, List, and Custom Search portlets are empty
until you click Set Up and choose the content you want to see. Other portlets
have data by default (examples include your calendar or your reminders).

Figure 4-5:
Click Set Up
to modify the
contents of
your portlets.

Portlets generate their content when you first log in. If you think the data has
changed, click the Refresh icon (circular arrows) in the top right of the portlet
to see the most recent information.

Comparing between dates

The Quick Date Selector lets you change the dates for everything in your
dashboard at once. To compare periods, choose a comparison option from

the Quick Date Selector drop-down list, such as This Qtr vs Last Qtr or This Qtr vs Same Last Year. On the other hand, you can keep it recent with Today vs Yesterday.

Flagging metrics that meet a threshold

The Key Performance Indicators portlet provides an easy way to show you how to flag metrics that exceed (or fall below) a given threshold.

To flag results that fall over or under your desired threshold:

1. **In the upper-right corner of the Key Performance Indicators portlet, click the down arrow and choose Set Up.**

   The Set Up Key Performance Indicators screen appears.

2. **Click Add Standard KPIs.**

   The Choose Standard Key Performance Indicators window appears.

3. **Select a key performance indicator.**

4. **From the Highlight If drop-down list, choose Greater Than or Less Than.**

5. **In the Threshold field, enter a value that you want to monitor.**

6. **Click Save.**

The dashboard refreshes to display the current value for the Key Performance Indicator. If the value for the KPI exceeds the threshold, a flag appears.

See the icon on the right side of your key performance indicator? That is the Refresh button. See the icon to the left of it? Click it to display a trend graph.

Display custom RSS feeds

Display custom RSS feeds from other sites with these steps:

1. **Choose Personalize Dashboard.**

   The Add Content Pane appears.

2. **Select RSS/Atom Feed.**

An RSS feed (that an admin has set up) is added to your dashboard.

Create shortcuts

The Shortcuts portlet includes shortcuts to all your favorite pages. So if you enter purchase orders all day, you can go straight to that screen (or any other of your favorite screens).

To add a shortcut to the shortcuts portlet (which is displayed by default):

1. **Go to the page you habitually visit.**

2. **In the upper-left corner of the page, select Add to Shortcuts from the star drop-down menu.**

   An Add Shortcut windows appears.

3. **Click Save.**

A link to this page is added to your shortcuts portlet.

Part II
Tracking Money and Resources

The 5th Wave   By Rich Tennant

"For 30 years I've put a hat and coat on to make sales calls and I'm not changing now just because I'm doing it on the Web in my living room."

In this part . . .

Keeping track of money is the key to profitability. Part II describes keeping the books (Chapter 5), invoicing customers and managing receivables as well as the flip side — paying your bills (Chapter 6) and managing inventory to make sure you can keep customers happy and your bottom line healthy (Chapter 7).

Chapter 5

Bookkeeping Basics

*I*n this chapter, you find out how transactions work and how to set up your chart of accounts and accounting periods — features you may not be familiar with but that are affected every time your financials change! Fortunately, when you're up and running, you probably won't have to think about them every day.

Similarly, you don't need to worry about understanding debits and credits unless you're a serious accounting user, but it's helpful to know how they affect your financials as you're doing business.

After that, you get into the practical side of bookkeeping, and read a few tips and tricks for handling your day-to-day banking activities — from writing a check to reconciling your bank balance.

You must be logged in using the Accountant or Bookkeeper role to access financial information for your company in NetSuite. If you aren't, you can't follow the steps in this chapter.

Accounting terms

Fortunately, you don't need a detailed knowledge of accounting rules and procedures to use NetSuite as your bookkeeping system, but knowing some basic accounting terms is helpful:

✔ **General ledger:** The record of all your company's financial history.

✔ **General ledger accounts:** The accounts used within your general ledger to categorize your financial history. In NetSuite, you see these simply referred to as _accounts_.

✔ **Transaction:** A record of a specific financial event or activity.

✔ **Posted:** Recorded in the accounting system. For example, when you write a check or send your customer an invoice, those events are recorded (posted) in your general ledger as transactions.

✔ **Transaction lines:** Transactions typically post to more than one account. Each transaction has multiple transaction lines, with each line posting an amount to a particular account.

✔ **Debit** and **credit:** Simply, debits and credits either increase or decrease the balance of a general ledger account. Within each transaction, the total amount of debits must equal the total amount of credits. Each amount on a transaction line may represent either a debit or a credit. Debits and credits are the fundamental building blocks of the double-entry bookkeeping system.

Managing Your Chart of Accounts

Your bird's eye view of the general ledger is known as the _chart of accounts_. As shown in Figure 5-1, the chart of accounts displays a list of names, account types, and balances of all your general ledger accounts.

Figure 5-1:
The Chart of Accounts lists all the accounts that are set up, as well as their balances.

Chart of Accounts

Edit	Number	Account	Type	Description	Currency	Foreign Currency Balance	Balance
Edit		Accumulated Depreciation	Deferred Expense				0.00
Edit		Customer Deposits	Other Current Liability				-100.00
Edit		Deferred Expense	Deferred Expense				9,065.00
Edit		Exchange Rate Variance	Other Expense				0.00
Edit		Failed ACH Transactions	Other Current Liability				0.00
Edit		GST/HST Liability	Other Current Liability				0.00
Edit		GST/HST on Purchases	Other Current Asset				0.00
Edit		GST/HST Payable	Other Current Liability				0.00
Edit		Intercompany Payable/Receivable CAD	Other Current Asset		Canadian Dollar	$0.00	0.00
Edit		Intercompany Payable/Receivable EUR	Other Current Asset		Euro	€0,00	0.00
Edit		Intercompany Payable/Receivable USD	Other Current Asset		USA	$0.00	0.00
Edit		Inventory In Transit	Other Current Asset				0.00
Edit		Inventory Returned Not Credited	Other Current Asset				800.00
Edit		Payroll Float	Other Current Asset				0.00
Edit		PST Expenses AB	Expense				0.00
Edit		PST Expenses QC	Expense				0.00

Show Inactives ☐   Report Style ☐   View Basic ▼

New   Print   Export - CSV ▼

To view your chart of accounts, from the Financial tab menu, choose Lists➪ Accounts.

Your chart of accounts in NetSuite contains many account types. Each account type groups together similar accounts that represent an aspect of your financial activities. For example, income accounts track the value of sales to your customers, while bank accounts track the amount of money you have in the bank.

Creating and editing accounts

From the chart of accounts, you can create brand new accounts or modify characteristics of your existing accounts.

You must have the role of Accountant to create or edit general ledger accounts.

Creating a general ledger account

To create a new general ledger account:

1. **From the Financial tab menu, choose Lists➪Accounts➪New.**

2. **Choose the type of account you want to create from the Type drop-down list.**

    If you select Bank from the Type drop-down list, you must also select a currency from the Currency drop-down list.

    Currency must be specified for bank accounts because the bank may be in a different country (Switzerland or Nigeria perhaps) and therefore use a different currency from your main NetSuite account.

3. **Enter a name for the account in the Name field.**

    If your company requires account numbers (a preference set at the company level in NetSuite), an account number is also required. See the later section "Assigning account numbers" for more information on account numbers.

4. **Enter any other details desired for this account.**

5. **Click Save.**

Editing an existing general ledger account

To edit an existing general ledger account, follow these steps:

1. **From the Financial tab menu, choose Lists➪Accounts.**

2. **In the Chart of Accounts list, click the Edit link next to the name of the account you want to edit.**

3. **Edit the text in the Name or Description fields.**

   Editing the text modifies account properties, such as the name or description.

4. **Click Save.**

Depending on which features you've turned on, you may be puzzled to see some accounts in your chart of accounts with a Non-Posting account type. Some types of transactions don't affect your financials because they represent business activities with no immediate financial impact. These are *non-posting transactions,* which are tracked in *non-posting accounts.* Although non-posting accounts may appear in your chart of accounts alongside posting accounts, they don't affect your general ledger.

For example, a sales order represents a commitment to sell goods or services, but it doesn't represent collecting money, fulfilling the goods, or recording revenue earned. Those specific financial events are recorded by separate posting transactions later (in the case of a sales order, those events might be recorded by a cash sale or an invoice).

Examining account registers

From the chart of accounts, you can click the name of a particular account to view that account's register, an example of which is shown in Figure 5-2. An *account register* gives you basic information about the transactions posted to that account, such as the posting date, the transaction number, and the amount.

Figure 5-2: View an account register.

Inventory Asset Register						
Date	Number	Payee		Increase	Decrease	Balance
	Type	Account	Memo			
16.10.2008	1			$2,193.00		$7,502,088.8
Edit	INV DIST	81400 - Other Expenses				
16.10.2008	1				$2,193.00	$7,499,895.8
Edit	INV DIST	81400 - Other Expenses				
16.10.2008	1			$2,193.00		$7,502,088.8
Edit	INV DIST	81400 - Other Expenses				
16.10.2008	1				$2,193.00	$7,499,895.8
Edit	INV DIST	81400 - Other Expenses				
16.10.2008	1			$2,193.00		$7,502,088.8
Edit	INV DIST	81400 - Other Expenses				
16.10.2008	1				$2,193.00	$7,499,895.8
Edit	INV DIST	81400 - Other Expenses				
16.10.2008	1			$676.20		$7,500,572.0
Edit	INV DIST	81400 - Other Expenses				
16.10.2008	1				$676.20	$7,499,895.8
Edit	INV DIST	81400 - Other Expenses				
16.10.2008	1			$686.00		$7,500,581.8
Edit	INV DIST	81400 - Other Expenses				
16.10.2008	1			$2,193.00		$7,502,774.8

Date all   From [ ]   To [ ]   Subsidiary Context Parent Company (Consolidated) ▼

1-Line ☐   Sort By date, type, document ▼   Open ☐

Refresh   Print   Email   Export - CSV ▼

The register, like many pages in NetSuite, uses footers to let you filter results on the page. The footer is what NetSuite calls the drop-down lists at the bottom of the page where you can change what data is displayed. On the footer for a register, you have several options for defining the data included and how the register displays:

- ✔ To **change the range of transactions displayed,** enter different start and end dates in the From and To fields, and click the Refresh button. You can also click the calendar icon beside the From and To fields to select a date from a pop-up calendar.

- ✔ To **view more transactions at once,** but with fewer details, select the 1-Line check box and then click the Refresh button.

- ✔ To **change how transactions sort,** choose a different option in the Sort By drop-down list and then click the Refresh button. By default, registers sort by transaction date, then by transaction type, and finally by transaction number.

Assigning account numbers

You may identify accounts by number as well as by name. Account numbering is useful for grouping related accounts within your chart of accounts and financial reports.

For example, expense accounts track the cost of your company's financial activities. You can assign each expense account a number between 6000–6999, and then create smaller groupings within that number range (such as numbering to identify certain types of expense accounts). Expense accounts that track utility costs can be assigned numbers between 6000–6499 and expense accounts that track travel costs can be assigned numbers from 6500–6999. You can also choose account numbers in drop-down lists or enter account numbers in data fields, for example, when you're entering transactions.

Assign account numbers to identify particular types of accounts by a number range. You must be an Administrator or have similar permissions to enable account numbers in NetSuite.

Follow along to use account numbers in NetSuite:

1. **From the Setup tab menu, choose Accounting⊅Accounting Preferences.**

2. **On the General tab, select the Use Account Numbers check box.**

3. **Click Save.**

When this preference is on, you can assign account numbers by editing each account. See the earlier section, "Creating and editing accounts."

When the Use Account Numbers preference is enabled, you must assign a number to any new accounts you create. You also have to assign a number to existing accounts if you edit them.

Running a general ledger report

Although an account register provides a detail of general ledger activity for a specific account, you can also get a report that shows the details for all accounts. Appropriately enough, this is the *general ledger report*.

To view the General Ledger report, as shown in Figure 5-3, choose Reports⇨Financial⇨General Ledger. You can change the date range that shows in the report by entering different start and end dates in the From and To fields in the footer of the report.

Figure 5-3:
The General
Ledger
report
shows the
details
for all
accounts.

Account	Type	Date	Num	Name	Debit	Credit	Balance	
General Ledger								
⊟ 2011 - Bank of Germany							$14.35	
Total - 2011 - Bank of Germany					$0.00	$0.00	$14.35	
⊟ 2012 - Germany 2							($38.09)	
Total - 2012 - Germany 2					$0.00	$0.00	($38.09)	
⊟ 10000 - Bank of the West-checking							($388,473.16)	
Total - 10000 - Bank of the West-checking					$0.00	$0.00	($388,473.16)	
⊟ 10100 - Investments							$100.00	
Total - 10100 - Investments					$0.00	$0.00	$100.00	
⊟ 10200 - Investments - Fidelity							$53.75	
Total - 10200 - Investments - Fidelity					$0.00	$0.00	$53.75	
⊟ 2010 - Bank of the East							$21.52	
Total - 2010 - Bank of the East					$0.00	$0.00	$21.52	
⊟ 11000 - Accounts Receivable							$1,264,883.73	
Total - 11000 - Accounts Receivable					$0.00	$0.00	$1,264,883.73	
⊟ 11200 - Delinquent Accounts							$968.91	
Total - 11200 - Delinquent Accounts					$0.00	$0.00	$968.91	
⊟ Inventory Returned Not Credited							$800.00	
Total - Inventory Returned Not Credited					$0.00	$0.00	$800.00	

Period This Period ▼ From Aug 2010 ▼ To Aug 2010 ▼ Subsidiary Context Parent Company (Consolidated) ▼

Refresh Customize   Options 🔍▼ □ □   Print Email Schedule Export - CSV ▼

Debits, Credits, and Journal Entries

When you create a transaction in the general ledger, in the language of accounting, you're also creating a *journal entry*. When someone refers to the journal entry aspect of a transaction, she means the financial impact — the debits and credits.

Debits and credits increase or decrease the balance of your accounts. That's only part of the story, however. The account balances are posted to the general ledger. The type of account determines whether they increase or decrease the balance:

- ✔ **Debits** increase the balance of an expense or asset account. They decrease the balance of an income, liability, or equity account.

- ✔ **Credits** have the opposite effect. They increase the balance of an income, liability, or equity account, and decrease the balance of an expense or asset account.

Every transaction must be *in balance;* in other words, the total amount of debits must equal the total amount of credits. NetSuite doesn't let you create a transaction where the credits and debits don't balance.

Use the GL Impact page to see the debits and credits for any transaction, as shown in Figure 5-4. (You might guess, correctly, that the GL in GL Impact is *general ledger.*)

Figure 5-4:
You can see
the general
ledger
impact for
a customer
invoice.

GL Impact									
Account	Amount (Debit)	Amount (Credit)	Posting	Memo	Name	Subsidiary	Department	Class	Location
11200 Delinquent Accounts	940.63		Yes	second account receivable	Craig Koozer, DDS	Parent Company	Sales	Dental	
40500 Sales		750.00	Yes			Parent Company	Sales	Dental	
50000 Cost of Goods Sold	100.00		Yes	Cost of Sales		Parent Company	Sales	Dental	
12000 Inventory Asset		100.00	Yes	Cost of Sales		Parent Company	Sales	Dental	
40500 Sales		125.00	Yes	Healthy tooth logo toothbrush		Parent Company	Sales	Dental	
50000 Cost of Goods Sold	25.00		Yes	Cost of Sales		Parent Company	Sales	Dental	
12000 Inventory Asset		25.00	Yes	Cost of Sales		Parent Company	Sales	Dental	
27150 Sales Tax Payable		65.63	Yes	Sales Tax	Montana Tax Man	Parent Company	Sales	Dental	

Total Found: 8

Seeing the debits and credits

To see the debits and credits for a transaction:

1. **View the transaction record in NetSuite by clicking the transaction name or number in a list.**

   Don't click the Edit button, or the GL Impact feature won't be available.

2. **Click the GL Impact link in the upper-right corner of the page.**

You can enter many different types of transactions in NetSuite. In accounting terms, all of these transactions post journal entries to your general ledger. Also, when you view an account register (see the earlier section, "Managing Your Chart of Accounts"), you can see the debits and credits posted to that account and the type of each transaction that posted to the journal entry.

However, keep in mind that a journal entry is the debits and credits for a transaction, such as a check or a cash sale; the journal entry *isn't* a separate record from that transaction — it's part of it.

You can also create a more general kind of journal entry that is not part of a transaction of another type. In this case, *journal entry* is the transaction type. You can create many different types of transactions in NetSuite, each of which has a specialized purpose. For example, a check is a type of transaction used to make a purchase or pay off a bill and always credits (decreases) your bank account balance.

The most generic transaction type in NetSuite is the *journal entry,* which may post debits and credits to any account. Journal entries have many possible uses; in particular, they're handy for making adjustments between accounts.

For example, you might create a general journal entry at the end of a fiscal year to take the balance of a single expense account and split it across two expense accounts to categorize the costs in more detail. This would be much easier than trying to split that balance by editing the transactions that posted to the original expense account throughout the fiscal year.

Creating a new general journal entry

To create a new general journal entry, as shown in Figure 5-5, follow along:

1. **From the Financial tab menu, choose Other⇨Make Journal Entries.**
2. **In the Date field, enter the date you want the journal entry to post.**
3. **Select or enter an account in the Account field.**
4. **Enter a debit or credit amount.**
5. **Click the Add button.**
6. **Click Save.**

If your credits and debits aren't balanced, you can't save the journal entry. The Out of Balance By fields show whether you have a credit or debit amount out of balance.

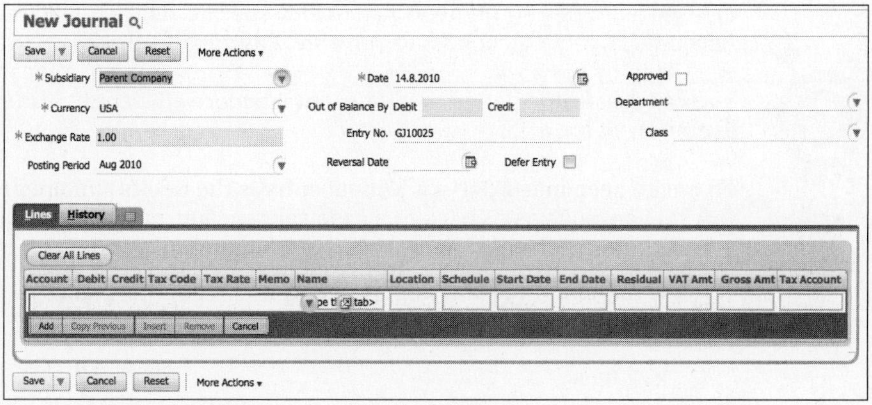

Figure 5-5:
A general journal entry.

Using Accounting Periods

Every transaction is assigned a posting date. When you search for or report on transactions, you look at a specific date range (for those transactions, even if that range is *all dates*). For example, if you run an income statement report for a particular month, it only includes transactions with posting dates during that month.

You may also assign an accounting period to your transactions, and search or report based on that accounting period instead of a date. Like a month, a period represents a certain range of dates. By default, new transactions are assigned to the period that contains their posting date, but you may choose to post them to a different period, without changing the date.

Assume, for example, that a vendor sends you a bill dated September 30, but you don't get it in the mail until mid-October. By that time, you've already closed your books for September, so you don't want this new bill to affect the September financials. With accounting periods, you can date the transaction September 30 but post it to the October accounting period, so that it affects the October financials instead.

Accounting periods also provide more control over closing your books. If you don't use periods, you can only lock all transactions on or before a certain date. Accounting periods allow you to lock specific categories of transactions — Accounts Payable, Accounts Receivable, Payroll, or All.

You can create one period at a time, but it's more efficient to set up an entire fiscal year at once.

To create accounting periods you must have the role of Administrator:

1. **From the Setup tab menu, choose Company⇨Enable Features.**

2. **On the Enable Features page, click the Accounting tab.**

3. **Select the Accounting Periods check box.**

4. **Click Save.**

5. **From the Setup tab menu, choose Accounting⇨Manage Accounting Periods.**

6. **Click a button depending on your preference:**

   • **New Period** creates an individual period.

   • **Set Up Year** creates periods for an entire fiscal year at once.

7. **Take the following steps based on what you chose in Step 6:**

   • If you're creating an individual period, enter a name in the Period Name field, and enter dates in the Start Date and End Date fields.

   • If you're setting up a year, select a month from the First Fiscal Month drop-down list, and enter the fiscal year in the Fiscal Year End field.

8. **From the Period Format drop-down list, choose the duration for each period within that fiscal year.**

9. **Click Save to create your accounting period(s).**

When you create periods for an entire fiscal year at once, NetSuite automatically creates a period hierarchy with the fiscal year at the top level, then fiscal quarters, and finally the individual accounting periods.

You only assign transactions to the lowest-level periods, not to a fiscal year period or a quarter. You use the higher-level types of periods when reporting on or searching for transactions.

Banking on It

Although only one aspect of your general accounting system, tracking everything that affects your bank and credit card accounts is one of the most crucial bookkeeping activities. The main reason is probably obvious — you need to know how much money or credit you have available to spend.

Making a deposit

One of the happier moments among your responsibilities as a bookkeeper may be putting money in the bank. In NetSuite when you want to make a deposit, usually those funds have been received on another transaction and posted to an Undeposited Funds account.

For example, a cash sale transaction might represent a retail sale in your store, for which the customer paid cash. You already have that money in hand, but it's not in the bank yet — hence the posting to the Undeposited Funds account.

When you're ready to deposit this money, record it by using the Deposit page shown in Figure 5-6. On the Deposit page, you specify which transactions you're depositing to transfer those funds from the Undeposited Funds account to your bank account.

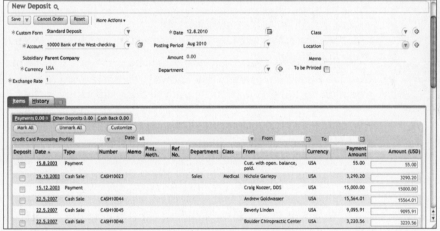

Figure 5-6:
The Deposit page is where money goes from Undeposited Funds to your bank account.

Recording a deposit

To record a deposit:

1. **From the Financial tab menu, choose Banking⇨Make Deposits.**
2. **Enter the date of the deposit in the Date field.**

   The field defaults to today's date.

3. **On the Items tab on the bottom half of the screen, click the Payments tab, and then check the Deposit check box for each transaction to deposit.**

   As you select each check box, notice that the Amount field updates to reflect the current total amount of the deposit.

4. **If some or all of the funds to deposit haven't previously been recorded in NetSuite, click the Other Deposits tab.**

   These amounts *aren't* in the Undeposited Funds account.

5. **On the Other Deposits tab, enter the amount in the Amount field and select the account from the Account drop-down list for each deposit.**

   If appropriate, you can also enter such information as the payor and method of payment in the Name field and Payment Method fields, respectively.

6. **If you're getting cash back, click the Cash Back tab.**

   This may occur when you deposit a check and get part of it as cash back.

7. **On the Cash Back tab, enter the amount in the Amount field and select the account from the Account drop-down list.**

   For example, you can select a bank account you set up to track cash.

8. **Click Save.**

To see a list of all the deposits you entered, from the Financial tab menu, choose Banking⇨Make Deposits⇨List.

Printing deposit slips

You can print a deposit slip that shows the total amount of cash and checks you're depositing. You can print your deposit slip in any of the following ways:

- ✔ When entering a deposit, click the arrow on the right of the Save button and choose Save & Print.

- ✔ When entering or editing a deposit, queue up a deposit slip to print later by selecting the To Be Printed check box and then clicking Save.

- ✔ You can print a deposit slip from the Deposits list of your deposit transactions by clicking the Print link to the right of the Date column.

When you want to print deposit slips you've queued, follow these steps:

1. **From the Financial tab menu, choose Banking⇨Print Checks & Forms.**

   The Print Checks & Forms page appears.

2. **Choose the Deposits link from the list of options.**

3. **Select the bank account you're depositing to in the Account drop-down list.**

4. **Select the Print check box for the appropriate deposit(s) in the list.**

5. **Click Print.**

Transferring money between accounts

If your business has more than one bank account, you may need to move money from one account to another. The bank account type also tracks cash belonging to the company, sometimes referred to as *petty cash*. You can use this cash to pay for business expenses rather than writing a check or using a credit card.

Use the Transfer page when you transfer money between bank accounts or withdraw cash from a bank account; see Figure 5-7.

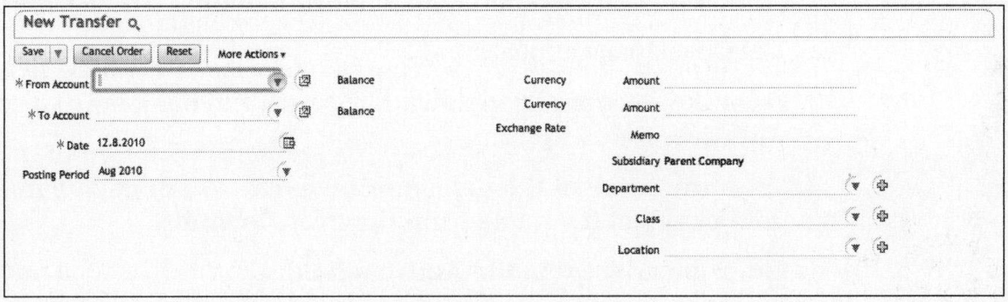

Figure 5-7:
The
Transfer
page.

Record a transfer of money in NetSuite:

1. **From the Financial tab menu, choose Banking⇨Transfer Funds.**

2. **In the From Account drop-down list, select the bank account from which you're withdrawing money.**

3. **In the To Account drop-down list, select the bank account you're transferring the money to.**

4. **In the Date field, enter the date you're transferring the money.**

5. **In the Amount field, enter the amount of money you're transferring.**

6. **(Optional) Enter a memo in the Memo field.**

7. **Click Save.**

To see a list of all the transfers you've entered, from the Financial tab menu, choose Banking⇨Transfer Funds⇨List.

Writing a check

A check is the most basic type of purchase transaction in NetSuite. When you write a check, the funds are deducted from your bank register balance and posted to an expense account or accounts.

Some of your purchases may be made on terms or credit, so you don't pay for them immediately. In that case, you enter a bill when the purchase is made, and pay it off later by writing a bill payment check. See Chapter 6 for more information.

You create several types of checks in NetSuite — paychecks, tax liability checks, bill payments — but for now you see the steps for the kind you use most often: a regular purchase check.

To write a check:

1. **From the Financial tab menu, choose Banking➪Write Checks.**

   The Check page appears.

2. **From the Account drop-down list, select the bank account you want to withdraw funds from.**

3. **Enter the name of the person or business you're paying in the Payee field or select the name from the drop-down list.**

4. **Enter the address in the Address field.**

5. **Select the period in the Posting Period drop-down list, and in the Date field, enter the date you want the check to post.**

6. **If you need to print the check, select the To Be Printed check box.**

7. **Enter the amount in the Amount field.**

8. **(Optional) Enter the check number in the Check # field and a memo in the Memo field.**

9. **Enter the amount in the Amount field.**

10. **Record either the expense account or the items purchased:**

    • *To record the purchase in an expense account,* click the Expenses tab and choose an expense account appropriate for your purchase from the drop-down list.

      For example, if you're buying a desk chair, you may choose a Furniture or Office Supplies expense account.

    • *To record the items purchased,* click the Items tab, select each item purchased, enter the quantity, and then click Add.

      You can use the Items tab to track the purchase of any goods or services set up as item records in NetSuite.

    Don't record the same purchase on both the Expenses and Items tabs because the purchase will be counted twice.

11. **Click Save.**

To see a list of all the checks you have entered, from the Financial tab menu, choose Banking➪Write Checks➪List.

You actually use the same Check page to record any kind of transaction (such as a wire transfer) that withdraws funds from your bank account. When you use a check this way, it's a good idea to enter a code in the Check # field (such as WT for wire transfer) and make sure you don't choose the To Be Printed check box.

Printing checks

When you record checks in NetSuite, you may want to print each one immediately, or enter a number of checks and print them all at once:

- ✔ When entering a check, you can immediately print it by clicking the arrow on the right of the Save button and selecting Save & Print. The check is assigned the number specified in the Check # field.

- ✔ When entering or editing a check, you can queue it to print later by selecting the To Be Printed check box and then clicking Save. In this case, the Check # field reads To Print until a check number is assigned when you print it.

- ✔ You can queue checks to print from your bank register. Just select the Print check box to the left of each check you want to print later.

Printing checks in your print queue

To print checks in your print queue:

1. **From the Financial tab menu, choose Banking⇨Print Checks and Forms.**

   NetSuite prints checks on blank check stock, which can be ordered from office supply vendors, including the supplier listed on the Print Checks and Forms page.

2. **Click the Checks link.**

   The Print Checks screen appears.

3. **Select the bank account from the Account drop-down list.**

4. **Select the Print check box for the appropriate check(s) in the list.**

5. **In the First Check Number field, enter the first check number you want to use.**

   You can select the Print Back to Front check box to print the checks in reverse order, finishing with the number you entered in the First Check Number field.

6. **Select an option from the Check Type drop-down list:**

   • **Standard** prints three checks per page with no voucher.

   • **Voucher** prints checks where the top third of each page is the check and the rest is used as a voucher.

7. **Click Print.**

You select the check type to use for a specific print job from the Checks print queue, as described in Step 5, but you can also set a company default to use unless you specify otherwise.

Setting the company default for printed check type

To set the company default for the printed check type, ask an administrator to set the preference in this way:

1. **From the Setup tab menu, choose Company⇨Printing, Fax, and Email Preferences.**

2. **On the Printing tab, under Check Printing, select an option from the Default Check Type drop-down list:**

   • **Standard**

   • **Voucher**

3. **Click Save.**

Putting it on plastic: Credit cards

Along with checks, another common way to purchase goods and services is to pay for them with a company credit card.

Create a separate credit card general ledger account for each company credit card, so that you accurately track your balances and reconcile them to the credit card statements from the bank or credit card vendor.

Making a purchase

Recording a credit card purchase in NetSuite is simple. The Credit Card page shown in Figure 5-8 is almost identical to the Check page.

To enter a purchase made with your company credit card:

1. From the Financial tab menu, choose Banking⇨Use Credit Card.

2. From the Account drop-down list, select the credit card account you're using to pay for the purchase.

3. In the Vendor drop-down list, enter or choose the name of the vendor you're buying from.

4. (Optional) Select the period from the Posting Period drop-down list.

5. Enter the date of the purchase in the Date field.

6. Enter the amount of the purchase in the Amount field.

7. (Optional) Enter a number in the Reference No. field and a note about the purchase in the Memo field.

8. If you're recording the purchase on the Expenses tab, go to Step 10. If you're recording the purchase on the Items tab, go to Step 11.

9. Click the Expenses tab and choose an expense account appropriate for your purchase from the drop-down list.

   For example, if you're buying a desk chair, you may choose Furniture or Office Supplies from the drop-down list.

10. Click the Items tab, select each item to purchase from the Item drop-down list, enter the quantity in the Quantity field, select a tax code from the Tax Code drop-down list, choose a Location from the Location drop-down list, and then click Add.

    You can use the Items tab to track the purchase of any goods or services set up as Item records in NetSuite.

    Don't record the same purchase under both the Expenses and Items tabs because — yep — you'll count the same purchase twice.

11. Click Save.

To see a list of all the credit card transactions you've entered, from the Financial tab menu, Banking⇨Use Credit Card⇨List.

The same Credit Card page used for charges also records returns or credits on your company credit card. To record a credit, simply select the Credit radio button at the top of the page instead of Charge, and follow the same steps as if you were entering a purchase.

You don't need to create a credit card account to track reimbursable purchases an employee makes with a personal credit card. These should be entered as expense reports, and the payment method doesn't really matter for your bookkeeping purposes.

Paying down your balance

You use the Write Check feature to pay down the balance of a company credit card. To write a check against your credit card balance, you have to enable the Expand Account List preference.

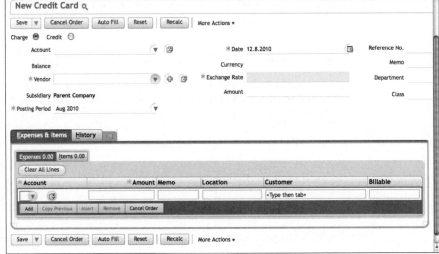

Figure 5-8:
The Credit
Card page
is similar to
the Check
page.

To turn on the Expand Account List preference, follow these steps:

1. **From the Setup tab menu, choose Accounting⇨Accounting Preferences.**

2. **Click the General tab.**

3. **Select the Expand Account List check box.**

4. **Click Save.**

To make a payment against your credit card balance, follow the steps in the earlier section, "Writing a check." When you reach Step 9, click the Expenses tab and select the credit card account from the drop-down list. To print the check, follow the instructions in the earlier section, "Printing checks."

The credit card statement you get each month isn't a bill, though it may seem like one because you have to make a payment on a specific date. A *bill* represents a specific purchase from a single vendor; a *credit card statement* may represent multiple purchases that occurred on different dates and from different vendors.

Enter your individual purchases with the Credit Card page; don't enter a bill in NetSuite for the whole statement — the accounting will be incorrect if you do.

Exploring bank and credit card registers

Each bank account has a bank register, in which you can view transactions posted to that account. See the earlier section, "Examining account registers," for general information about account registers.

Bank and credit card account registers include a couple of features not found in other account registers. Figure 5-9 shows a sample bank register.

- ✔ **Bank registers allow you to send checks to the print queue.** Choose the Print check box to the left of each check you want to print later.

- ✔ **Bank registers allow you to see whether transactions are cleared and reconciled.** If a transaction is cleared, you see a check mark in the Clr column in the register. If a transaction is reconciled, you see the reconciliation date in the Reconciled Date column of the register. (We discuss more about what this actually means in the upcoming "Reconciling accounts" section.)

Figure 5-9:
A bank account register reveals reconciled dates and clearance, Clarence.

Date	Print	Number Type	Payee Account	Memo	Payment	Clr	Reconciled Date	Deposit	Balance
30.3.2001		DEP	27250 - Payroll Taxes Payable : 401k Deductions Payable	PAYROLL NETLEDGER INC CO ID: xxxxx-11111		✔	31.12.2008	$0.01	$0.01
1.1.2002		GJ10001 GENJRNL	Scott Blosser 31000 - Owner's Investment	Owner's Investment		✔	14.1.2003	$250,000.00	$250,000.01
1.1.2002		GJ10002 GENJRNL	Sharon Sepulveda 31000 - Owner's Investment	Owner's Investment		✔	14.1.2003	$250,000.00	$500,000.01
1.1.2002		GJ10003 GENJRNL	Ed Baumann 31000 - Owner's Investment	Owner's Investment		✔	14.1.2003	$250,000.00	$750,000.01
4.2.2002		DEP	10300 - Undeposited Funds	Deposit		✔	14.1.2003	$20.00	$750,020.01
2.5.2002	✔	CASH10002 RCPT	Business Services, Ltd. - Split -			✔	14.1.2003	$7.50	$750,027.51
12.6.2002		PMT	Garrett Garrett, Esq. 11200 - Delinquent Accounts			✔	14.1.2003	$53.75	$750,081.26
9.10.2002		DEP	33000 - Opening Bal Equity	Account Opening Balance		✔	14.1.2003	$400.00	$750,481.26
15.12.2002	☐	1001 CHK	Luke Duke 14100 - Advances Paid	Payroll Advance	$5,000.00	✔	14.1.2003		$745,481.26
5.1.2003	☐	1002	Montana Property Management		$1,295.00	✔	14.1.2003		$744,186.26

Bank of the West-checking Register

Date [all] From [ ] To [ ]   Current Ending Balance: $173,482.59
1-Line ☐   Sort By [date, type, document]   Uncleared ☐   Find [<Type then tab>] Next Prev
Refresh   Print Email Export - CSV

Reconciling accounts

For each of your bank or credit card accounts, you usually get some sort of account statement periodically from the bank or financial institution. Most commonly, statements are mailed to you on a monthly basis, but the frequency may vary. You may also just get an e-mail notification and view your statement through online banking.

Reconciling your information in NetSuite with your bank statement is important to help ensure that the transactions you've entered accurately reflect the available funds in your bank account.

Reconciling can be a slightly tedious process, especially if you have many transactions every month, but in the long run, you have fewer errors if you stay on top of it. You never want to arrive at the end of a year or be in the middle of an audit and find that your reconciliations are wrong or incomplete!

Reconciling the statement with the register

Before you begin reconciling, do the obvious — look over your records and receipts to make sure you've entered all the bank and credit card transactions you know about.

To reconcile a statement with the register:

1. **From the Financial tab menu, choose Banking⇨Reconcile Bank Statement or Reconcile Credit Card Statement from the navigation menus.**

   The Reconcile Bank Statement page appears, as shown in Figure 5-11. If you're reconciling a credit card, the Reconcile Credit Card page appears instead.

2. **Choose the account you're reconciling from the Account drop-down list.**

3. **Enter the date on the bank statement in the Statement Date field.**

4. **Enter information in the Ending Statement Balance field.**

5. **Make sure the Last Reconciled Balance field matches the starting balance on your bank statement.**

   The Last Reconciled Balance field shows the (you guessed it) ending balance from the last reconciliation on that account. If all went well during that the prior reconciliation, your Last Reconciled Balance matches the starting balance on your current statement.

   Note that if you haven't reconciled that account before, the Last Reconciled Balance is 0.

6. **Click the Deposits and Credits tab and make sure each transaction on the tab matches your bank statement.**

   If your statement shows transactions that don't appear, and you're certain they weren't accidentally reconciled with another statement or posted to the wrong date, you can enter them on the fly. Enter transactions that decrease your bank account on the New Charges tab, and enter transactions that increase your bank account on the New Deposits tab. These are automatically reconciled with that statement when you click Save.

7. **Click the Checks and Payments tab and make sure each transaction matches the bank statement.**

   Now you're ready to get to the real work of reconciliation. As shown in Figure 5-10, transactions appear on the Deposits and Credits tab and the Checks and Payments tab. (They appear on the Payments and Credits tab and the Charges and Cash Advances tab if you're reconciling a credit card account.)

   These are all the unreconciled transactions in the account that have a posting date on or before the current statement date.

REMEMBER

You can't reconcile a transaction on a particular statement if its posting date is after the statement date.

8. **To reconcile a transaction on the statement, select the Reconcile check box on the transaction's row.**

   When you add transactions to the reconciliation, their values are added to the amount in the Reconciled This Statement field.

   When you've selected all the transactions on your statement, the amount in the Difference field should be 0. If so, the reconciliation is complete and successful, and the numbers in the Last Reconciled Balance plus the Reconciled This Statement fields equal the number in the Ending Statement Balance field.

9. **Congratulate yourself and click Save.**

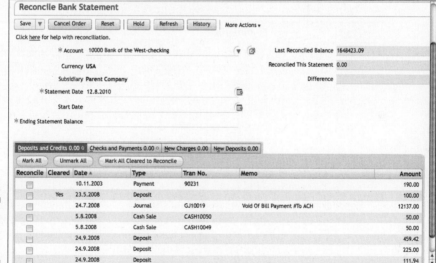

Figure 5-10:
A bank rec-
onciliation.

TIP

If you save a reconciliation with a mistake on it, don't panic. You can come back and fix it. Just return to the Reconcile Bank Statement page and enter the date of the statement you need to edit in the Statement Date field. Make your changes, and then click Save.

In your bank or credit card account register, you can see whether a transaction has been reconciled by whether a date appears in the Reconciled Date column. From the register, you can take a couple of actions related to reconciliation:

✔ Click a date in the Reconciled Date column to view that particular reconciliation statement.

✔ If a transaction has not yet been reconciled, click the Reconcile link to
  start a new reconciliation statement.

Reconciliation can be a long process and may take more than one session. Click the Hold button to save your progress on a particular statement without committing the reconciliation. In other words (drum roll . . .), the Hold button places the reconciliation process (drum roll . . .) on hold.

When you return, the reconciliation page loads the statement that was on hold, and you can continue. You can also access the on-hold statement by entering the date of the reconciliation in the Statement Date field on the Reconcile Bank Statement page.

Reporting on reconciliation

Use the three reports explained in Table 5-1 to examine reconciliations. These reports are only available if you have reconciled your bank account in NetSuite.

Table 5-1	Reconciliation Reports	
Type	**Explanation**	**To Run**
Reconciliation Summary	A summary-level description of a particular reconciliation statement. It shows the total amount of transactions you reconciled, any difference between that total and the statement ending balance, and the total of unreconciled transactions as of that statement date.	From the Reports tab menu, choose Banking/Budgeting⇨ Reconciliation.
Reconciliation Detail	Provides more details, including all of the information on the Reconciliation Summary report, plus a list of the actual transactions.	From the Reports tab menu, choose Banking/Budgeting⇨ Reconciliation⇨Detail.
Reconciliation History	Shows a list of your reconciliations with the statement balance, the total of the transactions reconciled, the previous statement balance, and the difference. It's a handy way to see all the reconciliations you've done for that bank or credit card account and whether they were successful.	Go to either the Reconcile Bank Statement page or the Reconcile Credit Card Statement page, and then click the History button.

Chapter 6

Invoicing Customers and Paying the Bills

*P*roperly managing accounts receivable (A/R) and accounts payable (A/P) is very important to the financial health of your business. If you don't bring in cash, you won't be paid, and if you don't pay your vendors, they're not likely to do business with you in the future.

With vendors you may have used a credit card to pay for something. If so, you purchased *on terms* — buying now and paying later. Businesses often extend a similar courtesy to each other by issuing invoices. An *invoice* is a sale on terms, meaning the merchant gives the customer a certain period of time to pay. If payment is overdue, the merchant may bill the customer for finance charges or other penalties.

In NetSuite, an invoice you send to a customer is simply an *invoice,* while an invoice sent to you by a vendor is a *bill.* In this chapter, we show you how to use NetSuite to manage customer invoices and vendor bills.

You must have a role like A/R Clerk or A/P Clerk (or a more powerful role, like Accountant, Controller, or CFO) in NetSuite to view and create invoices or pay bills. If you haven't been assigned one of those roles in NetSuite, you can't follow the steps in this chapter.

Getting What's Coming to You: Accounts Receivable

We start with the customer side of things, because that's the fun part of the business — putting money in the bank.

You perform three general types of activity when you manage A/R:

✔ Sending invoices to your customers

✔ Recording payments or credits

✔ Managing customers' A/R balances (in other words, knowing how much they owe you, what's overdue, and working with them to get their payments in)

The following sections discuss each activity.

Creating invoices and cash sales

An invoice describes a sale, including the customer's name, the account number, the date, what goods or services were sold, their prices, and the total amount owed.

You may use cash sales in addition to, or instead of, invoices in NetSuite. *Cash sales* are similar to invoices, but payment is received immediately, so the sale never goes through A/R. (Contrary to the name, the payment method doesn't have to be cash!) Real-world examples of cash sales include retail store sales or sales processed from Web store orders, where customers provide their credit card information during checkout.

Before you can add products or services to an invoice or bill, you must set them up as *items* in your NetSuite account. See Chapter 7 for more information.

Creating an invoice

To create an invoice:

1. **From the Customers tab menu, choose Sales➪Create Invoices.**

    The Invoice page appears, as shown in Figure 6-1.

2. **In the Customer field, type the name of the customer you're invoicing.**

3. **From the Terms drop-down list, select the payment terms for the invoice.**

    Terms automatically set the Due Date field. You may instead choose not to enter terms but set the Due Date manually.

Your NetSuite account comes with commonly used payment terms. To see how to edit or create your own terms, see the later section, "Setting up payment terms."

4. **On the Items tab, select the product or service you're selling from the drop-down list.**

5. **Fill in any other required fields, which (like all required fields) are shown in yellow.**

   Your settings may make fields such as Location required if your company uses multiple warehouses.

6. **Click the Add button.**

7. **Click Save.**

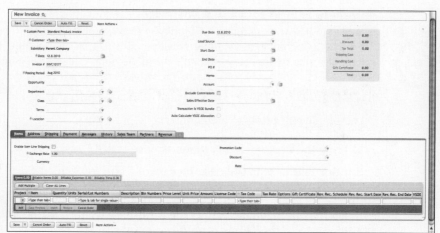

Figure 6-1:
Creating a
new invoice.

Creating a cash sale

Creating a cash sale is similar to creating an invoice, but you also enter payment details and don't select payment terms:

1. **From the Customers tab menu, choose Sales⇨Enter Cash Sales.**

2. **In the Customer field, enter the name of the customer you're entering a cash sale for.**

3. **Choose the correct radio button:**

   • **Undeposited Funds** if you're depositing the money later.

   • **Account** if the money will be deposited directly into a bank account (for example, a payment via credit card).

4. **On the Items tab, select the product you're selling from the Item drop-down list.**

   Both product and services are set up as items.

5. **Enter any other details (some fields may be required). Enter additional line items if needed.**

6. **Click the Add button.**

7. **On the Payment tab, select the appropriate Payment Method from the drop-down list.**

   If you chose the Account radio button in Step 3, choose the correct bank account from the Account drop-down list.

8. **Click Save.**

Assigning default terms to a customer

Terms define how a customer will pay you (for example, Due on Receipt or Net 30, meaning within 30 days). If you always want to give a customer the same payment terms on invoices, you can assign default terms in the customer's record. Then, whenever you create a new invoice for that customer, those terms automatically appear on the invoice.

To assign default terms to a customer:

1. **From the Customers tab menu choose Lists⇨Customers.**

2. **Click Edit next to the customer record you want to edit.**

   The Customer page appears.

3. **On the Financial tab, select the terms you want to assign to that customer from the Terms drop-down list.**

   The drop-down list includes standard terms such as Due on Receipt and Net 15 (due in 15 days). The terms you select will default on all invoices you create for this customer in the future, but you can change them on the invoice if you need to for any reason. For more information on terms, see the later section, "Setting up payment terms."

4. **Click Save.**

Assessing finance charges

How do you get your customers to pay their invoices on time? Since mind control isn't an option, one incentive you can offer is the promise of avoiding a *finance charge* (a late fee).

Before you start using finance charges, make some decisions about how you're going to calculate them:

✔ **How much interest will you charge?** This is calculated by applying an *APR* (annual percentage rate) against the customer's overdue balance, based on how past due the invoices are. (See the later section "Verifying finance charges" for an example.)

✔ **Do you want to apply a minimum finance charge amount?** If so, when you invoice finance charges, any customer whose calculated finance charge is less than the minimum is charged the minimum amount instead.

✔ **Do you want to offer a grace period beyond the due date?** If so, customers may pay their invoices a certain number of days after the due date without accruing any finance charges.

✔ **Do you want to apply finance charges to customers' unpaid finance charges?** This may occur if the customer is really late, and you've already billed him for finance charges.

✔ **Do you want to calculate finance charges starting from the due date of their overdue invoices, or go back to the invoice date?**

You must have administrator-type permissions to record global preferences like finance charge preferences. If you can't finagle getting those permissions yourself, ask your admin to set finance charge preferences for you.

Setting finance charge permissions

To set finance charge permissions:

1. **From the Setup tab menu, choose Accounting⇨Finance Charge Preferences.**

2. **Enter your finance charge APR in the Annual Rate % field.**

3. **From the Income Account drop-down list, select an income account to post finance charge invoices to.**

4. **If you're offering a grace period, enter a number of days in the Grace Period field.**

5. **If you're charging a minimum amount, enter it in the Minimum Finance Charge field.**

6. **If you want to calculate finance charges on unpaid finance charge amounts, select the Assess on Finance Charges check box.**

7. **Under Assess From, select the radio button that indicates what date to calculate finance charges from:**

   • **Transaction Date**

   • **Due Date**

8. **Click Save.**

When you've set up finance charge preferences, you can invoice your customers for the appropriate amounts.

Assessing finance charges and generating invoices

The next step is to drop the hammer and assess those finance charges. Because this can affect so many customers at once and generate a lot of support calls if it's not done correctly, only administrators or others gifted with similar permissions can assess finance charges.

To assess finance charges and generate invoices:

1. **From the Transactions tab menu, administrators choose Customers⇨Assess Finance Charges.**

2. **In the Date field, enter a date to calculate the outstanding finance charges due and create invoices that include the finance charges.**

3. **Choose the Assess check box for customers to invoice for finance charges.**

   You can see the date customers were last invoiced for finance charges.

4. **If you want to send these invoices to the print queue, select the To Be Printed check box.**

   The check box is near the top of the page. To read about the print queue, see Chapter 5.

5. **Click Save.**

In the Amount to Assess column, you can modify each customer's finance charge amount to invoice. A custom finance charge overrides the calculated amount. If the same overdue invoices are still open the next time you assess finance charges, the finance charge amount is calculated based on the number of days since the previous finance charge was assessed.

Verifying finance charges

How can you verify the finance charge amount is correct, before you invoice for it?

1. **Divide the annual rate by the number of days in the year.**

   You get the daily rate. Don't forget to count an extra day if it's a leap year.

2. **Multiply the daily rate by the customer's overdue balance.**

   The customer's overdue balance may consist of more than one invoice, in which case you need to multiply the balance of each invoice by the appropriate number of days.

3. **Multiply that result by the number of days between the finance charge and the due date (or the transaction date).**

4. **Round to the nearest penny (or whatever is the lowest denomination of your currency).**

   If your math is correct, the result will match the calculated finance charge amount.

Recording a customer payment

When customers pay their invoices, you create a *customer payment* in NetSuite and apply it to the invoices. This reduces the customer's A/R balance and closes out the invoices.

Creating a customer payment

To create a customer payment:

1. **From the Customers tab menu, choose Accounts Receivable⇨Accept Customer Payments.**

   The Payment page appears, as shown in Figure 6-2.

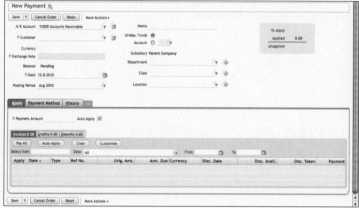

Figure 6-2: Recording and applying payments on the Payment page.

2. **In the Customer field, enter the name of the customer who made the payment.**

3. **Verify that the payment date in the Date field is correct.**

4. **On the Apply tab, enter the amount of the payment in the Payment Amount field.**

   Instead of entering the total payment amount, you can just select each invoice to be paid; the total calculates automatically in the Payment Amount field.

5. **Choose the Invoices tab from the Apply tab.**

6. **Select the Apply check box for each invoice to pay.**

   If the Auto Apply check box is selected, the payment automatically applies to as many invoices as possible, in the order they appear in the list. You can force Auto Apply by clicking the Auto Apply button.

7. **On the Apply tab, make sure no invoices are selected.**

8. **On the Payment Method tab, select a payment method from the Payment Method drop-down list.**

9. **Enter any other relevant information, such as check or credit card number, in the correct fields.**

10. **Click Save.**

A customer may make a payment without specifying which invoices to apply it to. At that point, contact the customer and verify what they intended. However, if you need to, you can record the payment first (for example, maybe you want to deposit the money into the bank right away). *On the Apply tab, make sure no invoices are selected before you click Save.* The total payment amount appears as Unapplied in the page header. When you find out which invoices to apply the payment to, edit the payment by clicking the Edit button, selecting the proper invoices, and saving it.

Editing the customer payment

Editing the payment doesn't change your accounting at all; your bank and accounts receivable balances remain the same. The only things affected are the status of the invoices and the status of the payment, which change from Unapplied to Applied.

Applying customer deposits

A *customer deposit* is another type of payment usually made before you create an invoice. (Sometimes, you might call this a *down payment* or a *deposit* on a large order.)

The accounting for a customer deposit is different from an unapplied customer payment. Customer deposits don't directly affect A/R. When first recorded, customer deposits increase the balance of a liability account called Customer Deposits.

Creating a customer deposit

To create a customer deposit:

1. **From the Customers tab menu, choose Accounts Receivable➪ Record Customer Deposits.**

   The Customer Deposit screen appears.

2. **In the Customer field, type the name of the customer who made the payment.**

3. **Enter the amount of the deposit in the Payment Amount field.**

You're liable to ask

What's a liability, you may ask? *Liabilities* are financial obligations the company has, whether it involves paying money or delivering goods and services that have already been paid for. Why the heck would customer deposits be liabilities? A deposit is, in essence, a prepayment, and it's a liability because it means the company owes the customer goods or services equal to the deposit, but hasn't delivered them yet. When there's a liability, someone, somewhere, can look at the company and say, "You owe me." Liability accounts are the accounts that track such liabilities.

4. **On the Payment Method tab, select a payment method from the Payment Method drop-down list.**

5. **Enter any other relevant payment details.**

6. **Click Save.**

Applying a customer deposit

To apply a customer deposit:

1. **From the Customers tab menu, choose Accounts Receivable⇨ Record Customer Deposits⇨List.**

   A list of customer deposits appears.

2. **Click the View link next to the relevant deposit.**

   The Customer Deposit page appears.

3. **Click the Apply button.**

   The Deposit Application page appears.

4. **Select the Apply check box next to each invoice you want to apply the deposit to.**

   The Apply check box is in the list at the bottom of the page.

5. **Click Save.**

The deposit application transaction removes (debits) the balance in your Customer Deposits account, and uses it to decrease (credit) your accounts receivable balance.

You can see the invoices that the deposit transaction was applied against on the Applied To tab.

Applying customer credits

Sometimes, instead of receiving payment for an invoice to close it out, you will credit it. This occurs when customers return product they bought before paying the invoice (or maybe delivery took too long and you offer them a partial credit as compensation). To handle this scenario, you create a *credit memo* in NetSuite.

Issuing credit memos involves giving money back to the customer. You need a role like Accountant to issue credit memos. If you don't have permission to issue a credit memo, ask an administrator to help you.

Crediting an entire invoice

If you need to credit an entire invoice, follow these steps:

1. **From the Customers tab menu, choose Customer/Receivables Reports⇨ Open Invoices.**

2. **Click the invoice number you want to see.**

3. **Click the Credit button.**

   A new credit memo is created for the appropriate amount and is automatically applied to the invoice.

Manually creating and applying a credit memo

To manually create and apply a credit memo:

1. **From the Customers tab menu, choose Credits and Returns⇨ Issue Credit Memos.**

2. **In the Customer field, enter the name of the customer you're crediting.**

3. **Select a location from the Location drop-down list.**

4. **On the Items tab, select what you're selling from the drop-down list.**

5. **Enter details like quantity and rate.**

6. **Click the Add button.**

7. **On the Apply tab, select the Apply check box next to the appropriate open invoice or invoices.**

   You may edit the credit amount to apply to each one, up to the open amount of the invoice.

8. **Click Save.**

Applying deposits and credit memos

You can apply both customer deposits and credit memos as part of the process of receiving and applying other customer payments. This task can be done by an A/R clerk because (unlike the procedure for creating and applying credit memos), it doesn't involve giving money back to the customer, which requires a role like an Accountant. This is just *applying* money that has already been sent from the customer (a deposit, what A/R folks like best) or given back to the customer and approved by someone else (like an Accountant).

1. **On the Accept Customer Payments page, click either the Deposits or the Credits tab on the Apply tab.**

2. **Select the customer deposits or credits you want to apply.**

3. **From the Invoices tab, select the invoices to apply the deposits (or credits) against.**

4. **Enter the rest of your payment as you normally would.**

5. **Click Save.**

   The appropriate deposit application transactions are created and credit memos are applied.

Knowing what they owe you

After you've sent invoices, you can just sit back and wait for the money to come pouring in, right? It's a nice thought, but you'll probably have to be more proactive, keeping track of which customers have open and overdue invoices, and reminding them of their obligations.

When you call customers about being paid, you need to know all the details:

- Open accounts
- Receivable balance
- Unpaid and overdue invoices

The following sections show you how to read the customer record and how to generate a report on A/R.

Reading A/R information in the customer record

You can easily access A/R information for each customer from the customer record in NetSuite.

To open a customer record, follow along:

1. **From the Customers tab menu, choose Lists⇨Customers.**
2. **Click Edit next to the customer's name.**

On the customer record, you find the following tabs.

The Financial tab

The Financial tab of the customer record shows the following:

- The customer's open balance
- The customer's overdue balance
- The number of days overdue for the oldest open invoice
- Balance on open customer deposits or sales orders not yet invoiced

What goes into the balances you see on the Financial tab? If you *post-date* an invoice — in other words, enter a future transaction date — that invoice is included in the open balance on the customer record, even though you may not think of it as part of the current balance. In other words, no date range filter is applied to these balances.

You can see the A/R balance as of a particular date if you create a customer statement or run an A/R Aging Summary report. (See the later section called "Reporting on accounts receivable.")

You can update the customer's credit limit and credit hold status. You don't want to keep extending credit to a customer who owes you too much. The decision about exactly what "too much" is may be automatically determined in preferences (Auto), or you may set the hold manually to On or Off on the customer record by making a selection from the Hold drop-down list.

The Sales tab

The Sales tab of the Customer record lists all of a customer's transactions. You can use the Billing Status and Type drop-down lists to further hone in on the information you're looking for.

For example, to see open invoices, choose Open from the Billing Status drop-down list and Invoice from the Type drop-down list.

Reporting on accounts receivable

NetSuite offers multiple reports to help you manage accounts receivable.

You run all the accounts receivable reports the same way:

1. **Choose the Customers tab menu⇨Customer/Receivables Reports.**

2. **Choose the appropriate report.**

The A/R Aging Summary report is the most important report you use when managing receivables and collections. This report shows a list of customers with open balances grouped into columns by the age of the invoices, as shown in Figure 6-3.

Each column represents the total amount for a particular date range. The report has columns for Current (today), 1–30 days old, 31–60 days old, 61–90 days old, and more than 90 days old.

You can change the range in the columns by entering a different number of days in the Interval field in the footer of the report. (The default setting is 30 days.)

Figure 6-3:
NetSuite offers multiple reports including the important A/R Aging Summary report.

Customer	Current Open Balance	13.7.2010 - 11.8.2010 (30) Open Balance	13.6.2010 - 12.7.2010 (60) Open Balance	14.5.2010 - 12.6.2010 (90) Open Balance	Before 13.5.2010 (>90) Open Balance	Total Open Balance
Craig Erickson	$0.00	$0.00	$0.00	$0.00	$415.00	$415.00
Craig Koozer, DDS	$0.00	$0.00	$0.00	$0.00	$19,381.83	$19,381.83
Dave Symonds	$0.00	$0.00	$0.00	$0.00	$909.99	$909.99
Elijah Tuck	$0.00	$0.00	$0.00	$0.00	$80.00	$80.00
Furman, Sally	$0.00	$0.00	$0.00	$0.00	$4,502.15	$4,502.15
Garrett Garrett, Esq.	$0.00	$0.00	$0.00	$0.00	($191.41)	($191.41)
Great Falls Emergency Clinic	$0.00	$0.00	$0.00	$0.00	$165.00	$165.00
Hamilton Emergency Clinic	$0.00	$0.00	$0.00	$0.00	$7,369.99	$7,369.99
Inactive customer with balance	$0.00	$0.00	$0.00	$0.00	$25.00	$25.00
Jebidiah Palm	$0.00	$0.00	$0.00	$0.00	$555,348.42	$555,348.42
Julie Kelly	$0.00	$0.00	$0.00	$0.00	$300.00	$300.00

Date today ▼ As of 12.8.2010 Interval 30 More   Find <Type then tab> Next Prev
Refresh   Customize   Options   Print Email Schedule Export - CSV ▼

The A/R Aging Summary report places invoices into columns based on the number of days between the report date and either the invoice or the due date (in other words, how overdue they are).

Administrators (or other privileged characters) can change this setting:

1. **From the Setup tab menu⇨Accounting⇨Accounting Preferences.**

2. **Choose the General tab.**

3. **Under Aging Reports Use, select the correct radio button:**
   - **Transaction Date**
   - **Due Date**

4. **Click Save to save the settings.**

You can click a subtotal or total amount in the A/R Aging Summary report to load a detail report of the invoices making up that total, or click the View Detail link next to the report title to run a complete A/R Aging Detail report.

NetSuite also provides A/R Payment History by Invoice and A/R Payment History by Payment reports to review your accounts receivable history. As you may guess from their names, these reports show all the payments applied to each invoice, and all the invoices each payment is applied against, respectively. Run the accounts receivable reports by clicking the Customers tab, then choosing the right report name under Customer/Receivables Reports.

Sending a statement of account

To send a customer a summary of what she owes, you can create a *customer statement* showing this information:

- The customer's A/R balance on a particular date
- The statement date
- A list of the open invoices
- The balance, split into fields representing the age of the invoices

Similar to the A/R Aging Summary report, each column shows the total open amount of all invoices in that range: Current (today), 1–30 days old, 31–60 days old, 61–90 days old, and over 90 days old.

You can remind customers of their open balance every time you invoice them. If you're not familiar with customizing transaction forms, you may want to read Chapter 5 first.

Generating customer statements

To generate customer statements:

1. **From the Customers tab menu, choose Accounts Receivable⇨ Generate Statements.**

   The Print Statements page appears, as shown in Figure 6-4.

2. **Click the Customize tab.**

3. **Set or modify the following statement options:**

   - **Statement Date and Start Date fields:** Statements will show transactions between these two dates. Any open balance prior to the start date is rolled into a single opening balance.

- **Include Zero Balances check box:** When selected, you can create statements for customers with a 0 A/R balance and transactions between the start date and the statement date.

- **Show Only Open Transactions check box:** When selected, only open invoices and credits are listed on the statement. (The balances are the same in either case.)

4. **Select the Print check box next to the customers you want to generate statements for.**

5. **Click the Print, Email, or Fax button.**

Figure 6-4: Creating customer statements from the Print Statements page.

Creating a single customer statement

If you need to create a single customer statement, it may be faster to use the Individual Statement page:

1. **From the Customers tab menu choose Accounts Receivable⇨ Individual Statement.**

2. **In the Customer field, enter the name of the customer you want to send a statement to.**

3. **Modify any other statement options, as you would on the Generate Statements page.**

4. **Click the Print, Email, or Fax button.**

You can instead view the Customer record and click the Generate Statement link in the upper-right corner of the page. This takes you to the Individual Statement page with the customer already selected.

Sending collections letters

When a customer doesn't pay on time, and the gentle hint of a statement of account doesn't help, you may call him or send a collection letter. Collection letters come in many flavors, but the general idea is the same: "You owe us money and you didn't pay us when you said you would. Please take care of it immediately." The letter can also explain the consequences if the customer doesn't make payment — finance charges, dealing with a collections agency, credit with your company being cut off, and so on.

You can use the Mail Merge feature to create collections letters and include specific information about each customer you track with NetSuite. If you're sending the collections letter via e-mail, you can even include a copy of the customer statement.

E-mailing a collections letter

Follow these steps to create a simple collections letter to e-mail to a specific customer:

1. **From the Customers tab menu, choose Lists⇨Customers.**

2. **Click the Edit link next to the customer you want to e-mail.**

3. **Choose the General tab.**

4. **From the Messages tab, click the Email button.**

   The Email Message window appears.

5. **Confirm the recipient's e-mail address on the Recipients tab.**

6. **On the Messages tab, enter a subject in the Subject field.**

7. **In the Message field, compose your letter.**

8. **To send a customer statement with your letter, choose the Include Statement check box on the Attachments tab.**

   You can also select other standard statement options. (See the earlier section, "Sending a statement of account.")

9. **Click the Preview button to look over your e-mail.**

10. **Click the Merge & Send button.**

    NetSuite sends the e-mail to the recipient.

Using CRMSDK tags to insert information

If you followed the steps in the previous section you may have wondered why you wouldn't just do that from your e-mail program. Here's where things get more interesting. You can use CRMSDK tags to dynamically insert information from NetSuite by typing the tags into your letter. *CRMSDK tags* stand for fields in NetSuite (like Balance Due and Last Payment Date).

To *dynamically insert* means that NetSuite automatically replaces the tag with the value of the tag. Assume the e-mail includes the tags for company contact, company name, balance due, and last payment date. In that case, the e-mail (with the appropriate CRMSDK tags) can say, "Joe Green at Ryan's Rentals, you owe us $4,075 and you haven't paid us since 8/19/2009!" The point is that you can say that generically, and NetSuite fills in all the details about the money you're owed.

CRMSDK tags save you time when sending e-mails in NetSuite. They're even more powerful when you're sending a lot of e-mail to all past-due customers, but this section provides a simple example of how to use them. If you want to e-mail all your customers, check the NetSuite Help Center for details (using the Help link in the upper-right corner of the screen).

You can insert CRMSDK tags (see Figure 6-5) into your e-mail so they can be swapped for real information when NetSuite sends the e-mail:

1. **Follow Steps 1–6 in the preceding section.**

2. **Type** Dear **(or whatever greeting you want to use).**

3. **Select Customer from the Field Type drop-down list.**

4. **Select Contact (Primary) from the Insert Field drop-down list.**

   NetSuite inserts an incomprehensible tag that is its way of saying this is the primary contact for this account.

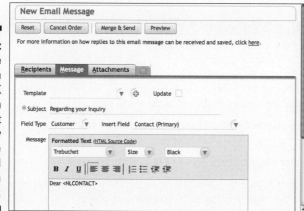

Figure 6-5:
NetSuite inserts a CRMSDK tag when you select an entry from the Insert Field drop-down list.

5. **Type a comma and press Enter to move down a line.**

6. **Write the rest of your e-mail in the same way, selecting the fields to insert from the Field Type drop-down list.**

7. **Click the Preview button to see how the message will look when it is sent.**

8. **Click Merge & Send.**

9. **Compose the rest of the text for your collections e-mail.**

10. **Click the Preview button to see how the e-mail will look (it appears in another popup window).**

11. **If you're happy, click the Merge & Send button.**

    Otherwise, modify the message if you want to add a little bit of vehemence to your request to pay up.

NetSuite inserts the values for each tag in the e-mail you send.

Paying the Piper: Accounts Payable

Perhaps A/P isn't as much fun as keeping track of what customers owe you, but it's equally important to the health of your business.

This section addressed the most common activities you perform when working with accounts payable — entering bills received from your vendors, paying or crediting those bills, and keeping track of your A/P balances.

To follow the instructions in this section, you need to have a NetSuite role of A/P Clerk or similar.

Recording vendor bills

A *bill* represents a specific purchase your business has made. It tracks the following:

- ✔ Vendor's name
- ✔ Date of the purchase
- ✔ Items or expenses purchased
- ✔ The amount

Depending on that vendor's payment terms, you may have to pay the bill immediately on receipt, or you may have a predetermined grace period.

Just as a cash sale is an immediate payment version of an invoice, a check is an immediate payment version of a bill; it has the same affect on your expenses, but takes money directly from your bank account instead of posting to accounts payable first. See Chapter 5 for more information about writing checks.

To create a bill:

1. **From the Vendors tab menu, choose Purchases⇨Enter Bills.**

   The New Bill page appears, as shown in Figure 6-6.

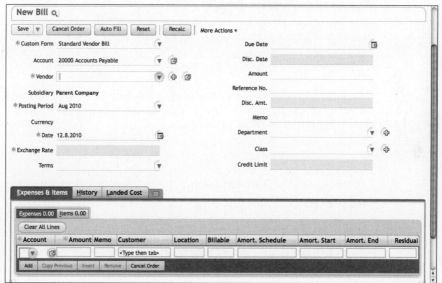

Figure 6-6:
Entering
a bill.

2. **In the Vendor drop-down list, type or select the name of the vendor you're purchasing from.**

3. **In the Date field, enter the date you want the bill to post.**

   It defaults today's date.

4. **Select the bill's payment terms from the Terms drop-down list.**

   The Due Date field calculates automatically.

5. **Enter the amount you owe in the Amount field.**

6. **If applicable, add any received discount in the Disc. Amt. field.**

7. **Choose the Expenses & Items tab.**

8. **On the Expenses tab, choose an appropriate expense account from the drop-down list.**

   For example, if you're buying printer paper, you may choose an Office Supplies expense account.

9. **On the Items tab, select each item to purchase, enter the quantity, and then click Add.**

   You can use the Items tab to track the purchase of any goods or services set up as item records in NetSuite.

Don't record the same purchase under both the Expenses and the Items tab, or you'll count the same purchase twice.

10. Click Save.

Paying your bills

You create a bill payment to close out a bill sitting in accounts payable. The bill payment represents payment from either a bank account (such as a check or an electronic transfer) or a credit card account.

Use the Start Date and End Date fields to see only bills due during a certain range of time. For example, if you want to see bills due on or after May 1, 2010, enter **5/1/2010** in the Start Date field.

To create bill payments:

1. From the Vendors tab menu, choose Accounts Payable⇨Pay Bills.

The Bill Payments page appears.

2. In the Date field, verify that the date of payment is correct.

3. In the Account drop-down list, select a bank account or credit card you will use to make the payments.

If you're paying from a bank account, select the To Be Printed check box to place your payments into the Checks print queue. (You can access this queue at a later time by choosing Accounts Payable⇨Print Checks and Forms and then clicking the Checks link.)

4. For each bill to pay, select the Pay check box.

5. If you aren't planning to pay the full open amount of each bill, edit the amounts in the Payment column.

Unlike a customer payment, you can't have an unapplied bill payment; a bill payment must always be fully applied to one or more bills.

6. Click Save.

For each vendor, a single bill payment is created and applied to all the bills you select to pay.

You have two other ways to create a bill payment, which may be useful in specific circumstances. These methods may be easier to use than sifting through the queue of bills from all your vendors on the Bill Payments page.

✔ **Pay a specific bill** by viewing that bill (for example, by clicking a bill in the Open Bills report) and clicking the Make Payment button. A bill payment is created with the appropriate amount and automatically applied to the bill.

✔ **To look at the open bills for one particular vendor and then make a payment,** from the Vendors tab menu, choose Accounts Payable⇨Pay Single Vendor. Select the vendor from the Payee drop-down list. The page lists bills for that vendor. When you select the Apply check box (next to one or more bills) and click the Save button, a single payment is created and applied against those bills.

Applying vendor credits

Sometimes a vendor issues you an A/P credit (for example, if you return items to the vendor that you were already billed for). You can apply a vendor credit to a bill to reduce the amount you owe the vendor, similar to a bill payment.

You can use the Bill Payments page to create bill payments and apply credits at the same time. The Type column on this page lets you see bills and bill credits. Select the check boxes next to a bill and a bill credit for the same vendor; when you click the Save button, the credit is applied along with bill payments created.

Keeping track of your obligations

Paying vendors on time is a good idea. You can use the Bill Payments page to manage upcoming payments.

Reading A/P information in the vendor record

You can easily access A/P information for each vendor on the vendor record in NetSuite.

To access a vendor record, follow along:

1. **From the Vendors tab menu choose Lists⇨Vendors.**
2. **Click the Edit link next to the vendor's name.**

On the vendor record, you find the following tabs:

✔ **The Financial tab** displays your balance with the vendor. Additionally, you can enter your credit limit with them. The balance for any unbilled orders for the vendor also appears. You can see the A/P balance as of a particular date if you run an A/P Aging Summary report. See the following section.

✔ **The Transactions tab** of the Financial tab lists all transactions for that vendor. You can use the Type and Billing Status drop-down lists to find specific transactions quickly.

Reporting on accounts payable

The A/P Aging Summary report, shown in Figure 6-7, provides a snapshot of your open payables, by vendor, grouped into columns by the age of the bills. The features of this report are basically the same as those of the A/R Aging Summary report, except this report covers payables instead of receivables.

You can

- Adjust the aging intervals
- Choose whether aging is based on transaction date or due date
- Drill down to the A/P Aging Detail report for more information on the transactions that make up each balance.

For more details, check out the section "Reporting on accounts receivable" earlier in this chapter.

Payment history reports are also available on the accounts payable side. The A/P Payment History by Bill and A/P Payment History by Payment reports display bill payments and credits applied against each bill, and the bills each payment/credit is applied to, respectively.

You can access all the reports described in this section (A/P Payment History by Bill; A/P Payment History by Payment; and A/P Aging Summary) by clicking the Vendors tab and selecting the appropriate report name under Vendor/Payables Reports.

A/P Aging Summary ⊙ View Detail						
Vendor	Current	13.7.2010 - 11.8.2010 (30)	13.6.2010 - 12.7.2010 (60)	14.5.2010 - 12.6.2010 (90)	Before 13.5.2010 (>90)	Total
	Open Balance	Open Balance	Open Balance	Open Balance	Open Balance	Ope Balanc
Acme Medical Supply	$0.00	$0.00	$0.00	$0.00	$37,459.02	$37,459.
ACME Shipping Co.	$0.00	$0.00	$0.00	$0.00	$14.00	$14.
Adam Fitzpatrick	$0.00	$0.00	$0.00	$0.00	$1,728.08	$1,728.
Allegro Medical	$0.00	$0.00	$0.00	$0.00	$209.97	$209.
Arkansas Department of Revenue	$0.00	$0.00	$0.00	$0.00	$11.00	$11.
BioPharm	$0.00	$0.00	$0.00	$0.00	$4,098.00	$4,098.
Dental Office	$0.00	$0.00	$0.00	$0.00	$5.00	$5.
Dr. Doug's Deteriorating Dental Supply	$0.00	$0.00	$0.00	$0.00	$425.00	$425.
Jonnie Cochoran Legal Supply	$0.00	$0.00	$0.00	$0.00	$1,036.90	$1,036.
Medical Resource USA	$0.00	$0.00	$0.00	$0.00	$12,137.00	$12,137.
Philips Medical Systems	$0.00	$0.00	$0.00	$0.00	$290,625.00	$290,625.
The Lab Depot, Inc.	$0.00	$0.00	$0.00	$0.00	$1,267.50	$1,267

Date today ▼   As of 12.8.2010   Interval 30   ☆ More   Find <Type then tab>   Next   Prev

Refresh   Customize   Options ⊙ ▼   Print   Email   Schedule   Export · CSV ▼

Done

Figure 6-7: The A/P Aging Summary report provides a snapshot of your open payables.

Sending and receiving electronic payments

You may never need to mail a paper check again! NetSuite provides two features that allow you to pay bills electronically:

- **The Online Bill Pay feature** allows you to issue payments from within NetSuite, similar to a personal online banking bill-payment system. If an electronic payment can't be made, the bill-payment provider mails a check on your behalf. You must enter a valid address on the vendor record to use this feature.

- **The ACH Vendor Payments feature** allows you to deposit funds directly into your vendors' bank accounts. Vendors' bank account information is stored in their vendor record.

You can make receiving payments faster and easier for your customers by accepting electronic payments through NetSuite:

- NetSuite is integrated with several credit-card processing gateways to allow you to charge credit cards directly from cash sales and customer payment transactions, or to refund a charge. You can enter a credit card number on each transaction, or store it in the customer record to use for future transactions.

- You may withdraw funds directly from a customer's bank account by using the Electronic Funds Transfer feature. The customer's bank information is entered and stored on the customer record.

Setting up payment terms

You can assign payment terms to customer invoices and vendor bills to set the due date automatically and to calculate discounts at payment time. You can use or edit the standard payment terms provided by NetSuite, or you can create your own.

Table 6-1 shows standard terms included in your account.

Table 6-1	Standard Payment Terms
Term	*Date Invoice/Bill Is Due*
Due on Receipt	On the transaction date
Net 15	15 days after the transaction date
Net 30	30 days after the transaction date
Net 60	60 days after the transaction date

(continued)

Table 6-1 *(continued)*

Term	Date Invoice/Bill Is Due
1% 10 Net 30	30 days after the transaction date, and is eligible for a 1% discount if paid within 10 days after the transaction date
2% 10 Net 30	30 days after the transaction date, and is eligible for a 2% discount if paid within 10 days after the transaction date

An invoice or bill without any payment terms is considered due on receipt. The due date is automatically set to match the transaction date, although you may edit it.

When you create new payment terms, you may base them on standard or date-driven rules. Both types of terms let you define a percentage discount that is available for early payment and the number of days after the invoice date that the discount is valid.

- ✔ **Standard term rules** allow you to set the number of days after the transaction date that the invoice will be due. This is the most straightforward type of payment term. For example, Net 15 means that the invoice is due 15 days after the transaction date.

- ✔ **Date-driven rules** allow you to specify a day of the month on which the invoice is due (for example, the 5th of every month). If this day is prior to the invoice date, the due date will instead be that day of the following month (the 5th of the following month). You can also have the due date move to the following month if the invoice date and day of the month due are within a certain number of days of each other; just set this to a certain number of days (2, for example). For example, if you buy something on the 3rd of the month, the invoice is due the next month on the 5th, not two days after you purchase something. (You may be familiar with this based on credit card statements, which have a closing date after which transactions appear on the next month's statement instead.)

Unlike many other setup tasks, you — yes you, the A/P clerk — can perform this task without the help of an administrator.

To create new payment terms:

1. **From the Setup tab menu, choose Other Setup⇨Accounting Lists.**

2. **In the Type drop-down list, select Term from the Type drop-down list.**

    The Type drop-down list is on the left side of the bottom of the page.

3. **Click the New button.**

   The New button is on the right side of the bottom of the page.

   The New Term page appears, as shown in Figure 6-8.

4. **Select one of the radio buttons:**

   • STANDARD

   • DATE DRIVEN

5. **In the Terms field, enter a name for this type of terms.**

6. **Enter a value in the Days Till Net Due or Day of Month Net Due field.**

7. **Enter the discount options in the following fields:**

   • **% Discount**

   • **Days Till Discount Expires** *or* **Day Discount Expires**

8. **Click Save.**

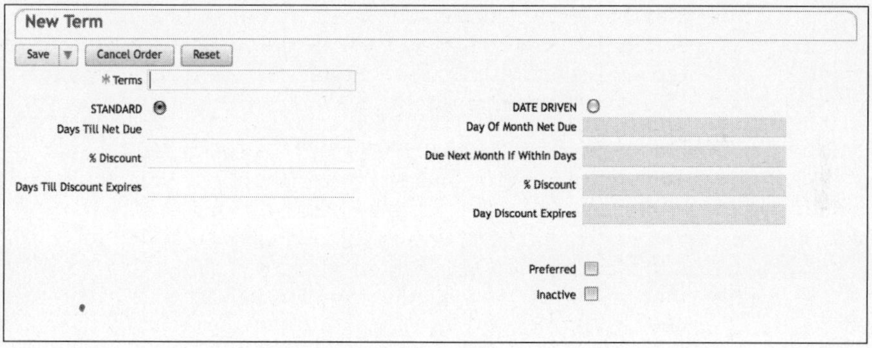

Figure 6-8: Setting up payment terms.

Chapter 7

Managing Inventory

• •

• •

To manage goods or services in NetSuite, you need to create *item records* to use with transactions and reports. This chapter helps you understand the purpose of different item types, how to set up items, and how to use NetSuite to manage your inventory.

Inventory involves a few different roles. Adding an item is often handled by a role such as Accountant (inventory certainly has significant accounting implications), while the work of transferring or adjusting inventory is often done by a role like Inventory or Warehouse Manager. As a result, the steps in this chapter specify what role you should have to perform the steps, whether Accountant, Warehouse/Inventory Manager, or Administrator (for setting preferences).

Understanding Item Types

You'll run into lots of item types in NetSuite and need to know when to use each. The following sections run down the various item types in NetSuite and, when there's more to say, where you can read more about them in other chapters of this book.

Goods and services bought and sold

Use these item types for goods and services you buy and sell:

- ✔ **Inventory:** *Inventory items* are physical goods you buy, stock, and sell. *Inventory on hand* represents an asset on your balance sheet. NetSuite automatically tracks your stock status as items are bought and sold.

- ✔ **Non-inventory:** Typically represents physical goods you buy and sell, but don't stock. To drop ship a product you don't stock, use a non-inventory item. You can find out more about drop shipping in Chapter 11.

- ✔ **Other Charge:** A more generic item type you may use for any goods or services you buy and sell. Gift-wrapping is one example.

- ✔ **Service:** Use these items to represent services you purchase and sell, and if you bill customers directly for your employees' time. You can learn more about service items in Chapter 12.

- ✔ **Gift Certificate:** When you sell a gift certificate item, a gift code is generated that a customer may use to pay for another sale later.

- ✔ **Download Item:** Customers may buy download items from you to gain access to files — such as applications, license keys, or informational documents — that you associate with the download item record. See Chapter 15 for more information.

Creating subtypes

When you create non-inventory, other charge, or service items, you must select a subtype that determines what you do with the item:

- ✔ **For Purchase:** You buy the items
- ✔ **For Sale:** You sell the items
- ✔ **For Resale:** You buy and sell the item (or service)

Grouping items

Some item types group items together into a single product. Some products may naturally be sold sometimes in a group (all of the Beatles albums), some may naturally come in a kit (like a magic kit), and others are assemblies (like a bike that isn't preassembled).

They differ by the way you count them in terms of inventory and in whether you can sell them in a Web store, as follows:

- **Item Group:** When you add a group to a purchase or sales transaction, individual lines are added for each member of the group, with a subtotal line showing the entire group's value.

  The price of a group is always equal to the sum of the prices of its members. When you fulfill an order for a group, each member item appears as a separate line item and you fulfill them as if they were sold separately. Groups can't be sold in a NetSuite Web store.

- **Kit/Package:** The greatest difference between groups and kits is that you may assign a price and revenue account to a kit, independent of the prices of its members.

  When you fulfill an order for a kit, it appears as a single line item — in other words, you can't fulfill different components of a kit at different times.

  Both kits and groups may contain inventory items, but don't have their own on-hand stock count. Kits can't be purchased, but they may be sold in a NetSuite Web store.

- **Assembly/Bill of Materials:** You build assemblies out of other items, then use them like regular inventory items — tracking how many are in stock, committing them to orders, and fulfilling them as a single line item.

  Assemblies may contain inventory, non-inventory, other charge, service items, or even other assemblies. You may stock assemblies by purchasing them as well as building them, and they may be sold in a NetSuite Web store.

Utility drawer-type item types

These are simply uncategorizable but very handy, like those things you put in your junk drawer along with the scissors and thumbtacks. Other item types and their uses include:

- **Discount:** You can add a discount item to a transaction to discount the line item immediately above it, or apply a discount item to the whole transaction.

- **Markup:** The opposite of discount items, you use markups to raise the price of an individual line item or an entire transaction. These markups can be hidden from the customer's view (whether printed or online).

✔ **Description:** You may use a description item to insert a memo, instructions, or a disclaimer between or below other line items on transactions. For example, for cigarettes, you may include the Surgeon General's warning as a description item. On a more positive note, on your green product line, you can add a description that thanks the customer for helping save the planet.

✔ **Payment:** You may add a payment item to a sales transaction to represent a down payment, reducing the amount due (of the customer payment for an invoice, or on the payment tab for a cash sale).

Creating Item Records

While each item type has its own properties and uses, most types share some basic properties. Walk through some of the properties of the items you'll use on a regular basis to buy and sell:

✔ Inventory

✔ Non-inventory

✔ Other charge

✔ Service items

Entering basic item information

You have to assign basic data to item records:

✔ **Item name/number** is used when you select the item to add it to a transaction and is displayed on inventory/item reports.

✔ **ID fields** are optional for item types that represent things you buy and sell:

- **Display name/code** is what your customers will see when you print a transaction with that item.

- **Vendor name/code** appears when you print purchase transactions.

✔ **Purchase descriptions** are shown and printed on purchase transactions.

✔ **Sales description** are shown and printed on sales transactions.

✔ **General ledger accounts** must be associated with every item you buy or sell. The association determines the accounting impact of that item on transactions. General ledger accounts come in one of two flavors (most of the time):

- **Income Account** records revenue when it is sold.

- **Expense Account** tracks cost of the item when it is purchased.

The accounts for inventory items work a little differently, but you get into that in this chapter's "Staying on ledger accounts" section.

Creating new items

To create new items, you should have the standard role of Accountant.

Follow along to create a new item:

1. **From the Financial tab menu, choose Lists⇨Items⇨New.**

   The New Item screen appears, which provides links to the various item types.

2. **From the list of item types, click the name of the item type you want to create.**

   See the section "Understanding Item Types" earlier in this chapter for a list.

   A screen appears with the name of the item type you select. For example, if you select Inventory Item, the Inventory Item screen appears. See Figure 7-1.

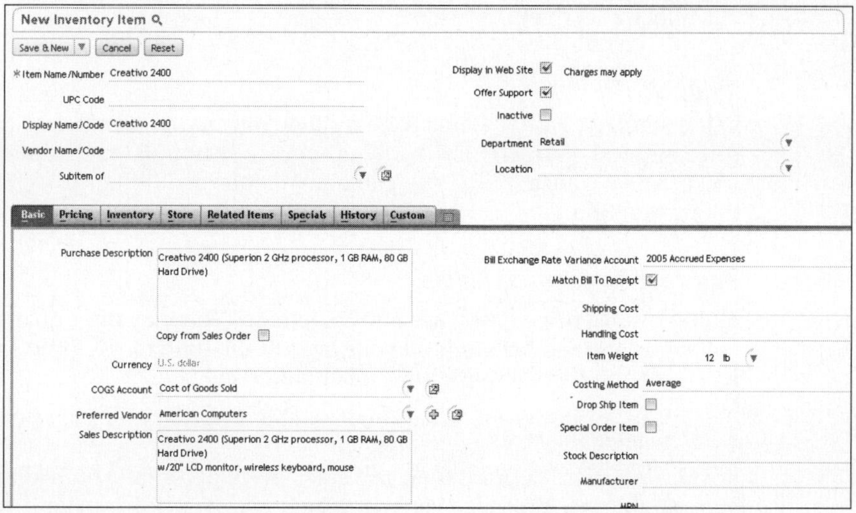

Figure 7-1: Your resulting screen depends on what item you're creating. Here, an inventory item is being made.

3. **Enter an item name/number.**

   This name or number will appear on inventory reports.

4. **(Optional) Enter a display name/code.**

   This is what your customers see when you print a transaction with that item.

5. **(Optional) Enter a vendor name/code.**

   This appears when you print purchase transactions.

6. **Click the Save button.**

Obviously, you can enter a lot more information about an item (price, for example, is information you're going to want to include). But like most things in life, pricing is more complicated than slapping on a 99-cent sticker. We cover pricing next.

Assigning item pricing

Use NetSuite to track many different kinds of pricing models for your items. In this section you read about the models available and how to set them up.

Before you just start typing in item prices, sit down and think about some things:

 ✔ What are the options.

 ✔ How they relate to the price models you're using today.

 ✔ How you can use these features to simplify or organize your pricing more effectively.

Single price level

In the simplest model, items have a single purchase and sales price. The price entered on the item record automatically populates the Rate field when you create a transaction. (You can always enter a different price manually on the transaction.)

Multiple sales price levels

Multiple sales price levels are more common. You may offer quantity discounts or special discounts to your biggest customers. Multiple sales price levels let you handle these types of situations.

Enabling multiple prices

If you want to track more than one sales price per item, your Administrator must enable the Multiple Prices feature:

1. **From the Setup tab menu, choose Company⇨Enable Features.**

2. **On the Transactions tab, select the Multiple Prices check box.**

When this feature is turned on, a Pricing tab appears on the item record. If you entered a sales price before enabling price levels, that price shows up as the base price level.

Associate customers with price levels

You can enter prices two ways:

- ✔ On the item record for each item.

- ✔ Predefined price levels, with a certain percentage discount or markup relative to the base price. Price levels then automatically calculate when you enter or modify the base price.

When you create a sales transaction, the price defaults to base price, but you may choose to do one of these instead:

- ✔ Select another price level, and the rate updates accordingly.

- ✔ Associate customers with price levels so that a different price level is selected by default on new sales when you select the customer.

To associate customers with price levels, take these steps:

1. **Edit a customer record.**

   Chapter 10 tells you how to do this.

2. **Choose the Financial tab.**

3. **Select from the Price Level drop-down list.**

You can go even further and assign default price levels on a per-customer, per-item basis by selecting combinations of item and price level under the Item Pricing tab under the Financial tab on the customer record.

To create and manage sales price levels:

1. **From the Setup tab menu, choose Accounting Lists.**

2. **In the footer, select Price Level from the Type drop-down list.**

   Now you can see your existing price levels, like those shown in Figure 7-2.

3. **Click an option:**

   - **Edit** to work with an existing price level.

   - **New** to create a new price level.

4. **Enter or change the following settings:**

   - **Price Level Name**

   - **Markup/Discount %** (relative to the base price)

   A *markup* is entered as a positive percentage value; a *discount* is entered as a negative percentage value.

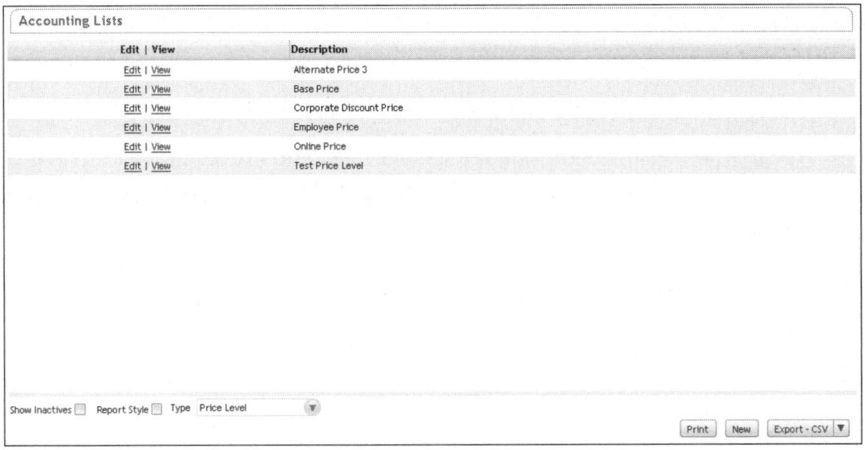

Accounting Lists

	Edit | View	Description
	Edit | View	Alternate Price 3
	Edit | View	Base Price
	Edit | View	Corporate Discount Price
	Edit | View	Employee Price
	Edit | View	Online Price
	Edit | View	Test Price Level

Show Inactives ☐   Report Style ☐   Type Price Level ▼

Print   New   Export - CSV ▼

Figure 7-2:
To see your existing price levels, click Price Level in the Type drop-down list.

5. (Optional) Select the Update Existing Prices check box.

Do this if you want to populate a new price level on existing items (or if you want to update pricing after changing the markup or discount for an existing price level).

6. Click the Save button.

Quantity pricing

You can set up discounts that automatically kick in when a certain number of items is sold in the same transaction.

Enabling quantity pricing

To use this functionality, an Administrator must first enable the Quantity Pricing feature:

1. From the Setup tab menu choose Company⇨Enable Features.

2. On the Transactions tab, select the Quantity Pricing check box.

Pricing columns

With quantity pricing on, the Pricing tab on the item record has multiple columns. The columns represent the following:

✔ The default discount percentage

✔ Default pricing, which shows a minimum sales quantity of 0

✔ Columns where you can enter numbers for the minimum to be ordered to receive a certain quantity price break (for example, 50 or 100)

Administrators can add more price break columns by modifying a company preference:

1. **From the Setup tab menu choose Accounting Preferences.**
2. **Choose the Items/Transactions tab.**
3. **Change the value for Maximum # of Quantity-Based Price Levels.**

   The default is 4.
4. **Click Save.**

Similar to using price levels, you can enter quantity-based prices manually for each item or have them calculated automatically by creating a quantity pricing schedule and assigning it to items.

Quantity pricing schedule

A *quantity pricing schedule* defines a table of sales quantity brackets and discount percentages that can be applied to multiple items. If you have a group of items that share a pricing model, creating a quantity pricing schedule is a great way to minimize the manual labor of entering and updating your prices.

Administrators set up quantity pricing schedules: From the List tab menu choose Accounting➪Quantity Pricing Schedules➪New.

Quantity pricing schedules have a couple of configuration options that add even more flexibility:

✔ **Use Marginal Rates** applies discounts only to the quantity that falls into each pricing bracket. For example, if you set up a schedule to give a 10-percent discount for 20+ widgets, and you sold 25 widgets, the first 20 units are priced normally, and the remaining 5 get the 10-percent discount. With marginal pricing you won't see any discount until you sell 21.

With *non-marginal rates,* all 25 widgets receive the 10-percent discount. Also, that discounted pricing kicks in when you sell 20.

✔ **Calculate Quantity Discounts** allows you to apply discounts based on different criteria of the sale. The discount may apply based on one of the following:

  • Quantity of one line item

  • Total quantity of the item sold across multiple line items

  • Total quantity of items sharing the same parent

  • Total quantity of any item assigned the same quantity pricing schedule

For example, assume a widget with a 10-percent discount over 20 units sold. If you set this field to calculate discounts based on overall parent quantity, and you sold 15 widgets and 15 of another item with the same parent, the 15 widgets get the 10-percent discount because all together you purchased 30 (more than 20) of items having the same parent item (you can set up items in a hierarchy so that some items are *related,* that is, they have the same parent).

Parent and child items relate to a special feature called Matrix Items; see the NetSuite Help Center for details.

Creating and Managing Inventory Items

Inventory items are more complicated than other types of items in NetSuite because you need all the cool features related to inventory.

Staying on ledger accounts

Unlike other items you buy and sell, an inventory item is associated with three general ledger accounts:

- ✔ Income account.
- ✔ Asset account. When you buy an inventory item, its value is posted to its asset account.
- ✔ *Cost of goods sold (COGS)* account. The COGS account is similar to the expense account on other item types, but the workflow of transactions is different. When an inventory item is sold/fulfilled, the current value of the item (per the costing method selected, described later in this section) leaves the asset account and is posted to the COGS account.

Keeping stock information

Stock status information about an inventory item is tracked automatically as you enter transactions. You can see the stock status of an item record on the Inventory tab or through inventory reports, which are described later in this chapter):

- ✔ **On Hand** is the quantity of the item you have in stock.
- ✔ **Available** is the quantity that has not yet been committed to open orders and so can be committed to new orders.
- ✔ **Committed** is the quantity committed to open orders awaiting fulfillment. Available + Committed = On Hand.

> ✔ **Back Ordered** is the quantity not committed to open orders. You may be waiting for these to arrive, or you may have not yet ordered them.

> ✔ **On Order** is the quantity on purchase orders that haven't yet been received.

Assigning costing methods

You must assign new inventory items a *costing method*. This costing method determines the value that's removed from assets and posted to COGS when the item is shipped to a customer.

NetSuite supports three standard costing methods:

> ✔ **Average:** Every time you receive an item, the average value of stock on hand for that item is recalculated. When the item is shipped, the value posted to COGS is its current average value. This is the simplest and most common costing method.

> ✔ **FIFO:** This stands for "First In, First Out." The exact cost and quantity of each purchase is tracked, and when the item is shipped, the cost of the oldest items in stock is posted to COGS.

> ✔ **LIFO:** This stands for "Last In, First Out." Similar to FIFO, exact cost of each purchase is tracked, but instead of using the cost of the oldest items at time of shipment, the newest items are used. This is the least commonly used costing method.

Keep these guidelines in mind:

> ✔ **Consult your accountant if you're not sure which costing method to use.** FIFO and LIFO are much less common and should only be used with certain types of product.

> ✔ **Set the correct costing method.** After you save a new inventory item record, you can't change its costing method! Otherwise, you'll have to recreate the item and delete or inactivate your other item record later. Costing calculations can get pretty complicated. For example, any time you create a transaction dated in the past that affects inventory, NetSuite must recalculate the costing impact on all subsequent transactions that use that inventory item.

> ✔ **Don't go *underwater* with your inventory.** In other words, don't enter transactions so that the number on hand is less than 0. If you do go below 0 and keep entering sales for that item, NetSuite will make a best guess at the cost based on the last sale of that item with a real cost. When you enter an adjustment or purchase to bring those items into stock, NetSuite will post correction lines to the general ledger to reflect the actual cost of the items.

Setting default accounting

If you're creating a lot of items and want to use the same accounting for all of them, an Administrator can set defaults for accounts and costing methods so you don't have to enter the same information on each item record.

Administrators can set default item accounts and costing methods:

1. **From the Setup tab menu choose Accounting⇨Accounting Preferences.**
2. **Select the Items/Transactions tab.**
3. **Select an account from the respective drop-down lists:**
   - Default Expense Account (for noninventory items)
   - Default Income Account
   - Default COGS Account
   - Default Asset Account
4. **Click the Save button.**

Setting and adjusting inventory levels

When you create a new inventory item, you can enter the current quantity you have in stock and its value on the item record. When you save the new item, NetSuite creates an *inventory adjustment* transaction that sets these starting stock levels.

To follow the instructions in this section, you must have a role of Warehouse/Inventory Manager.

Adjustments in NetSuite come in two flavors:

- ✔ **Inventory Adjustment:** A standard inventory adjustment records a positive or negative change to the quantity of items on hand as of the adjustment date. For example, if you had to throw out a defective item, you would enter an inventory adjustment with a quantity of –1.

- ✔ **Inventory Adjustment Worksheet:** Use a worksheet when you want to reset the quantity and value of items as of a particular date. For example, if you performed a cycle count in your warehouse and you found 10 items where NetSuite says you have 7, you could enter a worksheet for that item and enter a new on-hand quantity of 10.

Worksheets set your inventory in stone, so to speak, as of the worksheet date. If you enter an inventory transaction that's dated prior to the worksheet, the general ledger impact of the worksheet will change so that the total on-hand count and value, as of the worksheet date, don't change.

> In this sense, the inventory worksheet is a little like quick-dry cement: It sets the inventory valuation to an absolute value, regardless of how many transactions you post earlier that may otherwise affect that value. It adjusts the general ledger to ensure that the value as of the worksheet remains the same.

Creating a standard inventory adjustment

You can create a standard inventory adjustment by doing the following:

1. **From the Inventory tab menu choose Inventory⇨Adjust Inventory.**

2. **Enter a date.**

3. **Select an adjustment account.**

   The adjustment account posts the difference in value of inventory based on the quantity of the adjustment.

4. **Choose an item to adjust from the Item drop-down list.**

5. **Choose from the Location drop-down list.**

   See Figure 7-3.

6. **Choose a quantity to adjust in the Adjust Qty By field.**

   Enter a positive value to increase the quantity on hand or a negative value to decrease the quantity on hand.

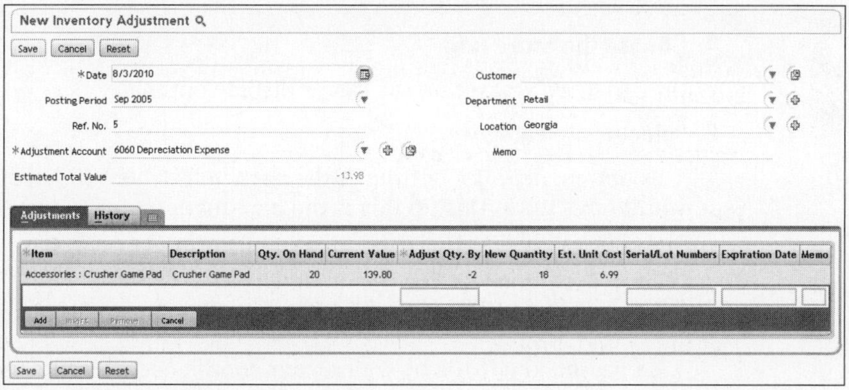

Figure 7-3:
To adjust inventory enter an item name, location, and quantity.

7. **Click the Add button.**

   Add more lines if you need to adjust more than one item.

8. **Click the Save button.**

Creating an inventory adjustment worksheet

To create an inventory adjustment worksheet:

1. **From the Inventory tab menu choose Inventory⇨Adjust Inventory Worksheet.**

2. **Enter a date.**

3. **Select an adjustment account from the Adjustment Account drop-down list.**

4. **In the list of items, enter the current quantity and value for any item you want to change.**

5. **Click the Save button.**

Making items available in the Web store

If you use a NetSuite-hosted Web store, publishing an item is simple:

1. **From the Inventory tab menu, choose Lists⇨Items.**

2. **Click Edit to the left of the item record.**

3. **Select the Display in Web Site check box.**

   See Figure 7-4.

4. **Choose the Store tab.**

   Here's where you set up the item's display options.

5. **Select a site category.**

   This option, near the bottom of the page, tells where the item appears in your Web site. Setting up this is the bare minimum. You may want to set up other useful properties:

   • Descriptions for the item that appear in the site

   • Item images

   • Search keywords by which your shoppers can easily find the item on your site

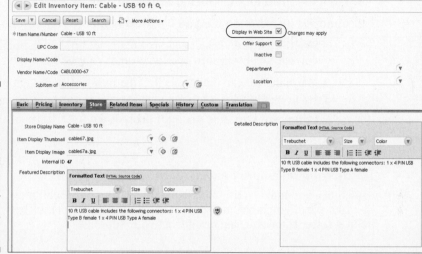

Managing multi-location inventory

If you stock and ship inventory in more than one warehouse or store, you can use the Multi-Location Inventory feature to more precisely keep track of your inventory using up to 50 locations.

Enabling multi-location inventory

An Administrator can turn on this feature:

1. **From the Setup tab menu choose Company⇨Enable Features.**

2. **Choose the Items & Inventory tab.**

3. **Select the Multi-Location Inventory check box.**

4. **Click the Save button.**

Distributing existing stock

NetSuite keeps track of the costing for each item on a per-location basis. The cost of items you buy and receive at one location doesn't affect the value or costing of items at another location unless you transfer the items there.

If you set up multi-location inventory when you first start using NetSuite, you can immediately begin entering inventory transactions and selecting locations for them. If you've used inventory in NetSuite prior to enabling multi-location inventory, you need to distribute your existing stock to locations before you start using the locations for inventory transactions.

1. **From the Inventory tab menu, choose Inventory⇨Distribute Inventory.**

2. **Choose a distribution method by clicking on the relevant link:**

   • **Simple:** You can select a simple distribution, which puts all your current inventory into one location of your choice.

   • **Manual:** You can enter specific quantities of each item to put in each location.

3. **Select from the Variance Account drop-down list.**

4. **Click Save.**

Transferring inventory between locations

Sometimes you may need to move inventory from one location to another. For example, if you have back orders to fill, transferring stock between locations is faster than ordering more from your supplier.

To record the transfer of items, you create an *inventory transfer* transaction:

1. **From the Inventory tab menu choose Inventory⇨Transfer Inventory.**

   The Inventory Transfer screen appears, as shown in Figure 7-5.

2. **Enter a date (if different from the default of today's date).**

3. **From the From drop-down list, select from where you're transferring inventory.**

4. **From the To drop-down list, choose where you're sending the inventory.**

5. **Choose an item to transfer.**

   The items are listed at the bottom of the screen.

6. **Enter the quantity in the Qty to Transfer field.**

7. **Click the Add button.**

   Add more lines if you need to transfer more than one item.

8. **Click the Save button.**

Figure 7-5:
To transfer inventory, enter the from and to locations, the item name, and quantity to be transferred.

Designating preferred vendors

Items for purchase or resale may be assigned a *preferred vendor* (the vendor that you most commonly buy the item from). The preferred vendor is used in a couple of scenarios:

- ✔ When you create a new purchase order or bill and add that item as the first line item on the transaction, the preferred vendor is automatically selected in the Vendor field.
- ✔ When you drop ship an item, and NetSuite creates a purchase order, the preferred vendor is used automatically.

You may also set up items to be associated with more than one vendor. To do so, an Administrator must first enable the Multiple Vendors feature:

1. **From the Setup tab menu choose Company⇨Enable Features.**
2. **Choose the Items & Inventory tab.**
3. **Select the Multiple Vendors check box.**
4. **Click the Save button.**

With this feature turned on, you'll see a Vendors drop-down list at the bottom of the Basic tab of the item record when you edit your items.

You can associate as many vendors as you like with each item and enter a default purchase price for each one. When you create a purchase transaction, select a vendor, and add your item, the price associated with that vendor is automatically pulled in.

If you're using the Multiple Vendors feature, you can still specify a preferred vendor; just select the Preferred check box next to the vendor you want to use as a default in the vendors list on the item record.

Buying Inventory

Depending on the processes in your company, you may use different transaction types to purchase inventory or other kinds of items.

For a quick, one-step purchase, you can create a bill, check, or credit card purchase transaction. If you put inventory items on one of these transactions, they're added to your on-hand stock and inventory assets as soon as the transaction is saved.

Using purchase orders to receive inventory

You create *purchase orders* if you want to keep track of when you order items, receive them, and are billed.

If you have the Advanced Receiving feature enabled, receiving and billing a purchase order are split into two steps and two transactions: the item receipt and the bill. If you don't use Advanced Receiving, the purchase order is received at the same time you bill it.

Administrators can set up advanced receiving:

1. **From the Setup tab menu choose Company⇨Enable Features.**

2. **Choose the Transactions tab.**

3. **Select the Advanced Receiving check box.**

To receive a purchase order:

1. **From the Receiving tab menu choose Receiving⇨Receive Order.**

2. **Click the Receive link next to the purchase order you want to receive.**

   You can select a vendor name from the Vendors drop-down list to filter the list.

   The Item Receipt or Bill screen appears, as shown in Figure 7-6. (Whether you do this on the item receipt or bill depends on whether you use Advanced Receiving.)

3. **On the item receipt or bill, enter the quantity of items you received.**

   The Items tab lists the quantity you were scheduled to receive. You can override this with the number of items you actually received.

4. **Click the Save button.**

Figure 7-6: To get a purchase order, choose the item and quantity on the Item Receipt page.

New Item Receipt 🔍											
Save ▼ Cancel Reset											
Customer **American Computers**						Posting Period Aug 2010				▼	
Created From **Purchase Order #1027**						Ref. No. 8					
*Date 8/4/2010						Memo					
Items & Expenses History											
*Exchange Rate			1.00		Currency **U.S. dollar**						
Items 0 Expenses											
Mark All Unmark All											
Select Item											
Receive Item	Vendor Name	Description	Location	On Hand	Remaining	Quantity	Serial/Lot Numbers	Expiration Date	Options	Rate	Currency
☑ Cable - USB 10 ft	CABL0000-67	10 ft USB A/B Cable	Bethesda ▼	20	50	50				8.99	U.S. dollar

Replenishing inventory and calculating demand

Arguably the most important aspect of managing your inventory business is the process of replenishing items: keeping the right quantity on hand at the right time so that you can fill orders as quickly as possible without a lot of unnecessary (and costly) stock on hand.

To simplify what would otherwise be a tedious and error-prone manual process, you can set up reorder points and preferred stock levels on your item records, and place purchase orders for the appropriate items and quantities with one click by using the Order Items page.

- ✔ **Reorder point:** When the stock level of an inventory item dips down to or below the reorder point, it's time to order more of that item. You can set the reorder point value above zero to give yourself a buffer of items to sell until the next shipment arrives.
- ✔ **Preferred stock level:** The quantity you want to have on hand after you restock the inventory item.

You can set or edit the reorder point and preferred stock level under the Inventory tab on your inventory item records. If you also use the Multi-Location Inventory feature, you may specify a different reorder point and preferred stock level for each location.

After entering reorder points and preferred stock levels, you can see which items need to be ordered on the Order Items page, which you can reach from the Inventory tab menu by choosing Inventory➪Order Items.

The quantity suggested to reorder under Order Items is calculated like this:

Order Items = Preferred Stock Level – Available Quantity – Quantity on Order + Back-Ordered Quantity

The Order Items page also fills in the preferred vendor and purchase price by default. When you click the Submit button, purchase orders are automatically generated. Items that share the same preferred vendor are consolidated into a single purchase order.

Once you're familiar with the concepts described earlier, consider using the Advanced Inventory feature. This feature automatically calculates reorder points and preferred stock levels for you based on past sales demand for your items and adds tracking of *lead time* (the average time to receive orders from your vendors), and the ability to add a safety stock buffer in addition to the reorder point. If you haven't already enabled this feature, talk to your friendly neighborhood NetSuite sales rep about adding it to your account.

Selling Inventory

As with purchasing, you can sell inventory items with a single transaction or using a more elaborate series of steps.

Enabling advanced shipping

Create a cash sale or invoice to record a sale in one step. You can create sales orders to record the sale in one step and fulfill and bill separately. Administrators can enable the Advanced Shipping feature to fulfill and bill a sales order as separate steps:

1. **From the Setup tab menu choose Company⇨Enable Features.**
2. **Choose the Transactions tab.**
3. **Select the Advanced Shipping check box.**

Sales orders are also recommended because they allow you to commit inventory prior to shipping it; in other words, it won't appear as available. That way you don't accidentally sell it twice. You can also use sales orders to track *back orders* (sales that cannot immediately be filled, but will be committed and shipped once more inventory comes in).

If you want to use shipping integration to print FedEx, USPS, or UPS shipping labels, you must use Advanced Shipping. You get into shipping in Chapter 11.

Managing committed items and back orders with sales orders

Options on the sales order determine how inventory should be committed to orders. Although this is relevant for salespeople or others who enter orders, those working with inventory should understand how this is determined.

For each item on a sales order, there is a Commit drop-down list. The value selected determines how stock is committed to the order:

- ✔ **Available Qty** ensures that any available stock is immediately committed to the order when you save it.

- ✔ **Complete Qty** means that the order should be committed only once you have enough of the item in stock to fill it completely. This can be useful if you don't want to ship partial orders; that way, items don't sit around committed to an order that won't ship yet, and you can sell them to another customer.

✔ **Do Not Commit** indefinitely defers stock being committed to an order. Salespeople may use this if someone places an order months in advance; closer to the desired ship date, they can edit the order and change the commitment setting.

If there aren't enough units available to commit to a sales order, or you choose to not commit, it's considered a back order. If Commit is set to Available Qty or Complete Qty on an order, it's automatically committed to fill the back order when more inventory is received.

For information on fulfilling orders, see Chapter 11.

Reporting on Your Inventory

The inventory report you'll probably use most frequently is Current Inventory Status. This report provides a snapshot of important stock metrics for each item: reorder point, preferred stock level, on hand, committed, and on order.

If you use multi-location inventory, the current inventory status may display a top-level summary across all your locations, or information about a particular location or locations.

✔ The **Physical Inventory Worksheet** looks similar to the *Current Inventory Status,* but only includes a list of items and the on-hand count for each. Print this out when you want to do a physical count in your warehouse, to reconcile against the inventory status in NetSuite.

✔ To determine which items are most profitable, use the **Inventory Profitability report.** This displays the cost and revenue for each item, along with the profit margin percentage and the percentage of total profit (across all your items) that each item represents.

✔ The **Inventory Revenue report** is similar to the profitability report, but only shows the revenue for each item and the percentage of total revenue for each item.

✔ To analyze the movement of inventory in and out of stock, and the costing implications, use the **Inventory Valuation report.**

✔ The **Inventory Turnover report** can be a useful tool for checking the efficiency of your inventory management. This report shows your inventory turnover rate (also known simply as *turn rate*) for each item and the average number of days supply of stock on hand, based on the turn rate.

Turn Rate = Cost of Sales (during the date range selected) / Average Value of Item

Average Value of Item = On-Hand Value on the Last Day of Each Month / Number of Months in the Report's Date Range

And how can you get to all these informative inventory reports? The answer, young Skywalker, is from the Inventory tab menu: Choose Reports followed by the report name.

Using Advanced Inventory Features

NetSuite provides a number of additional inventory features to handle more complex or specialized business needs. After you've implemented the basics, you may want to investigate the following features to see if they can help manage your inventory more effectively:

- ✔ **Bar Coding and Item Labels:** For all your items you can print labels (including a bar code of the item name/number or UPC code) and print a bar code on all your transactions with the transaction number. You can also scan item bar codes on the Order Fulfillment page to speed up the fulfillment process.

- ✔ **Matrix Items:** Sometimes you'll stock and sell an item that comes in multiple versions (for example, multiple sizes and colors), but need to track stock and pricing of each combination separately. You can create an item matrix for this purpose and search for the matrix on transactions or in the Web store, then select the combination of options for the particular item you want to sell.

- ✔ **Serialized Inventory:** When every physical unit of an item needs to be identified and tracked separately, use the Serialized Inventory feature. The exact cost of each serial number is tracked as you purchase and sell the item.

- ✔ **Lot Numbered Inventory:** Similar to serialized inventory, but each identifying number applies to multiple physical units of the item. For example, 10 bottles of a prescription drug manufactured at the same time may share the same identifying lot number.

- ✔ **Landed Cost:** Sometimes the true cost of inventory is more than just what you paid for the item itself. For example, there may be shipping or duty tax fees that you paid to receive the item. Use landed cost to assign these costs to the proper items and report on inventory profitability more accurately.

✔ **Bin Management:** By assigning items to a particular bin or bins, you can track exactly where all your inventory is stored and available within the warehouse.

✔ **Multiple Units of Measure:** You can assign different units to an item for sales, stocking, and purchase purposes. If your supplier sells to you in yards, but you sell in feet, the quantity on each transaction will make sense to its audience.

✔ **Assembly Items:** Assemblies allow you to track simple, light manufacturing in NetSuite. You can set up an assembly, or *bill of materials* item, as being made up of other inventory, assembly, non-inventory, other charge, and service items, and then build the assembly to put it into stock. Assemblies are treated like inventory for costing and sales purposes.

Part III

Marketing and Driving Sales

"The top line represents our revenue, the middle line is our inventory, and the bottom line shows the rate of my hair loss over the same period."

In this part . . .

*T*he best way to turn leads into customers is to dangle your products in front of them with marketing. But in order to really manage sales, you need to motivate your salespeople by giving them leads, quotas, and, of course, commissions. Meanwhile, you need sales forecasts that help you take an accurate pulse on the revenue.

Chapter 8 helps you hone your marketing efforts while Chapter 9 helps sales managers and administrators put sales force automation in place, with territories, quotas, and commissions. Important for all concerned, Chapter 10 helps sales reps turn leads into customers.

Chapter 8

Building a Campaign: Marketing Automation

In This Chapter

▶ Building marketing campaigns

▶ Offering coupon codes to increase sales

▶ Using keyword marketing

▶ Upselling related items

▶ Tracking ROI on marketing efforts

*N*etSuite lets you do absolutely everything you need to run your business. That key element doesn't stop at marketing. In this chapter, we show you how to create and track your entire marketing plan with campaigns, how to execute your campaigns by sending targeted e-mail or direct mail, and how to plan events to generate leads and sales.

Then, we describe how to track your marketing success by viewing the responses for e-mail campaigns and reporting on *return on investment (ROI)* (based on resulting sales and new leads that have joined your ranks). Don't miss the information about managing leads and the process to convert them into prospects and customers, which is further described in Chapter 10.

Many of the tasks in this chapter require administrator privileges, so keep your administrator nearby and well supplied with home-baked treats. Other tasks can be performed by those with roles such as Marketing Manager. We tell you when throughout this chapter.

Selling You on Marketing Campaigns

You can use *marketing campaigns* — strategies — in NetSuite to organize and track your entire bag of tricks for generating leads and sales:

- ✔ Ads placed in print or online
- ✔ E-mail
- ✔ Direct mail
- ✔ Telemarketing
- ✔ Events, such as conferences
- ✔ Keywords
- ✔ Any other lead-generating activity

Setting up a campaign domain

Are you going to send regular e-mail messages (such as monthly updates about featured products and coupons)? Then setting up a virtual domain for your e-mail campaigns is one of the most important setup steps. Setup includes a campaign domain used for both e-mail marketing campaigns and e-mail merges done via the Mail Merge feature.

Setting up your account to send e-mail campaigns takes several steps, and most of them are due to the ever-increasing regulations around e-mail marketing. These regulations protect both you and your customers, so you should follow them.

Buying a unique domain

Campaign domains are important so that your e-mail reputation remains separate from NetSuite's reputation. If someone uses NetSuite and breaks the rules, you don't want to be blocked as a result.

Your campaign domain needs to be different from your Web domain but can be a subdomain, such as mail.*yourdomain*.com. Once you set up a campaign e-mail domain, remove any reference to Netsuite.com. That reduces the chances of your e-mail being marked as spam or blacklisted by e-mail providers.

To set up a domain for e-mail campaigns, follow along in this section and the following subsections:

1. **Call your Domain Name System (DNS) provider.**

   If you haven't already bought a domain, you can buy one from your DNS provider.

2. **Explain what you need to do.**

   Simply say, "I want to forward my domain name to shopping.netsuite. com. Can you do a CNAME redirect for me?"

If the provider says yes, he performs the behind-the-scenes magic and may say something cryptic like "Okay, I'll set up a CNAME redirect for you." Depending on your DNS provider, forwarding your domain name may take some time. The DNS provider should give an estimate for when to expect the forward to be complete. Ask how you can tell when the job is done.

Don't send a campaign e-mail until you have set up the campaign in NetSuite, because (for example) the link to shopping.netsuite.com will be broken until the forward is completed.

Sometimes your provider can't use a CNAME redirect for both your Web domain and your e-mail campaign domain. If the DNS provider has trouble with a CNAME redirect, it can use a Record redirect to point your campaign domain to NetSuite using the IP address 63.209.28.41. A CNAME redirect is the preferred method, however, in case this IP address must change in the future.

We admit that we're throwing around technical terms here without a lot of context; every DNS provider is different, and we can't give you exact steps here. The point is that if you call your DNS provider and explain what you want to do, it can help you set it up.

Entering your domain name

After buying and getting a unique domain name, ask an Administrator to enter your domain name in NetSuite:

1. **From the Setup tab menu, choose Web Site⇨Domains.**

   The Set Up Domains page appears, as shown in Figure 8-1.

2. **In the Domain Name column, enter your e-mail domain.**

3. **In the Hosted As column, select E-mail Campaign from the drop-down list.**

4. **Click the Add button.**

5. **If you have a domain name beginning with www, repeat Steps 2–4 and enter your domain name again *without* the www.**

   For example, if you entered **www.companyname.com** the first time, enter **companyname.com** the second time.

6. **Click the Save button.**

   If you have more than one domain name to use for e-mail, you can repeat these steps and add multiple domain names used for e-mail campaigns.

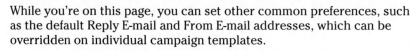

Set Up Domains							
Save Cancel							
Protocol	Domain Name	Hosted As	Web Site	HTML Hosting Root	Home Page	Redirect URL	Not-Found Page
http://	www.wolfeelectronics.com	Hosted Web Page	Wolfe Electronics	Live Hosting Files	Live Hosting Files : /index.html		
http://	wolfemail.com	E-mail Campaign					
http://		Web Store	Wolfe Electronics ▾				
Add *Insert* *Remove* Cancel							

Setting up a default domain

Even if you use only one domain name, you should set it up as your default domain name so you don't have to select a domain on every template you create. Marketing managers can do this task by:

1. **From the Setup tab menu, choose Sales & Marketing Automation⇨Marketing Preferences.**

   The Marketing Preferences page appears.

2. **From the Default Campaign Domain drop-down list, select the domain name you'll use most often when sending mass e-mail campaigns.**

   While you're on this page, you can set other common preferences, such as the default Reply E-mail and From E-mail addresses, which can be overridden on individual campaign templates.

   You can click the name of any field to read more about that preference.

3. **Click the Save button.**

Just when you thought you were done, you have one last thing to do — validate the address from which you send the campaign e-mails. (*Validating* is how NetSuite ensures that it adheres to high standards in e-mail marketing, setting you worlds apart from spammers and scammers for whom e-mail address forgery is a way of life. To validate the address is a way of checking that the person who sent the e-mail really did send it.)

Validating From and Reply To e-mail addresses

To validate your From and Reply To e-mail address, marketing managers can:

1. **From the Setup tab menu choose Sales & Marketing Automation⇨Campaign E-mail Addresses⇨New.**

   The Campaign E-mail Addresses page appears.

2. **Enter your campaign e-mail address in the Email Address field.**

3. **(Optional) Choose the Private check box if you want to be the sole person who can attach this e-mail address to a campaign**

4. **Click the Save button.**

   The authorization/validation code is sent to the e-mail address. The person who owns that e-mail address should look for the e-mail that NetSuite sends to do the next step in this process.

5. **Open the message containing the authorization code, and press Ctrl+C to copy the code.**

   Note: The owner of the e-mail address should click the link in the e-mail message to validate the address.

6. **Return to NetSuite and choose Setup⇨Marketing⇨E-mail Addresses.**

   The Campaign E-mail Address page appears with new fields, as shown in Figure 8-2. However, the screen you see will have the authorization code automatically filled in.

7. **Click the Edit link next to the e-mail address you need to validate.**

8. **Click in the Authorization Code field and press Ctrl+V.**

   You've pasted the code you copied in Step 5.

9. **Click the Save button.**

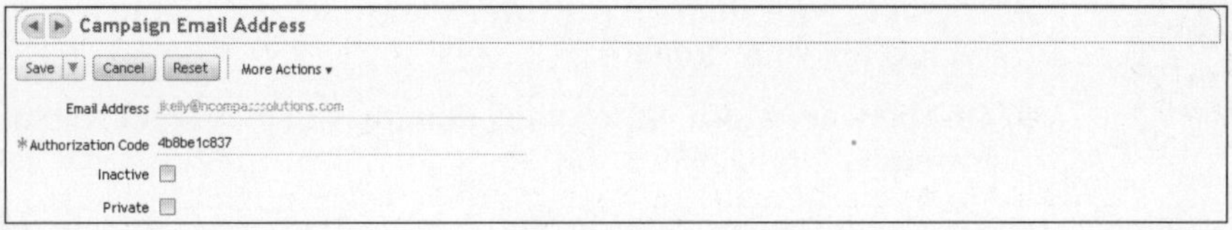

Figure 8-2:
After the e-mail address is validated, fields are added to the Campaign E-mail Address screen for authorization.

Using Domain Key Identified Mail (DKIM)

Another way to keep your campaign e-mail from being considered spam is to use Domain Key Identified Mail (DKIM).

Using DKIM is like using a hidden signature on your campaign e-mail that verifies your identity as a reputable marketer. You should first set up DKIM in NetSuite, then with your domain name provider. You can then verify the configuration in NetSuite. The following steps provide all the details.

Have an administrator set up DKIM in NetSuite using the following steps:

1. **From the Setup tab menu, choose Company⇨Printing, Fax & E-mail Preferences.**

    The Printing, Fax, and E-mail Preferences page appears.

2. **Click the E-mail tab.**

3. **In the Domain Keys section, select the Add DKIM to Mass Messages check box.**

    This inserts a DKIM header for all e-mail messages (both e-mail marketing campaigns and e-mail merge operations) you send in bulk from your account.

4. **In the Domain Selector field, type** selector1.

5. **In the Domain Name field, enter the domain name you're using when sending e-mail campaigns.**

6. **Next to Public Domain Key, click the Generate Key Pair link.**

    This generates the private and public domain keys and the full DNS entry.

7. **Open a new window in your browser, go to your domain provider's site, and log in to your account.**

    You have to switch between windows for the next few steps, where you set up DKIM with your domain provider.

    You may need a phone call with your domain provider to really follow these steps since every provider's procedures are a little different.

8. **Log in to your domain provider's account and create a new text record for your domain.**

9. **On the text record, enter your domain selector from NetSuite, followed by** .domainkey.

    If you entered selector1 in Step 4, you would enter **selector1.domainkey** as the TXT name.

10. **Go back to the NetSuite window and copy the information from the DNS Entry field.**

11. **Move back to the domain provider's page and paste it in as the TXT value.**

12. **Finish your work on the domain provider's page by clicking Submit or Have a Nice Day or Sayonara — whatever its closing button may say.**

13. **Move back to the NetSuite window and click the Save button.**

Now your fancy footwork is done.

If your domain is locked, you need to temporarily unlock it for your changes to take effect, which may take a few hours. Go for a long lunch if your domain provider says it'll take a while.

You're now ready to set up templates, create groups of recipients, and schedule those campaigns. Get some marketing done, people!

Creating a new campaign

Campaign records are created for any type of marketing that you want to track results for. Campaign events that you attach to campaign records can track the individual pieces of any activity your company does to bring in business, whether it is through online advertising, e-mail offers, direct mail, or other means. If you want to lump together several campaign facets for reporting, add these different aspects as campaign events.

Marketing managers can execute these steps themselves; no administrators are needed.

For example, say you have a big upcoming product and service package launch. You plan to market this new roll out with an e-mail campaign, post-card mail, Web site banner ads, newly purchased keywords for search engine optimization, new information brochures, and a booth at an upcoming trade show. You'd create a campaign record for the product package launch, and create individual campaign events under that campaign record for each of these marketing efforts.

ROI is tracked per lead source, and there is only one lead source per campaign. This means you can't track ROI for campaign events attached to a parent campaign. If you need to track revenue for individual events, you should create separate campaign records for each.

To set up a campaign record:

1. **From the Campaigns tab menu, choose Marketing⇨Marketing Campaigns⇨New.**

   The Marketing Campaign page appears.

2. **In the Title field, type a name for the entire campaign.**

   For instance, for the previously described example, you may enter *Widget X Product Package Launch.*

3. **(Optional) In the Category field, select a category for the campaign.**

   Campaign categories simply help you organize campaigns for lists, searching, and reporting. You can create your own categories from the Setup tab menu by choosing Sales & Marketing Automation⇨Campaign Categories⇨New.

4. **(Optional) From the Manager drop-down list, select a name.**

   Your name is selected by default. You may want to change this to another employee who's managing the campaign events associated with this campaign. She may need to receive a confirmation e-mail when an e-mail campaign has been sent.

5. **Complete the Start Date and End Date fields for the time the campaign events are in effect.**

   Entering these dates helps you filter lists and reports.

6. **(Optional) In the URL field, enter a Web address you may have set up for this campaign or for an online customer form you may have created.**

   Entering a promotional URL you're using for print, TV, radio, or Web banner ads, for example, lets you track your success in marketing reports based on the number of hits and purchases.

   If you're only using this campaign to send e-mail, leave the URL field blank so your reports track only activity generated from the e-mail. If you want to track an e-mail blast separately from other campaign events, you may want to create a separate campaign event for the e-mail blast.

7. **In the Base Cost field, enter the cost for the campaign, *excluding* the cost for any of the campaign events.**

   Costs for individual events are tracked separately on the Events tab. The Total Cost field adds the Base Cost to each event's cost for a running total.

8. **Enter your expected revenue from this campaign.**

   After the marketing campaign is over, you can run a report to compare the expected revenue to the actual revenue.

9. **(Optional) On the Related Info tab, select additional information about your goals for this campaign:**

- Vertical: What industries are you trying to reach? You can set up a list of vertical markets from the Setup tab menu by choosing Sales & Marketing Automation⇨Campaign Verticals⇨New.

- Audience Description: Who are you trying to reach? The MTV generation? The Pepsi generation? You can create campaign audience records from the Setup tab menu by choosing Sales & Marketing Automation⇨Campaign Audiences⇨New.

- Offer, such as a Promotion Code: What offers are available?

- Item: What are you selling?

10. **Click the Save button.**

After you set up your main campaign record, you can begin adding campaign events to it using the Events tab on this screen. However, most campaign events, such as e-mail and direct mail campaigns, require you to create target groups of customers (see the following section) and marketing e-mail templates (see the section following that) that can be uploaded or created directly within your account.

Putting your eye on the target

You can build groups of people to target for campaigns based on any number of criteria:

- ✔ Customers who recently purchased certain items
- ✔ Customers who recently submitted support cases
- ✔ Contacts recently added to your account

When creating target groups for e-mail campaigns, keep in mind these tips:

- ✔ **Set your criteria to *exclude* those who have Global Subscription Status set to Soft Opt Out or Confirmed Opt Out.** NetSuite filters these out automatically, but you can get a more accurate picture of who will receive the e-mail if you filter these out on the front end.

- ✔ **If your group is large, create test cells.** *Test cells* are subgroups that represent a percentage of your large group. When you set up an e-mail campaign event, first send it to your test cell (to make sure everything is working correctly) before sending it to the entire target group. You can also divide the group and send different offers to different test cells and evaluate their ROI.

Administrators must enable the feature before you can set up test cells. From the Setup tab menu, choose Marketing➪Preferences➪Marketing Preferences. Then choose the Campaign Test Cells check box.

Creating target lists

Administrators help you create target lists by creating groups:

1. **From the Lists menu tab choose Relationships➪Groups➪New.**

   The Create Group page opens.

2. **Choose the correct radio button:**

   • **Dynamic** forms your group based on search criteria.

   • **Static** lets you choose your group members one by one.

3. **Click Continue.**

   The Create Dynamic Customer Group appears.

4. **Enter a name for your group.**

5. **Select a saved search to find the leads who should be in your group.**

   For more information on creating saved searches, see Chapter 19.

6. **Click Save.**

If you create a dynamic group based on search criteria, you need to create a saved search of the type of people (such as customers) you want to group. Don't worry, though, you can create the search from the Create Dynamic Group page — just click the Add button next to the Saved Search drop-down list.

Subscription options

Every person or company with a relationship record in your account (customer, contact, partner, or vendor) has a Marketing tab on his record. Under this tab, the Subscriptions tab defines how you can contact this person via e-mail campaigns, as shown in Table 8-1.

✔ **Soft opt-in:** You send the customer e-mail by default, both e-mail about campaigns and an invitation to receive e-mail.

✔ **Soft opt-out:** You send the customer an invitation to receive e-mail.

✔ **Confirmed opt-in:** The customer has already told you that he wants to receive e-mail from you.

✔ **Confirmed opt-out:** The customer has already told you she doesn't want to receive any e-mail from you.

Table 8-1	Contacting Someone Via E-mail Campaigns		
Status	*Receive Campaign E-Mail?*	*Receive Opt-In Invitation?*	*Set By*
Confirmed Opt-In	Yes	Yes	Recipient only
Soft Opt-In	Yes	Yes	Manual or mass update
Soft Opt-Out	No	Yes	Manual or mass update
Confirmed Opt-Out	No	No	Recipient only

Potential recipients can choose which kind of e-mail campaigns they'd like to receive. With subscriptions you may, for example, get more people signing on to receive e-mail about sales and coupons for specific items, than you would if they could only opt in or out of *all* campaigns.

You can set up campaign subscription categories at Setup⇨Sales and Marketing Automation⇨Campaign Subscriptions⇨New.

Customers, contacts, partners, and vendors who opt out or are soft-opted out still get e-mail related to transactions or affecting their personal accounts with you.

Sending an opt-in invitation or confirmation e-mail is a best practice for converting soft opt-in and soft opt-out recipients to confirmed opt-in recipients, reducing the chances that your mail will be considered spam. In NetSuite, these invitation and confirmation messages are called *subscription messages,* and you can send them two ways:

You can customize the text used in these subscription messages:

1. **From the Setup tab menu choose Sales & Marketing Automation⇨Marketing Preferences.**

2. **In the Opt-In Confirmation Message field, change the text.**

   The text that shows up is used when sending confirmation e-mail to recipients who are soft-opted in.

3. **In the Opt-In Invitation Message field, change the text.**

   The text that shows up is used to invite those who are soft-opted out to begin receiving campaigns from you.

Recipients can also opt in or opt out of your campaign e-mail from the Customer Center, the My Account page of your NetSuite-generated Web Site, or by clicking the automatically included links in the footer of all campaign e-mail.

Mass update invite

You can search for recipients to invite and send them your invitation. For those who are soft-opted in, you can ask them to confirm their subscriptions. For those soft-opted out, you can invite them to start receiving campaigns.

Administrators can send subscription messages via mass update:

1. **From the Lists tab menu, choose Mass Update⇨Mass Updates.**
2. **Click the plus sign to expand the Marketing section.**
3. **Choose the type of recipient you want to send invitation e-mail to.**

One-off invite

Marketing managers (and just about anyone else) can send a single subscription message:

1. **Open the recipient or potential recipient's record.**
2. **Choose the Marketing tab.**
3. **Click the Send Subscription E-mail button or link.**

Creating campaign marketing templates

You should create marketing campaign templates for e-mail and direct mail marketing communication. You can create your templates two ways:

✔ As files outside of NetSuite and upload them to your account

✔ Written directly from the marketing template record

Marketing templates typically make use of CRMSDK (Customer Relationship Management Software Development Kit) tags, which act like the tags you use when you mail merge in Microsoft Word. In NetSuite, however, a CRMSDK tag is replaced with the corresponding information from the type of record it refers to without having to create a spreadsheet of data or import or export any information. The tag can include data from custom fields on the record if needed.

For example, you create an e-mail marketing template that begins with the following:

```
Dear <NLENTITYID>,
```

The <NLENTITYID> tag is automatically replaced with the first and last name or company name of each person in the target group.

Search NetSuite help for a list of CRMSDK tags.

Aside from relationship and employee records, you can use CRMSDK tags when sending mass e-mail about cases, transactions, or custom records. Setting defaults with CRMSDK tags is a good idea in case there's no data in a field for that record. You can do this in the following format:

```
Dear <NLENTITYID DEFAULT="valued customer">,
```

When you create your marketing template directly in your NetSuite account using the Text Editor feature (described in the following steps), NetSuite helps you insert these tags by giving you handy drop-down lists.

Creating an e-mail marketing template

Marketing managers can create an e-mail marketing template by:

1. **From the Campaigns tab menu, choose Marketing⇨Marketing Templates⇨New.**

   The Select Type page appears.

2. **Click Campaign.**

   The Campaign Email Template page appears.

3. **In the Name field, type a title for storing your template in NetSuite.**

   You may want to name it *Product of the Month,* for example.

4. **Choose the Send E-mail Preview check box.**

   This allows you to test your template and send the e-mail to yourself when you save this record.

5. **In the Subject field on the Template tab, type the subject that should show for your e-mail message.**

   For example, the subject may read *Columbus Day Sale!*

6. **Choose a radio button depending on which type of template you're using:**

   • **File:** If you've created your HTML template using CRMSDK tags, select the File radio button, and then select the New from the drop-down list to upload your file to the File Cabinet in a new window.

   Clicking the Documents tab automatically opens the File Cabinet.

   Your template file must include <html></html> and <body></body> tags in addition to all closing tags for your template to work with NetSuite.

   • **Text Editor:** Choose this radio button to create your message in a text field in NetSuite. To insert a CRMSDK tag, choose the type of record to pull from in the Field Type drop-down list, and then select the field you want to pull information from the Insert Field drop-down list, as shown in Figure 8-3.

7. **On the Restrict Access tab, select the Private check box.**

   That way only you can edit it. If you prefer, you can let others edit it by choosing a group from the Restrict to Group drop-down list.

8. **On the Marketing tab, enter who this e-mail should appear from in the From Name field.**

   Alternatively, you can choose the E-mail as Sales Rep check box to send this e-mail as though it's coming from each customer's sales rep (which is selected on each customer record). When you select this check box, the From name is the nickname that the sales rep has set under Home⇨Set Preferences, and the sales rep's e-mail address acts as the From and Reply To address.

9. **If needed, in the From and Reply to E-mail Address fields you can enter an e-mail address different from the default.**

   Keep in mind, however, that these e-mail addresses must be validated to be used with campaigns.

10. **In the Campaign Domain field, select the domain name you set up for e-mail campaigns.**

    For more information on setting up a domain name and validating an e-mail address, see the earlier section, "Setting up a campaign e-mail domain."

11. **(Optional) In the Subscription field, select a category.**

    This is the group that e-mails using this template should be grouped with.

Create subscription categories from the Setup tab menu by choosing Sales & Marketing Automation⇨Campaign Subscriptions⇨New. Customers can opt in or out of each subscription using the Subscription Center from the Customer Center page.

12. **Make sure the Track Outgoing E-mails check box is selected.**

    This ensures that statistics are tracked for how many messages are opened and clicked through.

13. **Click the Save button.**

Your marketing template is now saved and can be updated as needed by either saving over the file in the File Cabinet with a new version, or editing the text on the Template tab of the record. This template is now ready to be set up as a campaign event for a scheduled send out to a target group.

Creating a direct mail marketing template

Creating a direct mail marketing template takes a few steps, so hang in there!

1. **From the Documents tab menu choose Templates⇨Letter Templates⇨New.**

   The Letter Template screen appears.

2. **In the Name field type a name for storing this template.**

3. **On the Template tab, enter the subject of the mail in the Subject field.**

4. **If you haven't done so, click the Download link to download the sample source file.**

   This makes Microsoft Word work with NetSuite's CRMSDK tags.

   Heads up! Now you start creating your template in Microsoft Word.

5. **In Word 2003, choose Tools⇨Letters and Mailing⇨Mail Merge Wizard.**

   In Word 2007: Click this under Mailings tab, and then click the Start Mail Merge button. Select Step By Step Mail Merge Wizard from the drop-down list.

   Step 1 of the wizard starts.

6. **Select the Letters radio button, and then click Next.**

7. **Select the Use the Current Document radio button, and then click Next.**

8. **Select the Use an Existing List radio button, and then Existing List. Click Browse to select the source file you downloaded in Step 4.**

9. **Click OK through any dialog boxes that open, and then click Next.**

10. **Create your letter.**

11. **Add tags by using the Insert Merge Field tool on the Mailings or Mail Merge toolbar.**

12. **Close the Mail Merge wizard.**

13. **Save your completed template, with tags, as a DOC file.**

14. **In NetSuite, on the Letter Template page, select New from the File drop-down list, and upload your template document in the dialog box that appears.**

15. **(Optional) On the Restrict Access tab, choose the Private check box.**

    This makes this template record accessible only to you. Or you can restrict it to a certain group of employees by selecting the group name in the Restrict to Group field.

16. **Click the Save button.**

Your letter template is now available to be paired with a target group for a campaign event. Letter templates don't have to be associated with a subscription, which means that you can send valuable offers to all the customers as much as you want to.

Planning events: Setting up e-mail, direct mail, ads, and more

Campaign events are tracked on a *parent* (main) campaign. They can include all the tools in your belt for a certain campaign, tracking their success both individually and overall. Target groups and templates you create come together on campaign events.

If you haven't done so, create a parent campaign record as described in the earlier section, "Creating a new campaign." From the parent campaign record, you can start adding campaign events for your e-mail campaigns, mail outs, ads, and so on, as shown in Figure 8-4.

To add a campaign event:

1. **From the Campaign menu, choose Marketing⇨Marketing Campaigns.**

    The Marketing Campaigns list opens.

2. **Click the Edit link next to the campaign that this event should be added to.**

    The Marketing Campaign screen appears.

3. **On the Events tab, choose the tab related to the type of campaign event:**

- **E-mail:** Choose the E-mail tab. From the Target Group drop-down list, select your group of contacts or customers or select the test cell from this drop-down list if you want to send this in small batches (test cells are set on the group record), and select your e-mail marketing template from the Template drop-down list. Enter any associated cost, such as labor, in the Cost column.

To schedule the e-mail, select Execute from the Status drop-down list, and enter the date and time when the e-mail should be sent in the Date and Time columns. If a promotion code is being offered with this e-mail, select it from the Promotion Code drop-down list. More on promotion codes can be found at **http://www.dummies.com/go/ netsuitefd**. Click the Add button to add this campaign event.

- **Direct Mail:** From the Target Group drop-down list, select your group of contacts or customers, select the letter template you want to use from the Template drop-down list, and enter any associated cost and/or promotion code in the Cost field.

You execute direct mail campaigns using the Mail Merge feature. You can manually set the status here after sending mailers.

- **Other Events:** For ads, shows, conferences, and other marketing methods, you will likely only have need to enter a title in the Title field, a cost in the Cost field, and perhaps select a coupon code from the Promotion Code drop-down list.

You can create new channels for tracking your other events by choosing Setup⇨Sales and Marketing⇨Automation⇨Campaign Channels⇨New.

Figure 8-4: Create campaign events and set statuses on the Marketing Campaign record.

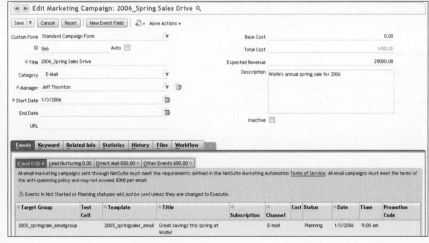

   **4. Click the Save button after adding the details of your campaign
      events.**

Your campaign event is automatically saved on the campaign record. For an
overview of the process of setting up campaigns and their events, see the
flow chart in Figure 8-5.

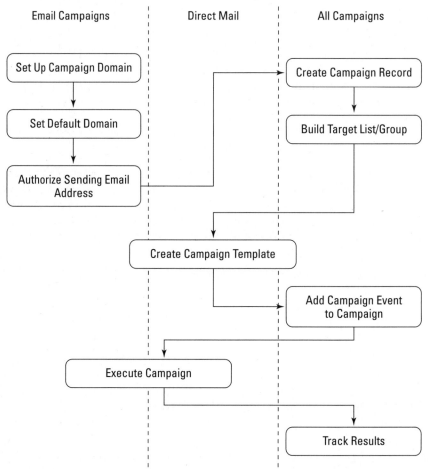

Figure 8-5:
Campaigns
are created
using this
process.

Keyword Marketing

Keyword marketing is a high bang for your buck search engine marketing technique that can be tapped in to for both keywords you naturally receive hits on but don't pay for, as well as keywords you are trying to capitalize on by paying for higher placement, or for ads when those keywords are used.

NetSuite offers a standard role just for handling these campaigns: the Marketing Keyword Manager. If you have this role, you, as well as the Marketing Manager, can perform the tasks in this section.

For example, you can track the success you have with keywords that you know work with your site already, and you can track your success with keywords you purchase though programs like Google AdWords. While natural keywords are automatically tracked using reports that come with the Advanced Web Reports feature in NetSuite, paid keywords are tracked by campaigns and then reported on marketing reports.

Because you need to provide a URL to search engines for each paid keyword, it is best to choose and set up your keywords in NetSuite before submitting keywords to search engines. If you already purchased keywords through a search engine, you may need to update the URLs for each of these with your search engine account. The URL is saved on the campaign record for the keyword.

Tracking keywords

You probably have more than a handful of keywords to track, and we know you don't want to enter them individually. That's why you can enter keyword campaigns (Campaign records specifically for keywords) in bulk or import them. When you create keyword campaigns in bulk, they all have the same start and end dates, and the same category. Before you import them, you need to prepare them in a spreadsheet in CSV format.

Creating keyword campaigns in bulk

To create keyword campaigns in bulk:

1. **From the Campaigns menu choose Marketing⇨Create Keyword Campaigns.**

   The Create Keyword Campaigns page appears.

2. **From the Category drop-down list, select the type of keyword campaign this is.**

   Here are just a few of your many choices:

   - TV

   - Referral

   - Paid Keywords

   Set up these campaign categories and add new ones from the Setup tab menu by choosing Sales and Marketing Automation⇨Campaign Categories⇨New.

3. **Enter the start and end dates for tracking these keywords in the Start Date and End Date fields.**

4. **On the Keyword tab, select and add each keyword with the following information:**

   - **ID:** Enter an ID for the keyword, if desired. This field isn't required.

   - **Search Engine:** From this drop-down list select the search engine from where the keyword was bought. Administrators can add to this list from the Setup tab menu by choosing Marketing⇨Search Engines.

   - **Family:** If the keyword is purchased in a group, select the name of the family, or group from this drop-down list. You can add family names from the Setup tab menu by choosing Sales and Marketing⇨Automation⇨Campaign Families⇨New. Families make it easier to view reports when you have a large amount of keywords to track.

   - **Keyword:** Enter the keyword in this field. It can be a single word, a phrase, or even a question.

   - **Cost:** Enter the amount you paid for the keyword in this field.

   - **Description:** Enter a description of the keyword or the campaign in this field if needed. For example, if you have a particular angle with one keyword variation versus another, you can document that in the description field (as in, "Targets female hair loss" for the keyword phrase "How can I regrow my lovely locks?").

   - **URL:** Enter the Web address associated with the paid keyword in this field. For example, if you buy a keyword related to an item, the URL is for the Item page instead of your Home page.

   - **Offer:** Select an offer related to the keyword from this drop-down list. You can add to this list from the Setup tab menu by choosing Setup⇨Sales & Marketing⇨Automation⇨Campaign Offers⇨New.

5. **Click the Add button.**

   If your next keyword is similar, you can click the Copy Previous button so you can modify that keyword more easily.

6. **On the Related Info tab, select the following:**

   • A vertical from the Vertical drop-down list

   • An audience from the Audience Description drop-down list

   • Any items associated with this group of keywords from the Items field

   You can add verticals and audience descriptions to these lists from the Setup tab menu by choosing Setup⇨Sales &Marketing⇨Automation⇨ Campaign Verticals or Setup⇨Marketing⇨(or Campaign Audiences)⇨ New. Verticals and audiences are used to report on and analyze keyword results.

7. **Click the Save button.**

All keywords are saved as individual campaigns. You can view and edit these campaigns from the Lists tab menu by choosing Marketing⇨Marketing Campaigns.

Importing keywords from a CSV file

To import keywords from a CSV file:

1. **From the Campaigns menu choose Marketing⇨Create Keyword Campaigns⇨Import.**

   The Import Assistant opens.

2. **Click the Select button next to CSV File.**

3. **Choose your file from your hard drive.**

   If you haven't already formatted your file, click the Campaign Keywords Template link to download a template that will help you fill in the right information.

4. **Click the Next button.**

5. **On the Field Mapping page, verify that all columns from your file on the left are mapped to NetSuite fields on the right.**

   To change mappings, click a line in the middle of the page and click a field name on the right or a column name on the left.

6. **Click the Run button.**

Your keyword import begins, and you see a status page that you can refresh to update the status of the import. You can leave this page, continue working, and check back on the status by choosing Setup⇨Import/Export⇨View CSV Import Status.

To submit your keywords with URLs to search engines, you may want to create a saved search for keyword campaigns for each search engine that lists each URL in the results. On the results page, those roles with permission to export search results can export the results list as CSV.

To create a saved campaign search, do this:

1. **Click the Search link in the header of the Campaigns list.**

   The Campaign Search page opens.

2. **Click the Create Saved Search button.**

Viewing keyword reports

You can now see the success of your paid keywords using the Sales by Paid Keyword and Leads by Paid Keyword reports.

To view keyword reports, choose Reports⇨Marketing⇨Sales by Paid Keyword. (Or choose Reports ⇨Marketing⇨Leads by Paid Keyword.)

You can view your ROI by using the Campaign ROI Analysis reports. See the upcoming "Measuring campaign ROI" section.

Because pay-per-click keywords have varying costs per number of clicks you get in a period of time, regularly update your cost on each keyword campaign record to ensure your ROI reporting remains updated.

Tracking Marketing Results

Perhaps the most important part of a marketing solution isn't how you get the campaigns set up or how you deploy the campaign, but pulling out the information on how the campaign did — looking at your campaign report card, in other words.

You can evaluate your marketing success in NetSuite in three places:

✔ **Campaign record:** On the Statistics tab of the campaign record, you can see the total revenue, ROI, profit, cost per lead and purchaser, leads generated, purchases generated. For e-mail campaigns, you also can see click-through rates and responses.

✔ **Customer record:** On the Marketing tab of the lead, prospect, or customer record, you can see which campaigns are targeted at the customer and you can see the customer's response.

✔ **Marketing reports:** Campaign response and ROI, lead source analysis, partner activity, lead source sales, and keyword reports give a full view of all marketing efforts across all leads and campaigns for the date range you define.

Track ROI by using the lead source field on customer records and transactions. The lead source field shows the campaign that generated the sale, and the associated campaign is credited in reports for producing that income.

The following sections describe how you can review and use campaign results in more detail.

Reviewing campaign responses

Campaign responses track what a customer did in reaction to your campaign. Non–e-mail campaigns can have the following responses, which you can track manually on the customer record or by using promotion codes:

✔ **Sent:** The campaign was sent, but no response has been recorded.

✔ **Received:** The campaign was received, but no action has been taken.

✔ **Responded:** The customer gave a response or submitted an online form.

✔ **Purchased:** The customer purchased because of the campaign.

E-mail campaigns can have the preceding response statuses, except for Received, in addition to the following responses:

✔ **Queued:** The e-mail hasn't been sent yet.

✔ **Opened:** The recipient received and opened the e-mail.

✔ **Clicked Thru:** The recipient clicked a link in the e-mail.

✔ **Failed — Invalid Address:** The e-mail was returned because of a bad address.

✔ **Failed — Content Spam:** The recipient or the recipient's e-mail provider marked the e-mail as spam.

✔ **Failed — Delivery Failure:** The e-mail was sent but not received because of reasons outside of NetSuite.

✔ **Subscribed:** The recipient subscribed to e-mail through an invitation e-mail.

✔ **Unsubscribed:** The recipient unsubscribed to e-mail through the unsubscribe link in a regular or invitation e-mail.

You can edit campaign responses per customer on each Customer record. To change a customer response (you may do that if you get a call about a campaign or you see a customer at an event), click the Add Responses button on the Customer record's Campaigns tab, and select the campaign and campaign event.

For e-mail campaigns, you must select choose the Track Outgoing E-mail check box on the e-mail marketing template to track the response automatically. Also, keep in mind that e-mail recipients who don't see your e-mail images or HTML will not have a response. Many e-mail providers block images by default. Unless a recipient chooses to download the images, the tracking pixel isn't downloaded, and the reports don't show the e-mail as opened or clicked through.

Measuring campaign ROI

ROI is tracked using the lead source field on transaction records. Because campaigns are chosen as lead sources when you have the Marketing Automation feature enabled, this means that a campaign selected as the lead source on a transaction is credited for the revenue of the sale.

The campaign can be credited in the transaction in the following ways:

✔ The default lead source method that you set at Setup⇨Marketing⇨Marketing Preferences in the Default Lead Source on Sales Transactions field

✔ The lead source selected on the customer record

✔ The lead source selected by the sales rep entering the order

✔ The lead source passed through a link the customer uses to get to your Web site

Because only parent campaigns — not campaign events — are used as lead sources, you can only track ROI for campaigns (not campaign events). You can track success with campaign events by viewing the responses (as discussed in the previous section), or by associating the event with a promotion code and viewing the Sales by Promotion Code reports.

Chapter 9

Setting Up Sales Force Automation

In This Chapter

▶ Setting up workflow and forms

▶ Capturing leads online

▶ Forecasting sales

▶ Paying commission

*L*eads are the very beginning of the sales cycle — your new and budding customers, just ripe for the picking. In NetSuite, you can bring in leads through marketing efforts or through imports, and you begin moving from lead to prospect and then on to customer.

Opportunities are an important part of the process of moving leads to customers. Using opportunity records, you can track each offer you make to a lead in an effort to entice them to buy. Opportunities allow you to play out a wide variety of different pricing, items, and service scenarios to find the perfect match for each lead.

Sales managers have the power to set up automatic lead assignment to sales reps, create statuses for leads, prospects, and customers, set up quotas and commissions, and create online forms for capturing leads online. Sales administrators can perform many of these tasks as well to help sales managers. If you have the Sales Manager or Sales Administrator standard roles, you can do the tasks in this chapter except where noted. (Commissions in particular are in the hands of sales managers alone.)

To set up commissions in NetSuite, you need the Incentive Management module. Talk to your friendly NetSuite sales representative if you don't have this feature installed. Your sales team will thank you for it.

Turning On Sales Force Automation

Given the title of this chapter, it won't surprise you that you'll need to turn on the Sales Force Automation feature if you want to, well, automate your sales force.

Administrators can turn on this feature:

1. **From the Setup tab menu, choose Company⇨Enable Features.**

   The Enable Features page appears.

2. **Choose the CRM tab.**

3. **In the Basic Features section, select the Sales Force Automation check box.**

4. **Click the Save button.**

Stages and Statuses: Closing In

Lead, prospect, and customer records are managed by stages and statuses. With the combination of a stage and status on each record, you can immediately get a read on the likelihood of a sale.

Stages help you keep track of where the person or company is in the sales process, and you can't edit them. The stages follow:

- ✔ **Lead:** You have contact information, but there have been no opportunities, estimates, or sales for this person or company.

- ✔ **Prospect:** Leads become prospects when an opportunity or estimate is created for the person or company. If you use the Lead Conversion feature, you can also manually convert a lead to a prospect or to a contact for an existing prospect.

- ✔ **Customer:** Prospects become customers when a sale is completed for the person or company.

Statuses can be created for each stage to help you keep an even closer eye on where the person or company is. Each status has a *probability,* which is the percentage estimate of a lead or prospect becoming a customer. You can create and edit statuses and set the default status for each stage.

These default statuses are included in NetSuite:

- ✔ **Lead-Dead:** The lead has given a definite "No."

- ✔ **Lead-New:** The lead is new, and you don't know if she has any interest.

- ✔ **Lead-Qualified:** The lead has shown some interest or comes from a qualified source.

- ✔ **Prospect-Closed Lost:** The prospect had a previous opportunity or estimate, and he is no longer interested.

- ✔ **Prospect-Opportunity Identified:** You know what the prospect is interested in and may have created an opportunity record for her.

- ✔ **Prospect-In Discussion:** You're in contact with the prospect about his interests.

- ✔ **Prospect-Identified Decision Makers:** You're in contact with the people who will ultimately decide whether to buy.

- ✔ **Prospect-Proposal:** You've made an offer to the prospect, perhaps in the form of an estimate.

- ✔ **Prospect-In Negotiation:** The prospect is interested in an offer or estimate you've made, but you're hammering out details.

- ✔ **Prospect-Purchasing:** The prospect is in the process of purchasing from you.

- ✔ **Customer-Lost Customer:** The customer used to buy from you but is no longer interested.

- ✔ **Customer-Renewal:** This is a current, paying customer who has renewed services from you.

- ✔ **Customer-Closed Won:** This is a current, paying customer.

You can delete statuses from this list and add new ones from the Customer Statuses list. From the Setup tab menu, choose Sales & Marketing Automation➪ Customer Statuses.

Creating Online Forms

Online forms are one of the most effective and easy ways to generate leads by capitalizing on your Web site traffic. When you create and post an online customer form, leads can submit their contact information when they are interested in your products or services. Records are automatically created in your account using that contact information — you decide whether these records are created as leads, prospects, or customers.

You can create an HTML form several ways:

- ✔ On your own using CRMSDK tags and uploading it to NetSuite
- ✔ From scratch using a text editor within NetSuite
- ✔ By customizing the default template in NetSuite

To create an online customer form by customizing the default template or inserting HTML:

1. **From the Setup tab menu, choose Sales & Marketing Automation⇨ Online Customer Forms⇨New.**

   The Select Type page appears

2. **Click the link for the type of form you want to create:**

   - **Default Form Template** for forms you want to create based on NetSuite's default template.

   - **Custom HTML Template** for forms you already created in HTML or forms you'd like to create in HTML within NetSuite using a code editor and field selector.

3. **Enter a title for the form.**

   This title appears at the top of the page when it's published online.

4. **If using the custom HTML template, skip to Step 6. If using the default template, enter a message in the Message field:**

   This message shows at the top of your form and can include up to 500 HTML characters.

5. **(Optional) Click the Detail Message tab to enter a longer message into the Detail Message field.**

   You can also enter a longer message to show at the bottom of the form on the Detail Message tab. The detailed message can include up to 4,000 HTML characters.

6. **If using a custom HTML template, choose from one of the following:**

   - Select the template you want to use in the Template field if it's already uploaded to the File Cabinet.

   - If you haven't already uploaded the template, select New to upload it in a new window using the File selection.

   - If you haven't created a template, select New in the Template field; in the new window select Text Editor. In the HTML Source Code, you can paste or type in HTML and use the Field Type and Insert Field tools to add the tags for fields from customer records to your form.

   For help creating a custom HTML template, look over the example later in this section.

7. **Select the Enable Online check box.**

   This enables links to this form online.

8. **On the Select Fields tab, select each field that you want leads to fill out; then click in the Mandatory column to select the Mandatory check box; click Add.**

Again, at a minimum choose these: Company Name, First Name, and Last Name, and Email. And make each mandatory since you'll need at least this much information.

The basics of your form are now created, and you should have an online form that looks similar to the one in Figure 9-1.

9. **To set preferences for how leads created by this form are handled, continue to the next section of steps.**

A confirmation screen appears, and then you are taken back to the Online Customer Form screen.

10. **Click the Preview button to see what your form looks like.**

Close the preview window.

11. **Click Save.**

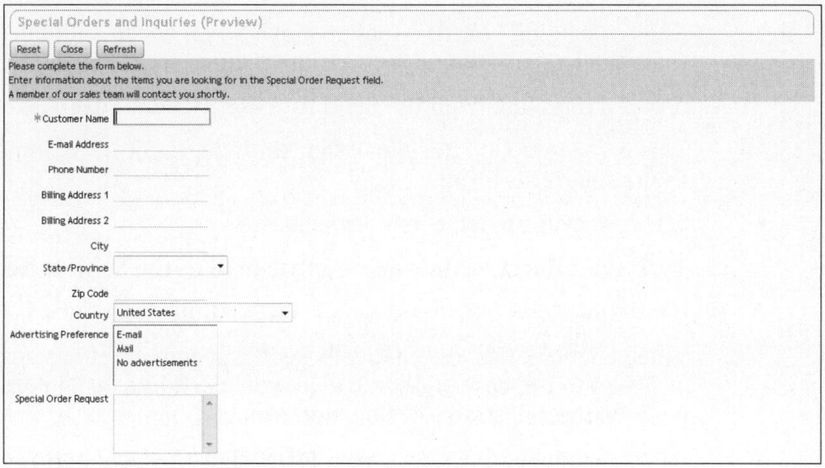

Figure 9-1:
This standard online customer form is ready to capture leads.

Special Orders and Inquiries (Preview)

Reset | Close | Refresh

Please complete the form below.
Enter information about the items you are looking for in the Special Order Request field.
A member of our sales team will contact you shortly.

* Customer Name
E-mail Address
Phone Number
Billing Address 1
Billing Address 2
City
State/Province
Zip Code
Country — United States
Advertising Preference — E-mail / Mail / No advertisements
Special Order Request

Setting up form workflow

Once you have an online form, it's possible to capture leads. But what happens after you capture those leads? Set up a *workflow* to assign the lead to the right person. The next steps hopefully take that person from being a lead to being a satisfied customer.

To set up workflow for your form:

1. **(Optional) If you've saved your form, click the Edit button.**

2. **Choose the Set Up Workflow tab.**

3. **(Optional) Select the Create Customers as Companies check box.**

   Do this only if most of your customers are companies, not individuals.

4. **Select the default status from the Set Lead Status drop-down list.**

5. **Select the lead source from the Set Lead Source drop-down list.**

6. **(Optional) Select the Allow Update check box.**

   Selecting the check box updates the Lead Source field if a record matching the submitted information already exists in your account.

7. **Choose from the Handle Duplicate Records drop-down list:**

   • **Always Create a New Record**

   • **Update the First Record Created**

   • **Update the Most Recently Created Record**

   • **Update the Most Recently Modified Record**

   You're deciding how to update records when a lead submits information that matches an existing record but includes some new information.

8. **Select a template from the Send Auto-Reply Email drop-down list.**

   This is the template the e-mail that should be sent to customers when they submit this form.

   Select New to upload a new template.

9. **Type the subject for this auto-reply e-mail in the Subject field.**

10. **(Optional) Select the Send Email Notification check box.**

    When enabled, this automatically sends an e-mail to the sales rep who's assigned to the case. In the Cc field, you can add e-mail addresses to copy on the sales rep's notification e-mail.

    If you're finished setting up your form, click the Save button. To set appearance settings, such as the color theme and font, continue on to the next section.

Setting up form looks

Forms should look like the rest of your Web site. You want your form to say "Fill me in, you handsome prospect!" With forms, as with interviews, first impressions count.

To set up the appearance of your form:

1. **(Optional) If you've saved your form, click the Edit button.**

2. **Choose the Set Up Appearance tab.**

3. **Choose from the Number of Columns Shown drop-down list.**

4. **Choose from the Color Theme drop-down list.**

   The theme can match your Web site and/or logo. If none of these color themes are suitable, administrators can create new color themes by choosing Web Site from the Setup tab menu.

5. **Select from the Font drop-down list.**

   Unfortunately, you can't add fonts to this list. The only way to use a custom font on a form is to create a custom HTML template for it.

6. **(Optional) Select the Unlayered Sections check box.**

   This means customers must scroll down to fill in more fields instead of organizing fields on tabs.

7. **Choose an option from the Button Alignment drop-down list:**

   • **Left**

   • **Right**

   • **Center**

8. **From the Form Logo drop-down list, select an image from your File Cabinet.**

   The image appears at the top of this form. Preferably, you'll choose your company's logo.

   To upload a new file, select New.

9. **Click the Save button.**

Linking up

A new tab is added to the record where you edit the properties of the form: the External tab. On this tab, you can find the Publishable Form URL for linking to your form. The Publishable Form URL can link to this form from your Web site, whether you use a NetSuite Web site or not.

To load the online form within the body of an existing Web page, you can use <iframe> tags, as in **<iframe src=https://forms.netsuite.com/yourform> </iframe>**.

You can also pass certain information into the form via the URL using URL parameters, which are listed in Table 9-1. For example, if you want to set the partner on a record by default, you can link to the form in this format, where [PARTNER] is the partner's name:

https://system.netsuite.com/app/site/crm/externalleadpage.nl?compid=AC CT000000&formid=1&h=1bdc80a058&partner=[PARTNER]

Table 9-1	Parameters That Pass Info Through a Linked Form to a Record
Field	*Parameter*
Company Name	&companyname=
City	&city=
Country	&county=
Email	&email=
Lead Source	&leadsource=
Login Password	&password=
Partner or Partner Code	&partner=
Phone Number	&phone=
Promotion Code	&promocode=
State	&state=
Zip/Postal Code	&zip=

Getting an example HTML template

Use the following example code to help you create a custom HTML template for your online customer form:

```
<NLFORM>
<HTML>
<Head>
<Title>OnlineLeadForm</Title>
<link href="/images/zengarden-sample[1].css " rel="stylesheet" type="text/css">
<style type="text/css">
</style>
</Head>
<Body>
```

```html
<table width="60%" border="0" align="center">
  <tr>
    <td bgcolor="#FFFFFF" valign="bottom" align="center" height="55">
      <p align="left"> <NSLOGO>
    </td>
  </tr>
  <tr>
    <td bgcolor="#FFFFFF" valign="middle" align="center" height="1">
    <hr color="#CCCCCC" align="left" size="1"></td>
  </tr>
    <tr>
    <td class="textll"><h1>
      <center>
         <span class="mainheader1 style1">Register With Us!</span>
       </center>
    </h1>
      <p align=Left> This is a sample online form template.
      <p> New leads would complete the fields below:
      <p><b>Name</b> <NLFIRSTNAME> <NLLASTNAME><br>
        Here you might enter special instructions.
      <p><b>Company Name</b> <NLCOMPANYNAME>
      <p><b>Email Address</b> <NLEMAIL>
               <p><b>Street Address</b> <NLADDRESS1>
      <p><b>City</b> <NLCITY>
      <p><b>State</b> <NLSTATE>
      <p><b>Zip/Postal Code</b> <NLZIPCODE>
               <p><input type="submit" value="Button Text"></p>
               <p align="center">
               <a href="http://www.linkbacktoHomePage.com">Company Home</a> |
               <a href="http://www.link1.com">Support</a> |
               <a href="http://www.link2.com">Help</a>
    </td>
  </tr>
</table>
</Body>
</HTML>
</form>
```

Assigning Leads to Sales Reps

When you set up automatic routing rules and assignments, new leads that meet your rule criteria are automatically assigned to the correct sales employees or teams. This is especially useful if the majority of your leads come in via online forms.

Setting up routing goes this way:

1. **Create sales rules, which are the criteria for the leads that will be routed.**

2. **Set up sales territories, which assign to the correct employees the leads that meet those rules.**

3. **Set up e-mail notification for employees to let them know they have a new lead.**

Creating sales rules and territories

Sales rules. Yes, that's true but it's not what NetSuite means by sales rules. *Sales rules* are basically saved searches using specific information from the lead record. You can create sales rules based on the lead's location, the subject of the lead's inquiry, or the lead's category, just to name a few criteria.

Keep in mind while you're creating rules that you can group rules when you create territories and decide if all the rules or just any one rule in the group must be met for the case to be assigned.

For example, you may create a rule for leads interested in a certain product and rule for leads in California. When you create the territory to assign the lead to a sales rep, you can choose that a lead must both be interested in that product *and* be from California to be assigned to John Smith, your local sales rep.

To create a sales rule:

1. **From the Setup tab menu choose Sales & Marketing Automation⇨ Set Up Sales Rules⇨New.**

   The Select a Customer Rule Field page appears.

2. **Click a link for the field that this rule will apply to.**

   This is similar to choosing a filter when you perform a search in NetSuite. Once you choose a field from the customer record, you can set criteria based on information for that field.

   When you choose a field, the Customer Field Rule page appears, as shown in Figure 9-2. The fields on each page depend on the type of field you chose for your rule.

3. **On the Customer Field Rule page, set the search criteria for your rule.**

4. **Click the Save button.**

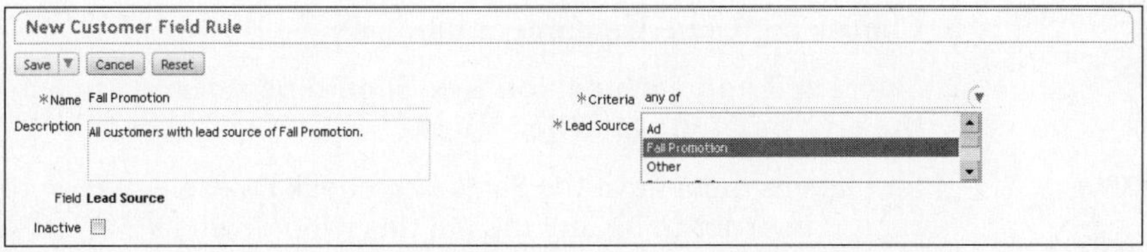

Figure 9-2:
Create
criteria for
the Lead
Source
field on the
Customer
Field Rule
page.

Continue setting rules with different criteria based on all the ways you may assign employees to leads. Once you're finished creating sales rules, you need to assign them to employees using sales territories.

Creating sales territory

Sales territory certainly implies geography, but territories can be far more flexibly defined than something like Northeastern United States. You may have a combination of geography and product line (or even numerous additional criteria) for creating a sales territory.

To create a sales territory:

1. **From the Setup tab menu choose Support⇨Manage Sales Territories⇨ New.**

    The Sales Territory page appears, as shown in Figure 9-3.

2. **Type a name and description.**

3. **Click one of the radio buttons:**

    • **Match All Rules** requires that all criteria of the rules you add must be met.

    • **Match Any Rules** requires that the criteria of any of the rules can be met in order for a lead to be assigned according to this territory.

    For example, you may set up a rule for customer names starting with S and a rule for company names starting with S and select Match Any Rule to catch all companies and customers beginning with S.

4. **Choose the Configure Rule Definitions tab.**

5. **Select and add each rule with criteria for leads that should be assigned to a certain person.**

6. **Choose the Lead Assignment tab.**

7. **Select and add each person who should be assigned to leads that meet the criteria of the attached rules.**

Employees must have the Sales Rep check box selected on the employee record in order to be included in this drop-down list. If you select more than one sales person, leads that come in meeting this criteria are assigned down the list, round-robin style.

8. **Click the Save button.**

Figure 9-3:
Combine
rules with
sales reps
on the Sales
Territory
page.

Sales Territory			
Edit Back More Actions ▾			
Name **San Francisco Area**			
Description **Area codes and customers from restaurant guide ad in the area**			
Match all rules **X**			
Match any rule			
Inactive ☐			

Rule Definitions ○ Assignment ○			
Apply Rule	**Field the Rule is applied to**	**# Sub Rules**	**Description**
Restaurant Guide	Lead Source	0	
San Francisco area	Phone Number	0	

Continue setting up territories for each set of criteria and person who needs to be assigned to leads. New leads are automatically assigned based on your criteria and groupings. Existing leads, prospects, and customers aren't affected.

Any customers who aren't assigned to a sales rep using your rules and territories are automatically assigned using the default round-robin territory, which distributes customers evenly among all sales reps. If you'd rather customers remain unassigned if they don't meet your criteria, you can edit and inactivate the default round-robin territory.

Reassigning existing leads, prospects, or customers

If you have outstanding leads that need to be reassigned because of employee changes, use the Territory Reassignment tool.

To reassign existing leads, prospects, or customers:

1. **From the Setup tab menu choose Sales & Marketing Automation⇨ Territory Reassignment.**

   A Mass Update screen appears.

2. **Choose the Criteria tab.**

3. **Create filters that apply to any leads, prospects, or customers that need to be reassigned.**

   The Filter drop-down list has many, many fields you can choose from. In some cases, a pop-up window appears with additional values. For example, if you choose Partner, a list of partners appears in case you want to further narrow the selection to a particular partner.

4. **Click the Preview button.**

   This displays which records will be updated.

5. **Deselect the check box next to any records that shouldn't be reassigned.**

6. **Click the Perform Update button.**

All leads, prospects, or customers who remain checked are updated to the new assignment.

Managing Quotas and Forecasts

You can set up monthly goals for sales reps or sales teams in NetSuite as *quotas*. Quotas can be

- ✔ Per item, class, or department
- ✔ Based on total sales

You can then view reports comparing the quota to the forecast to see how each sales rep or team is doing during the month, and you can base sales rep compensation on quota using commission schedules and plans.

Establishing quotas

Quotas set a bar for how much a rep should bring in each month. You can enter a yearly total and have it fill down per month, or you can vary each month based on seasonal demand. You can also choose to set quotas for specific items or classes.

To establish a quota:

1. **From the Forecast tab menu choose Setup⇨Establish Quotas.**

   The New Quota page appears, as shown in Figure 9-4.

2. **Select from the Rep drop-down list.**

   Only employees with the Sales Rep check box selected on the Employee record show in this field.

3. **(Optional) In the Item, Department, Class, or Location drop-down lists, make this quota for a specific area.**

   If you create quotas by class, department, and location, you can compare the forecast to quota using the Forecast reports available from the Reports tab menu.

4. **Do one of the following in the Total field:**

   • Enter a total for the entire year; then click the Distribute button. The total is dispersed evenly for each month.

   • Leave this field blank and enter the monthly quota in the January field. Click the Fill Down button to enter this quota for every month.

   • Leave this field blank and fill in each month's amount. The total will add up in this field.

5. **(Optional) Select the Team Quota check box.**

   Now this is the total quota for this sales rep and all of his or her subordinates.

6. **Click the Save button.**

Your quota is now set for this rep or this rep's team.

You can view current progress toward the quota using the Forecast page: From the Forecast tab menu by choosing Setup⇨Edit Sales Rep Forecast.

You can add several standard KPIs to your dashboard for a quick glance at quota standings. To do so, follow along:

1. **Click Personalize Dashboard (on the page where you'd like to add the KPI).**

2. **Click Key Performance Indicators in the Add Content pane on the left side of the page.**

3. **In the KPI portlet, click the Set Up link.**

   A window opens.

4. **Click the Add Standard KPIs button.**

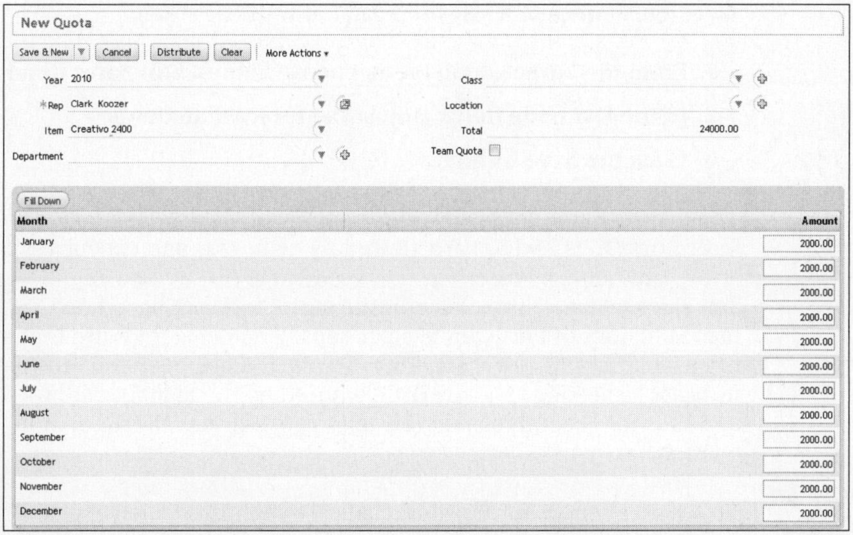

Figure 9-4:
Set up
quotas for
sales reps
on the New
Quota page.

Managing the forecast

The *sales forecast* is the sum of all sales and all expected sales for a sales rep in a period of time. More specifically, it's determined by the following:

- ✔ Current invoices
- ✔ Cash sales
- ✔ Unbilled sales orders
- ✔ Opportunities
- ✔ Estimates
- ✔ Potential for income

In NetSuite, you can finely tune forecasts by

- ✔ Setting probability amounts on opportunities and estimates.
- ✔ Setting minimum probability amounts with other settings on the Sales Preferences page, which you can reach from the Setup tab menu by choosing Sales & Marketing Automation⇨Sales Preferences.

Sometimes you need to change a sales rep's forecast for a more realistic picture of what he thinks will sell by the end of the month. Because the sales rep has the best feel for this, she can override the calculated forecast.

To edit his forecast, a sales rep can follow these steps:

1. **From the Forecast tab menu choose Setup⇨Edit Sales Rep Forecast.**
2. **In the Override fields, adjust the forecast amounts.**
3. **Click the Save button.**

The override amount is now shown on forecast reports and key performance indicators (KPIs), which are viewed by managers and executives.

The sales manager can also edit the entire forecast based on the performance history of her team of sales reps. If a manager knows that a certain rep often sandbags his forecast, for example, the manager can increase that rep's forecast as needed. The override entered by the manager shows on reports and KPIs for executives, but the sales rep still sees the amount he originally entered.

To set preferences for how forecasts are calculated and reported on, go to Setup⇨Sales & Marketing Automation⇨Sales Preferences, and click the Forecasts tab.

Show Me the Money: Commissions

You can reward for the sales that reps have closed by paying them *commissions* through NetSuite. NetSuite offers several options for how to pay commissions.

When you set up commissions, you create a matrix for how it is calculated based on the following:

- ✔ Items
- ✔ Percentages
- ✔ Linear or marginal scales
- ✔ Targets relative to percentage of quota

Sales reps can also watch their own commission payments grow using KPIs and commission reports.

Usually, sales reps are assigned to customers, and every time the customer makes a purchase, the sales rep is credited with the sale. However, you can override the sales rep responsible for a sale on the transaction itself if needed, and you can even set up sales teams where each rep gets a set percentage of the commission based on her involvement.

You can also reward partners with commissions using the same methods you do for employees, so we have included partners in these steps.

Enabling commissions

When you choose to pay sales reps commissions through NetSuite, you have the flexibility to set up some reps for commissions and leave others as ineligible. This helps keep your reports and commission pages clear of those reps who shouldn't ever receive commissions.

Sales managers can't perform the tasks outlined in this section; you have to be an Administrator to follow these steps.

1. **Enable the Employee Commissions feature from the Setup tab menu by choosing Company⇨Enable Features.**

    The Employee Commissions check box is on the (you guessed it!) Employee tab.

2. **Enable the Partner Royalties/Commissions feature from the Setup tab menu by choosing Company⇨Enable Features.**

    This feature must be enabled before you can pay partners commissions.

    Now set up sales reps for commission.

3. **Choose based on who gets the commission:**

    • **Employees:** From the Lists tab menu, choose Employees⇨Employees.

    • **Partners:** From the Lists tab menu, choose Relationships⇨Partners.

    The Employees or Partners list appears.

4. **Click Edit next to the person who should get commission.**

5. **On the Commission tab, select the Eligible for Commission check box.**

6. **Click the Save button.**

For partner records, this creates an identical Vendor record for the partner so that you can write checks to the partner.

You can set preferences for how commissions are handled at Setup⇨Sales & Marketing Automation⇨Set Up Commissions. Sales Managers can set these preferences, which include whether to include shipping items in commission calculations, requiring accounting approval, and the related expense account. These settings apply to both employees and partners.

Creating commission schedules

Commission schedules define how commission is calculated. After choosing the criteria commission is based on, you set up the specifics in a commission matrix that is used to calculate the commission rates for a set of thresholds.

For example, you may create a schedule for paying some employees or partners a flat rate of 5% per sales total and create another schedule for paying some employees or partners a linear rate of 10% of the profit for orders equal to or under $100 and 15% of the profit for orders over $100.

1. **From the Forecast tab menu choose Commissions➪Employee Schedules (Partner Schedules)➪New.**

   The New Commission Schedule page is shown in Figure 9-5. You set the formula for how much commission is paid on commission schedules. You can set up more than one if you pay different employees or partners at different rates.

2. **Type a name for the schedule.**

3. **From the Commission On drop-down list, select what to pay commission on:**

   - **Sales Amount**

   - **Alternate Sales Amount**

   - **Quantity**

   - **Inventory Profitability**

   - **Inventory Total Profit**

4. **From the Eligible Amount drop-down list, choose when commission is eligible to be paid out.**

   For example, you may allow 10 percent to be paid when the order is billed and 90 percent when the order is paid.

5. **Select a Calculation Scale radio button:**

   - **Flat Rate:** Paid at a flat dollar amount or percentage.

   - **Marginal:** Paid per sale within a given bracket. You set up brackets in the bottom part of the page.

   - **Linear:** Paid by bracket rate per total amount reached for all sales.

6. **(Optional) Select the Rate radio button and choose from the following:**

   - **Percentage**

   - **Amount**

Setting up a plan and assigning it to employees or partners are the key steps in making sure sales reps are set up to receive commission. Employees and partners can be assigned to only one plan at a time, and they must be assigned to a plan in order to receive payment.

You may have done this step by selecting the check box to create a commission plan when you created the commission schedule. In that case, you can skip creating a commission plan.

You set up commission plans this way:

1. **From the Forecast tab menu choose Commissions⇨Employee Plans (or Partner Plans)⇨New.**

   The New Commission Plan screen appears.

2. **From the Schedule drop-down list, select the schedules you want to combine.**

3. **From the Assign Plan to Employee or Partner drop-down list, select an employee or partner.**

4. **Type a name for your plan.**

   The name should help you remember who is on the plan.

5. **Click the Save button.**

Cutting the check

After you have set up schedules and plans and assigned your plans to employees and partners, commission amounts begin to be calculated on sales.

However, you must have commissions authorized before payment is made. This keeps commission payments from being automated without a double-check from management. Commissions are authorized from the Forecast tab menu choose Commission⇨Authorize Employee Commissions or Authorize Partner Commissions.

If you have the Require Accounting Approval of Employee Commissions preference enabled at Setup⇨Sales & Marketing Automation⇨Set Up Commission, an accountant or administrator must approve each commission payment before a check can be written.

Payments show up for accounting approval after they're authorized by management. Employee commissions are approved from the Forecast tab menu, by choosing Commissions⇨Authorize Employee Commissions or Approve Partner Commissions.

Commission checks can be automatically included in payroll checks if you process your payroll through NetSuite. To include commission in sales reps' paychecks, an administrator can set this option:

1. **From the Setup tab menu choose Payroll⇨Set Up Payroll.**

2. **Choose the Preferences tab.**

3. **Select the Pay Employee Commissions on Paychecks by Default check box.**

Chapter 10

Turning Leads into Customers

- -

In This Chapter

▶ Creating opportunities for leads

▶ Offering quotes from opportunities

▶ Converting quotes to sales

▶ Maximizing the customer record

- -

*I*n NetSuite, a *lead* represents a person or company. You have their contact information, but aren't sure if they're really interested in your products or services. A *prospect* is someone who has shown some interest but hasn't bought anything. An *opportunity,* on the other hand, represents an offer for a lead or prospect and behaves more like a transaction than a record although it has no accounting impact. An opportunity tracks the items that a prospect is interested in.

If you create an opportunity for a lead, it's automatically saved on the lead's record. Doing so changes the lead to a prospect by default. You can create a quote for a prospect based on the opportunity, and if the prospect decides to purchase, voila! She is now a valued customer.

Lead, prospect, and customer are all *stages* of the customer record. Within these stages, a lead, prospect, and customer can also have a *status,* which helps remind you where this person or company stands in terms of being close to a sale. A sales manager or administrator can set up new statuses and decide when a prospect moves from one status to another.

To follow the instructions in this chapter, you need (no surprise here) a sales role, such as Sales Manager. Where Sales Manager or Administrator level permissions are needed, we provide that clue.

Capturing the Elusive Lead

You have countless ways of luring an elusive lead to your company, most of which are covered in Chapter 8 on marketing. However, equally important to luring a lead is making sure you capture a lead's information and organize it in a way that helps you capitalize on your new-found relationship.

Coming your way

Leads can come into the system in a variety of ways, including the following most likely methods:

- ✔ **Online customer form:** If a manager has created and posted an online customer form on your Web site, a lead record is created any time someone fills out the form.

- ✔ **Online case form:** If your company accepts support requests online, people who haven't purchased before may use this form to submit questions. Their information is automatically used to create a lead record.

- ✔ **Web store purchase:** If you operate a Web store through NetSuite, anyone who makes a purchase through your Web store is saved as a customer record. However, if they enter information but do not complete checkout, they are saved as lead records.

- ✔ **Imported lists:** If you acquire lead lists, you can import these quickly into NetSuite if they are in comma-separated variable (CSV) format (you can save files into this format using Microsoft Excel). To import CSV files, have an Administrator go to the Setup tab menu and choose Import/Export⇨Import CSV Records.

- ✔ **Manual creation:** Sometimes, gold will fall in your lap, and an interested lead will just call you up, e-mail you, or strike up a conversation at your kid's soccer game. In these cases, you create a lead record yourself in NetSuite.

Creating a lead record

To create a lead record manually using any sales role:

1. **From the Leads tab menu choose Relationships⇨Leads⇨New.**

   The Lead screen appears.

2. **In the top part of the record, enter the lead's name and basic contact information.**

   The Status drop-down list defaults to LEAD-Unqualified, which is the only choice for a new lead.

3. **(Optional) On the General tab you can record any phone calls, tasks, events, and user notes.**

You may want to note what kind of latte the lead ordered or other details you want to remember for the next time you talk.

4. (Optional) Enter any other information you may want to on the Address, Financial, Qualification, and Marketing tabs.

The more information, the better.

5. Click the Save button.

You now have a record of the lead, which you can use to track all future communication and transactions. You can use all of the features for managing lead relationships discussed in the section "The Customer Record" later in this chapter.

Keep in mind that sales managers like to look at sales activity reports, which track how often leads, prospects, and customers are contacted via the record, including events, cases, campaigns, messages, calls, and notes. Since this is a great way for managers to know how sales reps are working to convert leads to prospects and customers, we certainly encourage you to use the lead record to initiate or log all of your interactions!

Going On Record about Opportunities

Creating opportunities is a wise step in the negotiating process not only because opportunities keep a record of your last offer to the lead but also because opportunities are included in the sales forecast. This helps give a big picture view of what sales are possible for the current month and what activities to prioritize.

An Administrator must first enable opportunities in your NetSuite account before you can access this record type. To enable opportunities, from the Setup tab menu, choose Company⇨Enable Features. On the CRM tab, under Sales, select the Opportunities check box.

You can create opportunities from the Opportunities tab menu by choosing Transactions⇨Opportunities⇨New.

Recording opportunities

On the Opportunity record, shown in Figure 10-1, you enter the name of the lead, set a status for the opportunity, set the probability that the opportunity will convert to a sale, and choose whether it should be included in the forecast. You can also add items to the opportunity (after all, they may want other things you didn't know about at first).

A few key fields on the opportunity require some explanation:

✔ **Status:** This is the status of this opportunity (not the lead or prospect). If a quote or order is created from this opportunity, the status is automatically updated.

✔ **Probability:** Percent chance that the lead or prospect will purchase. This typically defaults based on status.

✔ **Expected Close:** The date you expect the opportunity to result in a sale. This affects the forecast and pipeline reports as to what's expected to come in by the end of the month.

✔ **Forecast Type:** If you use the Advanced Forecasting feature, you can select whether this deal is included in forecast. It's included in the projected total unless you set the Range field.

• **Worst Case:** Worst Case opportunities are included in Worst Case, Most Likely, and Upside totals when you run forecast reports.

• **Most Likely:** Opportunities marked Most Likely are included in both the Most Likely and Upside totals when you run forecast reports.

• **Upside** (if the sale is completed): Opportunities marked Upside are only included in the Upside total when you run forecast reports.

✔ **Range:** If your account has the Advanced Forecasting feature and the Multiple Projected Amounts preference enabled, you can

• Set your projected amount as the Most Likely amount.

• Set a low and high amount for the Worst Case and Upside amounts.

✔ **Weighted Total:** This is the projected total multiplied by the probability percentage.

✔ **Est. Gross Profit:** This shows the revenue amount minus the Est. Cost.

Forecasting opportunities

Opportunities included in the forecast are based on these things:

✔ Your entries in these fields:

  • Forecast Type

  • Project Amount

  • Probability

  • Range

✔ Your preferences at Setup⇨Sales & Marketing Automation⇨Sales Preferences.

Table 10-1 shows some examples of scenarios that can occur.

Table 10-1	Potential Forecast Scenarios		
	Basic	*Advanced Forecasting*	*Adv. Forecasting with Mult. Projected Amounts*
Adv. Forecast Feature	No	Yes	Yes
Mult. Projected Amounts Preference	No	No	Yes
Minimum Forecast Probability	20%	N/A	N/A
Opportunity Amount	$1000	$1000 Most Likely	$1000 Most Likely, $500–1500
Opportunity Probability	30%	60%	50%
Weighted Total	Yes	Yes	Yes
Shows in Forecast	**$300**	**$0 in Worst Case; $600 in Most Likely and Upside**	**$250 in Worst Case; $500 in Most Likely; $750 in Upside**

Creating Quotes from Opportunities

Quotes are the next phase up from opportunities in the sales process. Quotes usually come into play when a prospect is interested enough to say, "I'm interested, but how much is this gonna cost me?" Prospects remain prospects when quotes are created, but the probability and status are upgraded when a quote is issued, depending on your account settings at Setup⇨Sales⇨Sales Preferences.

You can create quotes from scratch from the Opportunities tab menu by choosing Transactions⇨Quotes⇨New, which may be useful if you're working with an established customer or don't have the Opportunities feature. However, we recommend creating quotes from Opportunity records, which allows you to track the entire negotiation process.

Creating a quote from an opportunity has many benefits:

✔ You prevent duplicate entries in your forecast (which can happen if you have an opportunity and a quote that aren't linked).

✔ You can track all sales activity from the central opportunity to understand how things unfolded to date.

✔ You can attach multiple quotes to fit a few different scenarios for budget and needs.

Creating a quote from an opportunity

To create a quote from an opportunity:

1. **Choose the Opportunities List.**

2. **From the Opportunities tab menu, choose Transactions⇨ Opportunities.**

   The Opportunities list appears.

3. **Click the Edit link next to the opportunity you want to create a quote from.**

4. **On the Opportunity record, under General, click the Quotes tab.**

5. **Click the New Quote button.**

   The Quote page appears with the prospect's information already filled in.

6. **In the Status field, select the status that reflects the circumstances of this quote (listed here in order of likelihood of the sale):**

- **Closed Lost:** You probably won't use this for a quote, because it means all hope of a sale is lost.

- **Opportunity Identified:** You've identified the opportunity (also unlikely for a quote).

- **In Discussion:** The client is discussing the possibility of buying.

- **Identified Decision Makers:** The people who can approve the sale have been identified.

- **Proposal:** A proposal has been sent to the client.

- **In Negotiation:** The proposal is being debated in terms of price.

- **Purchasing:** Purchasing is in progress.

Each status is tied to a probability percentage, and the Probability field updates when you change the status. You can edit this percentage if needed to reflect the likelihood that the quote will result in a sale.

7. **In the Exp. Close field, enter the date you expect this quote to result in a sale.**

   You filter what shows in the forecast by expected close date.

8. **On the Items tab, select and add each item that you're quoting for the customer.**

   Items may default from the opportunity.

9. **(Optional) On the Messages tab, choose how to share this quote with the prospect:**

   - **Check to Be Printed:** Bring up this form in PDF format after saving.

   - **Check to Be E-mailed:** Send the form in HTML format to the e-mail address listed.

   - **Check to Be Faxed:** If you use e-Fax or Faxaway with your NetSuite account to fax the form to the number listed after saving.

   You can select a standard message to include with the quote in the Select Message field, or you can type a custom message to include in the Customer Message field.

10. **Fill in any other information as needed.**

11. **Click the Save button.**

When you create a quote from an opportunity, you have more control over your forecast because you can decide whether to show the original amount of the opportunity in the forecast or to show the amount of the attached quote instead.

To get a full picture of this, remember that the following transactions contribute to the forecast:

- ✔ Cash sales
- ✔ Invoices
- ✔ Unbilled sales orders
- ✔ Quotes set to be included in the forecast that haven't been converted to sales and exceed the minimum forecast probability (set from the Setup tab menu at Sales & Marketing Automation⇨Sales Preferences).

You can mark quotes to be included in the forecast on the Quotes tab of the opportunity in Edit mode or on the quote itself, using the Forecast Status drop-down list. Because the Advanced Forecasting feature allows for a range of amounts, the minimum forecast probability preference is not available when this feature is enabled.

- ✔ Opportunities with no quotes or with quotes set to not be included and that exceed the minimum forecast probability set at Setup⇨Sales⇨ Sales Preferences.

Managing multiple quotes

You can attach multiple quotes to an opportunity if you need to offer several different solutions to the customer or if you need to revise the quote several times and want to keep copies of the past quotes. While it is handy to attach multiple quotes to an opportunity, it can get hairy to remember how the forecast is affected.

- ✔ **Without Advanced Forecasting:** Choose one quote to include in the forecast. You can do this on the Quotes tab on the opportunity record.
- ✔ **With Advanced Forecasting:** Each quote should have a different forecast type: Worst Case, Most Likely, or Upside. The worst case quote will show in the worst case forecast; the most likely in the most likely forecast; and so on. If you have two quotes, one that's worst case and one that's upside, the worst case quote is included in the worst case *and* the most likely forecasts, and the upside quote is in the upside forecast.

Entering a Sales Order

When a prospect has received the quote that fits the bill, when she has gotten just the right marketing campaign, when she has had the right upsell suggestion, or something else strikes the urge to reach for the wallet, it's time to enter a sales order, cash sale, or invoice.

You can create these transactions in a few ways:

- ✔ From an opportunity's Closed tab
- ✔ Using the Sales Order, Cash Sale, or Invoice buttons on a quote
- ✔ Creating a sales order from scratch, as outlined later in this chapter (least common method)

Converting quotes or opportunities to sales orders is best because it tracks your full path to the sale and replaces the previous opportunity or quote in the forecast. It also automatically closes the related opportunity or quote.

Sales orders are usually created when either payment hasn't been received or goods haven't been shipped. Sales orders can be approved and then fulfilled separately. For more information on fulfilling sales orders, see Chapter 11.

Creating a sales order means you got the sale. You can create one from an opportunity or a quote (the best way if either of those exist) but if someone just happens to want something right away, you can enter the sales order right on the spot.

To enter a sales order:

1. **From the Opportunities tab menu choose Transactions⇨Sales Orders⇨ New.**

   The Sales Order screen appears.

2. **Type the first few letters of the customer name in the Customer field.**

   If only one customer name fits your input, that customer is filled in the field. Otherwise, you select the customer from a list.

3. **Enter the items and quantities.**

4. **Click the Save button.**

Lead Conversion for B2B

In addition to the automatic conversion of lead to prospect when an opportunity is created, you can use the Lead Conversion feature to convert leads to prospects. With the Lead Conversion feature enabled, you manage leads as individuals associated with a company, a more typical situation in business to business, or *B2B,* relationships.

Enabling lead conversion

Enable the Lead Conversion feature with these steps:

1. **From the Setup tab menu choose Company⇨Enable Features.**

2. **On the CRM tab, select the Lead Conversion check box.**

3. **From the Setup tab menu choose Company⇨General Preferences.**

4. **Make sure the Default Lead Type is set to Individual.**

The feature adds the Convert button to lead records, which manually converts a lead record in one the following ways (see Figure 10-2):

✔ New prospect record for the associated company with the lead added as a contact

✔ New contact record created for the lead and attached to a prospect or customer record already existing for the associated company

✔ Updated contact record that already exists with company record (in the case of a duplicate)

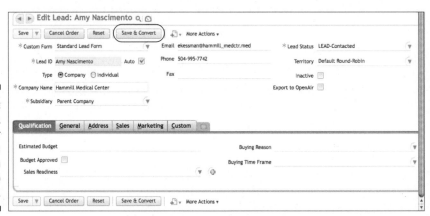

Figure 10-2: Click Save & Convert for automatic conversion of a lead to a prospect.

Rocking the Customer Record

The Customer record in NetSuite is your center for communication with your most important relationships.

NetSuite calls the customer record the 360-degree view because the customer record does so much more than just store your customer's name and contact information. One visit to a customer's record can tell you how long he's been using your products or services, how he came to be aware of your business, and any past e-mail, events, tasks, support cases, and phone calls related to the customer. In addition, you can view current and past opportunities and sales transactions, items the customer has purchased, and recommendations for items you can upsell to the customer.

Some optional features provide you with even more information about your customers:

- ✔ If you use the **Marketing Automation feature,** you can see what campaigns have been sent to the customer and what the customer's response was.

- ✔ If you use the **Customer Access feature,** you can see whether the customer has access to the Customer Center, where she can receive online support and perform some self-service tasks.

- ✔ If you use the **Web Site feature,** you can see when and how often the customer has visited your site. If your role has access, you can see where the customer stands with you financially and what price level the customer is offered.

In NetSuite, the form where you save your customer information is the same for leads, prospects, and customers, so when we refer to any of these, we're talking about the same record (including any customizations you may have added, of course). The page title will say Lead, Prospect, or Customer based on the stage of the customer in your sales process.

Contacts, activities, notes, and e-mail on records

Under the General tab of the customer record, you can find everything you need for communicating with your customer.

Contacts

You can add and view information for the main contacts at this company and define what role they have in communicating with you. For example, you probably have one person at the company who is the decision maker and one who is the primary contact (who you talk with most). If this is the same person, set the person as the primary contact.

If you already have a contact record created for someone, select that person's name in the Contact field, and click the Attach button to associate her with this customer. If you haven't yet created a record, click New Contact to create the record in a new window, as shown in Figure 10-3. When you save the new contact, it is automatically added to the customer record.

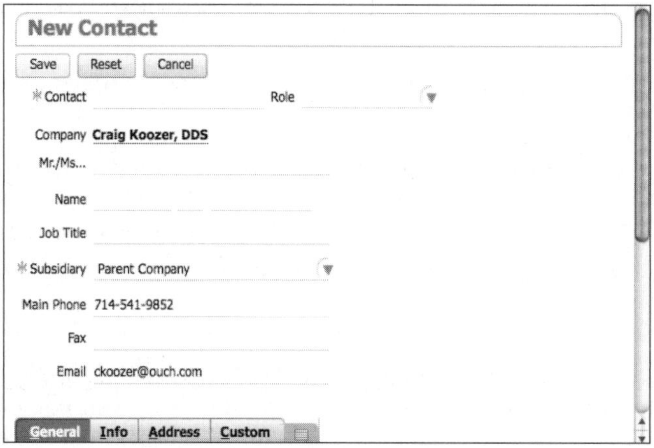

Figure 10-3:
Quickly create a new contact for a customer when you click the New Contact button.

Activities

From the General tab, you can view and handle all of your scheduling with this customer:

- ✔ **Tasks:** Click the New Task button to create a new task relating the customer in a new window. Tasks can include To-Dos that don't need to be completed at a certain time but should usually be completed by a certain date. For example, you may want to create a task to send the customer a birthday or thank-you card.

  If a task has been completed, you can still add it to the system for record-keeping and time-tracking purposes by clicking the Log Task button.

- ✔ **Events:** Like tasks and phone calls, you can create new events or log events that have already happened. You can invite customers and others to an event via e-mail and, if they have access to your account, the time is blocked on their calendars when they accept.

  It is also handy to see on your calendars which appointments are on the phone and in person using the phone and event icons, as shown in Figure 10-4.

✔ **Phone Calls:** Click the New Phone Call or Log Phone Call button to create new calls or log phone calls that have already occurred.

The main differences between phone calls and events are that events allow you to reserve resources, such as a conference room, and they allow you to set up recurrence patterns.

You can choose to have both tasks and phone calls show on your calendar, even if they aren't set for a specific time.

1. **From the Activities tab menu, choose Scheduling➪Calendar.**

2. **Click the Calendar Preferences link in the header.**

3. **Choose the Preferences tab.**

4. **Select the Display Non-blocking Phone Calls in Calendar check box.**

5. **Select the Display Non-blocking Tasks in Calendar check box.**

6. **Click the Save button.**

Meanwhile, back on the Customer screen, click the View History button on the Activities tab to see all tasks, phone calls, and events for the customer in chronological order.

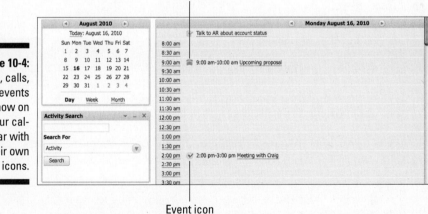

Figure 10-4: Tasks, calls, and events show on your calendar with their own icons.

User notes

On the User Notes tab of any record, you can add dated notes for anything regarding the customer that doesn't fit elsewhere on the record. For example, you may want to tell others who view the record why you changed something.

To add a note, do this:

1. **Click the New Note button.**
2. **Type your comments in the new window.**
3. **Click the Save button.**

System notes are automatically added by NetSuite to track what fields are changed and when the record is edited and by whom. If you don't add a user note explaining yourself, someone else can quite easily come and ask you some questions.

Messages

On the Messages tab you can send customers e-mail or save e-mails you get from customers. If you use the Mail Merge feature, you can also create letters or PDF documents for the customer from this tab and save them to the record.

To create an e-mail, letter, or PDF, click the corresponding button. A new window opens to create your message. If you are sending an e-mail, you can send an attachment as well. Click the Attach button to save a message you received from the customer to the record. You can also save any e-mail attachments you received from the customer when you save the message.

Files

On the Files tab, you can view and store any documents, such as contracts, images, or other important files related to the customer. All files are actually stored in your account's File Cabinet, but you can access them from the record when you attach them to the Files tab.

If your file is already uploaded to the File Cabinet, you can select the file in the Attach Existing Files field and click the Attach button.

If you haven't yet uploaded the file to the File Cabinet, follow these steps:

1. **Click the New File button.**

    A window opens.

2. **Type a filename.**
3. **Select a folder where it should be stored in the File Cabinet.**
4. **Click the Browse button and find the file on your hard drive.**
5. **(Optional) Select the Available Without Login check box.**

Do this if you need to link to this file at any time. (Bear in mind, however, that this means that anyone on the Internet can see this file if they get the link; they don't need a NetSuite login.)

6. **Click the Save button.**

Subcustomers

Subcustomers are companies that are considered a part of your existing customers. Creating subleads, subprospects, or subcustomers allows you to set up a hierarchy under a parent customer record. Subcustomer records are created and maintained exactly like customer records except that the parent record is selected in the Child Of field, and the subcustomers are available on the parent customer's record.

Projects

Projects allow you to track ongoing services for a customer with a start and end date. If you use the Advanced Projects feature, you can attach project tasks and milestones to a project in addition to tracking status and cost.

Projects can have their own tasks, events, calls, notes, files and time tracking attached to them, so be sure to associate an activity or other record with a project when appropriate (instead of attaching everything to the customer). This helps keep your records organized.

For more about projects and the Advanced Projects feature, see Chapter 12.

Time tracking

On the Time Tracking tab, enter time spent working with or for this customer that can be billed back to the customer. Click the New Time button to enter time for one instance, or click the New Weekly Time button to enter time for several different days in this week or previous weeks.

Opportunities and transactions on records

One of the most valuable assets of the customer record is the ability to view all opportunities in the pipeline, all past transactions, and all past items purchased. Not only can you access all of that information, you can also create new opportunities, quotes, and sales orders from the customer record.

This means that when you're talking with a customer, you can quickly check the Upsell tab on the Sales tab for items the customer may be interested in, check the Marketing tab for any interest he may have shown in current promotions, and immediately create and send him an opportunity or quote from the record.

Here are some handy shortcuts:

- ✔ To create a new opportunity for the customer, click the Sales tab, then the Opportunity tab, and click the New Opportunity button.
- ✔ To create other transactions for the customer, click the Sales tab, then the Transactions tab. You'll see buttons for New Quote, New Sales Order, and New Cash Sale so you can quickly create transactions for the customer in a new window.

Customer dashboard

The customer dashboard offers a graphical view of your customer record, complete with key performance indicators and snapshots that you can customize and move. While the customer record is perfect for digging in to the details of your relationship with a customer, the customer dashboard is perfect for getting an immediate health picture of the customer on one page with no tabs.

You can access the customer dashboard, shown in Figure 10-5, two ways:

- ✔ Click the dashboard icon from the customer list; see Figure 10-6.
- ✔ Click the View Dashboard button on the customer record.

Figure 10-5:
The customer dashboard shows reports, transactions, and KPIs specific to one customer.

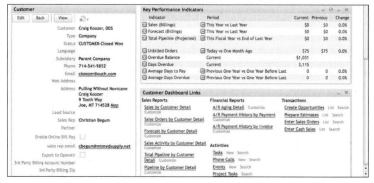

Click the Dashboard icon to display a customer dashboard

Edit	View		Name ▲		Duplicate	Primary Contact	Category	Subsidiary	Sales Rep	Partner	Status	Phone	Email
Edit	View	🖼	Aaron Rosewall-Godley				From advertisement	Parent Company	Mathew Christner	Commission Partner	CUSTOMER-Closed Won	504-789-1254	dsch
Edit	View	🖼	ABC Medical Supplies					Parent Company	Theodore Hosch		CUSTOMER-Closed Won		astou
Edit	View	🖼	Stours, Allen					Parent Company	Theodore Hosch		CUSTOMER-Closed Won		astou
Edit	View	🖼	Abdullah Bhupathiraju				From advertisement	Parent Company	Jessie Barto		CUSTOMER-Closed Won	504-987-5412	dsca
Edit	View	🖼	Abe Lincoln					Parent Company		Partner Kelly	CUSTOMER-Closed Won	789-678-5674	jkell
Edit	View	🖼	Abe Simpson		Yes	Erin Black	From advertisement	Parent Company	Jon Baker		CUSTOMER-Closed	504-231-1111	tadk

Customers   Inline Editing OFF

Sales Rep - All -   Stage Customer   From-To Aaron — Craig   Total Found: 117

Show Inactives   Style Normal   View General   Quick Sort   New | Print | Customize View | Export - CSV

Part IV
Taking Care of Your Partners and Customers

The 5th Wave   By Rich Tennant

"Ms. Lamont, how long have you been sending out bills listing charges for 'Freight,' 'Handling,' and 'Sales Tax,' as 'This,' 'That,' and 'The Other Thing?'"

In this part . . .

Getting customers is just half the battle; keeping them is the other half. Part IV tells you how to make sure customers are satisfied and happy, with the goods they ordered and with solid customer service when needed.

Part IV also describes how to work with your partners and manage projects (especially if you sell services as well as goods).

Chapter 11 provides details on fulfilling and shipping orders. If what you sell is services rather than (or in addition to) physical stuff, look at Chapter 12, which describes project management. Chapter 13 tells you how to manage your partners, who in turn help support your customers. Chapter 14 describes how to use NetSuite to provide excellent customer service and keep 'em coming back for more.

Chapter 11

Delivering the Goods: Fulfillment and Shipping

In This Chapter

▶ Fulfilling orders

▶ Shipping the goods

▶ Integrating with logistics providers

Knowing how to use NetSuite to generate leads and make sales. That knowledge doesn't do you much good unless you can deliver on what you promised. The next step is to find the items your customers ordered, pull them from the shelf, and ship them to the right address: fulfillment and shipping.

Feeling Fulfilled: Orders

Order fulfillment is pretty much what it sounds like — fulfilling what you promised when you accepted a sales order. Fulfillment involves removing an item from inventory to shipping it to the customer to complete a sales order. It also could be transferring an item to another location of your company.

With NetSuite, the fulfillment process varies based on whether you use the advanced shipping feature:

✔ Without Advanced Shipping, the fulfillment and invoicing are combined. When you fulfill an item, you create a customer invoice simultaneously.

✔ With Advanced Shipping, you have separate processes to fill orders and bill customers. You track your shipments separately from creating invoices.

Advanced Shipping is most commonly used, so if you sell items to customers, it's likely you will want to use it too.

In either scenario, always check order fulfillments against sales orders to track the status of items and orders. This ensures accuracy.

Getting started

Say you're the warehouse manager, and part of your job is to fulfill customer orders. The best way to get an overview of the order fulfillment process is to select the Shipping tab. The Shipping Links portlet shows the basic steps:

- ✔ Printing picking tickets
- ✔ Fulfilling orders
- ✔ Printing packing slips

Furthermore, if you use the Pick, Pack, and Ship feature (part of the Advanced Inventory module described in Chapter 7), you'll also see links to packing and shipping orders.

This chapter assumes you have the role of Warehouse Manager or Warehouse/Inventory Manager. You may not be able to follow the steps in this chapter if you have a different standard role. For setup options, you'll need the help of your Administrator.

Preferences you should know about

Before you plunge into the world of fulfillment, take care of some housekeeping items to ensure that your experience is more (ahem) fulfilling. This is important because setting preferences can save you a lot of time and aggravation down the road. These parameters likely will vary depending on your role and your company's business processes.

First, ask an administrator to set your preferences so that your account looks and acts as you want.

1. **From the Setup tab menu choose Accounting⇨Accounting Preferences.**

2. **Choose the Order Management Tab.**

There are many preferences; the following sections highlight some key features that are important to fulfillment and shipping.

Fulfill Based on Commitment

Now hear this! Fulfill Based on Commitment determines whether you can ship or fulfill orders when inventory hasn't been committed. Needless to say, a discrepancy between the number of items ordered and the number actually in stock can cause major havoc in your inventory tracking system.

Selling an item when you don't actually have the item in stock is known as an *underwater* sale. In other words, the on-hand quantity of the item is below zero. NetSuite recommends a best practice of setting the Fulfill Based on Commitment preference to Limit to Committed.

Default Items to Zero on Fulfillment

This feature is useful if you're using barcode scanning. You can scan each item individually to ensure an accurate count. Workers can scan each item one-by-one, and the system automatically tallies the correct quantity. This feature can be useful in large warehouse operations where lots of people are fulfilling large, multi-item orders. It is less exciting if your business generally fulfills single-item packages.

Order Fulfillment Confirmation Email

This preference allows you to send a confirmation e-mail informing the customer what was shipped upon fulfillment of orders. You can create a customized e-mail template. If you use the Web store feature, you can integrate the confirmation e-mail into your template: From the Setup tab menu, choose Accounting⇨Customize Fulfillment Email.

Advanced versus nonadvanced shipping

The fulfillment process differs based on whether you use the Advanced Shipping feature:

- ✔ Without Advanced Shipping, you use a single transaction to fulfill and bill sales orders.

- ✔ With Advanced Shipping, you use separate transactions to fulfill and bill sales orders. You also have the option to bill for items even if they haven't shipped: Enable a company preference called Invoice in Advance of Fulfillment.

Essentially, most NetSuite customers who ship physical goods use Advanced Shipping. Without Advanced Shipping, there is no item fulfillment.

An administrator must enable Advanced Shipping:

1. **From the Setup tab menu, select Company➪Enable Features.**
2. **Choose the Transactions tab.**
3. **Select the Advanced Shipping check box.**

Your lucky ticket

Fulfillment isn't like a traffic stop — getting a ticket is a good thing. A *picking ticket* are instructions for somebody in the warehouse to pull items from the shelf to fulfill an order.

Administrators can customize your picking tickets to make your warehouse operations more efficient. For example, you may want to organize tickets based on bin locations so your workers can avoid backtracking.

1. **From the Setup tab menu choose Customization➪Transaction Forms.**
2. **Click Customize next to Standard Picking Ticket.**

You can print tickets singularly or in bulk mode. Once printed, they disappear from the queue. If you don't entirely fulfill an order, the ticket stays in the queue until finished.

To print picking tickets:

1. **From the Shipping tab menu choose Shipping➪Print Picking Tickets.**
2. **From the Location drop-down list, select a location.**

   If you have multiple locations or warehouses, choose the one where the item should be picked.

3. **In the Print column, place a check mark next to the orders that need printed picking tickets.**

   Or you can click Mark All to print picking tickets for all orders on the page. See Figure 11-1.

4. **Click the Print button.**

   Now you can use picking tickets to pull the items you need to ship! (Or you can send Ralph to do it; he owes you one.)

You can also print a picking ticket by viewing the individual order and clicking the Print Picking Ticket button.

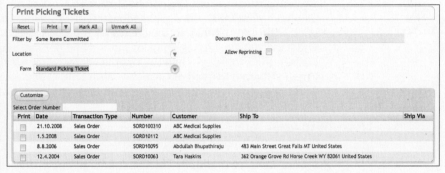

Figure 11-1:
Pick a location where the item should be picked and then check the ones you want printed.

Fulfilling orders

Fulfillment is basically the process of taking the item from the shelf, packing it, and getting it ready to ship to the recipient. In bureaucratic terms, this means pulling items from inventory, packaging them, and sending them to your customer. Sounds simple, but this is a major undertaking of logistics, organization, and information technology. NetSuite knits together these processes into an integrated workflow and makes them easier.

Fullfillment process

Take a walk through the fulfillment process:

1. **From the Shipping tab menu choose Shipping⇨Fulfill Orders.**

   The Fulfill Orders page appears, as shown in Figure 11-2.

2. **Select from where the orders should be filled from the Bulk Fulfill From Location drop-down list.**

   If there's too many orders to handle at once, you can narrow down the number of orders by selecting a particular customer or availability criteria from the Customer and Filter By drop-down lists, respectively.

3. **(Optional) Choose an option from the Filter By drop-down list:**

   • **Some Items Committed:** The list shows orders that have one or more items committed to be fulfilled. (This is the default.)

   • **Respect Ship Complete:** The list shows only the orders that are committed according to their Ship Complete setting. In other words, orders should be shipped only when all items are ready. This includes all orders that aren't restricted to ship complete. Orders that are marked Ship Complete appear only if all items are ready. Other orders will show if there are some items ready.

Say a customer orders 100 pairs of Groucho Marx glasses and 100 Groucho Marx mustaches (sold separately). Well, one isn't much good without the other so the customer requests Ship Complete. If you have 100 mustaches on hand but only 50 pairs of glasses, you can see the problem — half the people will wind up looking like Charlie Chaplin instead of Groucho. With Ship Complete, the order won't appear in your fulfillment queue until you have all items to complete the order.

- **All Items Fully Committed:** The list shows orders that have all items committed to be fulfilled.

- **Ignore Item Availability:** The list shows all open orders regardless of the availability of items on the orders.

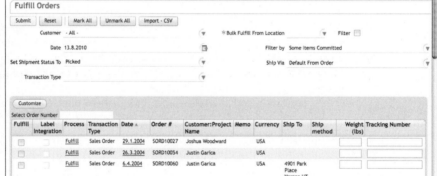

Figure 11-2:
You can customize the Fulfill Orders process by location, company, and filters.

Once you complete Steps 1 through 3, the page presents a list of orders pending fulfillment.

4. Select the Fulfill check box next to orders you want to fulfill.

Or you can click the Mark All button to select them all.

5. Click Submit.

The Job Status page appears, where you can check the status of the ful-fillments. See Figure 11-3.

Alternatively, you can fulfill orders one at a time. From the Sales Order page, click the Fulfill button to initiate fulfillment on a single order. You can also print a picking ticket by viewing the individual order and clicking Print Picking Ticket.

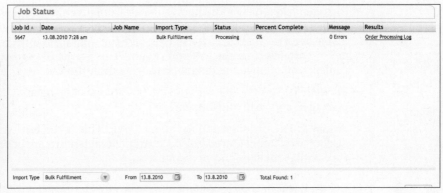

Figure 11-3:
You can
check the
status of an
order on the
Job Status
page.

Packing slips and return forms

Similarly, you can print a packing slip and return forms to include in shipments. To specify that packing slips should include a return form, ask an
administrator to do the following:

1. **From the Setup tab menu choose Company⇨Set Up Company⇨
   Printing, Fax, and Email Preferences.**

2. **Choose the Printing tab.**

3. **Select the aptly named Print Return Form with Packing Slip check box.**

Picked, packed, and shipped

Pick, Pack, and Ship is an optional feature that breaks the fulfillment process
into three steps. (Pick, Pack, and Ship requires another feature: Advanced
Shipping.) Using Pick, Pack, and Ship gives your business greater flexibility
in processing and tracking orders through the fulfillment and shipment processes. For example, a warehouse may have different teams of employees who
perform each step.

This feature allows the manager to track each shipment as it goes through
each stage of the fulfillment process.

Here's a brief description of the stages:

✔ **Pending Fulfillment:** This extra step breaks the nice rhythm of saying
  picked, packed, and shipped — but before you start, you need to print
  picking tickets so you know what to pick.

- **Picked:** *Picked* means the item is pulled from inventory. A worker takes the ticket, locates the item on the shelf or bin, and pulls it from the inventory. Picked status doesn't remove the item from inventory but *does* remove it from the available count. This marks the order as fulfilled (unless you change the default setting as described below).

- **Packed:** The picker delivers the items to the packaging area. Presto — packaged and ready for the carrier!

- **Shipped:** The order is sent to the recipient. This is the final stage. Orders aren't considered closed, and the item isn't removed from inventory until it reaches shipped status.

The Picked, Packed, and Shipped function allows you to track orders as they move through each step of the fulfillment process. You can view order status from the Transactions tab menu by choosing Sales➪Fulfill Orders➪List. You can filter the field using the Status drop-down list in the footer (Picked, Packed, Shipped, or Select All).

Flipping about Shipping Orders

Congratulations! You are ready to ship the order. This is the moment you — and your customers — have been waiting for. Shipping is just what it sounds like — except you don't necessarily need a boat.

NetSuite integrates with three of the major carriers: UPS, FedEx, and USPS/Endicia.

With NetSuite, shipping is integrated into the software. You can generate labels for the three major shippers (UPS, FedEx, and USPS/Endicia). NetSuite plugs directly into Web services of these three carriers so you can get real-time rate information, which reduces the cost and time associated with shipping.

You can:

- Generate shipping labels.
- Get shipments out the door faster.
- Track a shipping status.

Shipping basics

When you create a sales order, you specify the shipping method. But, as you know, stuff happens. Sometimes you need to change the shipping method on the fly. Thankfully, NetSuite allows you to change the shipping method at any point in the process.

Say a customer wants two-day air, and you mistakenly entered ground transportation. Now it's the day before the order is supposed to arrive, and you need to send it overnight. No problem: Change it at the fulfillment stage.

There are some things you need to understand about NetSuite and shipping, however. NetSuite offers two basic options, and the difference between them comes down to labels and, well, integration with your shipping carrier account:

✔ Non-integrated shipping

✔ Integrated shipping

Non-integrated shipping

In *non-integrated shipping,* you can do the following:

✔ Generate your own shipping labels.

✔ Work directly with your carrier.

✔ Enter tracking numbers and shipping weights (but these features aren't automatically populated as they are with integrated shipping).

✔ Print labels for sales orders, vendor returns, and transfer orders (but they won't have all those cool bar codes that the carriers put on there for you and that mean that your package can be whisked away by the carrier with no weighing or other delays). Shipping label integration gives you a sort of "labels-plus" functionality in that sense.

✔ Charge real-time rates; you just can't print carrier-specific shipping labels via NetSuite.

You can use non-integrated shipping even if you do use shipping label integration, but want to use a carrier or shipping method not integrated in your system.

As you fulfill each order, NetSuite adds the label to the queue to be printed. You can fulfill multiple sales orders and then print all the shipping labels at once.

To print labels for non-integrated carriers:

1. **From the Shipping tab menu choose Shipping⇨Print Checks and Forms.**

2. **Click Shipping Labels.**

   See Figure 11-4.

3. **Fill out the Starting Label number (if it is different from the default, which is 1).**

4. **Select the check boxes next to each order you want to print a shipping label for.**

   You can use the Mark All and Unmark All buttons to make this process easier.

5. **Click Submit.**

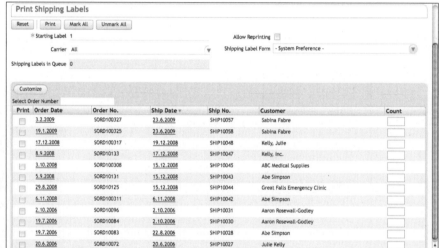

Figure 11-4:
To print non-integrated carrier shipping labels use the Print Shipping Labels form.

Integrated shipping

With integrated shipping, labels for your preferred carrier, shipping charges, tracking numbers, and other information are generated automatically, and your account with the shipper is automatically billed.

When you use integrated shipping, you can automatically sync your shipping operations with your carriers. The system automatically generates tracking numbers and shipping labels and gives you up-to-the-minute shipping rates.

Here are some of the main features:

- **Tracking numbers:** With integrated shipping, tracking numbers from FedEx, UPS, or USPS/Endicia are inserted when you fulfill an order (via Web services, in case you're curious).

- **Pick, Pack, and Ship:** As described earlier, you can enable the Pick, Pack, and Ship feature to break the fulfillment process into three steps. If you do this in combination with shipping label integration, you can designate the stage at which an order gets a tracking number and is charged to your shipping account.

1. **From the Setup tab menu, choose Accounting⇨Shipping.**

2. **In the Default Item Fulfillment Integration Stage field, select Picked, Packed, Or Shipped.**

✔ **Multiple locations:** When you have the Multi-Location Inventory feature enabled along with the Shipping Label Integration feature, you can set up different UPS and FedEx accounts for each location. As a result, each location can get real-time rates and correct labels for each warehouse. When the order is created, you designate the location from which it will be fulfilled. An Administrator can set up locations from the Setup tab menu by choosing Company⇨Locations.

✔ **Integrating with multiple carriers:** The default shipping carrier doesn't restrict you to using only that carrier. If you use multiple carriers, select the shipping option that you use most frequently as the default.

✔ **Shipping labels:** With the Shipping Label Integration feature, you can print — guess what? — an integrated shipping label ready to be processed by the related carrier. This label may also include a barcode.

Setting up integrated and non-integrated shipping options

To set up shipping, an administrator must follow these steps:

1. **From the Setup tab menu choose Setup⇨Accounting⇨Shipping.**

   The Set Up Shipping page opens, as shown in Figure 11-5.

2. **(Optional) Select the Charge for Shipping check box.**

   Check this option to automatically charge for shipping on orders. You must check this box to charge for shipping in your Web site.

3. **(Optional) Select the Charge for Handling Separate from Shipping check box.**

   Use this option if you charge a separate fee for handling orders.

4. **Select your main carrier from the Default Shipping Carrier drop-down list.**

   If you use multiple carriers, select the one you use most often as your default. You must set up an account for the default carrier (whether UPS, FedEx, or USPS) on the Carrier Registration tab before selecting the default carrier; see Step 6. You can register more than one carrier account with various carriers and toggle between them on orders.

5. **Choose from the Default Shipping Method drop-down list.**

   Choose the shipping method that should appear on bills and invoices. You can still choose any shipping method on transactions.

6. **Enter a default item weight, in pounds, for items without a weight specified.**

   Item weight determines shipping cost. If this field is left blank, NetSuite uses 1lb as the default weight.

   You will see tabs for carrier registration, preferences, and packages.

7. **Choose the Carrier Registration tab.**

8. **Register your account with one of the three major carriers: FedEx, UPS, or USPS/Endicia.**

   Special registration forms appear so that you can set up your account with the carrier you selected.

9. **Click Submit after you fill out the information needed to create the account.**

10. **Click the Submit button to save the preferences.**

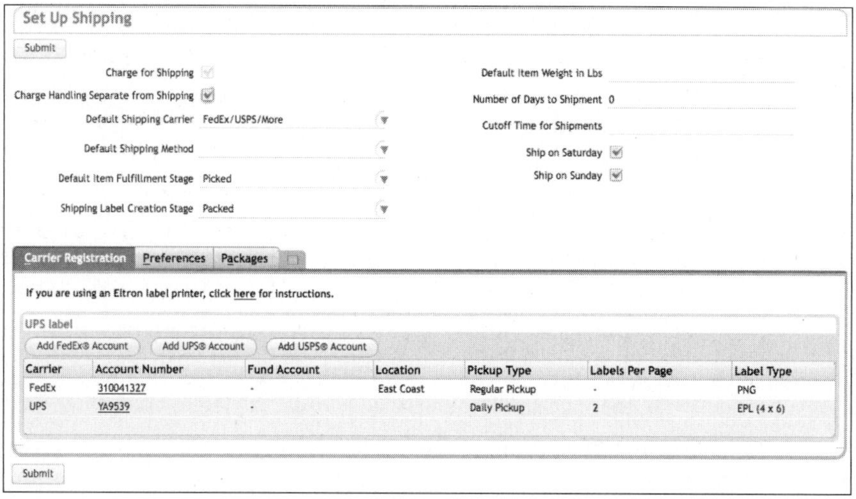

Figure 11-5:
To set up shipping and all its defaults, you must be an Administrator.

Other shipping stuff

Here are some other important options to consider when you're shipping.

Free shipping promotions

You can offer promotions for free shipping, perhaps if your customers buy certain items or reach a minimum order amount.

Certain items

To offer free shipping with certain items:

1. **From the Lists tab menu, choose Accounting⇨Shipping Items.**

2. **Click Edit next to the shipping item that should be free.**

   Or click New to create a new shipping item for the promotion.

3. **Choose the Free Shipping Items tab.**

4. **Select an item that should be offered without a shipping charge.**

   If you check the All Items Must Be Purchased check box on the shipping item, the order doesn't ship for free until all items selected are added to the order.

5. **Click Add.**

You can also click the Add Multiple button to quickly add several items. When one of these items is added to an order, the entire order ships for free.

Minimum order

To offer free shipping with a minimum order amount, you can create a coupon code, or promotion code:

1. **From the Lists tab menu choose Marketing⇨Promotion Codes⇨New.**

2. **Enter the code that customers will use as the Coupon Code.**

3. **In the Free Shipping Method field, select the shipping method to use.**

4. **Check the Available to All Customers check box.**

5. **In the Minimum Order Amount field, enter the total dollar amount a pre-tax order must meet in order for the promotion code to take effect.**

6. **Change the shipping rate to $0.**

7. **Click Save.**

Tracking numbers

Tracking numbers are the handy codes that let you trace an order from warehouse to the customer's door. These codes make logistics friendlier for everybody. With NetSuite, you can enter (or change) the tracking number when you fulfill an order. This number follows the order through the process and appears everywhere in the system.

UPS, FedEx, and USPS tracking numbers are entered automatically if you enable shipping label integration; and better yet, the tracking number functions as a live hyperlink: You can click the number and automatically be directed to the Web site that gives you an update on the status of the package.

You can also designate whether you want to send customers this link and tracking number in an e-mail as part of the shipping and fulfillment process.

To enter or view a tracking number on a fulfillment:

1. **From the Shipping tab menu choose Shipping➪Fulfill Orders.**

2. **Click Fulfill next to an order.**

3. **Enter the tracking number in the Tracking Number field; see Figure 11-6.**

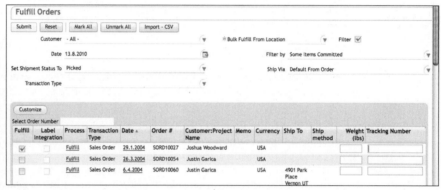

If you use shipping label integration, the tracking number automatically appears after you fulfill the sales order.

Multiple shipping routes

The Multiple Shipping Routes feature allows you to ship to several addresses and use different shipping methods on the same transaction. For example, Grandma wants to buy each of her four grandkids a nice wool sweater for Christmas. Sounds simple, but each child lives in a different state. Half the orders can go by UPS ground, but half need to go by air to arrive in time for Christmas. Oh, one more thing. You've had a run on these sweaters and have only two left in your New York warehouse so two others have to come from your California location.

No problem. With multiple shipping routes you can use unique combinations of the following elements:

- ✔ Shipping address
- ✔ Shipping method
- ✔ Origin address

This feature may be useful in many scenarios, such as companies with more than one warehouse or shipping to businesses with multiple sites.

Using the multiple shipping routes feature also affects the fulfillment process. Orders with multiple shipping routes automatically generate an item fulfillment for each address. Each shipping route represents its own pending item fulfillment with its own line in the fulfillment queue. Each shipping route also generates its own picking ticket.

An administrator must enable the Multiple Shipping Routes feature:

1. **From the Setup tab menu choose Accounting⇨Set Up Taxes.**

2. **Select the Per-Line Taxes on Transactions check box.**

   This enables taxes to be calculated for each line item in the order (since they may be delivered to different states).

3. **From the Setup tab menu, choose Company⇨Enable Features.**

4. **Choose the Transactions tab.**

5. **Select the Multiple Shipping Routes check box.**

   When the Multiple Shipping Routes check box is selected, shipping routes are automatically generated on the order based on the (origin) location, shipping address, and shipping method entered for each line item. These routes are visible under the Shipping tab of the sales order.

Chapter 12

Managing Projects

*B*usinesses sell goods and/or services. Goods are generally easy to define and manage, at least from a conceptual standpoint. They're physical inventory items that are usually tracked and priced on a per-unit basis. But what about services? They're not always as easy to track and price. Services may be related to goods (when someone from the electronics store comes to install your flat-screen television set) or services may be the only thing a firm offers (such as legal advice or software development).

Generally, services have three components:

✔ **Time:** Self-explanatory. Right?

✔ **Resources:** Individuals or entities — such as subcontractors — who actually perform the service.

✔ **Tasks:** Various goals that have to be achieved along the way. The entire set of tasks necessary to provide a particular service is called a *project.* A task or group of tasks whose successful completion moves the entire project forward is called a *milestone,* and the final milestone is often referred to as the *deliverable.*

So the electronics store sells a service that involves a technician (the resource) for two hours (the time) to install your television set (the task). By the same token, a law firm may supply a team of lawyers (the resources) each billable at their own rate for as long as it takes (the time) to write a contract (the task).

NetSuite has no standard project manager role, but you can create such a role. For some of the tasks described in this chapter, you can be a salesperson, the person who sells the project. For others, you will need Administrator privileges. And if you use project management a lot in NetSuite, you may want to define a role just for project manager, as discussed in Bonus Chapter 6 at **www.dummies.com/go/netsuitefd**.

If the only thing you're doing with time is billing it to clients, and you don't need to plan or track how time is used, then chances are you don't need any of the additional functionality for project management in NetSuite. In this case, you simply set up time and/or milestones as inventory items that can be added to customer invoices (see Chapter 6).

However, if you need to manage projects with multiple tasks and assign resources to each and allow time entry against those tasks, then you need one or both of two options within NetSuite: basic projects and advanced projects. To know more about these optional features, read on.

Priming Yourself for Project Management: Time and Billing

Painting a room is a classic example of a project. When's the last time you painted a room? It's made up of a series of tasks, all of which must be performed successfully in a specific order to achieve the desired outcome.

A typical painting project may consist of the following:

1. Choose the color and brand of paint.

2. Buy the paint and supplies.

3. Prepare the room.

    a. Cover the furniture and floor with drop cloths.

    b. Remove wall decorations.

    c. Prime the wall.

4. Paint the room.

    a. First coat.

    b. Second coat.

5. Clean up.

    a. Remove the furniture and floor covering.

    b. Re-hang the wall decorations.

Splitting a project into tasks is called the *Work Breakdown Structure (WBS)*. Notice that some tasks are groups of other, more detailed, tasks. Some of the tasks are independent, meaning that they don't rely on the completion of a prior task before they can be started or completed. Other tasks can't be started or completed until a prior task has been finished. Part of breaking down a project into tasks involves determining which tasks have dependencies and which do not.

In the case of painting a room, it's pretty intuitive. For instance, Task 3c (Prime the Wall) can't (or shouldn't) be started until the completion of Task 3b (Remove Wall Decorations). Task 3c is said to be *dependent* upon Task 3b, and the relationship between the two tasks is known as the *dependency*.

When you aren't so familiar with the tasks (and the practical implication of putting paint right on top of existing wall decorations), you may need to talk to the people who will be working on the project to determine which tasks are independent.

Table 12-1 shows the WBS with dependencies.

Table 12-1	Work Breakdown Structure (WBS) with Dependencies	
Task	*Description*	*Dependency*
1	Choose the color and brand of paint.	n/a
2	Buy the paint and supplies.	Task 1
3	Prepare the room.	Task 2
3a	Cover the furniture and floor with drop cloths.	n/a
3b	Remove wall decorations.	n/a
3c	Prime the wall.	Task 3b
4	Paint the room.	Task 3
4a	First coat.	n/a
4b	Second coat.	Task 4a
5	Clean up.	Task 4
5a	Remove the drop cloths.	n/a
5b	Re-hang the wall decorations.	Task 5a

In this WBS, tasks are dependent on other tasks at the same level (such as Task 2 depending on Task 1) and subtasks are dependent upon other subtasks within the same task group (such as Task 3c depending on Task 3b). This hierarchy tends to be the most streamlined way to organize a WBS. However, in NetSuite, you can make any task or subtask dependent on any other in the entire project, as you will see later in this chapter.

Adding resources

This WBS assumes you are doing this project alone. That's why preparing the room can't start until you buy the paint and supplies, unless, of course, you clone yourself! But what if a friend helps you? By adding the friend you now have two people (known in project management speak as *resources*) and you can divvy up the work. The dependencies on the WBS change because now someone can shop while the other person prepares the room. Since tasks can now be performed simultaneously, determine whether a dependent task must be completed first or whether it can be started at the same time and indicate finish-to-start or start-to-start on the WBS. This is called the *dependency type*.

If you're writing software instead of painting a room, the person testing the software can't start until the software has been created. The task of software development would then have a finish-to-start dependency type.

Table 12-2 shows the WBS with two additional columns: Dependency Type and Resource.

Table 12-2	WBS with Dependency Types and Resources			
Task	**Description**	**Dependency**	**Dependency Type**	**Resource**
1	Choose the color and brand of paint.	n/a	n/a	Kate
2	Buy the paint and supplies.	Task 1	Finish-to-Start	Kate
3	Prepare the room.	Task 2	Finish-to-Start	n/a
3a	Cover the furniture and floor with drop cloths.	n/a	n/a	Kate & Adam
3b	Remove wall decorations.	Task 3a	Start-to-Start	Adam

Task	Description	Dependency	Dependency Type	Resource
3c	Prime the wall.	Task 3b	Finish-to-Start	Kate & Adam
4	Paint the room.	Task 3	Finish-to-Start	Kate & Adam
4a	First coat.	n/a	n/a	n/a
4b	Second coat.	Task 4a	Finish-to-Start	n/a
5	Clean up.	Task 4	Finish-to-Start	n/a
5a	Remove the drop cloths.	n/a	n/a	Kate
5b	Re-hang the wall decorations.	Task 5a	Start-to-Start	Adam

The reason Task 3c is dependent on Task 3b, and Task 3b is dependent on Task 3a is that 3a and 3b both have to be completed before they can start on 3c (Prime the Wall). However, 3a and 3b can be done at the same time. Once the wall has been primed, Kate and Adam will paint the room together, one coat at a time. They will then assume separate chores in cleaning up the room.

Estimating time and costs

Assume you want to use the WBS to determine how long it will take Kate and Adam to paint the room. Then they need to assign a value to their time, so they can determine a fair price to charge their customer in order to earn a profit. Table 12-3 shows the WBS with three new columns: Hours, Rate, and Price with totals.

Table 12-3   **WBS with Dependency Types and Resources**

Task	Description	Dependency	Dependency Type	Resource	Hours	Rate	Price
1	Choose the color and brand of paint.	n/a	n/a	Customer	n/a	n/a	n/a
2	Buy the paint and supplies.	Task 1	Finish-to-Start	Kate	0.50	17.50	8.75
3	Prepare the room.	Task 2	Finish-to-Start	n/a	n/a	n/a	n/a
3.a.	Cover the furniture and floor with drop cloths.	n/a	n/a	Kate	0.25	17.50	4.38
3.b.	Remove wall decorations.	n/a	n/a	Adam	0.25	15.00	3.75
		Task 3a	Start-to-Start	Kate	0.75	17.50	13.13
3.c.	*Prime the wall.			Adam	1.00	15.00	15.00
		Task 3b	Finish-to-Start	Kate	1.50	17.50	26.25
				Adam	1.50	15.00	22.50
4	Paint the room.	Task 3	Finish-to-Start	n/a	n/a	n/a	n/a
4.a.	First coat.	n/a	n/a	Kate	3.00	17.50	52.50
		n/a	n/a	Adam	3.00	15.00	45.00
4.b.	*Second coat.	Task 4a	Finish-to-Start	Kate	2.50	17.50	43.75
		n/a	n/a	Adam	2.50	15.00	37.50
5	Clean up.	Task 4	Finish-to-Start	n/a	n/a	n/a	n/a
5.a.	Remove the drop cloths.	n/a	n/a	Kate	0.25	17.50	4.38
5.b.	*Re-hang the wall decorations.	Task 5a	Start-to-Start	Kate	0.75	17.50	13.13
				Adam	1.00	15.00	15.00
				TOTAL	18.75	230.00	305.00

*Project milestone

Now the WBS shows how long they expect things to take for each of them and what they will charge the customer. The rate chosen is based on Kate and Adam's perceived value of their time (Kate's rate is higher because she's managing the project), but if they were employed by a painting contractor the rate would be based on their actual wage plus any overhead (i.e., the **labor cost**).

For software development, you'd figure out the time it will take the developer to write the software, the tester to test the software, and the developer to fix any problems the tester finds. You'd also need labor costs for both the developer and the tester.

Also, in this example, you're looking at this project from a time and billing perspective, but not from a project scheduling perspective. If you were to further develop this WBS, you wouldn't only account for the resource's time and cost, but for the total time necessary to complete each task.

You can bill projects to customers a variety of ways:

- ✔ **Straight time:** Only a resource's time is accounted for and billed.
- ✔ **Time and materials:** The resource's time and any materials used or expenses incurred are billed.
- ✔ **Cost plus fixed fee:** The company's cost, including labor, materials, and expenses, plus an additional pre-negotiated fixed sum.
- ✔ **Fixed fee:** A flat rate for the deliverable.

Billing can occur at scheduled intervals (such as once a month) or when certain negotiated milestones are met.

NetSuite manages projects from a time and labor perspective. Notice in Table 12-3 that the customer is purchasing the paint and supplies, so this project only has to track time, not materials. If a contractor using NetSuite provides the paint and supplies, those materials would be accounted for as regular inventory (see Chapter 7).

Managing Service-Oriented Tasks

When you're managing a project, there are two kinds of tasks. There's the stuff you do (the tasks themselves) and then there's the stuff you do to enable people to do the tasks (schedule meetings, review sessions, phone calls, and create schedules). This section describes how to track basic tasks and how to handle supporting activities.

Tracking basic tasks

Even without enabling the optional project features, you can track basic tasks in NetSuite as they pertain to customers.

1. **From the Lists tab menu, choose Relationships⇨Customers.**

2. **Click Edit next to the name of a customer.**

3. **Click Task on the Create New bar at the top of the Customer page.**

   Figure 12-1 shows the New Task form. Here you can start setting up a basic WBS for tasks related specifically to this customer. They won't be grouped under a project umbrella, and you can't identify dependencies or create subtasks, but here's what you can do:

Figure 12-1: The New Task form enables you to create a new task for a customer.

- **Title:** Identify the task with a name such as Delivery, Installation, or Send Technician.

- **Assigned To:** Assign any employee in the system as a single resource for this task (required).

- **Start Date:** Establish when this task is to begin (required).

- **Due Date:** Establish when this task is to be completed (required).

- **Date Completed:** Identify when this task was completed.

- **Insert Before:** Place this task before another task.

- **Priority:** Set a priority for this task (Low, Medium, or High) (required).

- **Status:** Mark a status for this task (Not Started, In Progress, or Completed) (required).

- **Notes tab:** Include text describing this task in detail.

4. **Click Save.**

When you create a new task in a customer record and save, you will find the record on the Activities tab of the General tab for that customer. Figure 12-2 shows the Activities tab.

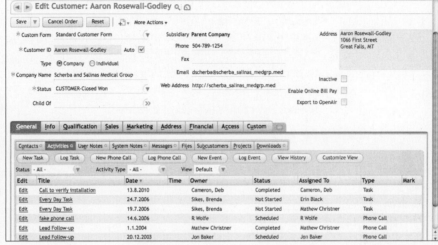

Figure 12-2:
You can see your new task on the Activities tab on the Customer page.

Handling activities

You manage tasks, events, and phone calls on the Activities tab.

Administrators can log the time spent on tasks for a client without turning on any additional features.

1. **Click the Time Tracking tab on the General tab in the Customer page.**

2. **Click New Time.**

Figure 12-3 shows the Time Tracking entry form.

On this form administrators enter time and billing information related to this customer. However, you can't relate this time to specific tasks on the Activities tab. What you can do:

- **Employee:** Select the resource that performed the work from this drop-down list (required).

- **Date:** Enter the date the work was performed (required).

- **Customer:** Change the customer for whom the work was performed from the drop-down list. It defaults to the current customer.

- **Case/Task/Event:** Associate this time with a particular activity such as a case, task, or event.

- **Billable:** Select this check box to mark this time as billable to the customer.

- **Service Item:** Use this drop-down list to select a Service Item, such as Delivery, Installation, or Repair.

- **Class and Location:** Use these drop-down lists to assign the time to particular areas within the organization for accounting purposes.

- **Duration:** How long did this task take? Use the two buttons to the right of this field to either start a timer while you work, or to calculate the time based on values you enter.

- **Supervisor Approval:** Select this check box if you have authority to approve the time entered.

- **Memo:** Describe the work performed.

3. **Click Save.**

Figure 12-3:
Click New
Time on
the Time
Tracking
tab of the
General
tab on the
Customer
screen (in
the house
that Jack
built) to
access
the Time
Tracking
entry form.

Enabling Project Features

Basic and advanced project functionality are discussed in this section.

You must be logged in as an Administrator to enable project features. To enable project features, from the Setup tab menu, choose Company➪Enable Features.

To enable basic project functionality, select Projects on the Company stab and click Save. This adds a new tab to the General tab on the Customer page called Projects. With this feature enabled, tasks can be created for projects (not just customers), and top-level information, including budget and accounting details, about the overall project can be tracked.

To enable advanced project functionality, see "Working with Advanced Projects" later in this chapter.

Setting Up Basic Projects

Once basic project functionality has been enabled in NetSuite, roles with the proper permissions (or Administrators) can create new projects and associate tasks with them.

To create a new project:

1. **From the Customers tab menu, choose Relationships⇨Customers.**

2. **Click Edit next to the customer name you want to assign this project.**

   Or create a new customer, if you wish.

3. **Select the Projects tab on the General tab.**

4. **Click New Project.**

   Figure 12-4 shows the New Project page.

Figure 12-4:
Reach the
New Project
page from
the Project
tab.
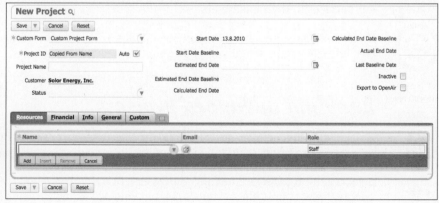

5. **Set up a basic project in the following fields:**

- **Project Name.**

- **Status.** Use the drop-down list to choose a status, such as Not Started, In Progress, or Completed.

- **Start Date.**

- **Project Manager.** Select an employee name from the drop-down list to designate a project manager.

6. **Click Save.**

You can access this project at any time: From the Lists tab menu, choose Relationships⇨Customers. Notice that when you get to the Customer list page, it now says Customers & Projects. The projects you create are underneath the customers with whom they're associated. Without Advanced Projects enabled, you can only create projects associated with customers.

You add tasks and time entries to projects using the exact same methods as you do for customers, as outlined earlier in this chapter.

After you save a project, you'll see one additional tab called Subprojects. You can add any number of project levels underneath this one and add tasks and time entries to it also.

Working with Advanced Projects

Advanced Projects is an add-on feature that is suitable for companies that sell services to their customers.

If you don't have Advanced Projects enabled in your account, contact your NetSuite sales representative to talk about this add-on feature.

Enabling advanced projects

You must be logged in as an Administrator to enable features. To enable project feature, from the Setup tab menu, choose Company⇨Enable Features.

Select both Projects and Advanced Projects. Don't worry; if you forget to enable Projects first, the system will warn you. Advanced Projects lets you designate employees and vendors as resources and assign them to projects, as well as build project schedules and view them in a graphical format called Gantt charts. It also adds menu items that allow you to create and edit projects independently from customers so you can set up reusable project templates.

Allocating resources (aka people)

After enabling Advanced Projects, you designate specific employees or vendors as *project resources* (a fancy term for those humans walking around drinking coffee in your office).

To designate an employee as a resource:

1. **From the Lists tab menu, choose Employees⇨Employees.**
2. **Click Edit next to the name of the employee you want to designate as a resource.**
3. **Click the Human Resources tab.**
4. **Select the Project Resource check box.**

   This check box was added magically when you enabled Advanced Projects for your account.

To designate a vendor as a resource:

1. **From the Lists tab menu, choose Relationships⇨Vendors.**
2. **Click Edit next to the name of the vendor you want to designate as a resource.**
3. **Click the Financial tab.**
4. **Select the Project Resource check box.**

   This check box was added when you enabled Advanced Projects.

Setting Up Advanced Projects

With Advanced Projects enabled, you can create and copy projects independently from customers. You can access projects by selecting Lists⇨Relationships⇨Projects. Figure 12-5 shows the Project page.

Figure 12-5:
Creating a
new project
indepen-
dently from
customers is
available
when you
enable
Advanced
Projects.

Creating a new project

To create a new project:

1. **From the Lists tab menu, choose Relationships⇨Projects⇨New.**

2. **Enter a name into the Project Name field.**

3. **Select someone from the Customer drop-down list.**

   In Advanced Projects, selecting a customer is brilliantly optional. Leave this field blank if you'd like to use this project as a template for other projects or if you have an internal project not associated with a customer. Click Save when you've filled in all the information you want to use in your template.

4. **Select from the Status drop-down list.**

5. **Indicate the start date for this project.**

   The end date is calculated automatically based on the task schedule.

6. **On the Resources tab, select from the Name drop-down list.**

7. **Click the Add button after each selection.**

   You can choose as many resources as you want, but you must click Add after every selection.

   Notice that you only see names of employees or vendors you've already designated as project resources in their respective Employee or Vendor pages. Unless overridden at the project level, only the resources you assign to the overall project are available as resources for its associated tasks.

8. **Click Save.**

9. **Select the Schedule tab on the Project page.**

10. **Add tasks to this project.**

    Read the following section for those steps.

Adding a task

To add a task:

1. **Click New Project Task.**

2. **Type a name for this project task.**

3. **Assign a parent task from the drop-down list, if appropriate.**

4. **Use the Insert Before drop-down list to specify where in the WBS this task will fall.**

5. **Type the number of hours you expect this task to consume in the Estimated Work field.**

6. **Choose from the Constraint Type drop-down list.**

    The constraint type specifies whether this task must begin on a specific date or if its start date is determined by the completion of a dependent task before it.

7. **If the constraint type is Fixed Start: Select a start date.**

    Otherwise the start date is automatically calculated based on this task's dependencies. In other words, the start date is the day after the last task is scheduled to finish.

8. **Choose the Assignees tab.**

9. **Choose from the Name drop-down list to assign employees or vendors as resources to this task.**

10. **Click Add after each assignment.**

11. **Choose the Predecessors tab.**

12. **If a task depends on the completion of another task: Select the dependent task from the Task drop-down list.**

    You can add more than one dependent task by clicking Add after each selection.

13. **Select the Dependency Type from the drop-down list on the Predecessors tab.**

    Select either Finish-to-Start or Start-to-Start for each dependent task in the list.

14. **Click Save to add this task to the project.**

If you've added more than one task to this project with dependencies and durations, click the View Gantt button on the Schedule tab to see a graphical representation of your project. Figure 12-6 shows an example of a Gantt chart.

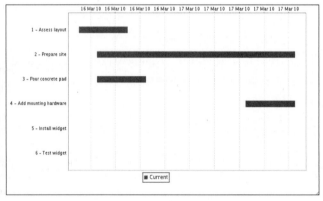

Figure 12-6:
You can view a Gantt chart in NetSuite on the Project page.

The Gantt chart is named for Henry L. Gantt (1861–1919), an American mechanical engineer who developed it to show planned and actual progress on large-scale construction projects. Gantt charts were used to great success on the Hoover Dam and the Interstate Highway System. Today they're used for just about every type of project imaginable, from launching the space shuttle to painting a bedroom.

Entering time

Enter time for projects using Advanced Projects in NetSuite:

1. **From the Lists tab menu, choose Relationships⇨Projects.**

2. **Click Edit next to a project name.**

3. **Click Edit next to a task name on the Schedule tab.**

4. **Click Time in the Create New bar.**

TIP

Integrating with OpenAir

NetSuite account holders using Advanced Projects can integrate with a powerful and robust project management system called OpenAir. When coupled with NetSuite, OpenAir provides you with enterprise-level project management, billing, and reporting features that allow you to do the following:

✔ Assign, schedule, and balance resources.

✔ Create detailed work breakdown structures.

✔ Analyze performance metrics.

✔ Process expense reports.

✔ Bill clients.

✔ Post project-related financial transactions to your general ledger.

For more information, visit www.openair.com.

5. **Fill out the Time form.**

   It's the same time entry form that we explain in this chapter's "Tracking basic tasks" section.

6. **Click Save.**

Chapter 13

Providing Excellent Customer Service

NetSuite has a very solid customer service and support solution to round out the customer relationship management features. Case automation preferences allow you to send the cases from the highest profile (or most difficult) customers to the smoothest talker, or escalate cases that have been open too long or concern certain subjects to experts or managers.

In this chapter, you find out about many of NetSuite's customer service features. You read about how to set up case rules so that cases can be automatically assigned as well as how to create cases.

To read how to create a knowledge base and how to help customers help themselves, check out this book's Web site at **www.dummies.com/go/netsuitefd**.

To follow the steps in this chapter, you must have a support role, such as Support Manager, Support Administrator, or Support Person. Where noted, you'll need an Administrator role.

Setting Up Case Routing and Notification

Before you accept customer service cases through NetSuite, consider any rules you want to set up for automatically routing cases to certain employees or groups. When you set up automatic routing rules and assignments, cases that meet your criteria are automatically assigned to the correct employees or teams. Automatic routing is especially useful if most of your cases come in by e-mail or online.

Setting up routing begins with creating case rules, which are the criteria for the cases that will be routed. Then, you set up case territories, which assign the cases that meet those rules to the correct employees. You can then set up e-mail notification for employees to let them know that they have a new case waiting for their response in the queue.

Creating case rules and territories

Case rules are basically saved searches using specific information from the case record. You can create case rules, just to name a few criteria, based on

- Number of days open
- Customer name
- Customer location
- Certain keywords in the incoming message

Keep in mind that you can group rules when you create territories and decide whether all the rules (or just any one rule) in the group must be met for the case to be assigned. For example, you may create a rule for a case about returns and another rule for a case from a customer in California. When you create the territory to assign the case, you can decide that a case must be regarding returns *and* from a customer in California to be assigned to John Smith, your West Coast return manager.

Create a case rule

You need to be a support manager to create a case rule:

1. **From the Setup tab menu choose Support⇨Set Up Case Rules⇨New.**

   The Select a Case Rule Field page appears.

2. **Click a link to select the type of information that you want to base your rules on.**

   The New Case Field Rule page (see Figure 13-1) appears after you choose a link. The fields on each page depend on the type of field you chose for your rule.

3. **On the New Case Field Rule page, enter a name for your rule in the Name field; then choose a criteria and select one or more values for the particular field.**

   For example, if you selected Customer as your field, you can create a rule that gives preference to a particular customer by choosing that customer from the list of customers.

4. **Click the Save button.**

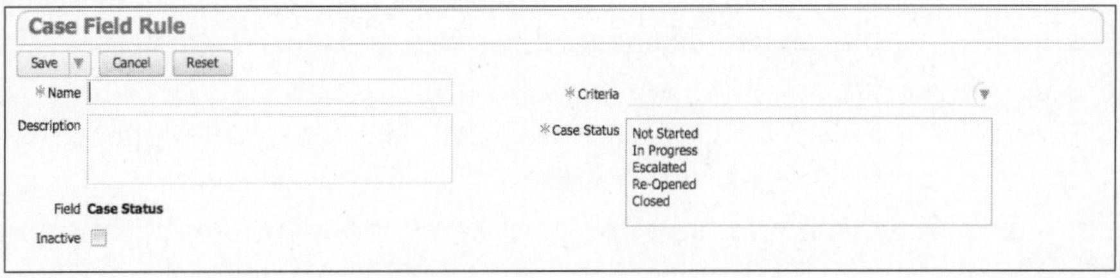

Figure 13-1:
Create crite-
ria for cases
that need
automated
assignment
on the Case
Field Rule
page.

Case Field Rule

Save ▼ | Cancel | Reset

＊Name |

Description

Field **Case Status**

Inactive ☐

＊Criteria ▼

＊Case Status | Not Started
In Progress
Escalated
Re-Opened
Closed

Continue setting rules with different criteria based on all the ways you may assign employees to cases. After you finish creating case rules, you need to assign them to employees using case territories.

Create a case territory

To create a case territory:

1. **From the Setup tab menu, choose Support➪Manage Case Territories➪ New.**

   The New Case Territory page appears, as shown in Figure 13-2.

2. **Type a name in the Name field.**

3. **Type a territory description in the Description field.**

4. **Select one of the radio buttons:**

   • **Match All Rules**

   • **Match Any Rules**

   This determines whether the criteria must be met on all rules you add (versus *any one* of the rules you add) to assign a case to this territory. For example, you may set up rules by customer name and company name and select the Match Any Rules radio button to cover all your bases. This way if the case came in with a customer name of Sam's Slightly Soggy Sandwiches or with a company name of Sam's Slightly Soggy Sandwiches, you'd still get the case assigned properly.

5. **Choose the Configure Rule Definitions tab.**

6. **From the Apply Rule drop-down list, select a rule with criteria for cases that should be assigned to a certain person or group.**

   You select one of the rules you defined earlier.

7. **Click the Add button.**

   Repeat as needed to add more rules.

8. **Choose the Support Assignment tab.**

9. **From the Support Rep drop-down list, choose each person or group that should be assigned to cases that meet the criteria of the attached rules.**

   Sally Sue Smith is the preferred sales rep for all support cases coming from Sam's Slightly Soggy Sandwiches problems.

   Employees or groups must have the Support Rep or Support Group check box selected on the record to be chosen here. If you select more than one support person or group, cases that come in with this criteria are assigned one by one down the list, round-robin style.

10. **Click the Add button.**

11. **Click the Save button.**

Figure 13-2:
Combine
rules with
support reps
on the Case
Territory
page.

Case Territory
Save ▼ Cancel Reset
* Name
Description
Match all rules ⦿
Match any rule ○
Inactive ☐
Configure Rule Definitions Support Assignment
* Apply Rule	Field the Rule is applied to	# Sub Rules	Description
▼
Add Insert Remove Cancel

Continue setting up territories for each set of criteria and person or group that needs to be assigned to cases. New cases are automatically assigned based on your criteria and groupings. Existing cases aren't affected.

Reassign existing cases

If you have outstanding cases that need to be reassigned because of employee or group changes, use the Territory Reassignment tool.

To reassign existing cases:

1. **From the Setup tab menu, choose Support⇨Territory Reassignment.**

   A mass update page appears.

2. **Choose the Criteria tab.**

3. **From the Filter drop-down list, choose cases that need to be reassigned.**

   For example, if an employee leaves the company or goes on vacation, you'll reassign her cases. In this case, you'd select Assigned To from the Filter drop-down list.

   A pop-up window with possible values appears.

4. **Enter or select the information you want, and click the Set button.**

5. **Click the Preview button.**

   Now you can see which cases are affected.

6. **Deselect the check box next to any cases that shouldn't be reassigned.**

7. **Click the Save button.**

Stilled-checked cases from this list are updated to the new assignment.

Setting up notifications for support reps and customers

Better customer service comes with talking to your customers. You can automate this process to some degree with e-mail notifications. NetSuite allows you to send automatic e-mail notifications via custom templates with the following actions:

- ✔ Confirm with the customer when a customer creates a case in the Customer Center.

- ✔ Notify the customer of different scenarios, including when a support rep creates a case internally for the customer. (Figure 13-3 shows a sample of this e-mail.)

- ✔ Notify the main support e-mail address when a case is created from the Customer Center.

- ✔ Confirm with the customer when a case is created using e-mail case capture (a feature that allows you to handle e-mails sent to an address like support@yourcompany.com).

- ✔ Confirm that cases are created for every case e-mail received.

- ✔ Confirm that cases have been created for everyone who received a CC of a case e-mail.

- ✔ Notify support reps when they're assigned to a case.

✔ Notify support reps when a case they're assigned to is updated.

✔ Notify employees who have cases escalated to them when the escalated case is updated.

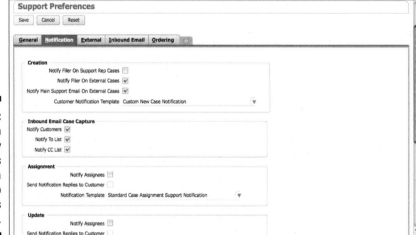

Figure 13-3:
You can notify customers when a support rep creates a case.

You can set up these notifications on the Support Preferences page:

1. **From the Setup tab menu choose Support⇨Support Preferences.**

2. **Choose the Notification tab.**

   You can set up automatic e-mail notification for case creation, inbound customer case capture (your support e-mail address), assignment, updates, escalation, and closure.

3. **Select the check boxes for those who should get the e-mail in each of these cases.**

4. **From the drop-down list, select templates for e-mail notifications.**

   Here is where you determine which templates are used in which situation.

5. **Click Save.**

   You can edit notification templates by choosing Setup⇨Company⇨ System Email Templates.

You can click any field to get a full description of the setting.

Allowing Customers to Submit Cases Online

If you want to offer customers the opportunity to submit questions and problems via the Web, you have two options. We encourage you to use them both:

- ✔ **Allow customers to submit cases through the Customer Center.** The Customer Center allows customers to log in to view past cases and submit new ones. The Customer Center is controlled by the Customer Access feature and discussed in detail in the next section, "Accepting cases through the Customer Center."

- ✔ **Create an online form that's linked to your Web site.** You can link to an online form whether or not you use a Web site built in NetSuite. Using an online form does not require a customer to be logged in — anyone who visits your site can click your link and fill out the form. Even better, the information is saved from the form in a Lead record if the site visitor has never registered with you before.

Accepting cases through the Customer Center

Customers can submit cases through the Customer Center when you enable both the Customer Support and Service and Customer Access features. Administrators should enable the features from the Setup tab menu by choosing Company➪Enable Features.

- ✔ On the CRM tab, select the Customer Support and Service check box.
- ✔ On the Web Presence tab, select the Customer Access check box.

By default, the case-entry form that customers use in the Customer Center (shown in Figure 13-4) is a slightly modified version of the case form you see in your very own NetSuite account when you contact NetSuite for support.

Before giving customers access to the Customer Center, or shortly after you enable the Customer Service and Support feature, customize the case form with any changes you want to make. For example, you may not want customers to see the Copy Employees field or have access to Escalation information.

You may also want to add fields to this form to capture all the details and be more effective at resolving the case. For information on customizing forms, see Chapter 25.

Figure 13-4:
You can customize the default external case form.

Use an online form for cases submitted through the Customer Center

You can use an online case form for cases submitted through the Customer Center. If you choose to do this, skip ahead to the "Accepting cases through your Web site" section to create your online form.

1. **From the Setup tab menu, choose Support➪Support Preferences.**

2. **Choose the External tab.**

3. **Select the name of the online form in the Default Customer Center Case Form drop-down list.**

Add fields to forms

Here's how to create fields you want to add to this form:

1. **From the Setup tab menu choose Customization➪CRM Fields➪New.**

   The Custom CRM Field page appears.

2. **In the Label field, type the name of the new field.**

3. **From the Type drop-down list, select what type of field this should be.**

   • **List/Record:** If customers will choose from a drop-down list. Form here, you must decide what type of list customers will select from.

   • **Long Text:** If this will be a large text-entry field.

4. **Select the Store Value check box unless this field will be display only.**

5. **On the Applies To tab, select the Case check box.**

6. **On the Display tab, choose from the drop-down lists:**

   • Insert Before

   • Tab

   • Display Type

   This setting decides how and where this field should be displayed.

7. **(Optional) On the Validation & Defaulting tab, choose the Mandatory or Check Spelling check boxes.**

8. **(Optional) Enter values in the Maximum Length and Default Values fields.**

9. **Choose from the Source List and Source From drop-down lists.**

   This sets your preferences for pulling information from other fields and records.

10. **On the Access tab, choose the Role tab.**

11. **Choose Customer Center from the drop-down list.**

12. **Click the Add button.**

13. **Click the Save button.**

Add or remove Customer Center form fields

Here's how to add or remove fields on this form:

1. **From the Setup menu tab choose Customization⇨Entry Forms.**

   The Custom Entry Forms page appears.

2. **Click the Customize link.**

   It shows up next to the Standard External Case Form link.

3. **Type a name for your custom form in the Name field.**

   Your custom form is saved as a new form, and this name helps you identify it.

4. **Leave the following fields set to their default settings:**

   • **Enable Field Editing on Lists** — Selected: This allows the form to be edited.

   • **Store Form with Record** — Deselected: Normally this check box is selected, but you don't want this used internally for external forms; you just want the data from the form.

   • **Form Is Preferred** — Selected: This selection makes this form the default in the Customer Center.

5. **On the Tabs tab, select the check boxes next to the tabs you want shown on the form.**

   For example, if you haven't created any custom fields to show on this form, clear the Custom check box to hide that tab.

6. **(Optional) Edit the name of a tab by typing the name in the Label field.**

7. **On the Fields tab, select the Show check box next to each field that should show on the form.**

   If you prefer, you can also do these things:

   - Select the **Mandatory** check box to make a field mandatory for submittal.

   - Choose how a field displays via the **Display Type** drop-down list.

   - Change the label by replacing the text in the **Label** field.

   We recommend the following changes as an example for customizing the external case form:

   - *Custom Form:* Deselect the Show check box.

   - *Contact:* Select the Mandatory check box.

   - *Email:* From the Display Type drop-down list; select Normal.

   - *Phone:* From the Display Type drop-down list; select Normal.

   - *Origin:* Deselect the Show check box.

   Select the Show check box next to each custom field that should show on your customized entry form.

8. **(Optional) On the Lists tab, select the Show check box.**

   On the Interactions tab, we recommend you select only the Show check box for Messages.

9. **(Optional) On the General tab, select the Show check box next to Files.**

   That allows customers to attach files (such as images). You can't add files to a case until the case is saved.

   If you choose to show the Files list, you may want to add a custom Help field using the previous set of steps, which explains how to save the case and then open it to add files.

   If you need to add custom behavior to this form, do so on the Custom Code tab. More information on custom code is in Chapter 23.

10. **On the Roles tab, select the Customer Center check box.**

11. **Click the Save button.**

If you select the Form Is Preferred check box, this form is automatically used in the Customer Center, and you're ready for the barrage of questions (never problems, of course) about your products or services.

If you don't make the form preferred, or if you have trouble getting the form to show in the Customer Center, set the form as the default for the Customer Center on the Support Preferences page:

1. **From the Setup tab menu, choose Support⇨Support Preferences.**
2. **On the External tab, select your form in the Default Customer Center Case Form drop-down list.**

Accepting cases through your Web site

If you want customers to submit cases through your Web site, you can create an online form that includes the information most important for creating a case. When customers submit this form, a case record in NetSuite is automatically created.

You can make a Web site case form one of three ways:

✔ Create an HTML form on your own by using CRMSDK tags and then uploading it to NetSuite.

✔ Create a form from scratch by using a text editor within NetSuite.

✔ Create a form by customizing the default template in NetSuite.

Create an online case form

To create an online case form:

1. **From the Setup tab menu, choose Support⇨Online Case Forms⇨New.**

   The Select Type page appears.

2. **Choose the link for type of form you want to create:**

   • **Default Form Template:** Create forms based on NetSuite's default template.

   • **Custom HTML Template:** Use forms you've already created in HTML or forms you want to create in HTML within NetSuite with a code editor and field selector.

3. **Enter a title for the form in the Title field.**

   This title appears at the top of the page when it's online.

4. **If you're using the default template, enter a message for your form in the Message field.**

   This message shows at the top of your form and can include up to 500 HTML characters.

You can also enter a longer message on the Detail Message tab. The detailed message, which shows at the bottom of the form, can include up to 4,000 HTML characters.

5. **If you're using a custom HTML template, choose from one of the following:**

   • Select the template you want to use in the Template drop-down list. This assumes it's already uploaded to the File Cabinet.

   • If you haven't created a template, choose New from the Template drop-down list. On the Template tab, choose the Online Form Template page and select the Text Editor radio button. In the HTML Source Code field, paste or type the HTML and use the Field Type and Insert Field drop-down lists to add the tags for fields from customer and case records to your form. Click the Save button when you finish.

6. **Select the Enable Online check box.**

   This allows you to link to this form online.

7. **On the Select Fields tab, select a field from the Title drop-down list.**

8. **Enter the title and size in the Title and Width fields.**

9. **Click the Add button for each field that you want customers to fill out when submitting a case.**

   Select the Mandatory check box to make it necessary for customers to fill in the field before they submit the form.

   The basics are now created, and you have an online form that looks similar to the one in Figure 13-5.

10. **If you're finished, click the Save button.**

    Note: If you want to set preferences for how cases are submitted by this form, continue to the following step list.

Figure 13-5:
A standard online case form.

Wolfe Online Case Form

Welcome! You can use this form to contact us with any questions or problems that you have.

First Name

Last Name

Company Name

Email

Phone Number

Subject

Incoming Message

Submit   Reset

We aim to respond to your question via email within 24 hours. If you prefer for us to contact you by phone, please specify this in your message. Remember that the more specific you can be about your problem, what you have already tried, and how we can reproduce the problem (if applicable), the more we are able to solve your case on the first response.

Set up workflow for your form

To set up workflow for your form:

1. **On the Set Up Workflow tab, select the Create Customers as Companies check box (if most of your customers are companies, not individuals).**

   This preference is only used if someone who doesn't yet have a record in your account creates a case using this form.

2. **From the Set Case Origin drop-down list, choose what should show as the origin on cases submitted with this form.**

   You can add selections by choosing the Setup tab menu and selecting Support⇨Case Origin Types⇨New.

3. **Select a template from the Template drop-down list.**

   This option is for e-mail that should be sent to customers when they submit a case.

4. **To send an e-mail automatically to customers who select this case, select new from the Send Auto-Reply Email.**

   Select New to upload a new template.

5. **Type the subject for this auto-reply e-mail in the Subject field.**

6. **Select the Send Email Notification check box to have an e-mail automatically sent to the support rep being assigned to the case.**

   In the CC field, you can copy any e-mail addresses on the support rep's notification e-mail.

7. **Choose an option from the Handle Duplicate Records drop-down list.**

   This determines how to update records when a customer submits a case with information that's different from what you have on record.

8. **If you're finished setting up your form, click the Save button.**

   Note: To set appearance settings, such as the color theme and font, continue to the following step list.

Change form appearance

To set up the appearance of your form:

1. **On the Set Up Appearance tab, choose the Number of Columns Shown field.**

   Many of these settings are straightforward, but if you get stumped on a field, you can always click it to get more information.

2. **Choose a theme from the Color Theme field.**

   For example, you can use a theme that matches your Web site or logo.

   If none of these color themes are suitable, create a new color theme by choosing Setup⇨Web Site.

3. **From the Font drop-down list, select the type to use for fields and text on your form.**

   Unfortunately, you can't add fonts to this list. The only way to use a custom font on a form is to create a custom HTML template for your form.

4. **(Optional) Select the Unlayered Sections check box.**

   Choose this if you want customers to scroll down to fill in more fields. This avoids you having to organize fields on tabs.

5. **From the Button Alignment drop-down list, choose the Submit button alignment:**

   • **Line up on the right**

   • **Line up on the left**

   • **Center of the page**

6. **In the Form Logo drop-down list, select an image from your File Cabinet to show at the top of this form.**

   Preferably, you'll choose your company's logo.

   To upload a new file, select New.

7. **Click the Save button.**

Edit form properties

An External tab, where you can edit the properties of the form, is automatically added to the record when you save an online case form.

To edit a form, follow these steps:

1. **From the Setup tab menu, choose Support⇨Online Case Forms.**

2. **Click the Edit link next to the form you want to change.**

   You see a new External tab.

3. **On the External tab, find the Internal Form URL and the Publishable Form URL for linking to your form.**

   • The Internal Form URL can link to this form from the Customer Center or link to internal support cases from your own account. For more information about internal case handling, see Bonus Chapter 7 at **www.dummies.com/go/netsuitefd**.

   • The Publishable Form URL can link to this form from your Web site, whether you use a NetSuite Web site or not.

Accepting cases by e-mail

The Email Case Capture feature in NetSuite basically sets up an e-mail address where you can forward case e-mail to be formatted into your NetSuite account's case form. Enabling the feature and setting up your e-mail account as required allows you to have customers send questions and problems to a specific e-mail address, such as support@yourcompany.com. E-mail going to this address is then automatically converted into cases.

Information is pulled from these parts of an e-mail to fill in the following fields in the case record:

- **Subject:** Subject of the e-mail
- **Date Created:** Date the e-mail is received by NetSuite
- **Company:** Company name with an e-mail matching the From e-mail address. If more than one company matches, the Anonymous Customer placeholder is used.
- **Contact:** Contact name with matching e-mail address
- **Email:** From e-mail address
- **Message from Customer:** Text of the e-mail message
- **Status:** Set to Not Started by default
- **Origin:** Set to Email by default
- **Priority:** Set to Medium by default
- **Assigned To:** Set using your case rules and territories

If you've set up rules and territories to assign cases to support reps, the cases are assigned as soon as they're converted. The case is then saved in the regular Cases list and saved on the customer's record whose e-mail address matches the From address. If the From address doesn't match a record in your account, the case is associated with the Customer record selected as your Anonymous Customer Placeholder at Setup⇨Support⇨Support Preferences on the Inbound Email tab.

E-mail messages larger than 10MB aren't accepted as cases, and no more than 10 e-mails are accepted every two minutes.

How you set up e-mail case capture depends on the type of e-mail server you use. NetSuite Help provides steps for Microsoft Exchange. Here are the basic steps you need to take:

1. **If you haven't already, create a Contact record for your support e-mail address, such as support@yourcompany.com.**

2. **From the Setup tab menu, choose Support⇨Support Preferences.**

   The Support Preferences page appears.

3. **Click the Inbound Email tab; select and copy the e-mail address you see after NetSuite Address.**

4. **Create another contact record for the NetSuite address where you will forward this e-mail.**

5. **Paste in the e-mail address you copied from your NetSuite account.**

6. **Reopen the contact record for your support e-mail address and set forwarding options for the contact you set up for the NetSuite address.**

7. **In your e-mail account, use forwarding rules to automatically forward customer messages (sent to support@yourcompany.com) to the NetSuite Address you copied.**

Getting a Handle on Customer Inquiries

Customer questions and problems can come into your account in a variety of ways. The most important thing to keep in mind is that you track them all in your account. If you take a case by phone or e-mail, be sure to log it in a case, even if this takes some customer and employee re-education.

Keeping your cases in NetSuite helps you do these things:

✔ See patterns for questions or problems across all customers.

✔ See what a specific customer has called in about.

✔ Quickly solve newer issues by seeing how past issues were resolved.

Because case information is stored on the customer record, sales reps can also quickly gauge how satisfied customers are by their case record and what additional solutions may raise satisfaction.

Creating a case

Cases can come at your support staff from a variety of directions, such as e-mail, online form submittal, Customer Center submittal, phone calls, and in-person conversations. If you have all your ducks in a row — as far as setting up a case form for the Customer Center, creating an online form, and accepting cases via e-mail — support reps should only have to create case records in two of those scenarios — phone calls and in-person conversations.

To create a case record:

1. **From the Cases tab menu, choose Customer Service➪Cases➪New.**

   The Case page appears.

2. **Type the subject of the case in the Subject field.**

   Name this very brief description something that helps you recognize which case this is. In fact, you may need to edit the subjects that your customers have entered, as they often like to enter subjects that read, "URGENT!" or "Help Needed Now!"

3. **Type the customer name in the Company field.**

   This associates the case with the customer and adds the case to the customer's record for future reference. This also allows you to select contacts attached to the customer record in the Contact field, which automatically fills in the Email and Phone fields.

4. **If you didn't select a contact with e-mail address and phone number, enter the e-mail address and phone number for the customer contact who should be contacted about this case in the Email and Phone fields.**

5. **Select a contact for the company that's submitting the case.**

   This automatically fills in the e-mail address and phone number. If you don't have a contact record created for this person, click the Add button next to the field to quickly create one or just enter the e-mail address and phone number manually.

6. **Select other information as needed from these drop-down lists:**

   - **Case Issue**
   - **Status**
   - **Priority**
   - **Origin**
   - **Type**

   You can add selections to these fields by choosing Setup⇨Support.

7. **On the Interactions tab, in the Message field, enter the problem or question.**

8. **If you already have a response to the customer, enter it in the Reply field.**

   - To send this response to the customer, select the Send to Customer check box.

   - To note the response you've given over the phone or to make another note about the case (such as a message left), deselect the Send to Customer check box and select the Internal Only check box. Selecting the Internal Only check box keeps the response off the customer's view of the case in the Customer Center.

   - To send a private message about the case to another employee, select an employee in the Copy Employees field is also a good way.

   You can default all case records to either select the Send to Customer or the Internal Only check box by choosing Setup⇨Support⇨Support Preferences.

9. **Click the Save button.**

All e-mail messages are sent when you save the case record.

When you save a case, it's saved to the Cases list where support reps can keep track of open cases and manage the communication with customers, as needed, until each case is closed.

Managing the case queue

A support rep's biggest nightmare and best friend is the Cases list, which you can view from the Cases tab menu by choosing Customer Service➪Cases. It can be a big nightmare if it's full of unhappy customers, but it can be a best friend if it helps organize and sort the cases so that nothing slips through the cracks.

Assign cases

If your case rules and territories don't catch all the cases that come in, or if you haven't set the rules just yet, the first order of business is to get unassigned cases into the right hands. Consider these links:

✔ **Grab:** If a support rep sees a case that she thinks she can handle, she can simply click the Grab link, as shown in Figure 13-6, to open the case and automatically assign the case to herself. This is better than clicking the Edit link because it keeps everyone else from trying to answer the case at the same time.

✔ **Edit:** If you're not quite sure whether you want to grab a case and you need to see more details, click the Edit link next to a case and manually choose the right support rep for the job in the Assigned To field. If you need to continue working on the case, however, be sure to save the case and reopen it for editing so that others working in the list can see that it's been assigned.

Figure 13-6: Clicking the Grab link from the Cases list automatically assigns the case to you.

Edit | View	Number	Grab	Subject	Priority	Status	Product	Module	Assigned To	Incident Date	Last Msg. Date	Awaiting Support Reply
Edit | View	49	Grab	test for emailing employees	Medium	Not Started				5.5.2006 2:14 pm	5.5.2006 2:15 pm	Yes
Edit | View	50	Grab	fake case	Medium	Not Started				14.6.2006 9:56 am		No
Edit | View	53	Grab	test3 Case	Medium	Not Started				3.7.2006 5:37 pm		No
Edit | View	54	Grab	test4	Medium	Not Started				3.7.2006 5:50 pm		No
Edit | View	55	Grab	test5	Medium	Not Started				3.7.2006 5:51 pm		No
Edit | View	57	Grab	testCase1	Medium	Not Started				27.7.2006 8:45 am		No
Edit | View	58	Grab	testCase3	Medium	Not Started				27.7.2006 9:24 am	27.7.2006 9:25 am	Yes
Edit | View	59	Grab	inbound test	Medium	Not Started				27.7.2006 9:30 am	27.7.2006 9:30 am	Yes
Edit | View	60	Grab	testCase6	Medium	Not				27.7.2006 9:45	27.7.2006 9:45	Yes

Cases — Inline Editing [OFF]

| Stage | Not Closed | Assigned To | - All - | Awaiting Support Reply | - All - | Total Found: 18 |

Show Inactives ☐ Style Normal View Status Quick Sort [New] [Print] [Customize View] [Export - CSV]

Only support reps can grab cases or be selected in the Assigned To field. Administrators can designate an employee as a support rep on the Human Resources tab of the employee record, found by choosing Lists⇨Employees⇨Employees.

Efficient queue management

Some quick tips for efficiently managing the case queue include:

- ✔ Use the Stage drop-down list to filter which cases you see; for example, select Open to see only open cases, or choose Not Closed to see both open and escalated cases.

- ✔ If you have lots of cases coming in regularly, you can

  - • Create groups marked as support groups.

  - • Use rules and territories to automatically assign cases to specialty groups.

  - • Use the Assigned To drop-down list on the Cases list to view only cases for your group.

- ✔ Use the Awaiting Support Reply drop-down list to show only cases that you need to respond to and to filter all cases that are still open but waiting on more input from customers.

- ✔ Click column headings to sort the list using different criteria (such as by last message date or priority).

- ✔ Create a custom view for the Cases list by clicking the Customize View button.

Set preferences

You can also set a few very useful preferences for managing your Cases list and case workflow. You can set the following preferences on the General tab of the Support Preferences page on (from the Setup tab, under menu, choose Support⇨Support Preferences and choose the General tab):

- ✔ **To re-open closed cases when a customer adds a new message,** select the Messages Reopen Closed Cases check box on the General tab, in the Preferences section. This closes a case when you believe you've answered a customer's question and but allows the customer to write back.

- ✔ **To lock closed cases and prevent them from being re-opened,** select the Lock Closed Cases After Lockout Period check box on the General tab, in the Case Lockout section. Then enter the number of days a case can remain available for re-opening before it's locked in the Period (Days) field. This prevents customers from responding to an old case with a new problem.

- ✔ **To set defaults for case statuses,** select statuses on the General tab, in the Defaults section when cases are new, assigned, re-opened, escalated, and closed. You can create and rename statuses from the Setup tab menu by choosing Support⇨Case Statuses.

When you're working in the case queue, keep in mind how customer support reports work. Likewise, if you're using reports to gauge success, keep in mind your standard case workflow. For example, if you leave cases open until the customer has confirmed the resolution, your Open Case Analysis reports will have a much longer average time for open cases than if you closed the case with your response, before receiving the customer confirmation.

View Customer Service reports by choosing Reports⇨Customers Service. These reports are excellent tools for keeping an eagle-eye view of how cases are moving along and how efficient the customer service team is.

Escalating cases

When you don't know the answer, it's nice to have a safety net. It's also handy to have someone higher up take the heat (and provide some professional smooth talking) and support you if something has gone terribly awry and needs fixing immediately. The ability to escalate not only takes pressure off a support rep who's already done all he can, but it makes the customer feel as though the problem or request is being taken very seriously, even if there's no current resolution.

By default, cases can be escalated to any employee with a record in your account. However, Administrators can limit escalations to support reps from the Setup tab menu by choosing Support⇨Support Preferences. On the General tab, select the Escalate to Support Reps Only check box.

To escalate a case:

1. **Choose Lists⇨Support⇨Cases.**
2. **Click the Edit link next to the case to escalate.**

    The Case record appears.

3. **In the Status drop-down list, change the case record to Escalated.**
4. **Click the Escalate tab.**
5. **In the Escalation Message field, add a brief description of the problem and what you need help with.**

    Select the person receiving should handle the escalated case from having to review all past messages and help her know why you are calling on her specifically.

6. **On the Escalate To tab, under Escalate, choose the employee who will handle this case.**

7. Click the Add button.

Be sure that an e-mail address fills in for this employee, or she may not be notified that a case has been escalated to her.

8. Click the Save button.

This case is now escalated, and your message is sent to the person the case has been escalated to. The case remains assigned to the original support rep, however, who can make sure the case is resolved.

You can set up escalation rules and territories to escalate cases automatically when they meet certain criteria, just as you can for case assignments. You may want to escalate cases because it's been a certain amount of time since the case was created or modified, for example.

You set up rules about escalation by choosing Setup⇨Support⇨Set Up Escalation Rules⇨New. Then, set up rules for escalating cases following the same steps as in the earlier section, "Creating a case." Choose Setup⇨ Support⇨Manage Escalation Assignment⇨New to set up assignments following the same steps as setting up territories in the earlier section, "Creating case rules and territories."

Part V
Selling Online

"Yes, I know how to query information from the program, but what if I just want to leak it instead?"

In this part . . .

It's no secret that an online presence is essential to running a successful business today. Whether your site simply tells people where to find you and what you do, or is a fully operational Web store, your site is one of the most cost-effective methods you can use to reach your market and find new leads and customers. Luckily, with NetSuite, you have the option to build a site completely integrated with your account or use a site you already have and integrate it with your NetSuite account. Either way, you can integrate the Web front-end of your business with your back office accounting seamlessly because like everything NetSuite, it is one sweet package.

Part V helps you decide which type of site is best for you in NetSuite, how to get it to match your company image, how to get your items and information published, and finally, how to maximize your exposure.

Chapter 14

Planning Your Web Site

In This Chapter

▶ Choosing your site type

▶ Using multiple Web sites

▶ Creating your Web address

*W*hen you're comfortable managing inventory, handling your accounting, and fulfilling sales orders, you're ready to optimize your company's selling potential on the Web. Even if you don't manage inventory, accounting, or orders, creating an informative site can increase your business exposure.

With NetSuite, whether you want to build a new site from scratch or use the near-perfect site you already have, you can integrate with the inventory, pricing, and customer purchase information you have in your NetSuite account. What better way to tailor your site than to use the valuable information you already have?

To follow the instructions in this chapter, you need a standard role like Ecommerce Manager or Administrator.

Surfing NetSuite Site Options

Sure you want your site to be beautiful and ready for the world in a record amount of time, but the more you can plan before publishing, the better your site will be.

Start by making some of the basic decisions that define where you'll go next in NetSuite. First, you must choose which type of site to use:

✔ NetSuite site

✔ Hosted site

✔ Combination site

✔ External catalog site integrated using the Web Site Developer's Kit (WSDK)

Table 14-1 gives you a preview of the options available with each type of site. The following sections explain each.

Table 14-1	Capabilities of Each Site Option			
Option	*NetSuite*	*Hosted*	*Combination*	*WSDK*
Integrate with NetSuite items	Yes	No	Yes	Yes
Integrate with NetSuite orders	Yes	No	Yes	Yes
Built-in themes/templates available	Yes	No	Yes	No
Customizable	Yes	Yes	Yes	No
Staging environment	No	Yes	Yes	No
Search forms	Yes	No	Yes	No
Lead capture	Yes	No	Yes	Yes
Usable with style sheet	Yes	Yes	Yes	No
Reports on page hits	Yes	Yes	Yes	No
Reports on shopping activity, such as item views	Yes	No	Yes	No

NetSuite sites

If you want a site (with the items and information in your account) that automatically integrates and is highly customizable, a NetSuite site is the best method for you. It's probably also the quickest type of site to set up.

The basics

With a NetSuite site, all you have to do is this:

- ✔ Enter your Item records with information on the Store tab.
- ✔ Set them to show online.
- ✔ Place them in a site category.
- ✔ Choose settings for your Web address and Home page.

  You can be live with a basic site within minutes, as shown in Figure 14-1.

Chapter 15 explains how to set up items in detail. In terms of customization for NetSuite site, you can rename your tabs and categories, add images and information, and change the site theme and color palette for a unique look and feel.

Site Builder module

If you use the Site Builder module, you can create custom site themes. Custom site themes provided by NetSuite allow you to build and save a completely custom and dynamic site within NetSuite. You can also tweak the default site themes to understand how themes are built, or to keep some aspects of a site while changing others. Chapter 16 describes how to use themes to change the look of your site.

The Site Builder module is an add-on for NetSuite. If you don't have Site Builder installed and would like to get it, contact your NetSuite sales person. The Site Builder module includes features such as Advanced Site Customization (which gives you the aforementioned ability to create custom themes), the ability to create external catalog sites, Advanced Web Search, and Google Checkout Integration.

Figure 14-1:
A custom and dynamic NetSuite site.

Pros of a NetSuite site

The biggest advantages to creating a NetSuite site follow:

✔ You don't have to build a site from scratch; the site is created using your data and preferences.

✔ You don't have to use HTML tags to enjoy integration with your account when items are updated or sold.

✔ The Web Site Setup Assistant makes creating the site simple; the Web Site Content Manager makes updating the site easy.

✔ A NetSuite site is the fastest to set up.

✔ Changes to the Web site are immediately published online.

Cons of a NetSuite site

The disadvantages to creating a NetSuite site follow:

✔ You can't fully customize it the way you can an HTML site.

✔ To customize the layout, you must know how site themes work as templates.

✔ The Web site is somewhat limited by the options available in NetSuite as preferences or site additions.

✔ You can preview after you change the site, but you can't preview the site while you edit.

Hosted sites

If you've already designed your HTML Web site, NetSuite can host it. Hosting your site with NetSuite is easy and lets you consolidate your site information; this way you also don't pay for third-party hosting. Also, it can make things a little easier should you decide to integrate some aspects of your site with your account using a combination site. (See the following section, "Combination sites," for more information.)

When you host your site in NetSuite, you can call the information available in item records, but you must use HTML attribute tags provided by NetSuite. Manually entering the tags and information for each item record can be a long and tedious process, so avoid it if you want to sell several items online. Instead, you can use a combination of a hosted site and an HTML site.

Pros of a hosted site

The advantages of a hosted site are

- ✓ A staging environment is available.
- ✓ A hosted site allows you to use an existing HTML site without changing it.
- ✓ A hosted site saves you the expense of third-party hosting.

Cons of a hosted site

The disadvantages of a hosted site are

- ✓ No automatic updates are made to the site when account information changes (unless you use NetSuite tags).
- ✓ You can't use NetSuite's shopping cart or online purchasing options on a hosted site.
- ✓ You can't gather information and create records for leads and customers when using a hosted site.
- ✓ You have to do a lot of manual setup if you haven't already created HTML pages or used NetSuite tags to integrate your item information.

Combination sites

If you like the integration and easy setup of a NetSuite site but want the familiarity of your current site's home page, a combination site provides the best of both worlds. Most people choose this option for their sites. Combination sites typically consist of a hosted HTML home page and NetSuite-generated inventory and checkout pages for integrated shopping.

Combination sites (see Figure 14-2) work by allowing you to host an HTML page as part of a NetSuite site. For example, if your complete site has the pages Home, Women, Men, Men, Children, and Sale, you can use NetSuite tabs with categories and items for the Women, Men, Men, and Children tabs and host HTML pages on the Home and Sale pages.

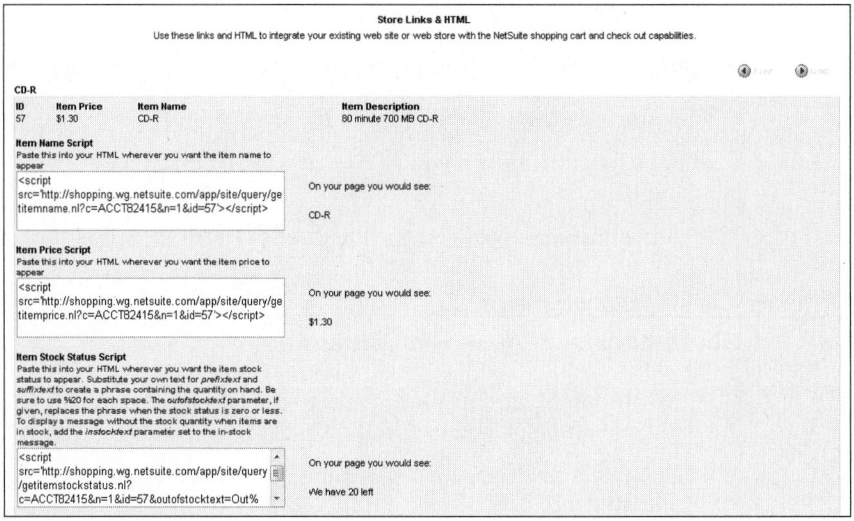

Figure 14-2:
A combination site has both NetSuite and HTML elements.

Pros of a combination site

The advantages to a combination site are

- You can mix custom HTML (see Figure 14-3) and NetSuite-generated pages.

- Item pages are automatically updated with changes while hosted pages remain static until you upload a new version.

Cons of a combination site

The disadvantages to a combination site are

- You can't stage and preview the entire site until it's live.

- You must take extra care to ensure a consistent look and feel across different page types.

Hosted Home tab   NetSuite tabs

Figure 14-3:
Hosting
your Web
site with
NetSuite.

External catalog sites with the WSDK

External catalog sites are a good option if you prefer to use a shopping site other than NetSuite but still want to integrate your items and orders with your NetSuite account. If you use the External Catalog Site feature, NetSuite provides a Web Site Developer's Kit (WSDK) that includes all the code you need to sell your items in another site.

The WSDK allows you to add scripts to your existing site to access NetSuite item information and the NetSuite shopping cart and checkout. You can then tell NetSuite what links to use to return to the shopping pages for a seamless look.

Pros of an external site

The advantages to using an external site are

- You're familiar with the site and system used.
- You can use your existing site and Web store.
- Item name, descriptions, and prices are automatically updated.
- It's relatively easy to convert an existing store to integrate with NetSuite's shopping cart and checkout.
- Web store orders are automatically incorporated into your accounting system, which is, naturally, NetSuite.

Cons of an external site

The disadvantages to using an external site are few, but here goes:

- ✔ Item pages may look different from checkout and shopping cart.
- ✔ No NetSuite reports are available on item views.

Spinning Multiple Web Sites

If one Web site isn't enough for you, you can use the Multiple Web Sites feature and run one or more of each kind of Web site, all integrated with your account data. This is useful if you want to operate one Web site for retail shoppers and one for wholesalers, or if you have one consolidated company with multiple brand identities.

When you have multiple sites, you can do the following:

- ✔ Have a different name, logo, look, and navigation for each site.
- ✔ Choose which items appear in each site by publishing items to a category set.

The Multiple Web Sites feature is part of the Multi-Site module, an add-on to NetSuite.

When you use multiple sites, your item names and descriptions, shipping methods, payment methods, and pricing information are the same for all sites. However, each site has its own shopping cart, checkout, and set of tabs and categories. When the same person buys from more than one store, that customer may create duplicate customer records.

If you enable this feature, you need to name and save a site record for each site you plan to publish before setting up your Web address and domain in NetSuite: From the Setup tab menu, choose Web Site➪Set Up Web Site➪New. You don't have to set any preferences right now; you just need to name each site so you can associate each site with a domain. For more information on setting up domains, see the following section, "Setting Up Your Web Address."

Setting Up Your Web Address

Regardless of which type you choose, every site needs its own Web address. You may want to wait to have your domain address show your NetSuite site until the site is ready for debut, but it's a good idea to get the domain name set up in your NetSuite account now.

Mastering your domain

If this is your first time setting up a Web site, the domain name is basically the same thing as the *URL* (Web address). For example, NetSuite's domain name is netsuite.com. Domain names are managed and sold by domain name registrars (DNRs), and are generally inexpensive, depending on the name you're after.

If you don't already have a domain name for your Web site, but you want to buy one, take these steps:

1. **Search for and choose a DNR online.**

2. **Using the DNR's site, search for available domain names and purchase one or more names.**

If you don't want to buy a domain name, you can skip this step and use a URL generated by NetSuite.

Setting up your domain name in NetSuite

Domain names can also be set up in NetSuite to have special promotional URLs for sales or marketing campaigns. You can set up multiple domains and specify the purpose for each. If you have more than one domain for the same Web site, you can set the primary domain for the site and set up the others as redirect URLs, so if visitors use a different domain to reach the site, the address automatically changes to the primary domain name.

To set up your domain name in NetSuite, ask your Administrator to follow these steps:

1. **From the Setup tab menu, choose Web Site⇨Domains.**

   The Set Up Domains page appears.

2. **In the Domain Name column, enter your registered domain name.**

3. **In the Hosted As column, choose from the drop-down list what this domain will be used for:**

   - **Web Store:** If you're setting up a NetSuite-generated site or a combination site.

   - **Hosted Web Page:** If you're setting up a site hosted in NetSuite.

   - **Redirect URL:** To forward this URL to your primary domain. For example, you may have mydomain.com set as a redirect URL to go to www.mydomain.com.

If you use the Multiple Web Sites add-on feature, you can set up a separate domain name for each site. However, you must first create a record for your site to assign a domain name to it:

1. From the Setup tab menu, choose Web Site⇨Set Up Web Site.

2. Enter an external and internal name for the site.

3. In the Web Site column, select the name of the site tied to that domain name.

4. **In the HTML Hosting Root column, choose one of the following:**

   • **Live Hosting Files**

   • **Staging Hosting Files**

If you're setting up a hosted site, the HTML Hosting Root refers to the folder where your site files are stored in the File Cabinet. You can upload files to the File Cabinet (to add to your site, for example). From the Home tab menu, choose File Cabinet.

You can define separate sites for your live and staged sites. If a domain is only used for a staged site, select Staging Hosting Files from the drop-down list, and store your staged HTML files in the Staging Hosted Files folder in the File Cabinet.

5. **If you're setting up a hosted Web page, choose the file from the File Cabinet in the Home Page column.**

6. **If you're setting up a Redirect URL, enter the primary domain to redirect to in the Redirect URL column.**

   For example, if this line is for mydomain.com set as a Redirect URL, enter **www.mydomain.com** here.

7. **In the Not-Found Page column, select the file from the File Cabinet that should show if a Page Not Found error occurs in your domain.**

   Your home page is used by default.

8. **Click the Add button.**

   Repeat Steps 2–8 to add as many domains as you have registered.

9. **When you finish, click the Save button.**

You can also use the Set Up Domains page to redirect traffic (including search engine crawlers) from inactive pages to new pages. For more information on redirecting Web sites, see Chapter 18.

When you're ready for your site to go live, point your domain to NetSuite. Do this using a CNAME redirect to shopping.netsuite.com from within your account with your domain provider. Contact your domain provider for further details about setting up a CNAME redirect.

If your domain name is added and your site has been set up with your domain provider to point to shopping.netsuite.com, you're ready to select your primary Web address. If you're setting up a NetSuite-generated site, this is the first step of the Web Site Setup Assistant, which you access by clicking Setup⇨Web Site⇨Web Site Setup Assistant. You can also select the primary domain on the Set Up Web Site page.

Setting your primary site URL

Administrators can follow these steps to set your primary site URL:

1. **From the Setup tab menu, choose Web Site⇨Set Up Web Site.**

2. **If you have multiple Web sites, click the Edit link next to the site you need to work with.**

3. **On the Setup tab, in the Web Site Basics section, select the main domain for your site from the Primary Site URL drop-down list.**

   Even if site visitors use an alternate URL to reach your site, this URL shows in the browser's address bar after the site opens.

4. **If you don't have a registered domain and want to use one generated by NetSuite, enter your site name as one word after http://shopping. netsuite.com/.**

   For example, if your site name is Roger's Pet Supplies, you may enter **rogerspetsupplies**, making your URL http://shopping.netsuite.com/ rogerspetsupplies.

5. **Click the Save button.**

Chapter 15

Adding Content to Your Site

*W*hen you use either a NetSuite-generated site or a combination of a NetSuite site and a hosted site, you can easily add tabs, categories, items, and information. You can use tabs as the separate pages in your site, and use categories to organize those pages. Then all you have to do is insert your items, and your pages are ready for customers!

To follow the procedures outlined in this chapter, you need to have a role of Ecommerce Manager or, where specified, Administrator.

Knowing a Site from a Store in the Ground

Most of the time, the terms *site* and *store* are used interchangeably. However, in NetSuite there is a difference:

- ✔ **Site:** Can display information, items, and images but doesn't allow purchasing. Requires the Web Site features.

- ✔ **Store:** Can display information, items, and images and includes a shopping cart and checkout for purchasing. Requires both the Web Site and Web Store features.

You can also decide the scope of what a site or store should display.

1. **From the Setup tab menu, choose Web Site⇨Set Up Web Site.**

2. **On the Setup tab, select one of the following from the Web Site Scope drop-down list**

   You're right, that's quite a few setup and Web site directions:

   - **Information Only:** Displays only information and images. For details on adding information, see "Being the Town Crier: Publishing Information" later in this chapter.

   - **Information and Catalog:** Displays information and items that you attach to categories but the items don't show prices.

   - **Information and Catalog, with Pricing:** Displays information, items, and prices but doesn't allow items to be purchased.

   - **Full Web Store:** Displays information, items, and prices; the items can be ordered and paid for via a checkout page.

Attempting to Organize

In NetSuite pages are called *tabs,* and each subsection that organizes a tab is called a *category.* For example, if Laura's Linens has tabs for Bed, Bath, and Windows, the Bed tab may have the categories Sheets, Bed Skirts, Pillow Cases, and Duvets.

With themes, your tab access links can look like the tabs of a filing cabinet, like buttons, or like regular links. Themes are discussed in more detail in Chapter 17.

Content Manager

The quickest and easiest way to manage your tabs, categories, and items is using the Web Site Content Manager. Ecommerce managers can access the Content Manager from the Web Site tab menu by choosing Publishing⇨ Content Manager. Figure 15-1 shows how you can update or add site pages quickly using the Content Manager.

The Content Manager is an option for adding and managing your site's content. You can easily use the New bar to add tabs, categories, items, information items, and forms. Use the frame to the left side of the page to view the organization and hierarchy. Click the + sign next to a tab or category to view the categories, items, information items, and forms published to that tab or category.

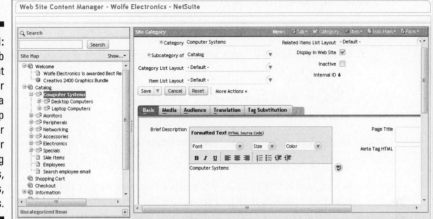

Figure 15-1:
The Web
Site Content
Manager
offers a
one-stop
shop for
adding or
updating
tabs,
categories,
and items.

You can also view your Web site content from the standard locations in
NetSuite in full screen view. The Content Manager is simply a handy place to
access all of these pages from one location.

Use these steps to access these pages outside of the Content Manager:

- **Tabs:** Web Site tab menu⇨Publishing⇨Tabs

- **Categories:** Web Site tab menu⇨ Publishing⇨Categories

- **Items:** Web Site tab menu⇨Publishing⇨Items

- **Information Items:** Web Site tab menu⇨Publishing⇨Information Items

- **Forms:** Web Site tab menu⇨Publishing⇨Publish Forms

Keeping tabs on things

Tabs represent your site pages, such as your home page, product pages, and
checkout. You can create as many tabs as you need to organize your information and items, but we recommend roughly two to four in addition to the
Home tab and Checkout tab.

You can create two types of tabs in NetSuite:

- **Presentation:** You can add categories, information, and items to presentation tabs.

- **Hosted:** You can display HTML pages from your File Cabinet on hosted tabs.

You create combination sites by using a mixture of these types of tabs.

Create a presentation tab

To create a presentation tab:

1. **From the Web Site tab menu, choose Publishing⇨Tabs⇨New.**

   The New Tab page appears.

2. **Click the New Presentation Tab link.**

   The Presentation Tab record appears.

3. **In the Label field, type the page name.**

   This name appears on the tab or link used to access this page.

4. **If you use the Multiple Web Sites feature, select the site where you want to publish this tab from the Web Site drop-down list.**

5. **Select a category from the Category List Layout drop-down list.**

   You're choosing design for the lists on your page. For more information on creating layouts, see Chapter 17.

6. **Select the alignment from the Welcome Page Portlet Alignment drop-down list.**

   Each presentation tab has a portlet containing links to its categories on the home page. This portlet appears only if you use a NetSuite-generated home page and not a hosted home page.

7. **Type text in the Greeting and Message fields.**

   The greeting serves as a heading for the tab, and the message is introductory text for the tab, which shows just under the greeting.

8. **Type a title in the Page Title field.**

   The page title is the name of the page when search engines return it, and the name shows at the top of the browser window when the page is being viewed.

9. **In the URL Component field, enter a name for this page as one lowercase word.**

   The URL Component is added to the URL when site visitors view this page. Using URL Components can help with search engine optimization. Example: www.netsuite.com/products.

   The URL Component field is displayed only after you turn on the Descriptive URLs feature.

10. **Enter meta tag information in the Meta Tag HTML field.**

    Adding the meta tags creates search engine optimization. Meta tag HTML contains a description and keywords, entered in the following format:

```
<meta name="description" content="This is the
description for this page">
<meta name="keywords" content="keyword, keyword,
keyword">
```

11. **Select the Display in Web Site check box.**

Selecting this check box publishes this page to all visitors to your site. To restrict your site to a specific audience, deselect this check box and choose who should see the site on the Audience tab.

12. **Click Save.**

Create a hosted tab

To create a hosted tab:

1. **From the Web Site tab menu, choose Publishing⇨Tabs⇨New.**

   The New Tab page appears.

2. **Click the New Hosted Tab link.**

   The Hosted Tab record appears.

3. **In the Label field, enter the page name.**

   This name appears on the tab or link used to access this page.

4. **If you use the Multiple Web Sites feature, select the site where you want to publish this tab from the Web Site drop-down list.**

5. **Enter a link for the page this tab should show:**

   - *To have this tab display another site with a separate URL, enter the URL in the Link URL field.*

     Entering a URL makes the tab label a link to the page. The full page opens in the same browser window, so be sure to put links back to the site on the page or add **'target=_blank'** to the end of the URL to open the page in a new window.

   - *To have this tab show an HTML file from your File Cabinet, select the file from the Web Site Page drop-down list.*

     If you choose this option, the page displays within your site, retaining the site's header, sidebars, and footer.

6. **Select the Display in Web Site check box.**

   Selecting this check box publishes this page to all visitors to your site. To restrict your site to a specific audience, deselect this check box and choose who should see the site on the Audience tab.

7. **Click the Save button.**

Conquering with categories

Categories help further organize tabs by dividing items into groups that make sense to your customers. Categories can be subcategories of other categories or subcategories of tabs, allowing you to set up a custom hierarchy.

To create a category:

1. **From the Web Site tab menu, choose Publishing⇨Categories⇨New.**

   The Site Category page appears.

2. **Enter a name for the category in the Category field.**

   This name shows in your Web site.

3. **(Optional) If you use the Multiple Web Sites feature, select the site this category should show from the Site drop-down list.**

   Selecting a site doesn't publish the category to that site but simply filters the list of tabs and categories available in the Subcategory Of drop-down list.

4. **From the Subcategory Of drop-down list, select the tab or category where this category should show.**

   For example, if this category is Short Sleeve Shirts, select the Shirts category.

5. **Select any custom layouts from the Category List Layout drop-down list.**

   This decides how lists of categories or items should show in this category. For more information on creating layouts, see Chapter 17.

6. **Select the Display in Web Site check box.**

   Selecting this check box publishes this category to all visitors who can see the category or tab it's published in. To restrict this category to a specific audience, deselect this check box and choose who should see it on the Audience tab.

7. **On the Basic tab, enter text in the Brief Description and Detailed Description fields.**

   If you need to know more about what to enter in a certain field, click the name of the field. The areas where descriptions show in the Web site are shown in Figure 15-2.

8. **At the bottom of the Basic tab, click the Item field double arrow.**

   The double arrow icon brings up List option.

Category name

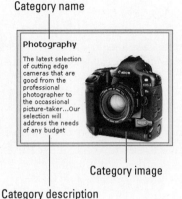

Figure 15-2:
The cat-
egory
name, brief
description,
and thumb-
nail image.

Photography

The latest selection of cutting edge cameras that are good from the professional photographer to the occassional picture-taker...Our selection will address the needs of any budget

Category image

Category description

9. **Click List.**

   The Choose Item list opens.

10. **Select the item from the list.**

11. **Click the Add button for each item that should show in this category.**

   You can quickly add multiple items:

   a. Above the Item field, click the Add Multiple.

   A window appears with items in the left pane.

   b. Click the items you want to add.

   They're copied to the right pane.

   c. Click the Done button.

   Back on the Item record, items must have the Display in Web Site check box selected and be assigned to a displaying category to be published in a site or store.

12. **On the Media tab, click the double arrow beside the Thumbnail or Image field.**

13. **Choose List to open the Choose Image list.**

14. **Select the thumbnails or images you want to show with this category.**

   The thumbnail image shows with this category when it's in a list of other categories. The regular image shows when visitors view the category. You can set up automatic image resizing from the Setup tab menu by choosing Other Setup⇨Image Resizing.

15. **Click the Save button.**

Debuting Items

To read more about offering downloadable files in your site either for purchase or for free, go to **http://www.dummies.com/go/netsuitefd**.

If you plan to show or sell inventory or service items in your Web site, you
need to get them gussied up for their debut. You do these things on the item
record tabs:

- ✔ Enter a formatted description of the item. You can use the text editor
  right on the page to specify font, size, color, alignment, and more. (If you
  prefer, you can enter the description formatted as HTML.)
- ✔ Set up images of the item.
- ✔ Set up online pricing.

Create or edit item records this way:

1. **From the Web Site tab menu choose Publishing⇨Items.**

2. **Click the Edit link next to the item you want online.**

3. **Select the Display in Web Site check box.**

4. **Select a category from the Site Category drop-down list.**

   The list is at the bottom of the Store tab, and selecting a category makes
   an item available online.

Store name and description

On an item record's Store tab, you can enter an item name and description
that show only in the Web site.

- ✔ **Store Display Name:** The store name for an item is the name of the item
  in the Web site. When the item is in a list, clicking the store display
  name opens the page for the item, where the description and images are
  displayed.

- ✔ **Store Description:** The store description shows under the item's store
  name when the item is in a list, as shown in Figure 15-3. It's best to keep
  this description brief but enticing to customers.

- ✔ **Detailed Description:** The detailed description shows on the item page
  when a visitor clicks the item's store name to view more information.
  This description can be entered in HTML or by using the rich text editor
  in Internet Explorer, and can be as long as you need it to be.

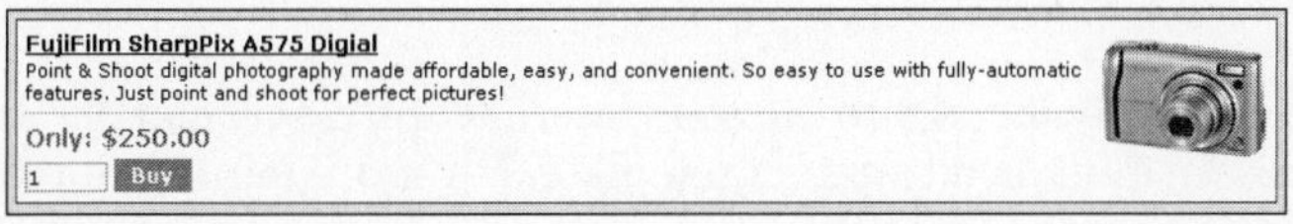

Figure 15-3:
The item's
store name
and store
description
show with
the item
thumbnail
image in
lists.

Item images

Before you can associate an image with an item, you must first upload the image to the File Cabinet. If you have many images for several items, you can save them in a .zip file and upload them to the File Cabinet.

To upload a .zip file of images to the File Cabinet, follow along:

1. **Click the Documents tab.**

   The File Cabinet appears.

2. **Click the Images folder.**

   The Images folder opens.

3. **If needed, click the New Folder button to create a new folder for your site images.**

   The new folder opens, where you can enter a folder name and click Save.

4. **Click the Advanced Add button.**

   The Advanced Add page appears.

5. **Click the Browse button.**

   The Browse button is next to the Zip Archive to Add field.

6. **In the Choose File dialog box, browse to and double-click your file.**

7. **Select the Unzip Files check box.**

8. **Select the Make All Files Available without Login check box.**

   This ensures that visitors in your site can see the images.

9. **If you already uploaded images, select the Overwrite Files with Same Name check box.**

10. **Click the Add button.**

    The File Cabinet appears with the unzipped files.

Attaching images to items

Each item can have one thumbnail and one full-size image displayed in the Web site. You can upload two separate images for each or use one image with automatic resizing.

If you use the Advanced Site Customization feature, you can display multiple images for an item using an item template. For more information on item templates, see Chapter 17.

To attach an image to an item, do this:

1. **From the Web Site tab menu choose Publishing⇨Items.**

   The Items list appears.

2. **Click the Edit link next to the item that needs an image.**

   The item record appears.

3. **On the Store tab, click the Item Display Thumbnail Image field double arrow.**

   Alternatively, click the double arrow beside the field, click the List icon, and then, from the file cabinet, select the image from the File Cabinet.

4. **Type the image name.**

5. **On the Store tab, click the Item Display Image field.**

   Alternatively, click the double-arrow beside the field, click List, and then select the image from the File Cabinet.

6. **Type the image name.**

7. **Click the Save button.**

   This image appears with the item in the Web site.

Resizing images

You may want to set up automatic resizing of your images. Automatic resizing allows you to set one size for images when they're shown as thumbnails or full size in different areas of your site. This prevents you from having to upload the same image in different sizes.

Digital photos larger than 5 megapixels (2584 × 1936 pixels or larger) can't be resized and won't be displayed in your site if you enable resizing. If your images are that large or larger, use a photo-editing program to resize or crop.

You can set up automatic resizing the following way:

1. **From the Setup tab menu choose Other Setup⇨Image Resizing.**

   The Image Resizing Setup page appears.

2. **In the Enabled column, select the check box next to each type of image that should have an automated size:**

   - Dense List Drilldown Image: Applies to images displayed when an item in a dense (one-column) list with an image is clicked.

   - Dense List Image: Applies to images displayed with items in dense lists.

   - Employee Image: Applies to images that show with employee names when an employee directory is published.

   - Web Site Category Thumbnail Image: Applies to category images for categories or subcategories in a list.

   - Web Site Drilldown Image: Applies to images displayed when a thumbnail image is clicked or when customers view item details.

   - Web Site Featured Item Thumbnail Image: Applies to images for items featured on the Welcome tab.

   - Web Site Related Item Thumbnail Image: Applies to item images in lists of related items.

   - Web Site Thumbnail Image: Applies to images displayed in graphical lists.

3. **Enter the maximum pixel height in the Maximum Height field.**

   Do so for each type of image.

4. **Enter the maximum pixel width in the Maximum Width field.**

   Do so for each type of image.

 Images are resized to meet either the maximum height _or_ the maximum width but not both. Keep the aspect ratio for the resized image the same as the original image or you'll end up with a distorted resized image. For example, if the original image was 800 pixels tall by 600 pixels wide, good thumbnail sizes are 80×60 and 160×120.

5. **Click the Save button.**

   Images are sized to meet your maximums for each enabled image display type.

Pricing it right online

For your site items, you can set up a variety of pricing options that depend on the customer currently logged in, a current sale, or a promotion code. For example, say a group of customers has been with your company through thick and thin. They've supported you since it started, and they're committed to you. Because they're your friends and supporters, you usually offer them a 10-percent discount on their purchases. Or perhaps you're starting a

Web site for the first time in conjunction with a physical location and want to drum up online sales. You decide to offer 5 percent off all online sales.

Online and customer-specific pricing

Using the Multiple Prices feature, you can set up multiple prices for a single item, including an online price. For an overview of this feature and the Quantity Pricing feature, see Chapter 7.

In the Web site, pricing is shown for the online price on the Pricing tab of item records. Customers assigned to a price level or a pricing group must log in to your site to view the special pricing.

Promotion and coupon codes

You can use promotion codes to offer discounts on orders online. For more information on creating promotion codes, see Chapter 11.

Here are a few suggestions for using promotion codes with a Web store:

- ✔ Get the word out on the promotion code with a marketing campaign. Letter and other print campaigns can print the promotion code, and e-mail campaigns can include links that tie in the promotion code.
- ✔ Include the promotion code in links on strategic referring sites, such as partner sites.
- ✔ Post instructions for using the promotion code on your site or through a Twitter or Facebook post. For example, "25% Off Through October 16th! Use Promotion Code BACK2SCHOOL at Checkout!"

To embed a promotion code in a URL, use the following format:

www.mysite.com/products?promocode=PROMOCODE

For example, where a promotion code is FREEACCT, the code would look like this:

www.netsuite.com?promocode=FREEACCT.

(Sorry to get your hopes up, but no, that particular promotion code doesn't work for your NetSuite account.)

To pass the promotion code discount through to your site, make sure the Pass URL Promotion Code to Checkout check box is selected. From the Setup tab menu choose Web Site⇨Set Up Web Site and select the Shopping tab.

When a happy site visitor clicks the link to visit your site, the promotion code is automatically applied when she checks out, as shown in Figure 15-4. (Site visitors who come directly, rather than through an e-mail link, will have to enter the promotion code; those who click an e-mail link with an embedded promotion code are lucky because a simple click on the link applies the promotion for them.)

Figure 15-4: Customers enter promotion codes in the Coupon Code field at checkout.

*Register ▸ Address ▸ Shipping ▸ Payment ▸ **Review & Submit***

Review and Submit Your Order

Your Shipping Address
Sample Customer
123 Main Street
Purchase, CA 12345
United States
[Change]

Your Billing Address
Sample Customer
123 Main Street
Purchase, CA 12345
United States
[Change]

Shipping Method
○ UPS 2nd Day Air AM®
○ UPS Next Day Air
◉ FedEx Express Overnight – $32.50
○ Shipping Weight Table
○ UPS Ground

Payment Method
Visa
*************4444
Exp: 11 / 2010
[Change]

Coupon Code [FALLPROMO25] [Apply]
If you have a coupon or promotion code, enter it here

Gift Certificate [   ] [Apply]
If you have a gift certificate, enter it here

Delivery Instructions [   ]

Associating related items

Showing a list of related items on an item page can raise sales by helping customers find the correct item if the item they are viewing is not quite right and by suggesting additional items, such as accessories.

You can relate items in your Web site:

✔ Manually relate one or more items to an item on the item record.

✔ Create a related items category to group related items together.

✔ Use the Upsell Manager to automatically relate items that are purchased together. (For more information on the Upsell Manager, see Chapter 11.)

To create a group of related items to attach to an item record, make a related items category: From the Setup tab menu choose Web Site⇨Setup Tasks⇨ Related Item Categories⇨New. Related items category groups allow you to create a set of items with similar characteristics that can quickly be associated with each item record in the group.

To relate an item or related item group to another item manually:

1. **From the Web Site tab menu, choose Publishing⇨Items.**

   The Items list appears.

2. **Click the Edit link next to an item.**

   The item record appears.

3. **On the Related Items tab, enter a description in the Related Items Description field.**

   This description shows above the list of related items. You can write something such as, "You may also like . . ."

4. **On the Related Items tab, select an item from the Related Item drop-down list.**

5. **Click the Add button for each item and category related to this item.**

   Click the Add Multiple button to add several items or groups quickly.

6. **Click the Save button.**

Complete these steps for each item that should be related to other items. When all items are related, decide where the related item lists should display.

To set display options for related items, take these steps:

1. **From the Setup tab menu choose Web Site⇨Set Up Web Site.**

   The Set Up Web Site page appears.

2. **Select one of the following from the Items to Upsell drop-down list (on the Upsell tab):**

   • **Show Only Upsell Items:** Select to show only automatically gener- ated related items based on what other customers have purchased with the item.

   • **Show Only Related Items:** Select to show only related items and related items groups selected on the Item record. If you choose this option, an item must have items selected on the Related Items tab of the item record for anything to show.

   • **Show Related Items First and Upsell Items Next:** Select to list related items specified on the item record before automatically correlated (upsell) items based on customer purchases.

   • **Show Upsell Items First and Related Items Next:** Select to list automatically correlated (upsell) items before related items selected on the item record.

   The option you select from the Items to Upsell drop-down list applies to items that show on item pages, under the description, as shown in Figure 15-5.

3. **In the Items to Upsell in Cart drop-down list, select from the same list of options described in Step 2.**

   This option applies to the list of items that can show under the shopping cart. The upsell and related items listed on the cart are based on the items that have been added to the cart.

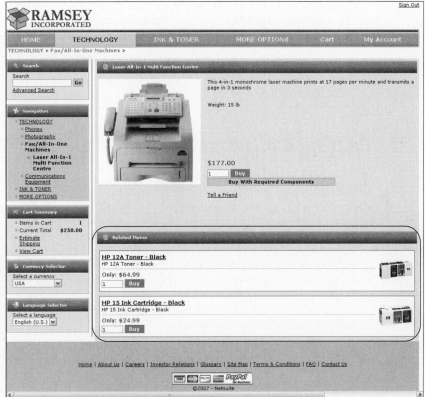

Figure 15-5:
Related
items and
upsell items
listed on
an item
description
page.

4. **In the Upsell field, enter a brief description or title that should show above automatically suggested items.**

    For example, you may enter "Customers who bought this also liked:".

5. **In the Related Items field, enter a brief description that should show above related items selected on the item record.**

6. **In the Display Minimums section, set preferences for the upsell items that should show with items and in the shopping cart.**

    Limit the number of upsell items that can show by using these settings:

    • *Minimum Correlation field:* The *correlation* is the percentage items are bought together. Enter the minimum percentage required to show the related item(s).

    • *Minimum Lift field:* The *lift* measures the amount an item is purchased with another item compared to how often it's purchased alone. A higher lift means a better correlation. Enter the minimum lift required to show the related item(s).

- *Minimum Count field:* The *count* is the number of customers who have bought both of the items. Enter the minimum count required to show the related item(s).

7. **Click Save.**

Featured or on-sale items

When you have items on sale (or items that you really want to sell), you can feature them on your Home page. This gives the items high visibility for all site traffic, making them more likely to sell. Stick to just a few feature items on your Home page. This accentuates the items and keeps site visitors from having to scroll too much.

When you feature an item, the store description and featured description are added to the Home page. If there's no featured description, the store's detailed description is used.

To feature an item, follow these steps:

1. **Select the Featured Item check box on the Specials tab of the item record.**

2. **Enter a description in the Featured Description field.**

When you feature an item, the item is added to a Specials category automatically. The Specials category lives in a place depending on how old your account is and how it's been customized. If you feature an item, make sure the Specials category is showing on a published tab.

To feature an item, select the On Special check box and enter a description in the Specials Description field (on the Specials stab of the Item record).

You can change the location of the Specials category and rename it to something like Clearance or On Sale at Lists⇨Web Site⇨Categories.

Mass updates are quite handy when you want to feature a group of items or put several items on sale. To search for items that need to be featured or placed on special and quickly update them all, go to Lists⇨Mass Update⇨Mass Updates. On the page that appears, click the General Updates link, and click the link for the type of item that needs updating, such as Inventory Item.

To quickly place items on sale, follow along:

1. **From the Lists tab menu choose Mass Update⇨Mass Updates.**

    The Mass Update page appears.

2. **Click the Items link.**

3. **Click the Update Item Prices link.**

4. **Choose from the Price Level drop-down list.**

5. **Enter a positive or negative dollar amount or percentage change in the Amount field.**

6. **On the Criteria tab, set your criteria for the items that should get this price change.**

Being the Town Crier: Publishing Information

Sometimes you want to send a message to your customers from your Web site. You can do this with *information items,* which let you publish formatted text or text snippets with images (in much the same way that you publish items). You can publish information items to any category, and they can accept HTML code.

To create and publish an information item:

1. **From the Website tab menu choose Publishing⇨Information Items⇨ New.**

    The Information Item page appears.

2. **Click a link:**

    • **Text and Image link**

    • **Formatted Text link**

    This determines whether you show text only or text and an image.

3. **Type a heading in the Name field.**

4. **Select the Display in Web Site check box.**

5. **On the Basic tab, type a summary in the Brief Description field.**

6. **In the Detailed Description field, enter the bulk of the information.**

   You can use HTML to enter this description. If you use rich text editing, click the HTML Source Code link to enter code. Set up rich text editing at Home⇨Set Preferences.

7. **Select a template from the Item Drilldown Template drop-down list.**

   For more information on item templates, see Chapter 17.

8. **(Optional) Enter information in these fields:**

   • **URL Component**

   • **Meta Tag HTML**

   • **Search Keywords**

   See the earlier section, "Keeping tabs on things," for details on entering meta tag information.

9. **From the Site Category drop-down list, choose a category and click the Add button.**

   Repeat until you've added all the categories under which this information item should show.

   For more information on creating categories, see the earlier section, "Conquering with categories."

10. **Go to the Media tab.**

11. **Click the double arrow beside one of the options:**

    • **Item Thumbnail**

    • **Item Picture**

12. **Click List.**

13. **Choose an image from the File Cabinet.**

    To upload a new file to use, click the double arrow and choose New.

14. **Click Save.**

The information publishes immediately to the chosen category on your Web site.

Getting Results with Site Search

If you want visitors to hand over their money, you have to help them find just the item they're looking for. When you set up search forms and published search results, customers can search your items, categories, and information.

The built-in search portlet is a global search for your Web site that customers can use to find tabs, categories, items, and information in your site. To show the standard search portlet, from the Setup tab menu, choose Web Site➪Set Up Web Site. On the Appearance tab, under Portlets, check the Show Search check box.

You have a few options for searches in your site:

✔ Choose *filters* (search criteria) for a search page.

✔ Choose filters for a search portlet.

✔ Publish the results of searches that you've run.

Enabling Advanced Web Search

Customizing search forms and portlets requires you to enable the Advanced Web Search feature:

1. **From the Setup tab menu choose Company➪Enable Features.**

2. **Click the Web Presence tab.**

3. **Select the Advanced Web Search check box.**

    The Advanced Web Search feature is part of the SiteBuilder add-on. If you don't have it installed in your account, speak with your NetSuite salesperson for more information.

4. **Choose Save.**

Creating a search form

When you search items in NetSuite, you can save both:

✔ The search criteria you set

✔ The fields you use to set the criteria (and that you want to use the next time you search)

The filters you save make a search form that your Web site visitors can use. This kind of custom search form lets customers search items by brand, color, size, or other custom attributes.

You can create a search form the following way:

1. **From the Web Site tab menu choose Search/Updates➪Saved Searches➪ New.**

    The New Saved Search page appears.

2. **Click the Item link.**

   The Saved Item Search page appears.

3. **Enter a title in the Search Title field.**

   The title should help you recognize the form when you choose it for publishing.

4. **Select the Public check box.**

   This makes the search form available for publishing in your site.

5. **Choose the Criteria tab.**

6. **Choose from the Filter drop-down list.**

   This sets criteria that limit the items that are searchable on the Web. For example, to create a search form on a media Web site that searches DVDs only, select Category as the filter; on the page that appears, choose DVDs from the list.

7. **Choose the Results tab.**

8. **Select items from the Field drop-down list.**

   The items you choose will have their information shown when search results are returned. For example, you may want search results to show Name, Image, Name, Image, Description, and Price.

9. **Click the Add button.**

10. **Choose the Available Filters tab.**

11. **Choose options from the Filter drop-down list.**

    The Filter drop-down list determines each field that visitors should have available for searching. For example, you can allow visitors to search by name, price, or keywords in the Description field.

12. **Click the Add button after each filter you select.**

13. **Click Save.**

Having a saved search form is great, but it isn't available on your site until you publish it.

Publishing a search form

To publish a search form in your site:

1. **From the Web Site tab menu choose Publishing⇨Publish Saved Search⇨New.**

   The Publish Saved Search page appears.

2. **Enter a name in the Title field.**

   This name shows in your site and is how visitors access the search page.

3. **From the Search drop-down list, choose the public saved search you're using as the search form.**

4. **Enter descriptions for the search page if needed in the Brief Description and Detailed Description fields.**

   Your descriptions may include instructions for how to use the search page.

5. **Select the Display in Web Site check box.**

6. **Click Save.**

Your site visitors are now much more likely to find exactly what they're looking for, and they can put those items in the shopping cart from the search results.

Setting your search preferences

Set your preferences for searches this way, and of course, you can always come back and modify them later:

1. **From the Setup tab menu choose Web Site➪Setup Tasks➪Set Up Web Site.**

2. **Choose the Basic tab.**

3. **Select the Show Uncategorized Items check box.**

   Selecting this option lets items that aren't published to a category show up in search results.

4. **Choose the Search tab.**

5. **Select options related to search.**

   Include whether categories and information items should be included in searches on your site.

6. **Click Save.**

Publishing search results

Instead of (or in addition to) your categorized items, you may want to publish items in groups based on search results. For example, you can publish search results for your site visitors for all blue items in addition to your basic site organization. This gives your customers an additional way to find the items they're looking for.

To publish a list of items based on certain criteria, you first create a public saved search in your account. For more information on creating saved searches, see the previous section.

After creating your saved search, do this:

1. **From the Web Site tab menu choose Publishing⇨Publish Saved Search⇨New.**

   The Publish Saved Search page opens.

2. **Enter a name for the group of items in the Title field.**

3. **From the Search drop-down list, choose the saved search.**

4. **From the Subcategory Of drop-down list, choose the category where the group results should be posted.**

5. **Click Save.**

After you publish saved search results, the results are automatically updated on your site when new items match the criteria of the search. This allows customers to always find the items that match their needs, even if your inventory changes regularly.

Chapter 16

Making Your Site Look Great

No one can deny that it's important to have a well-organized, visually appealing Web site. For customers who haven't seen you in person, the look and feel of your Web site represents your entire company's image. Luckily, if you create your site in NetSuite, you don't get a canned site with a limited set of options; you have a basic site structure with a myriad of options. This gives you all the glory of a professionally designed site without the sweat, tears, and empty pockets.

In this chapter, we show you how to use color themes and layout tweaks to customize your site's look. We also show you how to use advanced features to customize nearly every aspect of your Web site.

Only those with the role of Administrator can follow the steps in this chapter.

Looking Good

When managing a site with NetSuite-generated pages, you can use several options to customize your site's look and feel. The chart in Figure 16-1 shows you the overall workflow for changing a Web site's look with and without the Advanced Site Customization feature.

If you use the Advanced Site Customization feature, you may want to look over the "Using Advanced Site Customization Options" section of this chapter before applying themes or creating layouts.

None of the appearance settings is required. However, it's a good idea to review the various appearance settings in case you run into trouble with your site appearance.

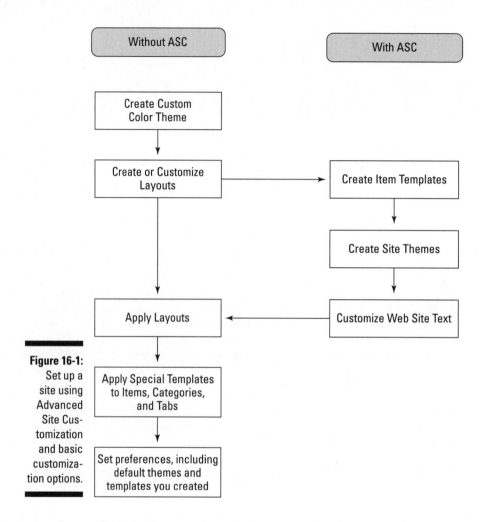

Figure 16-1:
Set up a
site using
Advanced
Site Cus-
tomization
and basic
customiza-
tion options.

Styling your site with themes

NetSuite includes a few built-in themes that you can apply to your site for a
fast setup. *Themes* are like templates in that they set the layout.

Themes also include the following:

- ✔ Templates for the item page
- ✔ Color theme
- ✔ Text size and font
- ✔ Look of the portlets, tabs, and buttons

To choose a theme for your site:

1. **From the Setup tab menu choose Web Site⇨Set Up Web Site.**

   The Web Site Setup page appears.

2. **Click the Appearance tab.**

   The Appearance tab has all the preferences you need to control the look and feel of a site created with NetSuite.

3. **Choose from the Web Site Theme drop-down list.**

   A *theme* is a design style that is applied to the various elements of your site. You can try the various templates on for size by clicking the Preview link to the right of the Web Site Theme drop-down list.

   The Web Site Theme drop-down list offers a number of different themes to choose from (courtesy of NetSuite), as well as any custom themes that you've created. Choose one of the built-in themes (as shown in Figure 16-2) or select None to have a plain site (as shown in Figure 16-3). Click the Preview link to the right of the Web Site Theme drop-down list to see how your site will look with that particular theme applied.

   If you have set up custom themes, they also appear in the Web Site Theme drop-down list. For more information on custom themes, see the later section, "Marching to the beat of your own theme."

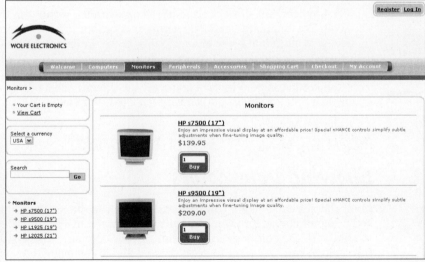

Figure 16-2:
This site uses the Round Edges theme.

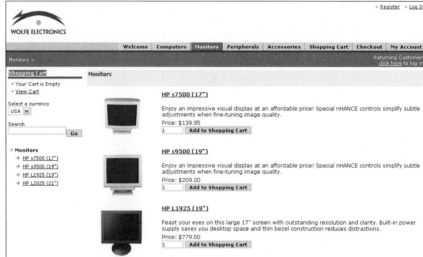

Figure 16-3:
This is the
same site
without
a theme
applied.

4. **Use the other fields, check boxes, and drop-down lists to change theme settings.**

For example, you can choose from the Web Site Color Theme drop-down list and the Web Site Font drop-down list while keeping the rest of the theme's aspects at their defaults.

To have the full effect of a theme, all appearance settings in the Colors, Web Site Templates, and Page/Fonts sections must be set to From Theme. Keep in mind that if you change one of these options and then change the theme, you still must set the drop-down list back to From Theme; choosing a theme doesn't override other changes you made (such as choosing Comic Sans as your font). If you want the theme in all its design glory, set all the options you've fiddled with back to From Theme.

5. **Choose Save.**

Showing your colors

Color themes can solidify your site with your products or branding. If you sell designer linens, for example, you may want to have a neutral color theme to showcase the coloring of your items. If your company logo contains signature colors, you may want to echo those colors to coordinate your site with your logo.

In NetSuite, you can choose from a variety of built-in color themes for use with your site, including any of the color themes used with the site themes and college school colors. You can also choose to create a color theme that is an exact match with your logo and other coloring.

Color themes were originally designed to personalize your NetSuite account. Therefore, the same color theme may not place color in the same places in your site that it will in your account. Make sure you preview your site after applying a theme to make sure everything is how you want it. Also, be sure that the text color contrasts enough from the background color on all pages in your site, including checkout. Otherwise, customers may not be able to read the text in your site.

You can apply color themes at Setup⇨Web Site⇨Set Up Web Site.

You can either apply an existing color theme or modify one from the Setup menu by choosing Web Site⇨Color Themes.

If you're ambitious (or picky) you can create your own custom color theme:

1. **From the Setup tab menu choose Web Site⇨Color Themes⇨New.**

   The New Color Theme page appears.

2. **Type a name in the Name field.**

   For example, you may enter Logo Color Theme.

3. **For each set of background and text colors, enter the hexadecimal code in the field that contains #FFFFFF.**

   The painting icon to the right of the fields lets you select a color instead (choices are rather limited).

4. **For these additional options, select the Advanced Editing check box.**

   If you're using a color match from a graphics program, you can enter the RGB or HSL codes. Entering an RGB or HSL code automatically sets the other codes for that field.

   More fields appear so that you can enter RGB or HSL values to match a color precisely.

   RGB stands for red, blue, and green. You can enter RGB color values to precisely define each color. RGB values range from 0 to 255 and there are three of them (just like the three fields that appear after RGB). Yes, you guessed it: Red goes in the first, green goes in the second, and blue in the third.

   HSL stands for hue, saturation, and lightness. Hue is the numerical value of the color on a color wheel (0 to 360 degrees). Saturation is a percentage; 100% means the color at its full strength. Lightness is also a percentage, but 0% is black, 50% is average, and 100% is white.

5. **Click the Preview button.**

   A sample site opens in a new window to show where the colors are used. You can close that window, keep making changes, and click the Preview button again to see the results. See Figure 16-4.

6. **When you're happy with the colors, click the Save button.**

Be sure that the text color contrasts enough from the corresponding background color. Otherwise, you may not be able to see the text in your site.

Heading options

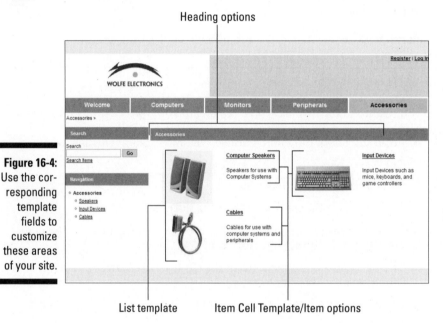

Figure 16-4:
Use the corresponding template fields to customize these areas of your site.

List template   Item Cell Template/Item options

Apply a color theme

Whether you choose to create a custom color theme or use one of the included color themes, you need to apply your theme to your site.

To apply a color theme to a site:

1. **From the Setup tab menu choose Setup⇨Web Site⇨Set Up Web Site.**

   The Web Site Setup page appears.

2. **Click the Appearance tab.**

3. **Choose an option from the Web Site Color Theme drop-down list.**

   The drop-down list is in the Colors section.

4. **Click Save.**

Your color theme is now applied to your live Web site.

Laying Out Your Space

You can customize layouts for pages that have item, category, and related item lists. Layouts save your settings for these things:

- Border style
- Column size
- Number of columns and rows
- Sorting
- More

Each site theme has four separate layouts:

- Item lists on presentation tabs
- Category lists on presentation tabs
- Related item lists on presentation tabs
- Item lists on Home tabs

You can create a new layout based on one of these layouts or create an entirely new layout.

To create or customize a layout:

1. **From the Setup tab menu choose Web Site⇨Layouts.**

   The Web Site Item/Category Layouts list appears.

2. **Click depending on your plan:**
   - **New** button (lower left): To create a new layout
   - **Customize** link (next to the layout you want to change): to customize an existing layout

   The Item/Category Layout page appears.

3. **Type a name in the Name field.**

   You choose this name when you apply the layout to list pages in your site.

   When you customize a layout, you're changing a *copy* of the layout. This requires you to enter a different name from the original.

4. **Enter settings in the Border Style, Column Width, Number of Columns, Number of Rows fields. You can also specify Row Height, Row Padding, and more.**

   Click the name of a field if you need an explanation of what the preference does.

5. **If you use the Advanced Site Customization feature, select the Use Templates check box.**

   Using templates allows you to use custom item/category templates to define how the list and each item in the list appear. When you use templates, the Heading and Items tabs disappear because you no longer need them.

   For more information on item/category templates, see the later section, "Item/category templates."

6. **If you don't use templates, clear the Use Templates check box and use the Heading tab to set how images and text align in lists.**

7. **If you don't use templates, use the Items tab options to decide how items appear in lists.**

8. **Click the Save button.**

Using Advanced Site Customization Options

If you have experience building Web sites or working with JavaScript and have the Advanced Site Customization feature available (and enabled) in your account, you have several customization options.

Because your advanced customization choices may affect other site appearance preferences, you should check out the set up process in Figure 16-1 of this chapter.

Marching to the beat of your own theme

Using Advanced Site Customization, you can either create a theme based on one of the built-in themes or create your own theme from scratch.

You get a few benefits from creating your own theme:

- ✔ You can design the shape, placement, and font of your tabs and buttons.
- ✔ You can set backgrounds or include images on your site's pages.
- ✔ You can design the header and footer.
- ✔ You can include scripts and other information.

✔ You can decide how bulleted lists appear.

  ✔ You can design the look and placement of portlets and sidebars.

Customizing a theme is a good option if one of these scenarios fits you:

  ✔ You want to use all of NetSuite's site features but want a fully customized site.

  ✔ You like one of the built-in themes but want to change one or two things about it.

Site themes pull information from your account using Web site tags that NetSuite provides. These Web site tags help define areas of the page so that NetSuite can work well with your site. Some of these tags must be used with certain HTML tags, and most of them must be used to have the correct content in your site and to integrate your Web site orders with your account. A list of NetSuite's Web site tags are available through the NetSuite online Help Center.

When you create a custom theme, you enter template code for the sections of the site that you want to change. Each section or aspect of the site that you can change is represented by each field on the Web Site Theme page.

Applying a style sheet

If you also enabled the Host HTML Files feature, you can apply a style sheet to your theme. Creating your theme then goes a little faster and makes connections between hosted or external pages less noticeable.

1. **From the Setup tab menu choose Web Site⇨Web Site Hosting Files.**

2. **Click the link for Live Hosting Files.**

3. **Click the link for the site folder.**

4. **Click the Add File button.**

   Browse to select your CSS file.

5. **When creating your theme (with steps in the following section), add your link to the Addition to <head> field.**

   You have to add your link to the CSS file using standard HTML codes. But our assumption is that if you've created a CSS file, this task will be all in a day's work for you.

Creating a custom site theme

To create a custom site theme:

1. **From the Setup tab menu choose Web Site➪Appearance➪Color Themes.**

   The Web Site Color Themes list appears.

2. **Click the option that fits your choice:**

   - **Customize** appears for themes that are built in and that you can change.

   - **Edit** appears for themes that aren't built in. Make sure you save them under another name so you don't overwrite the original theme.

   - **New** creates a completely new theme.

3. **Determine which templates and fields you want to edit.**

   The Color Theme, Drilldown Template, and Layout fields can be overridden on the Web Site Setup page. These preferences allow you to associate your other customizations with a theme so that the appearance settings are all saved in one package.

   For more information on color themes, see the earlier section, "Showing your colors." For more information on layouts, see the "Laying Out Your Space" section, earlier in this chapter. For information on drilldown templates, see the following section.

Item/category templates

Item templates are your ticket to a detailed item-information page with multiple images and custom formatting. You can use category templates to customize how items and categories look in a list, whether it's a list of items or a list of categories. Additionally, you can use item templates to customize the layout and design of pages for the items you sell and for information items (which lets you publish formatted text with images).

If you need to, you can create several templates for different circumstances and then apply the templates on individual records, layouts, themes, or via the Web Site Setup page.

When you create an item or category template, you use custom tags with attributes to pull information from items, information items, customer records, or color themes. Attributes are ways to tell NetSuite to pull in a particular piece of information or a particular image when it's displaying your site.

You can also choose from attributes to add to the page:

- ✔ Add to Cart button
- ✔ Quantity field
- ✔ Your company logo
- ✔ Out of Stock message

To create an item or category template:

1. **From the Setup tab menu, choose Web Site⇨Item/Category Templates.**

   The Web Site Item/Category Templates list appears.

2. **Choose one of the following:**

   - **Customize** link (next to a template): To create a new template from a built-in template.

   - **New** button: To create a new template from scratch.

   Customizing a template saves your changes in a new template and keeps the original copy of the template.

   When you see an Edit link next to a template, the template isn't built in. When you edit one like that, you must click the Save As button to save the edited version as a new template. Click the Save button to save over the current template.

3. **Enter a name for the template in the Name field.**

   Use a recognizable name when you apply it to areas of your site. For example, if you're creating this template for item lists, you may enter Item List Template.

4. **Enter any page scripts, meta information, or other header code in the Addition to <head> field.**

   The <head> field is part of the HTML in your file. HTML files have a head section and a body section.

   Adding code here means adding HTML code for elements you want to insert into the template.

5. **Enter the page template in the Template HTML field.**

   Template HTML is added to the existing HTML for the page. It must begin with <td> and end with </td>.

   Include tags to call information from your account. Use the tag formats and attributes that you get when you search for **Web Site Tags** in NetSuite's online Help center.

6. Click the Save button.

Your template is now saved, but isn't used in your Web site until you apply it.

Apply yourself

Like we said: You have to apply your templates and layouts before your Web site can use it.

1. From the Setup tab menu, choose Web Site⇨Set Up Web Site.

The Web Site Setup page appears.

2. Click the Appearance tab.

It includes a drop-down lists where you can select your new template. You can select templates or layouts for the following:

- Default Item Drilldown Template
- Default Item List

You can select layouts for:

- Default Item List Layout
- Default Category List Layout

3. Click the Save button.

Your templates and layouts are applied to your site. Like most Web development tasks, you may need to refresh your browser to see the fruits of your labor.

Customizing text

Another big advantage to using the Advanced Site Customization feature is the ability to customize almost all of the text in the site, including:

- ✔ E-mail messages, such as order confirmation
- ✔ Error messages
- ✔ Headings
- ✔ Drop-down list options for payment methods
- ✔ Alerts, such as Full Cart warnings

✔ Button labels

✔ Field labels

✔ Messages, such as items out of stock

Customizing these areas with your own text helps put your touch on your site. It allows you to add branding language or instructions or messages that are specific to your business. For example, if you call customers "clients," you can customize your messages and e-mail to remove or replace references to "customers."

To customize Web site text:

1. **From the Setup tab menu choose Web Site⇨Customize Text.**

   The Customize Web Site Text page appears.

2. **If you use multiple languages in your site, select the language you want to work with.**

   Your customizations are saved for each language you use. If you need to edit custom text, selecting the language brings up your saved customizations, which you can change and save over.

3. **The default text appears on the left side. Enter your text in the Customization field.**

   For example, if the default text reads "Selected Option Is Unavailable," your site can say, "You can't do that!" (Though seriously, we don't recommend anything that informal.)

   You may want to copy and paste the text from the Default Text field into the Customization field and then edit the text to help make sure any code and tags stay in place. Some fields provide an explanation for where the text is used in the Description field, so be sure to read these.

4. **Click Save.**

   You can also customize order fulfillment e-mail, but that's done on a different screen so people who don't use the Web site can still customize it. From the Setup tab menu, choose Accounting⇨Customize Fulfillment Email.

Chapter 17

Let the Shopping Begin

. . . .

In This Chapter

▶ Saving customer information

▶ Providing payment options

▶ Taking and customizing Web orders

▶ Giving customers access to their accounts

. . . .

Y ou can set how customers shop and buy merchandise from your site. This chapter is for those of you aiming to make big bucks on the World Wide Web.

Getting to Know Your Customers via Registration

Registration is the getting-to-know-you aspect of Web sites. After customers register, you can store information about them and suggest products they may be interested in. You can save their shipping and billing information. This section tells you what you need to know about registering customers on your site.

 To follow the procedures in this chapter, you need to have a role such as Ecommerce Manager or Administrator. Some tasks in this chapter require the help of an administrator and tell you that so you can go and bribe the appropriate person with homemade fudge.

New customer? Please register! Or not

Most people want to keep track of their customers so they

    ✔ Know who likes their products

    ✔ Can serve them better

    ✔ Can market to them

However, some users don't love filling out forms and creating a login.

For that reason, NetSuite gives you different ways to use registration on your site. See Table 17-1.

Table 17-1	Visitor Registration Options	
Registration Options	*Visitor Requirements*	*Leads Created*
Required registration	To buy something in your site, visitors must create a login and password.	Lead records are created with registration, and leads become customers when they place an order.
Optional registration	When buying something in your site, visitors can create a login and password for the next time or go straight to checkout without registering.	Lead records are created when visitors register, and customer records are created when an order is placed, whether they registered or not.
Disabled registration	Visitors can't create a login and password and must enter their information every time they buy something.	A customer record is created (every time an order is placed) with the information entered in checkout. Enable and use the Duplicate Detection feature at least quarterly if you use this option. Administrators can use the Duplicate Detection feature from the Setup tab menu by choosing Company⇨Duplicate Detection.
Allow only existing customers	To buy something, visitors must sign in with a login and password that were previously set up or provided to them.	No records are created with this option because customers must already have a record to check out.

You can choose which option is best for your site by going to the Web Site Setup page.

1. From the Setup tab menu, choose Web Site⇨Set Up Web Site.

2. **Click the Shopping tab.**

3. **Choose your registration method in the Customer Registration Is field.**

The options are described in Table 17-1.

You can restrict your entire site to those who have a login and password (see Figure 17-1) by checking the Password-Protect Entire Site check box.

The default customer category for lead, prospect, or customer records created through Web site registration is also set on the Web Site Setup page. On the Setup tab, in the Preferences section, choose the default customer category. You can create new customer categories.

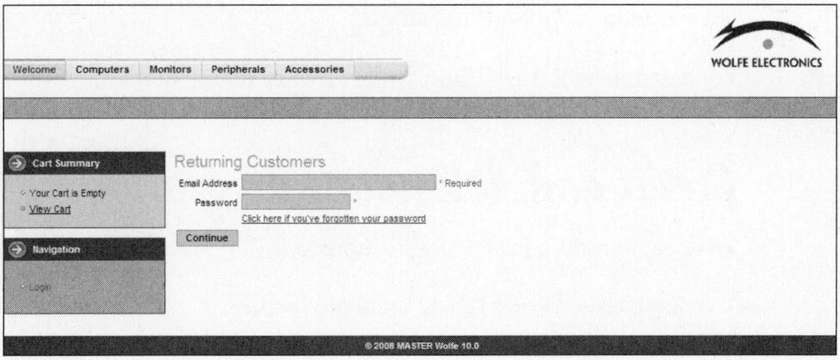

Figure 17-1:
When you password-protect your entire site, site visitors must log in to see pages.

Paying the Piper

You're not going to get very far in the world of e-commerce if you don't offer your customers at least a few ways to pay. This can be a little if you're new to the wonderful world of credit card processing, but once you know where payment methods are managed, you can add as many as you like and make them available online.

You can allow customers to pay in the following ways using your NetSuite cart and checkout:

✔ Credit or debit cards of these types (depending on how many types your processor accepts):

- Visa

- MasterCard

- American Express

- JCB

- • Solo

- • Switch

- • Discover

- • Diner's Card

  ✔ PayPal

  ✔ Invoice following an order

You can also offer PayPal Express Checkout or Google Checkout. If you use one of these methods exclusively, you may not need to set up the rest of your Web checkout, because customers will go straight to the Google or PayPal checkout. This book's Web site has more information on this topic: **www.dummies.com/go/netsuitefd**.

You need to be in the Administrator role to do the tasks in this section.

Credit and debit card processing

To accept credit cards in your Web site, you need to do a couple of things:

  ✔ Enable the Credit Card Payments feature.

  ✔ Create a payment method record for each type of credit card you want to accept (credit card types include, for example, MasterCard and Discover).

  ✔ Set up a merchant account that can integrate with one or more of the credit card processors offered with NetSuite.

You can choose from a few different processors, including

  ✔ CyberSource

  ✔ Merchant e-Solutions

Debit cards with a Visa or MasterCard logo are accepted and processed as credit cards in your store when you set up credit card processing. The charges are debited from the customers' checking accounts, but the charge is treated on your end just as any other credit card payment.

Enable the Credit Card Payments feature

Administrators can enable the Credit Card Payments feature the following way:

1. **From the Setup tab menu, choose Company➪Enable Features.**

   The Enable Features page appears.

2. **On the Transactions tab, check the Credit Card Payments check box.**

   The check box is in the Payment Processing section.

3. **Click Save.**

Create a payment method

Administrators can create a payment method for the Web site:

1. **From the Setup tab menu, choose Accounting⇨Accounting Lists⇨New.**

   The Add to Accounting Lists page appears.

2. **Click the Payment Methods link.**

   The Payment Method page appears.

3. **In the Payment Method field, type the payment you're accepting.**

   This name shows in your site, so name it after the type of card you accept, such as Visa.

4. **Check the Credit Card check box.**

   Selecting the check box tells the credit card processor to process the charge.

5. **Select how income from this payment method should be accounted for:**

   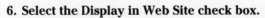

   • Group with Undeposited Funds

   • Deposit To (and then select an account from the drop-down list).

6. **Select the Display in Web Site check box.**

   If you don't check the Display in Web Site box, the payment method isn't available to customers in your site.

7. **Click the Save button.**

Choose a credit card processor

Credit card processors accept payments from your customers and do the math (so to speak) that lets money pass from the customer's card to your bank account. A credit card processor is a company that typically handles cards from all major credit card companies. (Of course they do charge you a transaction fee.)

To specify a credit card processor for your Web site, Administrators can follow along:

1. **From the Setup tab menu, choose Web Site⇨Set Up Web Site.**

2. **Under the General tab, select the credit card processor from the drop-down list.**

   If there are no entries in this drop-down list, an administrator should set up credit card processing from the Setup tab by choosing Accounting⇨Credit Card Processing. The drop-down list is populated with choices that have been previously set up in that location.

Save customer credit data

If a customer opts to save his credit card information on your site after registering, the credit card information is saved on the corresponding customer record, under the Financial tab. The credit card information is then available for quick payment the next time the customer buys something from your site, as shown in Figure 17-2.

Here's how to give customers the option to save credit card information with their profile:

1. **From the Setup tab menu, choose Web Site⇨Set Up Web Site.**

2. **On the Shopping tab, check the Display 'Save My Credit Card Info' Field.**

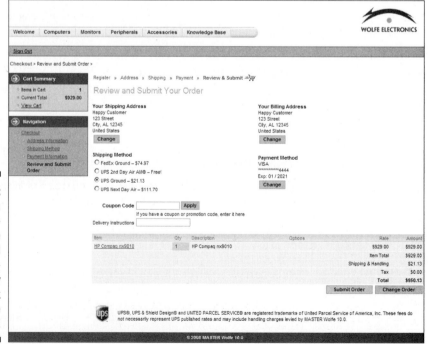

Figure 17-2:
When you let customers save credit card information, they can check out more quickly.

Paying later by invoice

Okay, you probably aren't going to do this unless you're taking donations (or really trust your customers), but you do have the option to take orders and have customers pay you later when you invoice them. (Actually, one real-world example is when customers order a service and you bill them later for that service.)

To allow customers to pay by invoice, do the following:

✔ Set your Web sales orders as Per Customer Basis to let customers choose between invoice and credit card.

✔ Set payment terms for invoicing on customer records that should be given this option.

Set up invoicing

To set up invoicing as an option in checkout:

1. **From the Setup tab menu, choose Web Site⇨Set Up Web Site.**

   The Web Site Setup page appears.

2. **Click the Shopping tab.**

3. **Under Checkout Preferences, choose Per Customer Basis from the Sales Order Type drop-down list.**

4. **In the Credit Card Form drop-down list, choose the transaction form to use when orders are placed with credit cards in the Web store.**

   Sales orders or cash sales are saved with the information from Web checkout on this form.

5. **Choose the transaction form from the Invoice Form menu.**

   This is the form that's used for orders when a customer chooses to be invoiced later.

   Sales orders are created with this form using the name, address, and item information from Web checkout.

6. **Click Save.**

Set invoice terms

To set terms for customers that are allowed to pay by invoice:

1. **From the Lists tab menu, choose Customers Relationships⇨Customers.**

   The Customers list appears.

2. **Click Edit next to a customer you want to allow to pay by invoice.**

   The customer record appears.

3. **Choose the Financial tab.**

4. **In the Terms menu, choose when payment should be due.**

   You can create new terms for this field at Setup⇨Accounting⇨ Accounting Lists⇨New⇨Term.

5. **Click Save.**

Customers with terms set now can choose Credit Card or Invoice on the Payment Information page during checkout, as shown in Figure 17-3. After a customer provides shipping information and submits the order, a sales order is created using the form you chose for invoices. You can then bill the order to create an invoice and send the invoice to your customer. See Chapter 5 for details on invoicing customers.

Figure 17-3: Established customers with set terms can choose to pay by invoice.

Shaping Up, Shipping Out

You can offer your customers shipping options specifically for Web orders so that you can deliver the goods in time for a price they like. In NetSuite, a shipping item record represents each shipping method you offer. For example, UPS overnight and USPS Priority Mail are examples of shipping items.

When you create a shipping item for each shipping method you offer, you can set the following options:

✔ Handling fees

✔ Free shipping with certain items

✔ Free shipping for orders totaling more than a certain amount

✔ Criteria for whether the method (such as order total and order weight) is available online

This section covers how shipping items work with the Web store. For detailed steps on setting up shipping, including shipping integration with UPS and FedEx, see Chapter 11.

Creating shipping items

Want to offer free shipping? Well, naturally you'll have to set that up, especially because you may not want to offer free shipping on baby grand pianos (guitar picks, yes; baby grands, no).

Administrators need to set up or adapt shipping items for use with the Web store and specify rules for how promotional shipping is offered.

To adapt an existing shipping item for the Web site, get your Administrator to:

1. **From the Lists tab menu, choose Accounting➪Shipping Items.**

   The Shipping Items list appears.

2. **Click Edit next to a shipping item you want to use on the Web site.**

   The shipping item record appears.

3. **Select the Display in Web Site check box.**

4. **On the Shipping and Handling Rules tab, check the Free if Total Is Over check box.**

   Now you can offer free shipping for orders totaling more than the amount you enter.

5. **In the Web Site Rules section, set criteria for when this shipping method is available in the Web store:**

   • *To make the shipping method available only when the total price is over or under a certain amount,* check the Available if Order Total is check box, select Over or Under, and enter the amount.

   • *To make the shipping method available only when the total order weight is over or under a certain unit or weight,* check the Available if Order Weight is box, select Over or Under, enter the weight, and select the type of measurement.

6. **On the Free Shipping Items tab, in the Item column, select an item that qualifies an entire order for free shipping.**

7. **Click the Add button.**

   You cannot offer free shipping for just one item. When free shipping is offered with an item, the entire order is eligible for free shipping with this shipping method.

8. **Repeat Steps 6 and 7 for each item that qualifies an order for free shipping.**

   Click the Add Multiple button to quickly add items to the free shipping list.

9. **(Optional) Check the All Items Must Be Purchased check box.**

   This requires that *all* the items added here are included on an order to qualify for free shipping.

10. **Click Save.**

This shipping item is now available for your customers during checkout.

Setting the default shipping method

If you have shipping items set up and set to display on your site, you can choose one of these methods as the default method. For example, you may want to select a default that is the easiest and most efficient method for your company to use.

Setting a default shipping method simply preselects the shipping method in the Web store checkout. Customers are still free to choose another shipping method that you offer.

To set a default shipping method:

1. **From the Setup tab menu, choose Web Site⇨Set Up Web Site.**

   The Web Site setup page appears.

2. **Choose the Shopping tab.**

3. **Choose a method from the Default Shipping Method drop-down list.**

   Only shipping methods that you create shipping items for and that are set to display in the Web site show in this list. For more information on how to set up shipping items, see Chapter 11.

   You also can set the other options in this section.

4. **Click Save.**

Default Web site shipping address options

You can require that customers enter a shipping address in the Web store, and you can let the shipping address show before the billing address. Both of these features can buy time for calculating shipping charges.

Require a shipping address

To require that customers enter a shipping address:

1. **Choose Setup⇨Web Site⇨Set Up Web Site.**

   The Web Site Setup page appears.

2. **Choose the Shopping tab.**

3. **Select the Shipping Information Is Required check box.**

   The check box is in the Shipping Page section.

Show the Shipping Address page first

To have the Shipping Address page show before the Billing Address page:

1. **From the Setup tab menu, choose Web Site⇨Set Up Web Site.**

   The Web Site Setup Page appears.

2. **Choose the Shopping tab.**

3. **Select the Ask for Shipping Address First check box.**

   The check box is in the Shipping Page section.

4. **Click Save.**

Restricting countries you ship to

You may want to limit the countries that can be selected on the Shipping Address page because of cost or the type of shipping methods you offer. This ensures that customers don't submit orders to be shipped to restricted countries.

To set the countries you do and do not ship to:

1. **From the Setup tab menu, choose Web Site⇨Set Up Web Site.**

   The Web Site Setup page appears.

2. **Click the Shopping tab.**

3. **Deselect the Web Store Ships to All Countries check box.**

   Clearing this box allows you to select countries in the next field. The check box is in the Shipping Page section.

4. **In the Countries Web Store Ships To drop-down list, select the countries you ship to.**

   Ctrl+click to select more than one country.

5. **Click Save.**

Now visitors can choose only the countries you selected.

Adding shipping cost to the shopping cart portlet

Customers often want to know what the total is while they're shopping. This helps them stay within budget without having to start checkout, and it helps keep your shopping cart and checkout abandonment rates down.

You can add a shipping estimate to the shopping cart portlet (a small area of the screen, like the areas on your home dashboard) to estimate the lowest possible shipping cost for your customers, allowing them to shop worry free. This shipping amount shows with the shopping cart portlet on all pages in your site, as shown in Figure 17-4.

Figure 17-4: The shipping estimate shows the least expensive shipping method in the Shopping Cart portlet while customers shop.

To add a shipping estimate to the shopping cart portlet:

1. **From the Setup tab menu, choose Web Site⇨Set Up Web Site.**

   The Web Site Setup page appears.

2. **Choose the Appearance tab.**

3. **From the Shopping Cart tab, select the Show Shipping Estimator in Cart check box.**

   This adds the shipping estimate to the bottom of the shopping cart portlet and to the bottom of the shopping cart page.

4. **Click Save.**

If you offer free shipping and the items in the cart qualify, the shipping estimator shows "Free!"

Taking Orders

When orders are submitted on your Web site, sales orders are created in your NetSuite account. The orders are created using the information the customer entered on the checkout pages. You can decide which form to use for Web site orders, in addition to other settings for Web orders covered in this section.

When an order is created in NetSuite from the Web site, it follows the same workflow as other sales orders:

Created⇨Approved⇨Paid⇨Fulfilled (Picked, Packed, Shipped)

The only difference is that regular sales orders have Billed after Fulfilled; The Web is the opposite in the common case of credit cards. However, it is a lot like any retail environment where you pay then receive the goods.

Crediting sales reps for Web orders

Most of the time customers come to your site via a link, an e-mail campaign, or a search engine. However, when an established customer who has a sales rep selected on her customer record buys something online, you may want to credit that sales rep.

For example, if your sales reps tend to have close relationships with your customers and talk with them about products and orders before the order is placed on the Web, the sales rep should certainly be credited for the sale.

Likewise, if there's typically a good bit of legwork after an order is submitted where the sales rep is in constant communication with the customer, the sales rep should also receive credit for managing the sale.

Here's how to ensure sales reps get credit for Web orders:

1. **From the Setup tab menu, choose Web Site⇨Set Up Web Site.**
2. **Choose the Setup tab.**
3. **Select the Credit Sales Reps for Web Orders check box.**

   The box is in the Preferences section.

Requiring a minimum order

Some companies sell very small or inexpensive objects or sell things in bulk but track inventory piece by piece (so orders may be larger, but still require a lot of overhead). If you fit into either of these categories, you may want to set a minimum order amount for your Web site. Setting a minimum order also helps you from being overcome by credit card processing fees.

If customers are placing $1.00 orders and you're charged a certain percent of each order processed with a credit card, you're not making the profits you should be. If the local coffee shop can set a $5 minimum charge, so can you! And you sure don't want to have to print and mail an invoice for a very small order; the postage alone can eat your profit!

To set a minimum order amount:

1. **From the Setup tab menu, choose Web Site⇨Set Up Web Site.**
2. **Click the Shopping tab.**
3. **Enter the minimum amount.**

All orders totaling less than this get an error when the customer tries to check out.

Legal jargon: Terms and conditions

Depending on the type of business you run, you may need to set the record straight about what you will or will not guarantee about your products or services. This can include such things as

- ✔ Return policy
- ✔ Contract details for service
- ✔ Warranty information

When you set terms and conditions, Web site customers must agree to them before they can check out and submit orders. Customers can view the terms and conditions in a pop-up window by clicking a link. This keeps all the text from filling up your checkout pages but keeps the legal stuff easily accessible for those people who must read every word.

To set terms and conditions:

1. **From the Setup tab menu, choose Web Site⇨Set Up Web Site.**

   The Web Site Setup page appears.

2. **Click the Shopping tab.**

3. **In the Review & Submit Page section, select the Require Terms and Conditions check box.**

   This requires customers to agree to your terms and conditions before they can check out in your site.

4. **In the Terms and Conditions HTML box, paste in the HTML code for your company's legal terms and conditions.**

5. **Click Save.**

A link to open your terms and conditions in a new window is added to the Review & Submit page.

Giving Customers Access

It's often beneficial to give your customers access to their account information. This allows customers to update their contact information when it changes and quickly reorder their favorite items.

Customers get access to account information when you enable the Customer Access feature and they register in your site. Once they have access, they see a My Account tab in your Web site. They also have the option of logging in through the NetSuite.com portal to access the Customer Center.

To give customers access a My Account tab:

1. **From the Setup tab menu, choose Company⇨Enable Features.**

   The Enable Features page appears.

2. **Click the Customer Access on the Web Presence tab.**

3. **Select the Customer Access check box.**

4. **Click Save.**

When you enable the Customer Access feature, customers see a My Account tab after they register on your Web site.

If you want customers to have access to this tab regardless of whether they register, make a change back on the Customer record. Ask an Administrator to select Lists⇨Relationships⇨Customers and edit the customer in question. Click the Access tab and select the Give Access check box. If you want to do this for all customers, an Administrator can perform a mass update for you.

Chapter 18

Fine-Tuning Your Site

In This Chapter

▶ Optimizing your site for search

▶ Reporting on results

▶ Adding popular options

*Y*our site is up and running. Now's the time to make things even better by making it easy for people to find your site via search engine optimization and reviewing some reports so you can see how visitors are using the site. This chapter provides details on how to do these things and more.

Optimizing for Search Engines

One of a site manager's most compelling goals is excellent search engine optimization. *Search engine optimization* makes your site higher in search engine results (free!); therefore, you get more traffic and more sales. Luckily, NetSuite makes it easy by adding some search-friendly features and by making some optimizing preferences and options available.

Letting NetSuite handle things

Here are a few things you can rest easy about because NetSuite handles them for you:

✔ **Automatic redirects:** NetSuite makes it easy to set up your site so that whether users enter www.mystore.com, www.mystore.org, or even plain old mystore, all roads lead to your home page. Technically, this is called a *301 redirect.* This type of redirect is friendly to search engines, rather like a concierge.

✔ **Page titles:** If you don't enter a custom page title, one is created from your company name and the tab name.

✔ **Short URLs:** NetSuite presents URLs to search engines in their simplest form.

✔ **No special characters:** NetSuite avoids special characters when creating pages to give the appearance of a *static page* (a page that doesn't change versus one that is dynamically created).

Taking some initiative

You can do a few things in NetSuite to improve search engine rankings:

✔ **Use descriptive names:** When you name tabs and categories, be as descriptive as possible. For example, if you mainly sell one type of item, instead of naming a tab Products, consider naming the tab after the products you sell.

✔ **Use descriptive links:** Instead of using *Click Here* for a link, title the link the same name as the page you're linking. For example, name the link *Seasonal Grilling Items.*

✔ **Use page titles:** Page title fields on Item, Category, and Tab records allow you to customize the page name.

✔ **Use meta tags:** Although meta tags aren't as widely used by search engines as they used to be, it still doesn't hurt to enter meta tag keywords that will help users find your site (similar to the kinds of words they'd enter using a Google search). *Meta tags* are hidden tags that exist just so search engines know to display your page when users search for certain terms. You can enter meta tags for the entire site from the Setup tab menu by choosing Web Site➪Set Up Web Site. Meta tags for tabs, categories, and items are entered on their individual records.

✔ **Use change:** Switch around your content often (and of course *often* depends on your level of ambition and the nature of your industry). Anytime you make changes, Google and its search engine friends will come and index your site again, putting it freshly near the top of the results pile.

✔ **Use fewer than five:** Make sure that all pages are accessible in less than five clicks from your home page. This helps improve usability.

✔ **Use internal links:** Include many internal links such as links to parent pages and subcategories.

✔ **Use Alt text for images:** Search engines don't have eyes. When they see an image, they see the filename. If you provide a textual description of that image, search engines can read "girls soccer cleats" rather than "image07276.jpg." Here's how:

1. **From the Document tab menu choose Files⇨Images.**

2. **Click Edit next to any image that needs to have a text description edited.**

3. **Type a description of the image in the Alt Image Tag field.**

4. **Click Save.**

Creating your doctype

The World Wide Web Consortium (W3C) is the organization that sets standards for the Web. Search engines rank sites better if the sites are W3C-compliant. This requires having a *doctype* (document type definition) tag at the top of your Web pages. It tells browsers and search engines the type of code on your site. For information on document type definitions, visit www.w3.org.

Create a doctype in the following format. For example, if you're using transitional XHTML 1.0, you document type declaration would be as follows:

```
<!DOCTYPE html PUBLIC "-//W3C//DTD XHTML 1.0 Transitional//EN"
"http://www.w3.org/TR/xhtml1/DTD/xhtml1-transitional.dtd">
```

You can enter your own doctype on the Web Site Setup page:

1. **From the Setup tab menu, choose Web Site⇨Set Up Web Site.**

2. **Click the Advanced tab.**

   The tab is shown in Figure 18-1.

3. **Type or paste your doctype code into the Document Type field.**

Figure 18-1: Enter your doctype on the Web Site Setup page.

Feeding the hungry customer

Customers are out there foraging for things to buy. Help them find you by submitting your wares to various shopping search engines via product feeds.

NetSuite can send product feeds to the following shopping engines:

- ✔ Google Base/Froogle
- ✔ Shopzilla
- ✔ Shopping.com
- ✔ Yahoo! Shopping
- ✔ NexTag

You get some upsides to submitting products to these sites:

- ✔ Item exposure from customers who are comparison shopping.
- ✔ Taking advantage of the advertising dollars spent by these sites for paid search listing.

A downside: Your items are up against competitors' items and prices.

Before you can set up product feeds in NetSuite, you must sign up as a merchant with the shopping engines that you want to use. You can then check out their instructions for whether to export your items in CSV or XML format.

Preparing for product feeds

To prepare items for product feeds, follow along:

1. **From the Lists tab menu, choose Accounting⇨Items.**

   The Items list appears.

2. **At the bottom of the Items list, select Feeds from the View drop-down list.**

3. **From the Type drop-down list, choose the item type you want to send.**

   Most likely, you'll choose Inventory Item.

   To quickly update your product feed information, you can use the Direct List Editing feature instead of editing each item record. To do so, enable the Direct List Editing feature. The steps in the following section help you do that.

4. **Click the Enable Editing link (in the header of the Items list).**

5. **Choose Yes or No for each product feed column that lists those two options.**

   - Click Yes to clear the check box for items you do *not* want to submit to a feed.

   - Click No to check the box for items you *do* want to submit to a feed.

   Once you move to another field, the check box changes to the word Yes or No depending on whether you selected or cleared the check box.

6. **For each product feed category column, enter the name of the related category from the shopping site.**

   Check the Shopping.com, Shopzilla, Yahoo! Shopping, and NexTag sites to enter the correct names for these categories.

7. **Click outside the list to save your changes.**

Your items are now prepared to export for product feeds. This happens on a different page and sends your data to spreadsheet files in the correct format.

Enable the Direct List Editing feature

Take this optional set of steps if you want to quickly update your product feed information.

1. **From the Setup tab menu choose Company⇨Enable Features.**

2. **If you want to include feeds to Yahoo! Shopping, click the Customize View button.**

3. **On the Criteria tab, limit the items that appear on the list.**

   For example, you may want to select Online and choose Yes to show only items that are ready to show in your Web site.

4. **On the Results tab, under Columns, select and add Yahoo! Shopping Product Feed.**

5. **Enter a name for your new custom view.**

   Type something easily identifiable, such as *Yahoo! Product Feed.*

6. **Click the Save button.**

The Items list reloads using your new custom view.

Submitting items to product feeds

To submit your items to product feeds:

1. **From the Setup tab menu choose Web Site⇨Product Feeds.**

   The Product Feeds page lists links for the supported shopping engines.

2. **Click the shopping engine you want to submit a product feed to.**

   A list of your items with their URLs appears in the format accepted by this shopping engine.

3. **Click the Export-CSV button.**

   This button has an arrow to the right so that you can select a different option (such as Export – Microsoft Excel or Export – PDF, as shown in Figure 18-2).

   The file type you should export to depends on the shopping engine. Check your account with the shopping engine for details on which file type to use.

4. **Log in to your account on each shopping feed site.**

5. **Import your item lists as directed on the shopping feed site.**

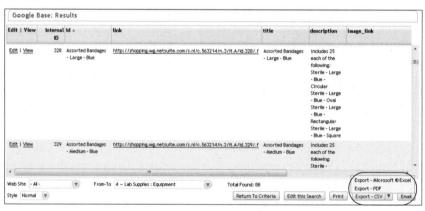

Figure 18-2:
Choose whether to export your product feed lists in XML or CSV format based on the shopping site's instructions.

Describing descriptive URLs

The Descriptive URLs feature in NetSuite does what its name says — it turns your long, hairy, number-filled URL (for item and category pages) into short, easy-to-remember, search engine-friendly URLs that actually describe the item or category they link to.

✔ A *generated URL* is created by a program, without regard to readability, and may look like this:

  http://www.netsuitestore.com/s.nl/sc.31/category.987/.f.

✔ A *descriptive URL* is also created by a program, but let's just say the developer was more sensitive to people being able to read URLs. The Descriptive URLs makes the preceding generated URL look like this:

  http://www.netsuitestore.com/electronics/cordless-phones

Using descriptive URLs helps make all your site pages more likely to show up in search engine results because of the use of 301 redirects from the non-descriptive URL to the new, descriptive one and because of hyphens (versus underscores) in the naming conventions.

Descriptive URLs are case sensitive. If you don't let the system create your descriptive URLs based on category and item names, set capitalization standards before you set up your URLs. All links to these pages must have the same capitalization standards. If your items are called Cordless Phones instead of cordless phones, the URL example earlier wouldn't work.

Setting up descriptive URLs

Administrators can set preferences for descriptive URLs including the tab and category name:

1. **Make sure your domain name is set up in NetSuite.**

   See Chapter 13 for how to do this.

   Now enable the Descriptive URLs feature.

2. **From the Setup tab menu, choose Company⇨Enable Features.**

3. **Click the Web Presence tab and select the Descriptive URLs check box.**

4. **From the Setup tab menu choose Web Site⇨Set Up Web Site.**

   The Web Site Setup page appears.

5. **Choose the Setup tab.**

6. **In the Preferences section, choose a format from the Descriptive URLs field:**

   • **/tab_name/category_name/item_name:** Shows the parent tab and category in the URL (which can help people who see the URL in print find the item using your site navigation).

   • **/item_name:** Shows just the item display name (which keeps the URL short).

7. **Click the Save button.**

To set all descriptive URLs to show the item display name:

1. **From the Setup tab menu, choose Web Site⇨Bulk Set URL Components.**

   The rather simple Bulk Set URL Components page appears.

2. **Select Set URL Components for all tabs, categories, and items based on Name.**

3. **Click the Save button.**

URL updates begin. You can check their status from the Setup tab by choosing Bulk Set URL⇨Status next to the Bulk Set URL Components link under Web Site. The Job Status page is shown in Figure 18-3.

Job Status						
Job Id ▲	Date	Job Name	Import Type	Status	Percent Complete	Message
7385	08/08/2010 7:23 pm	SET URL Components	Web Site Set Up	Finished	100%	0 tab(s) were updated. 4 category(ies) were updated. 0 information item(s) were updated. 9 item(s) were updated.

Import Type Web Site Set Up ▼   From 8/8/2010   To 8/8/2010   Total Found: 1

Figure 18-3:
The Job
Status page.

Setting an individual descriptive URL

You can set an individual descriptive URL for an item, category, or tab that differs from the display name:

1. **From the Lists tab menu, choose Web Site⇨Items, Tabs, or Categories.**

   The Items list appears.

2. **Click Edit next to what needs a unique URL.**

3. **In the URL Component field, enter the name that should show in the URL.**

   On the item record, this field is on the Store tab.

   For example, you may enter *Drops* for an item with a display name of Milk Chocolate Drops. This changes a descriptive URL that uses the item display name from www.netsuitestore.com/Milk-Chocolate-Drops to www.netsuitestore.com/Drops.

4. **Click the Save button.**

If an Administrator turns off the Descriptive URLs feature at Setup⇨Company⇨ Enable Features, all descriptive URLs revert to the previous format.

Redirecting: The 411 on 301s

When you move pages from one URL to another, it's important that your customers can still find your page. Think of a redirect as the virtual sign in the window of your old favorite hardware store. Just when you were afraid they'd shut down, you read, "Joe's Hardware has moved to a bigger and better location at 1234 S. Main."

301 redirects are the most search engine-friendly redirects.

No one knows where the 301 comes from (okay, probably someone knows), but it is interpreted as "moved permanently," which makes the search engine feel better about sending people to your new address. This is no temporary detour or wild goose chase; 301 means you're serious about your new digs. It also prevents the dreaded 404 Not Found error. Who knows what 404 means, but most of us know it's an ugly dead end.

To set up a 301 direct for a page that has changed URLs:

1. **From the Setup tab menu, choose Web Site➪Redirects➪New.**

   The New Redirect page appears.

2. **From the Domain Name field choose the domain this redirect applies to.**

3. **In the Redirect From URL field, enter the old URL.**

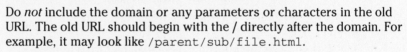

   Do *not* include the domain or any parameters or characters in the old URL. The old URL should begin with the / directly after the domain. For example, it may look like `/parent/sub/file.html`.

4. **In the Redirect To URL field, enter the new URL.**

   This URL can use any format. If it's on the same domain name as the main Web site, you can begin the URL with the / directly after the domain; if the domain name's entirely different, you can enter http://www.newsite.com/page.

5. **Click the Save button.**

Your redirect takes immediate effect, although it may take some time for search engines to index your new page. It's a good idea to keep both your old and new pages active for several days to allow engines to follow the redirect.

Your redirects are saved in the Redirects list for editing or deleting in the future.

Navigating sitemaps

Sitemaps link every other page in your site together, giving a full view of your entire site, like a directory. Sitemaps can be in XML format for search engine spiders to read and in HTML format for display on your site.

Having most or all pages linked from one page, as in an HTML sitemap, helps search engines find and index all the pages on your site rather than just your top-level pages.

NetSuite offers a sitemap generator to create an XML or HTML sitemap (or both if needed) that contains all the links of your site along with meta data (such as last modified date). It can handle up to 50,000 URLs per sitemap and will create multiple sitemaps if your site contains more URLs.

With the Site Builder add-on, you can enable the Host HTML Files feature. Even if you use a NetSuite-generated site, you must enable this feature to have access to upload your sitemap.

To enable the Host HTML Files feature:

1. **From the Setup tab menu, choose Company⇨Enable Feature.**

   The Enable Features page opens.

2. **On the Web Presence tab, click the Host HTML Files check box.**

   The Host HTML Files feature is enabled.

3. **Click Save.**

To generate a sitemap, follow these steps:

1. **From the Setup tab menu, choose Web Site⇨Sitemap Generator.**

2. **If you use the Multiple Web Sites feature, choose a site from the Web Site drop-down list.**

3. **In the Destination Folder drop-down list, choose the folder in the File Cabinet where the sitemap should be stored.**

   You should place this file in the highest level of the Web Site Hosting Files folder possible. By default, Live Hosting Files is selected.

4. **In the File Name field, enter the name of the sitemap file you're creating.**

5. **In the Index File Name field, create a name for the index file created (if multiple sitemaps need to be created).**

   Multiple sitemaps are created if your site contains more than 50,000 links. The sitemaps are linked to from an index file, which acts as a table of contents for the search engine spiders.

6. **Choose one check box:**

   • **XML Format** to create a sitemap in XML format.

   • **HTML Format** to create a sitemap in HTML format.

   If you check both boxes, two files are created, one for each file type.

7. **Select the Include Hosted Pages check box to include HTML pages in the Web Site Hosting Files.**

   An XML sitemap includes all hosted pages in your site as well as the tab and category pages generated by NetSuite when you check this box.

An HTML sitemap includes the hosted home page selected at Setup➪ Web Site➪Set Up Web Site as well as the tab and category pages generated by NetSuite.

8. **If your sitemap format is HTML, enter the number of columns to include in the Number of Columns in HTML Format field.**

   If your site format is XML, go to Step 9.

9. **Under XML Options, set the following preferences:**

   • **Change Frequency:** Select how often your site content is updated.

   • **Last Modified:** Select whether to include the date and time a file was last modified.

   • **Priority:** Select whether to automatically generate a priority for each page in your sitemap. When priority is automatically generated, the site hierarchy is used. Tabs are a higher priority than categories, and categories are a higher priority than items. You can set a priority for individual items on each item's record.

10. **In the Email Address field, enter an e-mail address to receive notification when the sitemap is complete.**

   When the sitemap file is created, it's automatically stored in the folder you selected in Step 3. You can submit the XML file to search engines using the links in your notification e-mail.

 It's a good idea to re-generate your sitemap after each site update and resubmit the sitemap to the major search engines. This helps ensure that your site's new content is properly indexed.

Using Reports to Improve Your Site

NetSuite has a number of amazing reports that can gauge how your site is performing (and make adjustments to make it perform even better). If you have the Site Analytics module, you have more than twice the number of original reports (for a very in-depth look at how customers arrive at and use your site) to make it the low-cost marketing and selling machine that a great Web site has the potential to be.

 While NetSuite's reports offer a complete view of what's going on with your site, they aren't just copies of what other solutions offer in Web reporting. For that reason, we encourage you to use third-party reporting tools to explore the differences in how data is gathered and to make comparisons.

 Tracking HTML and pixels provide data for reporting tools such as Google Analytics. You can place these tracking elements in any Greeting, Message, or Description field for items, categories, or tabs in your site. If you use Rich Text

Editing for fields, make sure you click the HTML Source Code link in these fields before pasting your code. That ensures your HTML doesn't display.

Basic reports

Everyone gets some basic reporting on their Web store's activities (see Table 18-1). Figure 18-4 shows the Page Hits by Category report.

Table 18-1	Basic Reports Included
Report Type	**Description**
Page Hits	Shows the number of hits by page or by category. Hits are counted by tracking unique customers with cookies. The Page Hits by Category report is shown in Figure 18-4.
Item Orders	Shows items ordered, how many orders per item, and how many customers ordered each item.
Page Views and Sales	Shows page views, placed orders, and revenue for each item, even if they are from the same customer(s).
Shopping Activity	Shows what which items customers put in their shopping carts and at what point they typically decide to purchase.
Cart Abandonment	Shows how often items are placed in the shopping cart but not purchased and helps you find potential kinks in the checkout process.

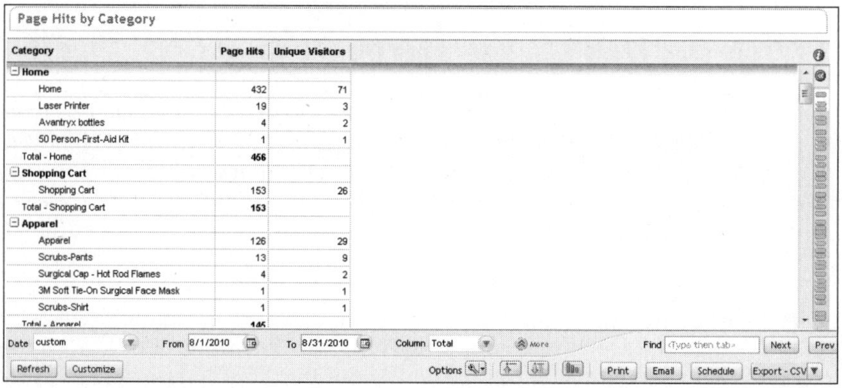

Figure 18-4: The Page Hits by Category report organizes page hits per item by category and subtotals hits by category.

To display these reports, from the Reports tab menu choose Web Presence, followed by the report name.

Site analytics reports

Site analytics takes the reporting another level deeper. How did the visitors get to your site (that's the referrer report)? How many of them are new visitors? What words did they use to search your site?

These reports are available if you have the Site Analytics module installed. Talk to your NetSuite sales person if you don't have this module installed. Table 18-2 lists the site analytics reports.

Table 18-2	Site Analytics Reports
Report Type	*Description*
Referrer Reports	Show which Web sites send customers to your site.
Keywords*	Show which keywords and keyword phrases customers use in search engines to find your site, hits per keyword or phrase, proceeds from those keywords, the number of leads created as a result, and the number of purchases.
Lead Conversion	Shows the percentage of visitors who register in your site (become leads) and then purchase (become customers).
New Visitor	Counts first-ever visits and first visits within a chosen period. Be aware that visitors without cookies enabled count as new visitors for every page visited. This may cause a large discrepancy in new visitor hits from other reporting tools.
Visitor Activity	Shows the date of the last visit and the number of pages viewed. Visitors who haven't registered show under No Customer, and registered visitors are listed by name.
Internal Search	Shows keywords used for searching within your site per customer.

These reports offer very valuable ROI analysis. Keep in mind these reports are different from similar ones in Google Analytics, which show higher hits per keyword. Google counts hits per keyword phrase and per phrase, where NetSuite counts per phrase or keyword.

Part VI
Dashboards, Searches, and Analytics

The 5th Wave   By Rich Tennant

"We're using just-in-time inventory and just-in-time material flows which have saved us from implementing our just-in-time bankruptcy plan."

In this part . . .

What should I do next? How am I doing? How is the company doing? You've got questions, and your data in NetSuite has answers. Part VI helps find and visualize the information you seek, both on a personal level and on a corporate level, with saved searches, dashboards, and key performance indicators (KPIs). Whether you're an inquisitive analytics newbie who just wants simple reports or a ninja data analyst, NetSuite easily and generously provides you with many ways to see where your business is and where it is going.

Chapter 22 describes saved searches, a key analytical feature whose simple name belies its power to find just what you want, again and again. Chapter 23 explains the power of dashboards, giving you clues on how to set up NetSuite to give you, at a glance, the insight you need to keep things moving the right way. Chapter 24 provides details on reporting and analytics, enabling you to slice and dice data and drill into it for additional detail.

Chapter 19

Realizing the Power of Saved Searches

A s a NetSuite user, you will repeatedly have to call upon the same data set. It's the nature of many a manager's job to monitor specific areas of the business and share their findings with others, often on a regularly scheduled basis. To assist you with this task, NetSuite has a number of pre-built searches that you can use to access those data elements that are so important to doing your job. In addition, you can create your own saved searches tailored to your specific needs and share the results with your colleagues, co-workers, and even customers, if you so desire.

Saved searches serve a valuable function in NetSuite's arsenal of data access tools, as they are the basis for a wide variety of other features, including list views, report snapshots, and custom KPIs, which are discussed in Chapter 20.

A *saved search* is a reusable search definition that includes:

✔ **Search criteria:** What and where to search

✔ **Results:** What data elements to retrieve

✔ **Layout options:** How to present the results

✔ **Available filters:** An optional way to further narrow the results once they're presented

In addition, users who have the publish search permission can share search results with other users in a variety of ways:

- ✔ Assigning an audience and roles for a particular search
- ✔ E-mailing searches to specific recipients based on the results

Revving Up for a Saved Search

You can start a saved search any of the following ways:

- ✔ **Create Saved Search:** Click Create Saved Search on any search page.
- ✔ **Save This Search:** Click Save This Search on any search results page.
- ✔ **Saved search menus:** Depending on your role and permissions, any or all of the following methods may be available to you to start a Saved Search.
  - • From the Transactions tab menu, choose Management⇨Saved Searches⇨New.
  - • From the Lists tab menu, choose Search⇨Saved Searches⇨New.
  - • From the Reports tab menu, choose Saved Searches⇨All Saved Searches⇨New.

Defining a Saved Search

Of course, you first have to define a saved search. The following sections step through a simple example of how to define and view a saved search.

For this example, start a saved search:

1. **From the Reports tab menu, choose Saved Searches⇨All Saved Searches⇨New.**

2. **Select a search type from the list of links that appears.**

Setting general search options

A saved search starts to function as soon as you choose the search type and the Saved Search definition page opens. Click the Preview button to see what results this saved search would produce if you make no changes to it. Figure 19-1 shows the Saved Search definition page.

The Saved Search definition page is actually titled Saved *Search Type* Search. For convenience, we refer to it as the Saved Search definition page in this chapter.

Figure 19-1:
Define
the saved
search on
this page.

Saved Budget Search			

Reset | Save ▼ | Cancel | Preview

* Search Title Custom Budget Search   Available as List View ☐

ID   Available for Reminders ☐

Public ☐   Show In Menu ☐

Criteria | Results | Highlighting | Available Filters | Audience | Roles | Email | Execution Log 🗔

Use this tab to specify criteria that narrow down your search.

Use Expressions ☐

Standard | Summary

*Filter	*Description	Formula
▼ 🗔		

Add | Insert | Remove | Cancel

Look at the fields on the Saved Search definition page. You may see some or all of the options listed here depending on the search type you selected:

- ✔ **Search Title:** A default name is chosen, but you can change it. Because saved searches can appear in multiple places and have multiple uses within NetSuite, pick a descriptive name specific to this particular search.

- ✔ **ID:** Leave this field blank. It is automatically filled in by NetSuite when you save the search. If you provide an ID, NetSuite stores it at the end of the words customsearch. If you don't provide an ID, NetSuite numbers the search customsearchXYZ, where XYZ is a three-digit number.

- ✔ **Public:** Select this option to make this search available to all users. See "Making searches public" later in this chapter for more information.

Limiting viewers

Some roles can publish saved searches for others to use. This can come in handy, but obviously has its pitfalls as well. If you don't have the tabs and options described in this section, then you don't have the permission to publish your searches so that others can use them. Consider that less to worry about. (Of course, if you need this permission, you can always talk to your administrator.)

If a saved search has confidential information, don't make it public. Restrict who sees the search by first leaving the Public check box blank.

From there make selections on the Audience tab to define a more limited audience. List boxes appear where you can select multiple options. There are list boxes for roles, departments, partners, subsidiaries, groups, and employees. After making your choices, click the Save button.

- ✔ **Available as List View:** Select this option if you want the saved search to appear in the View drop-down list when viewing lists of the same search type. *Note:* When this option is selected, this saved search won't appear in the Saved Searches menu. In that case, you must go to the List view for the search type in order to edit this saved search. In the List view, select this search from the View drop-down menu and then click Edit View.

- ✔ **Available as Dashboard View:** This option lets you add a saved search to your dashboard as a Custom Search portlet. Remember to click the Customize This Page link that appears in the upper-right corner of the home page to add a portlet.

- ✔ **Available as Sublist View:** Choose this option if you'd like this saved search to be available as a sublist view for the corresponding search type. In NetSuite, many lists drill down to individual record forms that contain sublists within them. For example, the Activities list drills down to various different forms, such as the Task, Event, or Phone Call forms. Each of these has a tab called Notes with a sublist embedded in it. Another example of a sublist is the list of contacts for a customer. You can create a customized view for such a sublist by defining a saved search for the User Note search type and selecting this option. See Figure 19-2 for an example of a sublist.

- ✔ **Available as Reminders:** When selected, this option makes this saved search available on the Set Up page of the Reminders portlet. In other words, you can set up a saved search to look for transactions that match certain criteria so that you can be reminded to follow up. For example, you might search for customers whose products were installed two weeks ago, and create a reminder to follow up and see how things are going.

- ✔ **Show In Menu:** Select this option to display this saved search title in the Reports⇨Saved Searches menu, making the search easy to find.

- ✔ **Available as Product Feed:** This option is available when using the Item search type and allows you to export the results in a specific format so that they can be uploaded to various shopping comparison engines such as Google Base or Yahoo! Shopping.

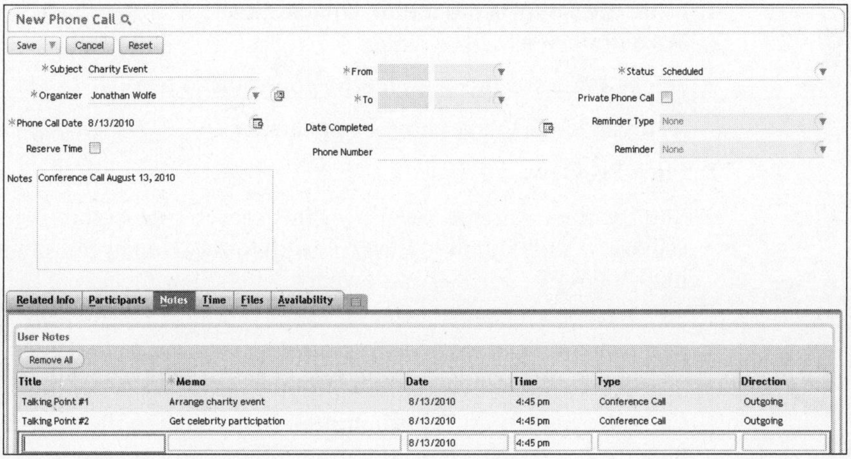

Figure 19-2:
This is a
sublist.

Developing search criteria

The term *search criteria* refers to search result boundaries. Part of the search criteria is already defined by *where* you are looking. If you are looking at a list of students in a grade school, then *grade school students* would already be one boundary of the data. But say you want to see how girls are performing academically; then an additional search criteria would be *female,* and since you want to see the top performing students in that subgroup, an *average of B+ or above* would be added to the search criteria. For a record to be found by this search of *grade school students,* it would have to match *a gender of female* AND *an average of B+ or above.* Otherwise, it won't appear in the results. In this example, *grade school students* are the search type, *gender* and *average* are the data fields, and *female* and *B+ or above* are the values to match.

Search criteria consists of the following:

- ✔ **Search type:** Where to look for the results, such as the customer record.

- ✔ **Data fields:** The fields within that record to search on, such as the state where the customer is located.

- ✔ **Values to match:** The values that field can have to be included in the search. CA would search for customers in California.

Looking at underlying data

To take a look at the underlying data before you start searching:

1. **From the Reports tab menu, choose Saved Searches⇨All Saved Searches⇨New.**

2. **Select a link for the search type you want to use.**

   A screen for that search type appears.

3. **Click Preview.**

   You see the unfiltered results for this search type before you set any criteria. (Cool! You didn't even search for anything yet and you can just look at data!)

   It's possible you won't see any results, perhaps because you don't have permission to see any of the underlying records. In that case, start another search using a search type that has data you can access.

4. **Click the Return To Criteria button to go back to the Search Definition page.**

5. **Click the Criteria tab.**

   Note the two tabs in the criteria section: Standard and Summary. This section focuses on the Standard tab. The Summary tab is discussed later in this chapter in "Summarizing data."

6. **Continue to the steps in the following section (or click Save and come back later when you have more time).**

   You're going to learn more about search criteria in the next section. Standard criteria may not sound exciting, but they are very useful, so keep reading.

You can always click the Save button to save your search and then edit it again later.

Setting standard criteria

In NetSuite, _standard criteria_ refers to a data filter that searches through individual records only, without applying any calculations or groupings to those records. In other words, standard criteria don't calculate or aggregate the data in any way before presenting it. It simply presents any record on the results page that satisfies the specified standard criteria.

Standard criteria are basic but still powerful. Think of the possibilities:

✓ Find all prospects whose deal value is more than $1 million.

✓ Find all support cases that haven't been touched in 72 hours.

✓ Find all employees who can take over that shift you don't want to work this weekend.

Think of other quandaries like these that a quick saved search can answer.

Figure 19-1 shows the Standard tab on the search definition page. Notice that the Use Expressions check box is deselected. With that option turned off, three columns appear below it:

✔ **Filter:** The data field or the formula type to be searched.

✔ **Description:** The values to search for in a data field or formula.

✔ **Formula:** The formula expression to be searched.

The simplest type of search to conduct is a data field that's equal to a particular value (or example, finding all customers in California).

1. **Start up a saved search as outlined earlier.**

2. **Click the Standard tab on the Criteria tab.**

3. **Select a data field from the Filter drop-down list.**

   Try to select one that will have some kind of text in it if you want to follow along.

   A window pops up after you select the data filter. The first field in that window is a drop-down list of comparison operators that are appropriate to the data field you select.

4. **Select a comparison operator from the drop-down list.**

   Depending on the data type of the field you select as a filter, the next field or set of fields that appear will fall into one of the following categories:

   • **A value list:** A list of appropriate values for the data field you select, such as Customers, Accounts or Items. Click on the values you wish to select. Use shift-click and ctrl-click (command-click on Mac) to select multiple values. *Note:* Just because a value appears on the list doesn't mean it will be found by this search. The values in the list come from the primary tables that store such data and may not appear in the area of NetSuite where you are searching.

   • **A date or date/time selector:** When you select a date field as a filter, the pop-up window will display date or date/time selectors to populate the value fields. Click the button next to a date field to call up a calendar from which to select a date and click the drop-down list to select a time of day.

   • **A number value field:** Type a numeric value into this field to create a number comparison. Use a minus sign (-) for negative numbers.

5. **Select (or enter) a value to compare.**

   If you selected Any or All as a comparison operator, you won't need to enter a value.

6. **Click Set to add this criteria to the criteria list.**

You return to the search definition page.

7. **Click Preview to see your results.**

A few outcomes are possible:

- **You didn't get results:** Click Return to Criteria and check the data filter and values you entered to make sure they exist in the unfiltered search. If necessary, clear the search filter by selecting the criteria that you just entered and clicking Remove. Then click Preview again to see the unfiltered results once more.

- **You didn't get more than one result:** Click Return to Criteria and select a data filter and value that returns multiple records.

- **You got more than one result:** Excellent! Look at the data fields that have differences in the data between records and make note of those different values. You'll use them to build a more complicated search.

Building a more complicated search

From the preceding steps, you can continue following here to add another criterion to your standard search:

1. **Click the Standard tab on the Criteria tab.**

You can find it on the search definition page.

2. **Select a second data field from the Filter drop-down list.**

A pop-up window appears.

3. **In the pop-up window, set a second criteria.**

4. **Click Set to add this criteria to the standard criteria list.**

5. **Click Preview to see your results.**

6. **Click Return to Criteria.**

You're returned to the search definition page.

The default operation when adding multiple criteria is for the separate lines, or *clauses,* to be joined by the word AND. In other words, both criteria have to be true for a particular record to appear in your results.

On the Criteria tab of the search definition page you can add multiple criteria lines that will continuously narrow down your search results. You can add as many lines as you like. However, even the most complicated searches will usually not require more than four or five standard criteria.

Choosing the results to display

Figure 19-3 shows the Results tab on the search definition page with the Columns tab selected.

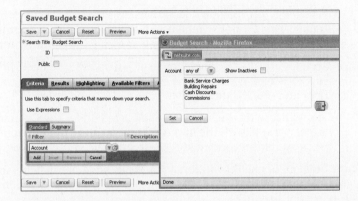

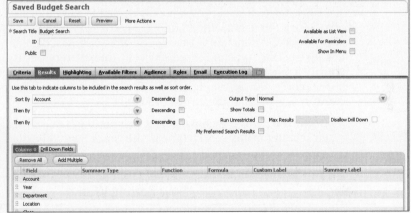

Figure 19-3:
Set up columns to display.

Setting general options for results

Look at the drop down lists:

- ✔ **Sort By and Then By and Then By fields:** Three drop-down lists indicate the sort order for the results. Next to each is an option for Descending if you'd like to reverse the sort order for that selection. Table 19-1 demonstrates how sort orders work.

- ✔ **Output Type:** This selection determines how your results will appear on the screen. Four types of output are available:

- **Normal:** This is the default saved search format. It presents an interactive list with column headers that can be clicked to change the primary sort order. Provided that you have the permissions, this format provides Edit and View buttons for accessing underlying records. You can also select what part of the list you'd like to view based on the primary sort order by using the drop-down list at the bottom of the results page.

- **Report:** This format is similar to Normal, but is more suitable for printing because it contains fewer screen graphics and buttons.

- **Grid:** Identical to Normal, however it displays grid lines, much like a spreadsheet, which can be easier to read (especially if there's a lot of numerical data).

- **Graph:** Presents the first two fields listed under the Columns tab as a bar graph, with the first field representing the horizontal x-axis and the second field representing the vertical y-axis.

✔ **Show Totals:** Choose this option if you'd like all numeric fields to show a grand total at the bottom of the output. Totals can be added to any output except Graph.

✔ **Run Unrestricted:** This option is only available to Administrators. It provides restricted users with limited access to specific records for a specific purpose. For instance, this option would allow a data entry clerk to look up a certain type of record so avoid entering a duplicate. You can indicate a number in Max Results when Run Unrestricted is selected. If more records are returned than are limited by the Max Results field, you see More... printed at the end of the list.

✔ **My Preferred Search Results:** Select this option to make this the preferred search for this search type in the Quick Search portlet.

Table 19-1	How Sorting Works	
First Selection Sorts Everything . . .	*Second Selection Sorts Within First*	*Third Selection Sorts Within Second*
Name	*Grade*	*Homeroom*
Adam	10	Room X
Adam	10	Room Y
Adam	11	Room Y
Adam	12	Room X
Barbara	9	Room X
Barbara	9	Room Y

First Selection Sorts Everything . . .	Second Selection Sorts Within First	Third Selection Sorts Within Second
Barbara	11	Room X
Charlie	9	Room X
Charlie	10	Room X
Charlie	10	Room Y

Setting up columns to display

Look at the Columns tab in Figure 19-3, which displays a default set of columns based on the search type selected when you started the saved search process.

You can remove all of the columns by clicking Remove All. Or, you can add several at a time by clicking Add Multiple and then Ctrl+clicking (⌘+click for Mac users) to select multiple fields to add to the list.

The first thing you can do with the existing columns is change how they appears in the search results page:

1. **Select the second field in the list.**

2. **Place the mouse over the six dots positioned to the left of the field name.**

3. **Click and drag this field up to the first position.**

   Notice that an insertion line travels along with the mouse to show you where the new position will land.

4. **Click Preview to see the results.**

Alternatively, you can select a field, then click Move Up or Move Down to change its order in the list.

You can also add new fields to display in the search results:

1. **Click the Results tab on the search definition page.**

   There should be a new line on the bottom of the Results tab so you can add another criteria.

2. **If you don't see a new line, click the Click Here to Add a Line link.**

3. **Make a selection from the Field drop-down list.**

4. **Click Add.**

   A new, blank line is automatically added.

5. **Make another selection from the Field drop-down list.**

6. **Click Preview to admire your results.**

7. **Click Return to Criteria when you're done oohing and aahing.**

8. **Click Save to preserve your hard work.**

See how easy that is? You're now ready to start creating and saving your own saved searches, but stay tuned because there's more to know. In the next section you read how to turbocharge these searches with some advanced features.

Advancing Your Searches

Just when you thought you couldn't do anything else with a saved search, alas, along come the advanced features! Of course, you probably guessed this because you saw more on the screen than was being discussed.

Summarizing data

In addition to searching through individual records and outputting them in a detailed format, you can summarize results by grouping data together based on common values in fields and even search through summarized results to present only those groups that satisfy your criteria.

For example, you can see total head count by department, or only see departments that employ ten or more people, or see both, if you wish.

To produce a summary saved search:

1. **Click the Results tab on the search definition page.**

2. **In the Columns list, choose a numeric field for which you would like to see a total value.**

   For example, select a field such as Amount or Balance. If an appropriate numerical field isn't on the list, add one by selecting it from the Field drop-down list.

3. **Select Sum from the Summary Type drop-down list for this field.**

4. **Click Add or Done below that field.**

5. **Click Preview to see the resulting summary field.**

Notice that only one record and only one column of data appear on the results page. This single record represents the grand total of all the records in the data set. When you specify summary fields, only those fields with summary types will appear in the results. All other fields become superfluous.

Adding a group for subtotals

Add a data grouping to see subtotals:

1. **Click the Results tab on the search definition page.**

2. **Choose a field you'd like to use as a data grouping.**

   For example, you may want to group by Company or Department or Cost Center. Choose a column in which many of the records have duplicate values so that the results are grouped into several "buckets."

   Choosing a column in which every record has a unique value will not produce meaningful results.

3. **Select Group in the Summary Type drop-down list for that field.**

4. **Click Done to accept your changes.**

5. **Click Preview to see the subtotaled results.**

This time, notice that two columns with multiple records appear on the results page. The first column represents the field you grouped by while the second column, labeled Sum of *<fieldname>*, has the subtotals for the numeric column for each group with a grand total at the end of the list. Before you leave this screen make note of some of the values in the Sum column. We'll use these to create search criteria for the summarized data.

You can select any of the following calculations as a summary type:

- **Count** can be used on any data type.

- **Sum** can only be used on numeric fields, including Currency and Percent.

- **Minimum** can be used on any data type.

- **Maximum** can be used on any data type.

- **Average** can only be used on numeric fields, including Currency and Percent.

However, summary calculations work best when paired with another field using Group as a Summary Type.

Searching summarized data

As stated earlier, sometimes when you only want to see summarized results that meet certain criteria. Before you can search through summarized data, you must set up at least one summary field. Summary searches work best on grouped data. Otherwise, the only value that will be searched is the overall aggregate result such as a grand total.

Search based on summarized data:

1. **Click the Criteria tab on the search definition page.**

2. **On the Standard tab, select any criteria and then click Remove directly beneath it.**

   Note: Standard and Summary search criteria can be used in the same Saved Search. This step is just to keep the search simple while you're learning.

3. **Select the Summary tab.**

4. **From the Summary Type drop-down list, choose Sum.**

   Always be sure to choose the same summary type as a field you calculated on in the Results tab. If you chose to sum a numeric field on the Results tab, choose Sum here.

5. **From the Field drop-down list, choose the same field you calculated on in the Results tab.**

   For example, if you chose to sum the Amount field, choose Amount here.

   A pop-up window appears so you can specify an operator for the field.

6. **Choose an operator from the drop-down list.**

7. **Type a number in the Value field.**

   Use a value that will narrow the search results but not eliminate them. For example, if values ranged from 1 to 100, choose a number in between those two values, like 50.

8. **Click Set.**

9. **Click Done or Add below the Summary Criteria line you're working on.**

   Sometimes it says Done, sometimes it says Add. Either way, it lets you go on to the next step.

10. **Select Save & Run from Save drop-down list to see your summary search.**

11. **Click Edit this Search to return to the search definition page.**

Et voila! That is how you create a summary data saved search and how you search through summary data to retrieve only groups that match your summary criteria. Take a bow.

Using available search filters

One great trick you can pull with saved searches is using search filters that will appear as drop-down lists on your results page so that you can narrow the search results on the fly. This is a clever way to provide flexible results when you don't know exactly what "view" of the data you're going to need to see each time you run the search. Search filters save you from having to edit the saved search each time you want to see a different subset of the data.

You can even include filters for fields that you haven't selected on the Results tab. Just know that if you're using summary fields, the summary result are also filtered. For example, if you select a summary count of employees by department and add a search filter of Status to the page, the count will change depending on whether you've selected Active, Inactive, or All in the Status filter drop-down list on the Results page.

To add a filter to a saved search:

1. **Select the Available Filters tab on the search definition page.**
2. **Select a field from the Filter drop-down list.**
3. **Select Yes or No from the Show in Footer drop-down list.**

   While any field can be used as a search filter, only non-numeric fields can be shown in the footer of a results page. Additional functions of search filters are discussed in the later section, "Ways to use saved searches."

4. **Click Add.**
5. **Select Save & Run from the Save drop-down list.**

Look at the bottom of the results page to see the filter you just added. It will appear as a drop-down list with the unique values of the field you're filtering. Choosing from this drop-down list will change the results on this page. Footer filters even work when you're using a graph as your output type.

Calculating formulas

The ability to calculate formulas boosts a saved search's power and flexibility. Although they're generally employed by more advanced users, you can do some simple things with them that are quite useful. You can use formulas to run "what-if" scenarios. For example, what if you increased your budget by 5 percent? You can include the actual budget in one column and a calculated budget in another. You can also develop search criteria using formulas.

Data types

As you begin reading about calculating formulas, it's important to know a little about data types. NetSuite uses several different data types that are stored differently and are dealt with differently by saved searches. Table 19-2 lists the data types you will deal with in saved searches and how they're used in formulas.

Table 19-2   Data Types and How They're Used in Formulas

Data Type	Description	Notes	Returns . . .	How It Appears in a Formula
Numeric	Any real number between -9,999,999,999.99 and 9,999,999,999.99	Negative numbers are formatted with a minus sign.	. . . a real number without any punctuation other than a decimal point where required.	{NumberField}=-123.456;
Currency	Same as Numeric	Same as Numeric	. . . a real number formatted to two decimal places with commas where required.	Same as Numeric
Percent	Same as Numeric	Same as Numeric	. . . a real number formatted with a percent sign (%).*	Same as Numeric
Date	Any Gregorian calendar date between 4/1/1601 and 12/31/9999	—	. . . a date result formatted as specified under Setup tab men u↪Company↪Pre ferences↪General Preferences	{DateField}=01/31/2008
Date/Time	Any date/time between 4/1/1601 12:00 a.m. and 12/31/9999 11:59 p.m.	—	. . . a date/time result formatted as specified under Set up↪Company↪Pre ferences↪General Preferences	{DateField}=01/31/2008 7:01 am
Text	Any alphanumeric text such as customer name or street address	—	. . . an alphanumeric string of characters.	{Company Name} = NetSuite

Results of percent formulas are automatically multiplied by 100, so factor this into your calculations.

NetSuite, like other products such as Microsoft Excel, has pre-defined formulas called *functions* that accept parameters in order to calculate specific values.

Perhaps the most important thing to bear in mind is that most functions work with only one or a few data types. Generally, NetSuite will warn you if you are trying to pair a function or formulas with the wrong data type.

Calculating formulas in results

For this example, use the Saved Search you developed in the preceding exercises. Begin by clearing out the previous search criteria on both the Standard Criteria and Summary Criteria tabs by going to each tab and clicking Remove on each item listed, if any. Next go to the Results tab and remove the Group and Sum summary types by choosing the blank selection from the Summary Type drop-down list. Now, add a new field to the bottom of the list:

1. **Select Formula (Numeric) from the Field drop-down list.**

2. **Click Add.**

   This activates the Formula field on this line.

3. **Click the Formula field on the line you just added.**

4. **Click the Set Formula button next to the field.**

5. **In the Formula field, type** *1.05 **after the field name you just selected.**

   If you selected the Amount field in Step 6, the field will look like this: {amount}*1.05. This shows the value in the Amount field increased by five percent.

6. **Click Set.**

7. **In the Custom Label field, type** 5% Increase.

8. **Click Done.**

9. **Select Save & Run from the Save drop-down list to see your results.**

Make note of the results in the calculated column.

Searching with formulas

Using formulas in search criteria is a powerful way of discovering things in your data that you may not see without them. Formulas can test or augment data to uncover conditions in your business that may not be obvious otherwise. They can be used for forecasting and experimenting with what-if scenarios. Formulas are your friends.

If you included calculated results in your saved search, you may want to search through those results for specific records. For instance, if you've calculated a budget increase of five percent, you may want to see where those dollar amounts have exceeded a certain threshold (say $100,000).

Return to the Criteria tab in your search definition page and remove any criteria that may be there. Also, remove any criteria from the Summary tab, if any exists. Start with a clean slate:

1. **On the Standard Criteria tab, select Formula (Numeric) from the Field drop-down list.**

2. **In the pop-up window, select the same field you included in your calculation on the Results tab.**

   If you selected Amount in the calculation on the Results tab, select it again here.

3. **In the Formula field, type** *1.05 **after the field name you just selected.**

   If you selected Amount in Step 2, the formula should look like this: {amount}*1.05.

4. **Select a comparison operator from the Formula (Numeric) drop-down list.**

5. **Type a number in the Value field.**

   Use a value that will narrow the search results but not eliminate them. For example, if values ranged from 1 to 100, choose a number in between those two values, like 50.

6. **Click Set.**

7. **Click Preview.**

Refining a search with And/Or expressions

When you use more than one search criteria in a saved search, the default action in NetSuite is to join the various criteria together by using the expression And. This means that *all* the criteria have to be true in order for a record to be found by a search (as in, if you clean your room AND vacuum, you can go to the mall).

If you use the word Or instead, it creates an entirely different search (and gets you the mall quicker too). In this case, you only have to fulfill one condition or the other, not both.

The phrases on either side of And or Or are often referred to as *clauses,* much the same as the clauses you learned about in English class in grade school.

Think of it this way: When the word And is used, it tends to reduce the number of records found by the criteria listed before it, but when the word OR is used, it tends to increase the number of records found by the criteria that are listed before it. The word Or is most often used when searching the same field for more than one value, as when you want to see customers in either California or New York (since the same field can't be equal to both values at once).

However, NetSuite allows you to search with the terms Any or Any Of to find any *one* value in a list of values in the same search criteria, which creates an Or search without actually using the word.

But there certainly are cases you will need the flexibility offered by saved searches to join two or more clauses together by explicitly stating And or Or.

To use And/Or, on the Criteria tab, select the Use Expressions check box. Selecting this check box adds extra columns the Criteria list. The And/Or column appears on the right side of the list. The values can be (you guessed it) And or Or.

When explicitly using And/Or, the most common mistake is to get confused when stating the formula in plain English. You say, "I want to see all customers in New York and California." But remember that one field can't be equal to two values at the same time, so you have to translate it as Customer State = "NY" OR Customer State = "CA".

Highlighting data in search results

Sometimes you want to see a full set of data with certain conditions high-lighted, such as a customer report showing a red flag next to customers with a particularly high balance. Accomplishing this is rather simple in NetSuite.

1. **Select the Highlighting tab on the search definition page.**
2. **On the Highlight If tab, click the Set Filters icon (a diagonal up arrow) next to the Condition field.**
3. **In the pop-up window, select a field from the Filter drop-down list.**
4. **In the new pop-up window, select a comparison operator from the drop-down list.**
5. **In the Value field, type a value that you'd like to highlight.**
6. **Click Set.**

   This will close the last window that popped up.

7. **Click Set again.**

   This will close the first window that popped up.

8. **Back on the Highlight If tab, select an icon from the Image drop-down list.**

9. **In Text Color Chooser, select a color.**

   You may want white if you're going to choose a colored background in the next step.

10. **In the Background color chooser, select another color.**

    Just don't choose the same color for text and background, or this will be invisible (the opposite of highlighting).

    Select contrasting colors in Steps 9 and 10, which will make the highlighted items stand out.

11. **Select Bold in the next column.**

12. **Type some text in the Description field if you want to verbally flag highlighted results.**

13. **Click Preview.**

You can add as many conditions as you'd like and make each one as complex as you'd like. It's one more way that NetSuite helps you illuminate your data — literally.

Being Generous with Your Saved Searches

Provided you have a publish search permission of at least the Create level, you will have two more features on your search definition page. These features allow you to share your saved searches, sparing you (and your colleagues) from duplicate work:

   ✔ **Public option:** Share your search with everyone in your organization.
   ✔ **Audience tab:** Share your search with selected groups in your organization.

Making searches public

Only users with at least the Create level of the publish search permission are able to make searches public. When you select the Public option on the search definition page, all users can see results for public searches. However, only the search owner (usually its creator) and Administrators can edit a public search.

Select the Allow Audience to Edit option on the Audience tab to indicate that those who can view the search results can edit the search itself.

Even public searches aren't available to customers, vendors, and partners (advanced partners excepted). However, if for any reason such users can run a published saved search, they would only see their own records.

Defining an audience

If you have the correct permissions, you will see the Audience tab, which you can use to restrict who can run a saved search and see its results. By default, only the creator of a saved search can initially edit and run it. It is up to the saved search owner (typically the creator, unless ownership has been reassigned by an Administrator) to define any additional users who can edit or run the search.

If you want other audience members to be able to edit a saved search, select the Allow Audience to Edit option on the Audience tab.

You can define your audience by selecting individual Roles, Employees, Partners, or Groups. Make selections from these lists by clicking the desired value. Press Ctrl+click (⌘+click for Macs) to select multiple values on a list. You can also choose the Select All option at the top of an Audience list if you want to grant access to the entire list.

Ways to use saved searches

Once you've created your saved search, use it in a variety of ways throughout NetSuite:

- ✔ **List Views:** When you enable the Available as List View option on the search definition page, the saved search is available on the View drop-down list in the List View for that particular search type.

- ✔ **Sublist Views:** When you enable the Available as Sublist View option on the search definition page, the saved search is available in the View drop-down list in the Sublist View for that particular search type.

- ✔ **Basic Search Forms:** A saved search can be used by someone (who has the right permissions) using the Publish Form page to create basic search forms that can be published on a Web site or intranet site.

✔ **Global Search Results:** Your saved search appears when queried in global search results (if you have the correct permissions).

✔ **Custom KPIs:** You can use a saved search as a custom KPI in the following:

- **KPI Portlets**
- **KPI Meters**
- **KPI Trend Graphs**
- **KPI Scorecards**
- **Report Snapshots**

Chapter 20

Exposing Metrics on Your Dashboard

*A*t its most basic level, accounting is about record keeping. In decades past, record keeping consumed most of an accounting department's time. Compiling standard reports such as financial statements and balance sheets consumed the rest of it. Dedicated bookkeepers, often depicted wearing green visors and sleeve garters, toiled over leather-bound journals and ledgers.

But ain't technology grand? Today, when your customer buys something from you through the Internet, NetSuite records the entire transaction automatically. In fact, depending on your business model, NetSuite can handle all of your company's processes end to end, from buying supplies to delivering products. Instead of arduously maintaining records you can mine them for precious nuggets of wisdom. Businesses have gone from being producers of vast quantities of data to consumers of it.

This chapter lays the foundation for leveraging NetSuite's powerful set of analytical tools that can distill your data into the rich knowledge needed to propel your company forward.

Harnessing the Power of Key Performance Indicators

Key performance indicators (KPIs) are quantifiable and measurable — repeat, quantifiable, and measurable — *metrics* that companies use to determine how well they're achieving their pre-determined goals. "Gross Sales" is quantifiable and measurable. "Way Cool" is not. Although "Way Cool" may be a stated goal in your business plan, and laudable at that, it doesn't make for a good KPI because there's no objective way to measure it.

A *metric* is simply a standard of measurement. Within NetSuite, it's a way of turning your raw data into useful information from which you can draw valuable insight about your business. One way to think of a metric is as an answer to a question about your data. Who are my top salespeople? How do they compare to each other? How do they compare month to month? How do they compare to each other month to month? All of these questions and many more can be answered using metrics.

NetSuite has over 75 pre-designed standard KPIs built in to it that you can set up in the Key Performance Indicators portlet on your dashboard. The standard KPIs available to you depend upon which role you're using; the KPIs can each be viewed in four different ways, which are discussed in this chapter:

- ✔ **Summary:** This most basic view of a KPI is presented in a one-line summary format in the Key Performance Indicators portlet.

- ✔ **Meter:** A KPI Meter presents data in a graphic that closely resembles a gauge on your car's dashboard. This view appears in its own specialized portlet.

- ✔ **Trend graph:** This view is a line graph that shows the KPI data values on the y-axis with time intervals on the x-axis. It appears either in a pop-up or in its own specialized portlet.

- ✔ **Scorecard:** A KPI Scorecard provides comparisons among multiple KPIs over multiple date ranges or accounting periods. Spreadsheet-like formulas can be added to Scorecards that include KPIs and functions in their expressions. To use it you must enable this view before you can use it. Once enabled, you add a specialized Scorecard portlet to your dashboard.

You discover more about each of these views in detail later in this chapter.

Once you have added a KPI to your dashboard, you can review the basic metrics at a glance and drill down to the detailed data that supports it. (Simply click it.) In short, KPIs place a tremendous amount of analytical power right at your fingertips. And if that's not enough, you can create custom KPIs for your very own pie-in-the-sky KPI.

When to use a KPI

The two best times to set up a KPI are

- ✔ When you can have an impact on the data.
- ✔ When the data can have an impact on you.

In other words, it doesn't make any sense to track something that you have no control over or that otherwise has no effect on how you do your job. If you're a Marketing Director tracking the Gross New Leads KPI and it dips below a pre-determined threshold, then you can take some action to try to drum up more leads. But what's a Customer Service Manager going to do with that same information? Customer Service likely has little or nothing to do with lead generation, nor does Gross New Leads have any effect on how that department performs its duties. The customer service manager is better off using the Cases Escalated and Cases Closed KPIs.

Most often, a company uses many KPIs to achieve the primary goals of the organization at large. For instance, the president probably has an eye firmly fixed on the Profit KPI as the company's primary goal. The chief financial officer looks at specific KPIs as they relate to profit such as cost of goods sold (COGS), while the sales director monitors the Quota KPI among others, all in the pursuit of the same goal — higher profits. Practically every NetSuite user can find a standard KPI that accurately reflects his or her own contribution to the bottom line.

Adding the Key Performance Indicators portlet

If it's not already there, add the Key Performance Indicators portlet to your dashboard:

1. **Click the Customize this Page link.**

   The link's on the upper-right side. The Add Content pane opens.

2. **Click the Key Performance Indicators link.**

3. **Click the X in the upper-right corner of Add Content window.**

   The window closes

Note: If Key Performance Indicators appears in the list in bold type with a green check mark next to it, then it is already on your dashboard. See Figure 20-1.

Figure 20-1:
Add the Key
Performance
Indicators
portlet
to your
dashboard.

Choosing KPIs

Once the Key Performance Indicators portlet is on your dashboard, you need to add one or more KPIs to make it worthwhile. After all, an empty portlet isn't very useful, is it? Standard KPIs appear as one-line summaries in your portlet.

To add summary KPIs, click the Set Up link near the bottom of the Key Performance Indicators portlet. The Set Up Key Performance Indicators window opens as shown in Figure 20-2.

Figure 20-2:
Set up KPIs.

To add other KPIs, follow these steps:

1. **Click the Add Standard KPIs button.**

   The Choose Standard Key Performance Indicators window opens, as shown in Figure 20-3. Depending on the number of KPIs available, you may see an additional drop-down list that allows you to jump to a particular segment of the alphabetized list.

2. **Click the text to select a particular KPI.**

   The KPIs you choose populate the list on the right. You can select as many as you wish, but pick at least three so you get enough experience with layout options and features.

Figure 20-3:
Choose
standard
KPIs.

3. **Click Done.**

   You're done now, unless you want to work on the layout of your KPIs, as described in the next section.

4. **Click the Save button.**

Setting KPI layout options

After you choose KPIs, you'll see one row for each KPI you selected from the list in the Set Up Key Performance Indicators window. Notice that the same set of fields and options appears on each row. Corresponding to the numbers in Figure 20-4, Table 20-1 details what each of those fields and options means and how each one sets layout options.

Table 20-1	Fields and Options in the Set Up Key Performance Indicators Window	
Indicator in Figure 20-4	**Name**	**Description**
1	Mover	Click the six small dots (to the far left of each KPI row) to drag the selected row up or down to change its order in the list, or click Move to Top or Move to Bottom to put the selected row in one of those locations.
2.	Help	Click the question mark icon for detailed help on the selected KPI.

(continued)

Table 20-1 *(continued)*

Indicator in Figure 20-4	Name	Description
3	Key Performance Indicator	Identifies the selected KPI.
4	Range	Use this drop-down list to select a point in time (such as today) or a date range (such as this fiscal month) from the list of dozens of pre-defined date ranges.
5	Highlight if . . .	Highlight a row of data in the KPI portlet if it's greater than or less than a particular number that you set in the Threshold column. Highlighted data appears in the KPI portlet in bold followed by a red flag. Leave this field blank if you don't want to highlight this KPI.
6	Threshold	Set the number above or below which you want to have a particular KPI highlighted.
7	Compare	Select this option if you want to compare the period you specify in the Range column with another period you indicate in the Compare Range column.
8	Compare Range	Specify the period that you'd like to compare to the value you enter in the Range column. Use the drop-down list to access dozens of pre-defined ranges. For example, you may choose to compare today with one month ago.
9	Remove this KPI	Click the X to remove this KPI from the list.

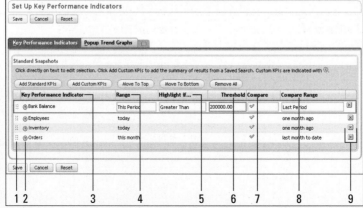

Figure 20-4: Setting the layout options on Key Performance Indicators.

Setting up KPI comparisons

In many cases, a KPI is automatically set to compare two periods by default. In the Set Up Key Performance Indicators window, set up a comparison for a particular KPI:

1. **Select the Compare check box.**

2. **Select a date range from the Compare Range drop-down list.**

Your KPI portlet must be in the center column of your dashboard in order for comparison data to appear. Comparison data doesn't appear in KPI portlets that are placed in the left or right columns of the page.

Highlighting KPIs

You can make data stand out on the page if it's over or under a pre-determined threshold. In the Set Up Key Performance Indicators window, highlight the data for a particular KPI:

1. **Select Greater Than (or Less Than) from the Highlight If drop-down list.**

2. **In the Threshold field, type a number above or below which you want this KPI to be highlighted.**

   The KPI appears in the portlet in bold with a red flag next to it if the data surpasses the threshold you've set.

3. **Click the Save button.**

Viewing your KPI data

Your selected KPIs will appear in the KPI portlet on your dashboard after you click Save. Using the corresponding numbers in Figure 20-5, Table 20-2 describes what you're seeing.

Table 20-2		KPI Portlet Options
Indicator in Figure 20-5	*Name*	*Description*
1	Refresh KPI	Click this icon (circular arrows) to refresh the data in this particular KPI. Or you can click the Refresh All link near the bottom of the KPI portlet.
2	Indicator	Identifies the KPI.

(continued)

Table 20-2 *(continued)*

Indicator in Figure 20-5	Name	Description
3	View Graph	Click this icon of a graph symbol to see your KPI presented as an interactive graph. Among the most powerful features in NetSuite, this button appears for any KPI for which comparison values can be set up, whether a comparison for that KPI is actually set up or not.
4	Period	Specifies the date range to which the KPI pertains.
5	Current	Shows the current KPI for the date range indicated in the Period column.
6	Previous	Shows data for the period specified by the compare range, if you select the Compare option when setting up the KPI.
7	Change	Indicates the percentage change between the periods.

Figure 20-5:
This Key Performance Indicators portlet has selected KPIs.

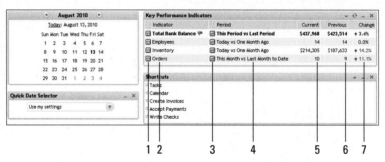

Drilling down to the details

In NetSuite, you can access a KPI's supporting detail instantly by clicking the number in either the Current or Previous columns of the KPI portlet to see the raw data that was used to calculate it. This is referred to as *drill down*.

If you're curious about what makes up the number in your Profit KPI, click it to drill down to the financial statement from which it is drawn. If your Employees KPI is showing 28 last month and 31 this month, drill down to the employee roster to see the three people who make up the difference. In many cases, the screen you drill down to can be drilled down even further.

Measuring Performance Using KPI Meters

A KPI Meter resembles a speedometer and appears in its own portlet as a graphical representation of a KPI that is already in your KPI portlet. You can add as many as three KPI Meter portlets to your dashboard. You can format each KPI Meter to handle KPI data for a date range comparison or a highlighted threshold (regardless of how the KPI is originally set up in your KPI portlet). However, when you first add a KPI to a KPI Meter, the KPI will assume the layout options you have set up in the KPI portlet.

To add a KPI to a KPI Meter, the KPI must first appear in your KPI portlet.

KPI Meters are particularly helpful for monitoring those KPIs that are critical to your job performance. Similar to an airplane cockpit that has the most important gauges right where the pilot can see them, a KPI Meter can alert you when to take action. For instance, a production manager monitoring the Inventory KPI Meter can take corrective steps if quantities creep too low or too high.

KPI Meters provide the most useful information when you configure them to highlight a threshold. The threshold number will appear at approximately the one-third or two-thirds mark on the meter depending on whether you have chosen Less Than or Greater Than, respectively, from the Highlight If drop-down list on the Set Up page. The left limit of the meter then represents 0 percent and the threshold mark represents 100 percent. The needle indicates where in relation to those two points the actual data falls.

Special KPI Meters

You can use three special KPI Meters in addition to the ones that are provided by default in your KPI portlet:

- ✔ Actual vs. Forecast
- ✔ Actual vs. Quota
- ✔ Forecast vs. Quota

When you select one of these in a KPI Meter, you may get the message "Please set up this meter." This message means you need to add one or both of the supporting KPIs to the KPI portlet in order to use this KPI Meter. See Table 20-3 for a list of the supporting KPIs for each special KPI Meter.

Table 20-3	Using Special KPI Meters
To Use This Meter . . .	*. . . Place These KPIs in Your Key Performance Indicators Portlet*
Actual vs. Forecast	Sales, Forecast (Alt. Sales)
Actual vs. Quota	Sales, Quota
Forecast vs. Quota	Forecast (Alt. Sales), Quota

Adding a KPI Meter portlet to your dashboard

To add a KPI Meter portlet, follow along:

1. **Click the Customize this Page link on the page you want to customize.**

   The Add Content window opens.

2. **Click one of the listings for KPI Meter.**

   You can add up to three, which is why you see KPI Meter listed three times.

3. **Close the Add Content window by clicking the X in the upper-right corner of the window.**

   Figure 20-6 shows the KPI Meter portlet on the dashboard.

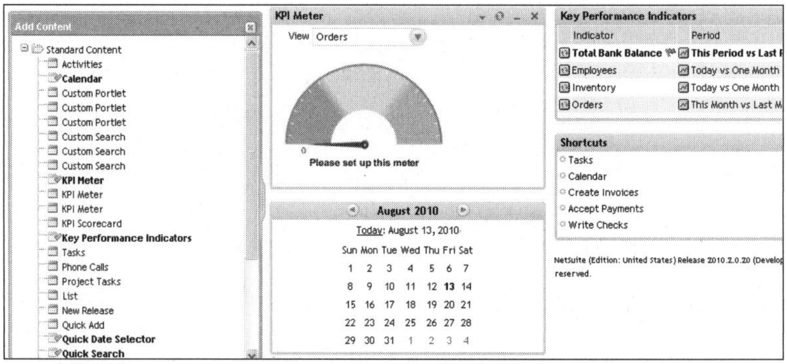

Figure 20-6: The KPI Meter portlet appears on the dashboard.

Setting up your KPI Meter

Set up one of the KPIs in your KPI portlet:

1. **Select a KPI from the View drop-down list in the KPI Meter portlet.**

2. **Click the Set Up link.**

   By default, the details on the KPI Meter Set Up page will be the same as in the KPI portlet for any given KPI. Figure 20-7 shows an example of the KPI Meter Set Up page.

3. **Select a value from the Highlight If drop-down list.**

4. **Type an appropriate number in the Threshold field.**

5. **Select the Compare check box.**

6. **Select a period from the Compare Range drop-down list.**

7. **Click the Save button.**

Figure 20-7:
Setting up a
KPI Meter.

 Pay attention to the relationship between the KPI Meter portlet and the KPI portlet. When you change the Set Up parameters for a particular KPI in one, it changes the Set Up parameters for that KPI in the other. However, the changes for the other portlet (the one you didn't edit directly) don't take effect until you refresh that portlet's data by clicking Refresh (or, if there's more than one, Refresh All).

Monitoring Activity Through Trend Graphs

In NetSuite, a *trend graph* is a line graph that shows the differences in KPI data values over time. The y-axis shows the selected KPI's values, and the x-axis represents the time interval. You can change the time interval as needed to daily, weekly, monthly, quarterly, or yearly. You can also export a trend graph to a spreadsheet.

As the name implies, a trend graph is best used to examine changes in data over an extended period of time to discover patterns of behavior *(trends)*. This differs from the Summary KPI and the KPI Meter, which both represent snapshots of data at specific points in time. The trend graph is a reflective look at the data that can answer broader questions: When are our best selling seasons? Are sales increasing? Which way are costs moving?

NetSuite's trend graphs display in two different modes:

✓ **Pop-up trend graphs** display in their own windows when a View Graph icon is clicked.

✓ **Trend Graph portlets** display continuously in their own portlets on the dashboard.

Setting up pop-up trend graphs

To set layout options for all pop-up trend graphs, follow along:

1. **Click the Set Up link in the KPI portlet.**

2. **Click the Pop-up Trend Graphs tab.**

3. **Select one or more of the following options for your graph (shown in Figure 20-8):**

   • **Show Rolling Average on Pop-up Trend Graphs:** By default, trend graphs show a solid line and shading for the actual data. Selecting this option adds a dotted line that represents a rolling average of the data.

   • **Show Last Data Point on Pop-up Trend Graphs:** Trend graphs display data through the last closed period unless you choose the Show Last option, in which case pop-up trend graphs show the very latest data even if a period is still open in NetSuite.

   • **Include Zero on Y-Axis:** Y-axis values begin with an approximation of the lowest value in the data set. Choosing this option shows y-axis values starting at 0.

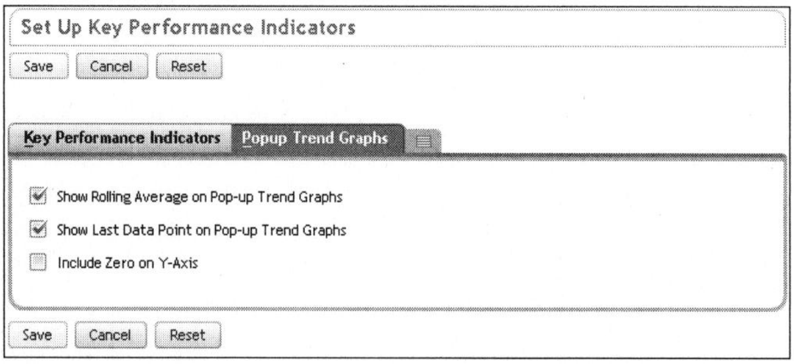

Figure 20-8:
Setting up
pop-up
trend
graphs.

Set Up Key Performance Indicators

Save   Cancel   Reset

Key Performance Indicators   Popup Trend Graphs

☑ Show Rolling Average on Pop-up Trend Graphs

☑ Show Last Data Point on Pop-up Trend Graphs

☐ Include Zero on Y-Axis

Save   Cancel   Reset

Displaying a pop-up trend graph

Pop-up trend graphs are available from the KPI portlet for all standard KPIs for which the Compare feature is available. Figure 20-9 shows the View Graph icon in the KPI portlet. You can also enable the View Graph icon in the KPI Scorecard, which is covered later in this chapter. In Figure 20-10, notice that the pop-up Trend Graph page is interactive.

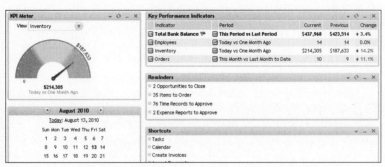

Figure 20-9: The View Graph icon appears in the Key Performance Indicators portlet.

Different KPIs display different time-interval options.

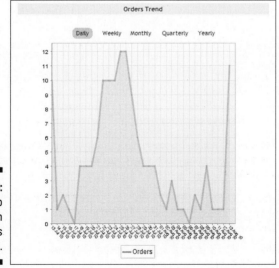

Figure 20-10: The pop-up Trend Graph page is interactive.

Adding a Trend Graph portlet to your dashboard

A Trend Graph portlet functions the same as a trend graph pop-up except that you can permanently attach the portlet to the dashboard.

You can add up to five Trend Graph portlets to your dashboard:

1. **Click the Customize this Page link on the page you want to customize.**

   The Add Content pane opens.

2. **Scroll down and click + to expand the Trend Graphs folder.**

   The remaining number of trend graphs you can add to your dashboard is listed in parentheses next to the folder. If no trend graphs are currently on your dashboard, you will see (5 available). Which trend graphs are available depends on which role you're using.

3. **Click the trend graph you want to display.**

   The trend graph is immediately added to your dashboard. Repeat if you'd like more trend graphs on your dashboard.

4. **Click the X in the upper-right corner of the Add Content pane.**

   The Add Content pane closes, and you're done.

Setting up a Trend Graph portlet

A Trend Graph portlet is functional as soon as you add it to the dashboard, but you can change its appearance and how it presents the data. Figure 20-11 shows the Trend Graph portlet Set Up page, which is opened by clicking the Set Up link near the bottom of the portlet. The following options can be selected on the Set Up page:

- **Trend Type:** Select Daily, Weekly, Monthly, Quarterly or Yearly from the drop-down list to change the default period for this Trend Graph portlet.

- **Show Average:** By default, Trend Graph portlets show a solid line andshading for the actual data. Selecting this option adds a dotted line representing a rolling average of the data.

- **Average Window:** This number represents the window of data to average based on the date range selected in the Trend Type field. For example, if you selected weekly and enter 3 as the window, the data points on the y-axis represent a 3-week average.

✔ **Show Last Data Point:** Trend Graphs show data through the last closed period. When this option is selected, Trend Graph portlets show the very latest data even if a period is still open in NetSuite.

✔ **Include Zero on Y-Axis:** Y-axis values begin with an approximation of the lowest value in the data set. Selecting this option shows y-axis values starting at 0.

✔ **Color:** Click here to change the color of the primary trend line and its shading.

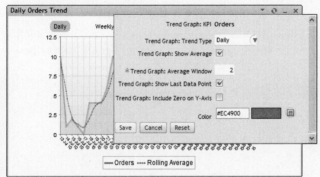

Figure 20-11:
You set up options on a Trend Graph portlet.

Taking a tour of a trend graph

Figure 20-12 shows a Trend Graph portlet on the dashboard. Trend graphs offer the following features:

✔ **Time Period:** Click one of these buttons (Daily, Weekly, Monthly, Quarterly, or Yearly) to change the time period for which the trend graph is drawn.

✔ **Trend Line:** This line shows the trend for the raw data for this trend graph for the period indicated. You can set the color for this line on the Set Up page.

✔ **Average Line:** If selected on the Set Up page, this optional line shows the average trend in specific time increments that can be chosen on the Set Up page.

✔ **Y-axis Origin:** You can set the y-axis to originate with 0 on the Set Up page. Otherwise, the y value origin is based on an approximation of the lowest value in the data set.

✔ **X-axis Values:** The x-axis represents the time intervals over which the trend is graphed. These intervals change depending on the time period you select.

✔ **Refresh:** In a Trend Graph portlet, click this button to refresh the data set and redraw the graph, if necessary. This button doesn't appear in a trend graph pop-up. To refresh the data in a trend graph pop-up, close and reopen the pop-up.

✔ **Set Up:** In a Trend Graph portlet, click this link to access the Set Up page (see "Setting up a Trend Graph portlet"). This link doesn't appear on the trend graph pop-up. To set up a trend graph pop-up, see "Setting up Pop-up Trend Graphs" earlier in this chapter.

✔ **Export:** Click this link to export data to a spreadsheet, such as Microsoft Excel. (See "Exporting data from a Trend Graph," described next.)

Figure 20-12: A Trend Graph portlet is shown on the dashboard.

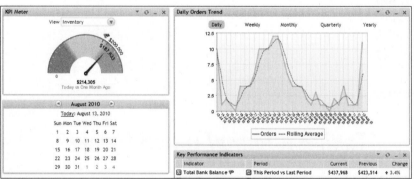

Exporting data from a Trend Graph

Click Export at the bottom of the Trend Graph page, whether a pop-up or a portlet, to create a text file in comma-separated values (CSV) format of the current trend graph view. See Figure 20-13 for an example of the file. You can save this file to disk or open it in your browser, provided you have Microsoft Excel or some other spreadsheet software installed on your computer.

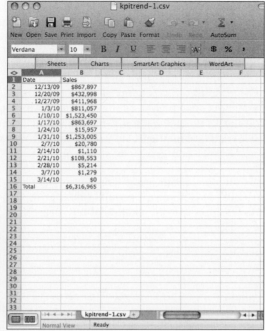

Figure 20-13:
Trend graph
data can be
exported to
a spread-
sheet.

Grading Your Business with KPI Scorecards

KPI Scorecards are a clever way to illuminate your data because they combine multiple KPIs over multiple date ranges or accounting periods. The underlying strength of KPI Scorecards is their customizability: Scorecards can be modified to include spreadsheet-like formulas using KPIs and functions in their expressions and can display KPI data in many ways, including trend graphs. They slice! They dice! They even julienne!

You wouldn't necessarily use a KPI Scorecard to determine whether to take immediate action (although you can, if you wish). Instead, it is a more sophisticated way to monitor the health of your business. Think of a Scorecard as a fancy piece of medical equipment monitoring your company's vital signs. To stretch the medical metaphor, if you were a doctor monitoring someone's blood pressure, and the pressure suddenly shot up dangerously high, you wouldn't take action based solely on that one piece of information. You would look for a specific cause before administering treatment. In the same way, the KPI Scorecard can show ratios, percentages, and trend lines that would lead you to investigate further if they don't fall within expected ranges.

A prime example of this "medical monitoring" concept is the Financial Ratios Scorecard, which is pre-built in NetSuite. It groups together the kind of key financial metrics that CFOs and CEOs get excited about and includes the following comparative KPIs:

- ✔ Current Ratio
- ✔ Receivables Turnover
- ✔ Days Sale Outstanding
- ✔ Inventory Turnover
- ✔ Days Inventory on Hand
- ✔ Asset Turnover
- ✔ Profit Margin on Sales
- ✔ Return on Assets
- ✔ Return on Equity
- ✔ Debt to Total Assets
- ✔ Debt to Equity

By default, you can display this scorecard in your KPI Scorecard portlet only if you have permission to view the Trial Balance report. However, Administrators can modify this scorecard's definitions to create a custom Financial Ratios Scorecard, including granting permission to additional users to display the scorecard.

Enabling the KPI Scorecards feature

You must enable this feature in your account before you can use it and only Administrators can enable features. To enable KPI Scorecards:

1. **Log in as Administrator.**

2. **From the Setup tab menu, choose Company⇨Enable Features.**

3. **On the Company tab, select KPI Scorecards.**

4. **Click the Save button.**

If the Enable Features option isn't available on your Setup tab's menu, you lack the necessary permission to do this. Ask your Administrator to enable the KPI Scorecards feature.

Adding a KPI Scorecard portlet to your dashboard

To add the KPI Scorecard portlet to your dashboard, do this:

1. **Click the Customize This Page link on the upper-right side of the page you want to customize.**

   The Add Content window opens.

2. **Click KPI Scorecard.**

3. **Close the Add Content window by clicking the X in the upper-right corner of the window.**

If KPI Scorecard appears in the list in bold type, then it's already on your dashboard.

Creating a KPI Scorecard

Once you've added the KPI Scorecard portlet to your dashboard you can create a new scorecard:

1. **From the Setup tab menu, choose Customization⇨KPI Scorecards⇨ New.**

   This menu option is only available if the KPI Scorecards feature is enabled. See "Enabling the KPI Scorecards feature" earlier in this chapter.

2. **Type** Sample Scorecard **in the Name field.**

Using a unique, descriptive name will save you a lot of time later when you go looking for that KPI Scorecard you just created. Be aware that NetSuite will allow you to duplicate the name of an existing KPI Scorecard.

3. **In the Content section of the page, select a standard KPI from the drop-down list.**

4. **Click Add.**

The current KPI is saved and a new line is created.

5. **Select another KPI from the drop-down list.**

   For this exercise, select a KPI that you would like to see in relation to the first one. For example, if you chose the Sales KPI for the first selection, choose the COGS KPI for the second, as the difference between the two indicates a gross margin.

6. **Click Add.**

7. **In the new line, select the same KPI as in Step 3.**

   In this example, you will compare the first KPI to the second.

8. **On the same line, select the same KPI as in Step 5 from the Compare Value To drop-down list.**

9. **On the same line, select Variance (Percent) from the Comparison Type drop-down list.**

10. **Click Add.**

11. **On the same line, type** Pct Change **in the Label field.**

12. **Click Add.**

13. **In the Date Ranges section, select This Month from the Range drop-down list.**

    If the Date Ranges section has a plus sign (+) next to it, click this to expand the section.

14. **Click Add.**

15. **In the new line, select Last Month from the Range drop-down list.**

16. **Click Add.**

17. **In the new line, select This Month from the Range drop-down list.**

18. **On the same line, select Compare With Previous.**

19. **On the same line, select Variance (Percent) from the Comparison Type drop-down list.**

20. **On the same line, type** Monthly Change **in the Label field.**

21. **Click Add.**

22. **Click the Save button.**

The new KPI Scorecard is now available for you to add to your KPI Scorecard portlet.

Setting up a KPI Scorecard

Once you create a KPI Scorecard, you must set it up in a KPI Scorecard portlet. Figure 20-14 shows the KPI Scorecard Set Up page. You can open this page by clicking the Set Up link near the bottom of the portlet. You choose from the following options on the Set Up page and click Save to view your changes in the KPI Scorecard portlet:

- ✓ **KPI Scorecard:** Select the KPI Scorecard you want to display in the portlet from the drop-down list.

- ✓ **Restrict To:** Select the scope of the data that you would like to see in the KPI Scorecard. The KPI Scorecard can reflect all data, only the data relevant to your team, or only the data where you are tagged as the owner. Select an option from the drop-down list:

  - All

  - My Team

  - Only Mine

- ✓ **Orientation:** Select how you want the data oriented from the drop-down list: KPIs on Left or Data on Left.

- ✓ **Show Trend Graph Icon:** Select this to option to display the pop-up Trend Graph icon.

- ✓ **Show Date Row:** Select this option to display the dates for the periods covered by the KPI Scorecard. The dates will appear in a single row above the data.

Figure 20-14:
A KPI Scorecard must be set up in a KPI Scorecard portlet in order to be useful.

You may have to scroll down to find the Save button in the KPI Scorecard Set Up page.

Using formulas in a KPI Scorecard

One of the best reasons to use a KPI Scorecard is to embed formulas composed of KPIs and functions to analyze your data in ways the folks at NetSuite could never dream up.

KPI Scorecard formulas come in three flavors:

- ✔ **Currency** will add a currency symbol to the result. For U.S. dollars, it will add a dollar sign ($).
- ✔ **Numeric** will have no punctuation other than commas and a decimal point where appropriate.
- ✔ **Percent** will format the output as a percentage, including multiplying the result by 100 and adding a percent sign (%).

Notice that all three types only format the result. Don't be misled: Even though there's a type called Numeric, all three types have to do with numbers. You can't create formulas that return date, Boolean, or character type results in KPI Scorecards. If you don't know what those types are, don't worry. You can't use them anyway.

For argument's sake, pretend you'd like sales numbers rounded up to the nearest thousand. So, do this to add a formula to your Sample Scorecard:

1. **From the Setup tab menu, choose Customization⇨KPI Scorecards.**

2. **Click Edit next to the name of the KPI Scorecard you wish to edit.**

   If you were following along with the previous steps, it's named Sample Scorecard.

3. **In the KPIs section, select Formula (Currency) from the drop-down list.**

   A new line is automatically inserted at the end of the KPIs section when you enter Edit mode.

4. **In the Formula field, type this:** ROUND({SALES},-3)/1000

   The ROUND() function takes two parameters. The first parameter, {SALES}, is the Sales KPI, and the second parameter, -3, indicates that you want to round up to the thousands. Dividing by 1000 removes the trailing zeros, as is often done on financial reports.

5. **Type** Sales (000's) **in the Label field.**

6. **Click Save.**

7. **Return to the page containing your KPI Scorecard portlet.**

   If necessary, click Set Up in the portlet and select the scorecard you just edited if it's not already visible.

8. **Click Refresh to view the results of your formula.**

You have added a formula to your KPI Scorecard! The crowd goes wild! Time for a victory lap around your desk while someone plays fanfare on a kazoo.

The Formula field can be somewhat temperamental when used in conjunction with the Function and Field drop-down lists. If you're used to using spreadsheet software, you'll notice that the behavior between these drop-down lists and the field isn't as elegant as editing formulas in a product like Microsoft Excel. Any value that you select from the drop-down lists will be appended to the end of whatever is already in the field regardless of where the cursor was last in the field. That can be a bit frustrating. The drop-down lists are useful for looking up available formulas, functions and their parameters, but will require some cutting and pasting in the field when you select items from them.

Building Custom KPIs

If none of the standard KPIs suit your needs, you can create a custom KPI based on a saved search. In NetSuite, there is no limit to how discrete or how specific a KPI can be. If the data is there and changes periodically, chances are it will support a KPI.

Custom KPIs are based on Custom Saved Searches. In order for a Saved Search to serve as a Custom KPI, there are several things to pay attention to depending on how you want the KPI data displayed:

- ✔ **Record counts:** To simply display the number of records returned by search results in the KPI, any Saved Search will suffice.

- ✔ **Summary data:** In order to display summary data such as sum (total), count, average, minimum, or maximum, the search must contain a summary type defined for an appropriate field on the Results tab of the Saved Search form.

   If more than one field is defined as a summary type on the Results tab in the Saved Search form, the KPI will display the data for the first summary field that *isn't* defined as Group. (There's not a simpler way to put it, so re-read the last sentence as often as it takes for you to get it.)

- ✔ **Summary search filters:** Because KPI calculations don't include groupings, KPIs can't enforce summary search filters. The results for the KPI may differ from a Saved Search's results if the Saved Search includes any summary search filters.

✔ **Summary search filters:** Because KPI calculations do not include groupings KPIs cannot enforce summary search filters. The results for the KPI may differ from a Saved Search's results if the Saved Search includes any summary search filters.

✔ **Comparing time ranges:** To display a comparison of data for different time ranges, or to use the data in a KPI meter, trend graph, or KPI Scorecard, the search must:

• Not have a date range defined as search criteria.

• Have only one field with a summary type (such as group, sum, or count) defined.

• Have a date column defined as a Filter on the Available Filters tab of the Saved Search form.

✔ **Using Periods:** If you selected the Use Periods option for a scorecard, you must specify a Period filter as an Available Filter in the Saved Search for it to appear as a Custom KPI in the scorecard.

Adding a Custom KPI to a KPI portlet

Once you verify that a Saved Search meets the criteria for a Custom KPI, you can add it to a KPI portlet:

1. **Click Set Up in the KPI portlet.**

2. **Click Add Custom KPIs.**

3. **Select the Custom KPI from the list.**

   Click the name of the Custom KPI you wish to select.

4. **Click Done.**

5. **Set up the Custom KPI with your desired options.**

6. **Click Save.**

Once a custom KPI (or any KPI, for that matter) has been set up in a KPI portlet, it is available for use in a KPI Meter. To use a Custom KPI in a KPI Meter, select it from the View drop-down list in the KPI Meter portlet. Click Set Up to choose layout options.

Displaying a Custom KPI in a Trend Graph portlet

To display a Custom KPI in a Trend Graph portlet:

1. **Click Customize this Page.**

2. **Expand the Trend Graphs folder.**

   Click the plus sign (+) next to the folder.

3. **Select Custom KPI #1.**

   Or select the next available Custom KPI in the series. There are 10 in all.

4. **Close the Add Content window by clicking the X in the upper-right corner.**

5. **Click Set Up in the new Trend Graph portlet.**

6. **Select the Custom KPI you wish to display from the Custom Trend Graph drop-down list.**

7. **Set the other layout options as desired.**

8. **Click Save.**

Showing a Custom KPI in a KPI Scorecard

To show a Custom KPI in a KPI Scorecard:

1. **Click Edit in the KPI Scorecard portlet where you want to add the Custom KPI.**

2. **In the Content section of the KPI Scorecard, select a Custom KPI from the Custom KPI #1 drop-down list.**

   To add up to 10 Custom KPIs, select them in order from the respective drop-down lists labeled Custom KPI #1 through Custom KPI #10.

3. **In the KPIs section, select Custom KPI #1 from the KPI drop-down list.**

4. **Click Add.**

5. **To add additional Custom KPIs, repeat Steps 2–4.**

6. **Click Save.**

7. **Return to your KPI Scorecard portlet**

8. **Click Refresh to see the newly added Custom KPI.**

Seeing Your Business Through Report Snapshots

A *report snapshot* shows summary data from one of the many pre-built reports provided by NetSuite through a Report Snapshot portlet on your dashboard. NetSuite allows up to 10 Report Snapshot portlets on a dashboard at any one time.

The Report Snapshot portlet is a keyhole view of a standard report for a given date range since it only looks at a given number of records taken from the top or bottom of the report. It includes a View Report link for you to access the underlying detail. Many of the snapshots allow you to configure the number and order of results, as well as choose the format that best suits your needs.

By now, you may be wondering why there's often a limit to how many of an item you can add to a dashboard: three KPI Meters, five trend graphs, ten report snapshots, and so on. This is to avoid creating a performance bottleneck on the system. Too many portlets refreshing data at the same time can slow your dashboard down dramatically, which probably wouldn't make you happy. The folks at NetSuite want you to be happy.

Use a report snapshot for those standard reports that you access most frequently and which have the greatest impact on your daily or weekly affairs.

Which report snapshots you can access depends on the role you're using. In addition to standard report snapshots, roles with access to sales reports can view Sales Management Snapshots that are rolled up to different management levels. There are three Sales Management Snapshots:

- ✔ **Sales Managers by Sales Orders:** Based on the Sales Orders by Sales Rep Summary report, this snapshot displays the approved sales order totals for each manager and sales rep in a selected date range.

- ✔ **Sales Managers by Forecast:** Based on the Forecast vs. Quota report, this lists the quota, actual sales, calculated forecast, and override forecast for each manager and rep in a selected date range.

- ✔ **Sales Managers by Sales:** Based on the Sales by Sales Rep report, this snapshot shows sales revenue by each sales manager in the selected period range.

Adding a Report Snapshot portlet to the dashboard

To add a Report Snapshot portlet, follow along:

1. **Click the Customize this Page link on the page you want to customize.**

   The Add Content window opens.

2. **Scroll down and click + next to the Report Snapshots folder.**

   The number of Report Snapshots you have left to add to your dashboard is stated in parentheses next to the folder.

   If no Report Snapshots are currently on your dashboard, it says (10 available). Which Report Snapshots are available depends on your role.

3. **Close the Add Content window by clicking the X in the upper-right corner of the window.**

Setting up a Report Snapshot portlet

A Report Snapshot portlet works as soon as you add it to the dashboard, but you can change several aspects of its appearance and how it presents data. Figure 20-15 shows the Report Snapshot portlet Set Up page. Open this page by clicking the Set Up link near the bottom of the portlet. The following options can be selected on the Set Up page:

- **Date Range:** Select the date range you wish the report snapshot to display from the drop-down list.

- **Display Type:** Select whether you want the report snapshot to display as a list or a graph.

- **Display Order:** Select whether you want the results to be from the top of the report or the bottom of the report.

- **How Many:** From the drop-down list, select how many items you want to display from the report.

- **Layout:** If you chose to display the report snapshot as a graph, here you can select what type of graph you would like to see.

- **Color:** If you chose to display the report snapshot as a graph, click here to change the graph's primary color.

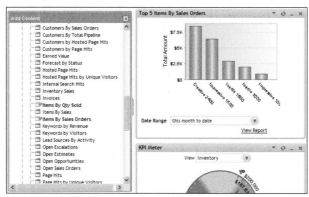

Chapter 21

Reporting and Analytics

*1*t's time to unleash your inner artist! Getting data out of the system and into a presentable format is probably one of the most satisfying aspects of using a system like NetSuite. The inherent value in any business software is the ability to analyze the data it contains. There's nothing like that "Oh, wow!" moment when you suddenly see your information in its clearest form. Even the simplest report can have a great deal of impact if it illuminates a corner of your business that had remained hidden.

The gathered information is really all about informed decisionmaking. Do you stop, stay the course, or change direction? Ultimately, a report is only so much ink or screen clutter if it can't answer that question. A well-designed report does so much more than list a bunch of boring facts and figures. It sells a point of view and influences perception.

NetSuite's onscreen reports are interactive and can be output in a variety of document formats, including print, CSV, and PDF to name a few. Lots of pre-defined reports come standard with NetSuite and will suit most users' needs. Many of these standard reports have parameters you can change on the fly to hone in on the data you want.

Getting Started with Reports

To access reports, you must have the correct permissions. If you don't see the Reports tab on your Home page, check with your Administrator. You may have the Reports tab, but may not see some reports or report types. Permissions define whether you can view or modify report formats and whether you can view or modify the underlying data.

For example, to view the Sales by Customer report, you need the Sales Report permission. To drill down to the customer record from that report, you need permission to view that record.

Setting preferences for reports

As a NetSuite user, you can set preferences that tell the system just how you want report functions to operate.

1. **From the Home tab menu, choose Set Preferences.**

   The Set Preferences page opens.

2. **Click the Reporting/Search tab.**

3. **Change the options you want to set:**

   • **Report by Period:** Tell NetSuite whether you'd like to use Reporting Periods for All Reports, Financials Only, or Never. Selecting Never toggles between using dates and the accounting periods transactions are posted to.

   • **Print Company Logo**

   • **Display Report Title on Screen**

   • **Display Report Description**

   • **Default Bank Account:** This preference only affects the Bank Register and Bank Balance reports.

   • **Show Forecasts as Weighted:** This option shows the weighted forecast value rather than the total projected forecast values on reports.

   • **Minimum Forecast Probability:** This preference only shows up if you haven't selected Advanced Forecasting for your NetSuite account. It sets the minimum forecast probability in your Forecast and Pipeline Performance Indicators reports. Forecast results will be greater than or equal to the value entered here.

Administrators set company-wide preferences: From the Setup tab menu choose Accounting⇨Accounting Preferences.

Table 21-1 shows the preferences and their locations on the Accounting Preferences page.

Table 21-1   **Setting Company-wide Reporting Preferences**

Preference	Tab	Section	Description
Cash Basis Reporting	General	General Ledger	Select this option to use cash-basis accounting instead of accrual basis for your reports. You also can set this option on the Report Customization page.
Aging Reports Use	General	General Ledger	Select whether you want to age bills and invoices by the Due Date or the Transaction Date.
Include Reimbursed Expenses in Sales and Forecast Reports	Items/ Transactions	Sales & Pricing	If this option is selected, transactions that affect expense accounts are included in sales and forecast reports.
Include Shipping in Sales and Forecast Reports	Items/ Transactions	Sales & Pricing	This option includes shipping costs in sales and forecast reports.
Transaction Types to Exclude from Sales Reports	Items/ Transactions	Sales & Pricing	Select transactions to explicitly exclude from sales reports. Use Shift+click or Ctrl+click (⌘+click on Macs) to select multiple transactions.
Transaction Types to Exclude from Forecast Reports	Items/ Transactions	Sales & Pricing	Select transactions to explicitly exclude from forecast reports. Use Shift+click or Ctrl+click (⌘+click on Macs) to select multiple transactions.

Report types

When you access the Reports page — from the Reports tab menu, choose Reports Overview — a number of submenus classify the reports by type. The first three listed are present for just about everyone who has access to this page:

- ✔ Saved Reports
- ✔ Scheduled Reports
- ✔ Saved Searches

The rest depend on your role and the permissions available to that role, but they may include:

- ✔ Financial
- ✔ Revenue
- ✔ Banking/Budgeting
- ✔ Payroll
- ✔ Employees/HR
- ✔ Time & Billables
- ✔ Purchases
- ✔ Vendors/Payables
- ✔ Inventory Items
- ✔ Order Management
- ✔ Customer/Receivables
- ✔ Commissions
- ✔ Sales
- ✔ Sales Orders
- ✔ Forecast
- ✔ Customer Service
- ✔ Issue Management
- ✔ Marketing
- ✔ Pipeline Analysis
- ✔ Web Presence
- ✔ Integration

Finding and Accessing Reports

Perhaps the first step to determining if there's a useful report out there for you is knowing how to find reports.

You can find an existing report in NetSuite three ways:

- ✔ **Browse the Reports page:** From the Reports tab menu, choose Reports Overview to go to the Reports page. In the Report Links portlet, click + next to a menu to see a list of reports for that topic (or click Expand All to see what's under all submenu headings).

- ✔ **Click the Find link:** In the Report Links portlet, type a keyword that appears in the title of a report to see all reports with that word. All Reports submenus are searched automatically and found report titles appear with that keyword highlighted.

- ✔ **Use Global Search:** Type the full title or just a keyword in the Global Search link at the top of the window to find all relevant items in NetSuite, including reports.

After you find the report you need, choose one of the following actions:

- ✔ Click a report's name to run it.

- ✔ Click the Customize link next to it to go straight to the Report Builder where you can change formatting and choose data elements to suit your needs.

- ✔ Click the Customize link (or Edit link, as the case may be) next to a financial report to open the Financial Report Builder.

- ✔ To create an ad hoc report, from the Reports tab menu, choose New Report (or from the Reports tab menu, choose Reports Overview and click the New Report link).

Running Reports

Running an existing report, whether it's a standard report, saved ad hoc, or financial report, is a simple matter of clicking the report name on the Reports page or in a Global Search results list. NetSuite's on-screen reports are highly interactive, allowing you to change filter settings and output options directly from a report's results page.

Some reports may take several minutes or longer to produce results. If you see a thermometer running that looks like it's going to take some time to complete, click Alert Me When Ready, and you'll get an e-mail notification including a link to your results when the report is ready.

Summary and detail reports

Reports listed directly underneath the submenu headings on the Reports page are summary versions. Reports that also have detail versions will display a Detail link just beneath the report name. Many summary reports that don't list a specific detail version can be drilled down to a detail page. For example, almost all reports have drill-down capability to transaction or individual item record pages, such as Customer or Vendor pages. Figure 21-1 shows an example using the standard Forecast by Customer Summary report that has an accompanying detail version.

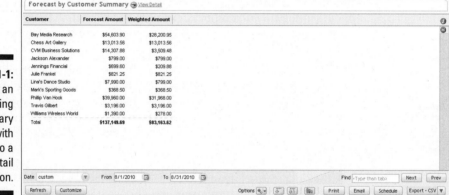

Figure 21-1: Run an existing summary report with a link to a detail version.

The title of the report is at the top of the page. Next to that is the View Detail link, which appears anytime there's an accompanying detail version of a summary report. Below that are the column headings, followed immediately by the data. By clicking the View Detail link, you see the results in Figure 21-2. You also see detail for individual summary records by clicking the numbers in the numeric column (Weighted Amount). A View Detail balloon appears whenever a detail report exists for a particular record. You return to the summary report by clicking View Summary or Return to Summary.

Customer	Type	Sales Rep	Probability	Date	Exp. Close Date	Forecast Amount (grand total)	Weighted Amount (grand total)
Forecast by Customer Detail ⊙ View Summary							
⊟ Bay Media Research							
111	Sales Order	Sam R Cruz	100.00%	8/13/2010		$1,798.00	$1,798.00
4	Opportunity	Sam R Cruz	50.00%	8/1/2010	8/3/2010	$52,805.90	$26,402.95
Total - Bay Media Research						**$54,603.90**	**$28,200.95**
⊟ Chess Art Gallery							
112	Sales Order	Mark Grogan	100.00%	8/5/2010		$13,013.56	$13,013.56
Total - Chess Art Gallery						**$13,013.56**	**$13,013.56**
⊟ CVM Business Solutions							
113	Sales Order	Mark Grogan	100.00%	8/12/2010		$809.88	$809.88
5	Opportunity	Mark Grogan	20.00%	8/1/2010	8/3/2010	$13,498.00	$2,699.60
Total - CVM Business Solutions						**$14,307.88**	**$3,509.48**
⊟ Jackson Alexander							
1034	Invoice		100.00%	8/10/2010		$799.00	$799.00
Total - Jackson Alexander						**$799.00**	**$799.00**
⊟ Jennings Financial							
6	Opportunity	Mark Grogan	30.00%	8/13/2010	8/13/2010	$699.60	$209.88
Total - Jennings Financial						**$699.60**	**$209.88**

Date custom ▼ From 8/1/2010 To 8/31/2010 Find ‹Type then tab› Next Prev

Refresh Customize Options Print Email Schedule Export - CSV

Figure 21-2:
Click View
Detail and
see the
results with
a link to a
record.

Expanding or collapsing data

Reports often produce data in a hierarchical fashion. In other words, they display data starting with more generalized records and group-related records just beneath them in an increasing level of detail. Think of each top-level record as a Russian babushka doll in which one doll is nested inside another.

You can expand or collapse each level of data:

- ✔ Click + or - next to each record to either expand or collapse that particular line.

- ✔ Click Options at the bottom of the results window, and then select a level from the Expand Level drop-down list.

- ✔ Use the Expand or Collapse buttons at the bottom of the results page to expand or collapse the entire report one level at a time.

Navigating through a report

When the results for a particular report exceed one page, use the Report Navigation pane (to the right side of the report window) to jump directly to specific records in the report. Mouse over a marker to see the record it represents and click it to go directly to that record in the report. See Figure 21-3.

Mouse over the Information symbol at the top of the navigation bar

to see the total number of data rows produced by this report and the range of rows currently visible in the results window.

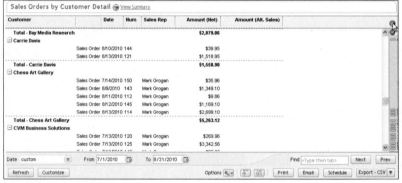

Figure 21-3: Jump to specific records and see total number of data rows.

Footer filters

In the footer area of nearly all reports are options for filtering data. These options often include date drop-down lists and date pickers to change, narrow, or expand the date range for which a report is being run. If a report is based on accounting periods (fiscal year, quarter, and the like), then an appropriate drop-down list appears in place of date options.

Click More next to the footer filters to see additional filter options. These may include additional drop-down lists to further refine results based on different field values, such as Customer or Vendor name.

After you change settings in a report's footer, click Refresh to see the results of the new filter.

Finding records

A Find field is at the bottom right of all reports to help locate specific values anywhere in the entire report:

1. **Type the value in the Find field.**

2. **Click Next or Prev.**

   The Finder searches forwards or backwards through the report and highlights the nearest found value. It highlights the search string in yellow on the report.

3. **Click Next or Prev to continue searching.**

Setting results options

Click the Options button at the bottom of the results page to access the following settings:

✔ **View:** Select Report-Plain or Report-Grid to turn grid lines on or off.

✔ **Expand Level:** Select the level of detail you want to see in the report. Selecting Expand All displays all details; Collapse All shows just the summary-level information. Some reports have multiple levels of detail, and for these you can select 1, 2, or 3 to view progressively more detailed results.

✔ **Display Title:** Reveal the full report title, including company name and the date range at the top of the results page.

✔ **Show drill-down balloons:** Display a balloon announcing whether a drill-down report exists when you mouse over a particular record.

Selecting output options

In addition to viewing your data on the results page, you can output the data in different ways:

✔ **Graph:** Clicking this button on the summary page produces a graph of the data using the first column of data on the x-axis. By default, the first column of numeric data is used as the first y-axis. You can set the following options in the Graph window:

   • **Type:** Choose one of three chart types from the drop-down list: Bar Graph, Pie Chart, and Line Graph.

- **Show:** Select a text column from this drop-down list to be charted on the x-axis.

- **vs.:** Select which numeric column to chart on the left y-axis.

- **Also show:** Select which numeric column to graph in addition to the first.

- **TOP:** Choose how many values to chart on the x-axis.

- **2nd Y-axis:** This option produces a second y-axis on the right for the column chosen from the Also Show drop-down list.

✔ **Print:** Click this button to produce a WYSIWYG preview of your report and activate your computer's print function. The output shows exactly what you've formatted on the results page, including what level you have expanded or collapsed the records.

✔ **E-mail:** This activates a window from which you can e-mail this report by setting options on the following tabs:

- **Recipients:** From a list of recipients who registered within your NetSuite account, choose who should receive this report. You can't e-mail reports to addresses that aren't registered in your NetSuite account.

- **Message:** Type a message that all recipients of this e-mail will see. Select the Send Report as Attachment option on this tab if you'd like to send the report as an attachment rather than in the body of the message.

- **Attachments:** Select any additional attachments you'd like to send with this report.

✔ **Schedule:** Click this button to e-mail this report sometime in the future (either on a one-time or recurring basis).

✔ **Export:** Use this drop-down list to produce a file from this report in one of the following formats:

- **.CSV:** Comma-Separated Values is a raw-text format that can be opened by practically any spreadsheet, database, or word processing program. CSV is the simplest method of exchanging data between software systems.

- **.PDF:** Portable Document Format is a non-editable version of the printed report in digital format suitable for sending via e-mail or posting on the Web or intranet.

- **Microsoft Word:** This editable version of the report uses the table features in MS Word.

- **Microsoft Excel:** This format exports all rows of the report regardless of the expand/collapse level in use, but it hides currently collapsed rows when the export is executed. Choose Format➪Rows➪Unhide in MS Excel to display the hidden rows.

Starting a New Report

Most of your reporting needs are likely to be fulfilled by NetSuite's self-contained, pre-built reports using footer filters and other options that you can set at runtime and have a wide array of output options. However, when you must create your own report, NetSuite has provided a powerful set of tools that make the task as simple or as complex as your skill and experience allow. It's actually very easy to create a feature-rich report with only a few clicks of the mouse.

Figure 21-4 shows a New Sales Report page. To see how quickly you can produce a dynamic, interactive report in NetSuite try the following:

1. **From the Reports tab menu, choose New Report.**

   The New Report page opens.

2. **Click a metric name, any metric name.**

   Humor us.

   NetSuite assumes that you're writing a report to measure something (a *metric*). Selecting a metric first narrows down the overwhelming amount of data. You can also write reports that don't measure things, like customer contact sheets, but these are usually fairly simple and, lucky for you, the NetSuite report writer is geared toward a much more complicated task.

3. **Select the format of the report by choosing a radio button:**

   • **Summary** subtotals the data selected from the Metric drop-down list in Section 1 and creates one row of data for each unique value in the field selected in Section 3.

   • **Detail** shows the individual records that make up subtotaled values in a summary report.

   • **Matrix** creates an array that subtotals the data selected in the Metric drop-down list by the field selected in Section 3, and then again by another data field whose values become headings for additional columns.

4. **Select how you want to subtotal the report.**

   From the Component drop-down list, choose the primary data field by which you want to subtotal, then from the Field drop-down list, select the secondary field for subtotals.

   If you select Matrix as the report type, a fourth section is added to the New Report page. Otherwise, skip to Step 6.

5. **Select how you want to summarize the data across columns from the Column drop-down list.**

6. **Click the Run Report button.**

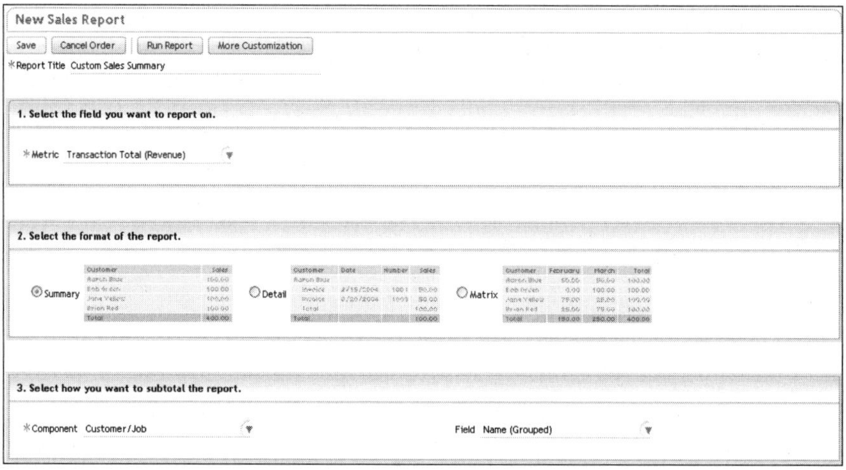

New Sales Report

Save | Cancel Order | Run Report | More Customization

*Report Title Custom Sales Summary

1. Select the field you want to report on.

*Metric Transaction Total (Revenue) ▾

Figure 21-4:
You can create your own report from one of the New Report pages.

2. Select the format of the report.

⦿ Summary   ○ Detail   ○ Matrix

3. Select how you want to subtotal the report.

*Component Customer/Job ▾   Field Name (Grouped) ▾

Isn't that amazing? The folks at NetSuite have worked very hard to protect you from having to know very much about report writing.

You see this New Report page only when you're creating a report. As soon as you click Run Report, Save, or More Customization, this page disappears. Any further changes are made in the Report Builder. However, you don't have to save your work yet, because you haven't done very much to get this far. Once you make your selections, just click Run Report. If you're not satisfied at this point, simply start over from the Reports tab menu, choosing New Report and re-selecting the metric you had previously chosen. Within a couple of seconds, you're back at the beginning. You can save it later after you've done more customizing.

Customizing an Existing Report

Now that you've created a report, use the Report Builder to customize and add complexity to it. You can access the Report Builder in any one of the following ways:

- ✓ **Reports page:** Click Customize when it appears next to a report name on the reports page.

- ✓ **Global Search result:** Click Edit when it appears next to a report listing in a Global Search result.

- ✓ **New Report page:** Click More Customization on the New Report page.

- ✓ **Results page:** Click Customize on a Results page.

If you only have View permissions for Report Customization, you will see Customization and Edit links but get an error when you click the links. Also, if you have Create permissions, rather than Edit permissions, you will have access to the Report Builder and can preview reports, but you can't run or save them. However, Preview and Run are virtually the same.

At the top of the Report Builder page are four links:

- Edit Columns
- Filters
- Sorting
- More Options

Just below these links is the Name field, which contains the title you gave on the New Report page and which can be changed at any time here.

Editing columns

Figure 21-5 shows the Edit Columns page, which is where the Report Builder first lands. The Edit Columns page has two panes: Fields and Report Preview.

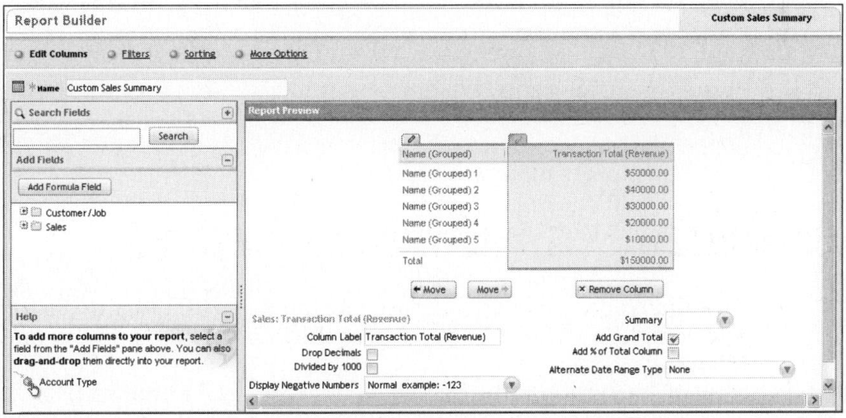

Figure 21-5: The Report Builder page is where you begin to customize your reports.

Fields pane

This pane is divided into three sections:

- **Search Fields:** Type any part of a column name into the Search field and click Search to locate all field names containing that keyword.

✔ **Add Fields:** You can browse a list of fields in the Add Fields section. Field names may be in folders that you open by clicking + next to the folder name. Click or drag-and-drop fields from the Add Fields pane to the Report Preview pane to add them to the report.

✔ **Help:** This section presents details about fields as you mouse over them.

The folders, also known as *report components,* usually map to a particular record in NetSuite. In some cases, they may combine fields from multiple records or even add calculated fields, depending on the type of report. Subfolders most often represent a specific record, which is linked to the top level record or component. For example, a Transaction component has a subfolder for Item. This is basically the same as doing a join in Saved Search (see Chapter 19).

Report Preview pane

The second pane is the Report Preview, which isn't actually a full preview of the report but more of a focused glimpse of the columns that you choose, showing their order and formatting options.

You select a column for editing by clicking directly on it or on the Edit symbol tab attached to it.

The first column on the left is the column you selected in Section 3 of the New Report page, and it has text information. If you haven't selected any other columns, the second column on the report is the Metric field you chose in Section 1 of the New Report page; and it has numeric data.

Column options

Depending on the type of column you select, a set of options specific to that column appears directly underneath:

All columns offer the following options:

✔ **Column Label field:** Type a name for the column as you would like it to appear on the report. This field defaults to the column name within NetSuite.

✔ **Move buttons:** You can change the order of a column by clicking the Move Left or Move Right buttons. You can also move columns by dragging-and-dropping them with the mouse.

✔ **Remove Column button:** Click here to remove the selected column from the report.

The first and second columns offer the following two, respectively:

- ✔ **First column:** Will have a Group option if you want to subtotal data by the unique values in this field.

- ✔ **Second column:** Will always have a Group With Previous column option if you want to also group data by this field. The second grouping is nested within the first. For instance, if you want to group a sales report by Customer and then by Sales Rep, there is a row of data for each customer name and then, beneath each customer, is the name of each Sales Rep associated with that customer.

Numeric columns offer these options:

- ✔ **Drop Decimals:** This option rounds the result to the nearest whole number.

- ✔ **Divided by 1000:** This option rounds results to the nearest thousand, which is commonly done on financial and business reports.

- ✔ **Display Negative Numbers:** This drop-down list determines how negative numbers will be displayed, whether with a minus sign, parentheses or as an absolute value.

- ✔ **Negatives in Red:** Selecting this option will display negative numbers in red.

- ✔ **Summary:** This drop-down list defines how summary rows are calculated. Select Sum, Count, Minimum, Maximum, or Average.

- ✔ **Add Grand Total:** This option determines whether a grand total is calculated at the bottom of this column.

- ✔ **Add % of Total Column:** This option add an extra column which calculates a percentage of the total for each row of data in the report.

- ✔ **Alternate Date Range:** Select an alternate date range that applies to this column only. For example, on a Sales by Customer report, you can set up a column for gross sales amount and another column for gross sales amount for the last fiscal year. That way, any date range you choose in the report filter will always automatically compare the first column to the date range in the second.

Adding a formula column to a report

In the Add Fields section of the Fields pane in the Report Builder is a button labeled Add Formula. Click this button to add a column that will calculate the values from two other numeric columns.

All of the formatting options available to a numeric column are also available to a formula with the following additions:

- **Formula Type:** Use this drop-down to specify what calculations you'd like to perform between the two columns. Select from:
  - **Difference x-y**
  - **Percent Difference of ((x-y)/x)*100**
  - **Percent Difference of ((x-y)/y)*100**
  - **Ratio x/y**
  - **Percent Ratio (x/y)*100**
  - **Multiply x*y**
- **x:** Choose which numeric column you want to represent x in the formula above from the drop-down list.
- **y:** Choose which numeric column you want to represent y in the formula above from the drop-down list.
- **Apply Formula to Grand Total:** Select this option to apply the formula to the grand total. Otherwise, the grand total will simply be a sum of the column's results.

Filtering data

When you select the Filters link in the Report Builder, a new set of panes opens similar to the panes on the Edit Columns page. Figure 21-6 shows the Choose Filters pane in the Report Builder.

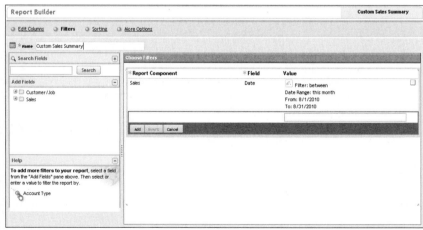

Figure 21-6:
Select the Filters link to open a new set of panes.

Fields pane

The pane on the left is the Fields pane from which you select the fields you would like to filter.

✔ Type any part of a column name into the Search field and click Search to locate all fields containing that keyword.

✔ Browse a list of fields in the Add Fields section. Field names may be in folders (which you open by clicking + next to the folder name). Click the name of a field to add it to the filter list.

✔ The Help section presents details about fields as you mouse over them.

Choose Filters pane

The pane on the right is the Choose Filters pane. Each field that you're filtering will appear on its own line in this pane.

✔ Click the line to display the filter selections.

✔ Select which type of filter you would like to use from the Filter drop-down list.

✔ Depending on which field you've chosen and which filters you employ, a value field may appear that is specific to that filter type. It may be a field, a drop-down list, or a date picker. Enter the value you want this filter to compare against to include or exclude records for this report.

Sorting records

Click the Sorting link in the Report Builder to open a new set of panes. Figure 21-7 shows the Sorting page in the Report Builder.

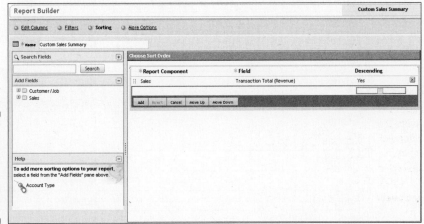

Figure 21-7:
Choose your sorting options from the Sorting page.

Fields pane

The pane on the left is the Fields pane from which you select the fields you would like to filter.

✔ Type any part of a column name into the Search field and click Search to locate all fields containing that keyword.

✔ Browse a list of fields in the Add Fields section. Field names may be contained in folders which you open by clicking + next to the folder name. Click the name of a field to add it to the sorting list.

✔ The Help section presents details about fields as you mouse over them.

Choose Sort Order

Sort order specifies how the information on the report appears. It can be alphabetically by name, numerically by date or revenue, or whatever other order you choose. (Customer's middle initial would be a new twist on sort order, though probably not very useful.)

If no sorting is specified, the records are presented in what is known as *natural order* — the order they were entered into NetSuite. Once you select a field to sort, whether you'd like that column sorted in descending order (Z to A or 9 to 0).

The sort order is very important, which is why you can move a selection up or down in the list by clicking Move Up or Move Down directly beneath an entry in the Sorting list.

Table 21-2 demonstrates how sort orders work.

Table 21-2	How Sorting Works	
First Selection Sorts Everything	**Second Selection Sorts Within First**	**Third Selection Sorts Within Second**
Name	*Grade*	*Homeroom*
Adam	10	Room X
Adam	10	Room Y
Adam	11	Room Y
Adam	12	Room X
Georgia	9	Room X
Georgia	9	Room Y
Georgia	11	Room X
Kate	9	Room X
Kate	10	Room X
Kate	10	Room Y

Setting additional options

The More Options link appears at the top of the Report Builder. This is separated into two sections, Report Options and Audience. Figure 21-8 shows the Additional Options page in the Report Builder.

Report options

Available report options depend on which metric you selected when you started the report. You may see some of these report options:

- ✔ **Show Zeros:** This option displays records in your report for which there is a zero value in all numeric columns. When this option isn't selected, all numeric columns across the board have to contain a value of zero in order for the record to be excluded. When this option is not selected, any record that contains a value of 0 in all numeric columns across the board are excluded.

- ✔ **Web Store Sales Only:** Choose this option if you only want sales completed online to be included in your report.

- ✔ **Open Transactions Only:** Select this option to only include open transactions on your report.

- ✔ **Activity Only:** This option includes only records for which there was activity during the selected period.

- ✔ **Below Reorder Point:** Choose this option to see only items that are due for reorder.

- ✔ **Show On Reports Page:** This option displays the report title under the Saved Reports heading on the Reports page.

✔ **Allow Web Query:** Choose whether you want this report to be exportable as an Excel Web Query. If so, a new option (Export-Excel Web Query) appears in the Export button on the results page of this report. Export-Excel Web Query produces an IQY file suitable for import into Microsoft Excel.

✔ **Show Currency Symbol:** This option shows a currency symbol on currency-type numeric fields.

✔ **Expand Level:** Select the default expand level for this report from the drop-down list. You can always change the expand level from the results page.

✔ **Owner:** Administrators can change the owner of a report by selecting a name from the drop-down list.

Audience

Specifying an audience for the report determines who can view it. Set the audience for the report by selecting values from the following four lists:

✔ Roles

✔ Employees

✔ Groups

✔ Partners

You can choose the Select All option above any of the Audience lists to make the report available to everyone on it. Click an individual value in a list to select it, or Shift+click (⌘+click for Macs) to select multiple values from any list.

Using the Financial Report Builder

Financial reports are highly-structured, formal documents bound by laws, rules, and norms. No one should attempt to edit or create financial reports in NetSuite without the close supervision of an experienced accounting professional. The permissions to use the Financial Report Builder should only be granted to someone with an accounting background, or the designee of someone with an accounting background. Although Administrators automatically have the required permissions to create and edit financial reports, they should leave this task to, or seek the direction of, a qualified individual. In any case, senior management should always be made well-aware of any changes, additions or deletions in the financial reporting system of the company.

Although financial reports for other countries are included in NetSuite OneWorld, this section focuses on the U.S. versions. U.S. financial reports that are included with NetSuite conform to Generally-Accepted Accounting Principles (GAAP) as established by the Financial Accounting Standards Board (FASB). GAAP-compliance, however, doesn't guarantee that the reports will satisfy every company's specific issues. Various factors affect how financial details are laid out on balance sheets, cash flow statements, and income statements, including industry norms and practices, state rules and regulations, governing bodies such as the Securities and Exchange Commission (SEC), and Federal law, not the least of which is the Sarbanes-Oxley Act of 2002 (SOX). In other words, there are a lot of cooks in this kitchen, so NetSuite has wisely included a quick and easy way of editing these documents to help address all of their tastes.

Accessing the Financial Report Builder

You require both the Financial Statements permission and the Report Customization permission in order to edit financial statements in NetSuite. Once you have these permissions, there are several ways to access the Financial Report Builder:

- ✔ **From the Reports tab menu, choose New Financial Report.** Click the name of a financial statement type on the list on the New Financial Report - Select Financial Statement page.

- ✔ **From the Reports tab menu, choose Financial.** Select a financial statement from the submenu, and click its Customize link. Most, but not all, reports listed here will open in the Financial Report Builder. A few will open in the regular Report Builder.

- ✔ **From the Reports tab menu, choose Banking/Budgeting.** Select a document from the submenu and click its Customize link. Most, but not all, reports listed here will open in the Financial Report Builder. A few will open in the regular Report Builder.

- ✔ **Run a financial statement.** On the results page, click the Customize button.

- ✔ **From the Reports tab menu, choose Financial⇨Row Layout Assignment.** Click Customize or Edit next to a financial statement.

- ✔ **Click the Edit link next to any saved financial statement on the Reports page under Saved Reports.**

Editing a financial report

The first page that you land on in the Financial Report Builder is the Edit Layout page. The existence of the Edit Layout page is the primary difference between the Report Builder and the Financial Report Builder. Figure 21-9 shows the Edit Layout page for a balance sheet. The other links, Edit Columns, Filtering, Sorting and More Options are identical between the two.

The reason for two different report builders is simple: Each type of report (regular and financial) has different layout requirements.

✔ **Regular reports** use the same layout options for all rows/sections, usually hierarchical with subtotals.

✔ **Financial reports** need more complex layouts with different types of grouping to accommodate the nested sections within many financial reports, as well as calculated rows, special text, complex filtering, and so forth

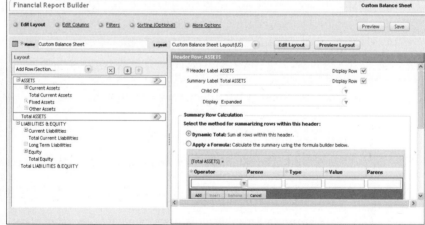

Figure 21-9: The Edit Layout page is the first page you reach in the Financial Report Builder.

Only some fields can be edited:

✔ **Name field:** It's populated with default text. Change this or accept it, as you wish.

✔ **Layout field:** If other fields on this page aren't editable, choose a different custom layout from this drop-down list. The layout on this page may be a standard layout, a custom layout shared by multiple custom financial statements, or a non-shared custom layout which is only used in one custom financial statement. When customizing a standard financial statement, its standard layout is copied to a new, editable layout automatically.

You can't edit a standard layout. When a shared custom layout is open on the Edit Layout page, all editing functions are disabled until you click the Edit Layout button. When you click this button on a standard layout, a pop-up window asks for the new name for this custom layout (with a default name supplied). The standard layout is then copied to a new layout which you can edit.

To rename a layout:

1. **From the Reports tab menu, choose Financial⇨Financial Row Layouts.**

2. **Click Enable Editing.**

   Only custom financial report names will become editable.

3. **Select the custom financial report you would like to change and type the new name.**

Below Name and Layout options are two editing panes.

Layout pane options

The first one on the left is the Layout pane. This pane acts like an outline of your report and serves a similar purpose for the row layout in a financial report as the Report Preview does for column layout. The following options are available in the Layout pane:

✔ **Add Row/Section drop-down list:** If this type of financial report accepts additional rows or sections, then this drop-down list will be enabled. The types of rows or sections that can be added include:

  • **Header and Summary Rows:** Header rows are linked to summary rows and are used to aggregate related child rows of data contained between them. Summary rows can dynamically sum all row amounts, or calculate the rows based on a more complex formula.

  • **Financial Section:** Financial sections are subsets of data on a financial report that consist of header, detail and summary rows.

  • **Formula Row:** Formula rows calculate data from other rows in a financial statement.

  • **Text Row:** A text row can display static text, such as a footnote, or be used to insert a blank line between sections of a financial statement.

  • **Add Reference Row:** Use a reference row in a Balance Sheet or Cash Flow Statement to insert a value referenced from a section or row in another financial statement.

✔ **Delete button:** This button deletes the selected row or section.

✔ **Mover buttons:** These buttons move a selection up or down in the layout hierarchy:

  • **Move Up**

  • **Move Down**

Edit pane options

Below the Move Up and Move Down buttons is the Row/Section layout for this financial statement. Click a row in the layout to select it for editing in the Edit pane on the right. Notice that when you select a section header, it's accompanying summary row is automatically selected also.

The Edit pane will change depending on the type of row or section selected in the Layout pane. Some of the tasks that can be completed for each row/section type follow.

Header and Summary rows

For header and summary row in the report, you can determine how and whether it appears as follows:

- Edit the Header and Summary row labels.
- Choose whether to display Header or Summary rows.
- Specify if this section is nested in another section.
- Specify the expand level for this section.
- Choose whether the summary row will display a dynamic total (an automatic formula that sums everything between the header/summary rows). Choosing Apply a Formula allows you to define a custom formula for the summary row instead.
- Set formatting options for the Header and Summary rows, including font, line, and color.

Financial section

For each financial section of the report, you can

- Edit the Header row labels for the section.
- Specify if this section is nested in another section.
- Specify the expand level for this section.
- Determine primary and secondary grouping of the data in the financial section. Usually financial sections are automatically grouped by account.
- Set formatting options for the Header, Total, and Account rows within the section, including font, line, and color.
- Set the sort order for the accounts listed on the report.

Account section

For each account section you can

- Edit the Header row labels for the section.
- Specify if this section is nested in another section.

✔ Specify the expand level for this section.

✔ Determine primary and secondary grouping of the data in this account section.

Usually financial sections are automatically grouped by account.

✔ Define which transactions will be reflected in this financial report. Specify individual accounts, a dynamic list of accounts, or combinations of account, class, department, location, customer, or item that will filter the transactions that show up in this section.

By setting a dynamic list of accounts, you can include all accounts of a particular type, such as Income, so that whenever a new Income account is created it will automatically appear on the report. However, you may have several groupings of Income accounts you want to show in different financial sections. If one group of these income accounts is numbered in the 4000s, you can set a Section criteria of *Account Number starts with 4* so whenever you create a new general ledger account within that numbering, it will automatically get picked up in the correct section in your financials.

✔ Set formatting options for the Header, Total, and Account rows within the section, including font, line and color.

✔ Set the sort order for the accounts listed on the report.

Formula row

To further specify a Formula row

✔ Edit the Formula row labels.

✔ Specify if this row is nested in another section.

✔ Set formatting options for the Formula row, including font, line, and color.

✔ Create the formula by specifying the following three options:

- A math operator
- Whether the value is a constant or another row
- The actual constant or row to use

As many calculation lines as necessary can be added to the formula. Parentheses can also be specified to identify the order of operations.

Text row

To add information to a Text row

✔ Edit the text for this row.

✔ Specify if this row is nested in another section.

✔ Set formatting options for the text row, including font, line, and color.

Reference row

For Reference rows, you can

✔ Edit the Reference row labels.

✔ Specify if this row is nested in another section.

✔ Choose the financial report and row from which to reference the data.

✔ Select the relative date range for which the data should be referenced. The referenced date range is defined relative to the date range for the current financial statement. When the date range for the current financial statement is changed, the date range for the referenced field changes accordingly.

✔ Set formatting options for this row, including font, line, and color.

To commit all of your changes, click Save. To see the results of your changes, click Preview. The results page for a financial report behaves identically to other reports.

See "Running Reports" earlier in this chapter for more information about the Report Results page.

Part VII
The Part of Tens

The 5th Wave   By Rich Tennant

"Bad news – Buddy flipped the van, spilling eight crates of samples into rush-hour traffic. Good news – the van flipped logo-side up."

In this part . . .

Many good things come in The Part of Tens. Here you find ten differentiators for NetSuite, ten tips for a successful implementation, and ten frequently asked questions. Okay, in some cases there are 12. We couldn't help ourselves.

Chapter 22

Ten-Plus Key Differentiators

*W*hat makes NetSuite different? How will you love it? Let us count the ways.

Full-Circle Order Processing

Where other applications provide only one piece of the puzzle, such as generating leads, NetSuite handles every part of the order process. You can import a lead list, e-mail the list to drive them to your site (also created in NetSuite), and have them automatically converted to customers when they buy something in your site. You'll then find the sales order already there in your account, where you can approve it, fulfill it, and invoice it. And the accounting for all these steps is taken care of for you!

Even better, you can then replenish your stock by reordering the items you sold; you then receive the items and pay the bill. If the customer has any problems or questions, he can submit a support case, which you can track in NetSuite, and you can process a return or refund if necessary. Furthermore, all this information about the client is viewable by looking at the customer record for that client.

Your Web Site and Your Back Office: Together at Last

The Web opened whole new markets for companies, but the software running Web sites and the software running the back office weren't integrated. With NetSuite, your Web shop and your accounting are all one big happy family, with Web shops and profit and loss statements living happily as one.

Make NetSuite Suit You

No matter what you want to customize in NetSuite, from the names of the fields to the colors on the screens, everything's up for grabs. You can change it to suit just how you do business — enabling features, renaming fields, adding custom fields, and just generally tailoring NetSuite until it's a perfect fit. Also, much of the customization can be done by business users; you don't have to be a technogeek to change it up.

Data and Analytics, Delivered

NetSuite's powerful analytics features range from the dashboards where you monitor important indicators at a glance to saved searches that help you find just the information you need. Call it business intelligence for everyman (and woman). Your data analysts will be happy for two reasons: First, they can get all their data hungers met with powerful capabilities (like embedded SQL); they'll also be happy because you won't be asking them for help all the time. Analytics and reporting become self-service, letting people answer their own questions and leaving the hard stuff to analysts.

Bring Me Your Tired, Your Weary, Your Data

Like the Statue of Liberty, NetSuite welcomes all the data in. You can import files from Quickbooks (using an option called "Send Us Your Quickbooks File") or from any platform using comma-separated variable (CSV) format. So whether you buy a mailing list or want to import items from a new vendor, you can easily bring your data into NetSuite — no typing skills required. The feature you need here is called the CSV Import tool. For more information on this important tool, see Chapter 2.

Rolling Up Is Just as Fast as Rolling Down

Consolidating monthly and quarterly results can be tricky and time consuming. Add the complexity of mergers and acquisitions and see if you can improve your time to close. Not likely.

Amazingly, with NetSuite you can. Consolidation is faster and more flexible than with any other major ERP software package on the market today. You won't dread end-of-month and end-of-quarter any more, whether you're consolidating results from one company or 100 subsidiaries in 5 regions. (That last bit applies to users of NetSuite OneWorld, the multicurrency version of NetSuite for companies that do business globally.)

Hey, What's That?

How many times have you looked at a screen and said to yourself, "What the heck does *that* do?" The good news is that in NetSuite, clicking a field name reveals the answer to that question. Plus, if you click the Help link (in the top right of every screen), NetSuite tries to take you to just the page you need based on where you were when you clicked. And while we're on the topic of help, did we mention that the Help system has more than 1.5 million words and more than 3,600 topics, all wonderfully searchable? (We looked up a lot of pretty obscure things while writing this book, and we found every single topic, preference, or option we wanted to know about in the Help Center.) And in case you don't see a feature we mention in this book, searching for that feature in the Help system will show you whether that feature has been enabled in your account. Help isn't static; it tailors itself to your account setup and your role. Such a sensitive Help system!

Get Me Where I Need to Go — Now

Often you work on something and that isn't the end of it. You change an employee record, and the employee wants something else updated. You work on an opportunity, and more activities need to be recorded. NetSuite feels your pain and puts something quick and easy on your home dashboard so you can get back there quickly.

The Recent Records portlet is a handy, clickable list of the records you've touched most recently. Another usability feature we love is typeahead. Start typing a customer's name, and NetSuite comes back with completions. Most applications don't do that, so getting used to this feature may result in being miffed at other applications that aren't as helpful.

In the Cloud, but Locked Down

The best part of NetSuite security is definitely something you can't see: NetSuite's data centers are bastions of corporate security. They have SAS 70 Type II Compliance, a security certification that's extremely difficult to qualify for. (Most security admins just give up and go home after they realize how rigorous the certification process is; few companies get this certification on their own.) If anyone ever audits you (heaven forbid), you can point directly to NetSuite's SAS 70 Type II Compliance and call that security level your own. Also, NetSuite implements the Payment Card Industry Data Security Standards (PCI DSS), a best practice for locking down e-commerce transactions that flow through your NetSuite Web site.

Bonus Chapter 6 provides some great advice about security that you can set up in NetSuite. Visit **www.dummies.com/go/netsuitefd**.

Roles and Permissions

Because NetSuite holds every part of your business data, it's important to limit who has access to what. You don't want salespeople with information about everyone's payroll history, for example. NetSuite's fully customizable roles let you control who can see what parts of your data; that way they can use the resources they need for their job but nothing more. Customers, vendors, and partners all have roles to view their own data securely.

Don't Just Sell Products — Sell Projects!

Project management comes in three sizes within NetSuite: small, medium, and large.

In the small size, you don't need to sign up for any additional functionality. You simply start tracking tasks and time, albeit separately from each other. You can relate the two by upgrading to medium functionality when you turn on Projects on the Enable Features page and create customer-specific Work Breakdown Structures (WBS). But, wait, there's more! If you turn on Advanced Projects, you can set up full-featured projects and subprojects complete with scheduling and Gantt charts. If you want to go extra large, take advantage of NetSuite's integration with (and ownership of) a product called OpenAir, a professional services automation suite for project-based businesses.

Work-Life Balance

The more ways you can make sure your work gets done, the more time you have for writing your Great American Novel or going to your kids' soccer games. Here are some of the ways that NetSuite helps you get stuff done:

- **Carry it with you.** NetSuite integrates with your browser (of course) but you can also access your account from the iPhone, Palm, or BlackBerry.

- **Glance at your dashboard.** The Reminders portlet helps make sure every process gets completed.

- **E-mail yourself.** You can have saved searches and reports e-mailed to you on a schedule or even e-mail yourself a snapshot of your dashboard.

- **Check your Outlook.** NetSuite integrates with Microsoft Outlook, so any e-mail that comes to your inbox can go right to the appropriate record in NetSuite; calendar entries can also be synced with Outlook.

Chapter 23

Ten Tips for a Successful Implementation

*Y*ou need to keep a number of things in mind when you're implementing NetSuite, and many vary depending on your company type and the features that you plan to use. Regardless of the type, size, or features you use in NetSuite, however, the advice in this chapter helps you achieve a smooth transition and future success.

Consider Investing in Hired Help

Whether you choose NetSuite Professional Services or a NetSuite partner, getting professional implementation help from someone with extensive NetSuite experience and proven implementation methods is well worth your money.

Try to choose services from someone who has worked with a variety of business types and sizes to be sure that your needs are considered.

Professional and consulting services probably cost less up front than you might think, and the consultant can apply project-management skills, give you a realistic time estimate, and almost certainly prevent a major mistake or two that would otherwise cost you time or money down the road.

Know Your Requirements

It's important to know your business requirements and know whether each area of NetSuite — specifically CRM and ERP — fits your company. NetSuite is extremely customizable, but you must be aware of your company's exact needs so that NetSuite or an implementation partner can assess what NetSuite can do for you. Also keep in mind that your business requirements shouldn't necessarily equal your business processes — focus on what you need an end result in order to achieve results. There may be multiple ways to meet your goals.

Be Open Minded

Taking advantage of a completely integrated product that can serve all of your business needs in one place may require a change in your current processes and workflows. We strongly encourage you to remain open minded, even if it means changing the way you've always done things. After all, why look for a new solution if you're only interested in doing things the way you always have? Become intimately familiar with the best practices of NetSuite, and you can start letting go of the best practices used with your previous tool.

Heed Advice

This may go without saying, but if you a hire professional service or an implementation partner to help you, heed her advice! She's been there and done that, and she knows that down the road you'll be calling her, begging for a bail out when things go awry.

NetSuite can be easy to set up and fun to experiment with. However, most actions in the system have an equal and opposite reaction, so if you aren't aware of the accounting implications of the processes you're using (or the experiments you're running), you're likely to need some help figuring out just where things got tangled up.

Get What You Pay For

We hate to see people buy NetSuite and only use it for one part of their business while paying for separate sales, marketing, or Web solutions. Unless there is a unique situation where a feature can't meet your business requirements, you should absolutely use NetSuite to its fullest potential and take advantage of the One System model.

The uniqueness of NetSuite is the automation that occurs between your Web, CRM, and ERP without you having to customize integration between programs or install software on multiple machines. Capitalize on your investment and get the full experience with NetSuite by using all the features that apply to your business needs.

Remember That Time Is on Your Side

Be sure to set reasonable time expectations for moving into NetSuite. Often, implementing an entirely new software solution can be like building a house: Whatever the initial time estimate is, you are wise to double it! Setting unreasonable time constraints on something this important is likely to lead to dissatisfaction — something you definitely want to avoid. You need requirements and processes defined, customization and scripting added, data imported, and training, training, training. The time estimate isn't only for a hired professional but also for your internal resources while you assist in the process and learn the new system.

Know the Possibilities

NetSuite is extremely customizable — you can customize records, forms, fields, scripting, and even more with Web services. Before you assume that something can't be done or something doesn't fit your needs, check out what's possible with customization. You can add and remove fields on pages, create completely new pages, create new roles with custom access to pages and forms, and do endless things for processes and workflows. You also can pull out data in pretty much any way you can think of with custom reports and saved searches — and have that data e-mailed to you regularly.

Many partners have their own solutions built on NetSuite, which you can sift through at www.suiteapp.com. With a quick search or post in the NetSuite User Community, you may also find that someone else has done the legwork for you and knows how to do just what you need to accomplish in NetSuite.

Keep Your Training Wheels On

Investing in training not only improves your satisfaction with NetSuite, but ensures you're using NetSuite to its fullest potential and prevents you from having to change things later. Company-wide training can ensure that everyone is on the same page with processes and adoption. Similar to the implementation advice, whatever you think you need, double it! And when training is over, you can still keep going with additional training courses as well as free training. Make sure you keep up to date with new releases by checking out Release Notes, Help, NetSuite Central, the NetSuite User Community, and NetSuite's newsletters and webcasts.

Keep It Simple

One major mistake is customers having more features available than they need. You can be overwhelmed and slowed by too many features, pages, and fields in your NetSuite account.

After you establish your needs and ensure you're making the most of NetSuite's complete integration, turn off any features that you know you won't need. This helps simplify your workspace and makes it easier to find what you need. Additionally, if the default roles in NetSuite don't quite match the roles of your employees, take advantage of the ability to customize roles so employees don't have to sift through pages they don't need.

Take Baby Steps

When implementing NetSuite, it's best to take it slow and roll out your conversion in stages. Change management is a big factor, and even with the best of systems and planning, you don't want everything to change overnight. We recommend you start with back-office changes, such as accounting and inventory management, and then roll out more customer-facing features, such as order management, customer records, customer access online, and your Web site. Also, heed your users! Get them involved early and give them a sense of ownership and ability to make the UI work for them.

Chapter 24

Ten Frequently Asked Questions

*T*eachers say it again and again: There's no such thing as a silly question. If one person has a question, ten more probably do too. Here are ten of the most frequently asked questions we get at NetSuite. (Plus you get the answers too, at no additional charge!)

How do I log in?

Signing into NetSuite is easy:

1. **Go to** www.netsuite.com.

2. **Click Customer Login.**

   The words appear near the top of the screen.

   If you've logged in before, enter your username (usually your work e-mail address) and password.

3. **(Optional) Select the Remember My E-mail Address check box.**

   This way you don't have to fill in your username the next time you log in. You'll have to enter your password every time no matter what.

4. **Click Login and away you go!**

How can I add something to my shortcuts?

You can add two types of links to the Shortcuts portlet on your home dashboard:

- ✔ A link to a page within NetSuite.
- ✔ A link to an external Web page (that should cover all the bases!)

Add a NetSuite page to your Shortcuts portlet this way:

1. **Go to the NetSuite page you'd like to add as a shortcut.**
2. **Click the Add to Shortcuts link.**

   The link is in the upper-right corner of the screen.

   The Add Shortcut dialog box opens.
3. **Type a name for the shortcut.**

   Or you can accept the default.
4. **Click Save.**

If the page you want to link to in NetSuite is one of the few without the Add to Shortcuts link, you can still add it by following the procedure for adding an external Web page:

1. **Click the New Shortcut link.**

   The link is near the bottom of your Shortcuts portlet.

   The Add Shortcut dialog box opens.
2. **Type a name for this shortcut.**
3. **In the URL field, type (or copy and paste) the URL for the shortcut.**
4. **Click Save.**

You can't add duplicate NetSuite pages to the Shortcuts portlet. If you try to save an existing shortcut under a new name it will overwrite the existing shortcut, because NetSuite uses the actual page name or URL as a unique identifier for the shortcut. NetSuite is one smart cookie — you must admit.

How can I e-mail an invoice to someone who isn't the main contact?

If you interact with someone who needs a copy of an invoice (or sales order or quote), you can e-mail it to him quickly just by filling in an e-mail address, typing a quick message, and attaching the invoice.

1. **Open the document he needs a copy of.**
2. **Click the Messages tab.**
3. **Click the Email button.**

   An Email Message dialog box opens.

4. **Type in an e-mail address for the recipient on the Recipients tab.**

   Or, if one is available, accept the default e-mail address.

   Add some addresses, such as yours, to CC if you like.

5. **Click the Message tab.**
6. **Complete the Subject field and type a message in the Message box.**
7. **Click the Attachments tab.**
8. **Select the Include Attachments check box.**
9. **Click the Merge & Send button**

The button's near the top of the window. Away that invoice (or sales order or purchase order or quote) goes!

The message you sent now appears on the history for this record; NetSuite automatically keeps track of messages you send this way.

How can I add something to my dashboard?

Dashboard items appear in portlets.

To add a portlet to your dashboard:

1. **Click Customize This Page on the page where you want the portlet to appear.**

   The Add Content dialog box opens.

2. **Select the portlet type.**

Many types of portlets (Calendar, Tasks, and Reminders) present useful data when you put them on your dashboard. Chapter 20 covers the dashboard in detail and Chapter 4 describes personalizing many aspects of NetSuite, including your dashboard.

Why don't I see that field/screen/option?

The fields, screens, and options you see in NetSuite depend on a few different factors:

- ✔ Your role in NetSuite
- ✔ The form being used (whether a standard or custom form)
- ✔ The features turned on in your account
- ✔ Cool customizations that someone has created for your account

NetSuite is wonderfully malleable, and you can make it fit your needs exactly. This flexibility means that things don't always look the same for everyone.

Great news though: NetSuite's help is not only context sensitive, but configuration sensitive. It knows what options you have enabled in your account and the permissions for your role. For example, if you search for a preference, the menu path tells you how to get there from your account and your current role. Click Help in the upper-right corner, and when the NetSuite Help Center opens, tell it what you're looking for.

How can I send marketing e-mail that isn't marked as spam?

You send an e-mail to a prospect, and what happens? You hit her spam filter, and your valuable offer is never received.

How can you avoid having your e-mail marked as spam? The best practice is to set up a campaign domain (marketing.*yourcompany*.com) and set up DomainKeys Identified Mail (DKIM), which marks your e-mail as coming from a reputable marketer (not a Nigerian who needs to use a U.S. bank account). NetSuite requires DKIM for companies that send more than 10,000 marketing e-mails a month, but it is highly recommended for everyone. For step-by-step information on how to send marketing e-mail, see Chapter 11.

Why are there repeated lines in my search results?

WARNING!

Any time a search record or transaction record has multiple lines, you can wind up with repeated lines in your search results for that transaction.

NetSuite generously wants to give you everything in your search results. But you may want just the main line for any transaction.

1. **From the Reports tab menu choose New Search⇨Transaction.**

   There are other methods for getting to the Main Line option, but this is a surefire way.

   The New Transaction Search dialog box opens.

2. **Look for a Main Line option.**

   It has radio buttons that say Yes, No, or Either.

3. **Click the Yes radio button.**

This restricts your search to main lines and avoids repeated results.

You can also avoid repeated lines by including **Main Line = True** in your search filters.

When a record can map to more than one result, you'll see that result more than once. If you include an address in a report, and the customer has multiple addresses, you'll see multiple lines. The solution in this case is to limit the search to a more specific field (default shipping address or default billing address, for example).

How can I open a new window while keeping the same session?

The answer to this question is probably something you already know: Right-click any link on your NetSuite window to open it in a new window or a new tab — two NetSuite windows for the price of one. You never have to leave your current NetSuite window to do this. You simply right-click a link, and there you go.

How can I get an audit trail?

The trails in NetSuite are plentiful. Most records in NetSuite provide their own audit trail: a record of who added them, changed them, or e-mailed them, for example. (If Fred tries to take credit for Wilma's sale, you can see just who did what by looking at the history on the Sales Order, for example.) Check out the History tab on any transaction or the General tab on any record, and look over their tabs. The System Notes tab shows you who created and updated the transaction or record and when (which is important from a control perspective).

But for a big-picture audit trail, administrators (and others with big-shot permissions) can get an audit trail this way:

1. **From the Transactions tab menu choose Management⇨View Audit Trail.**

2. **Click the Submit button.**

You get a complete audit trail of all changes or narrow your selections by user, transaction type, action type (create, change, or even delete), account, and date range. Sherlock Holmes loves this.

How can I control which fields and columns print on a form?

It's up to you to decide which items print on a form (if your role permits such changes).

1. **From the Setup tab menu, choose Customization⇨Transaction Forms.**

2. **Click Customize or Edit next to your preferred form.**

3. **On the Lists tab, select or clear Show check boxes for each field on the transaction form.**

You can make more advanced changes by editing the PDF layout from the Setup tab menu by choosing Customization⇨Transactions⇨PDF Layouts.

Index

• R •

reading
  A/P information in vendor records, 103
  A/R information in customer record, 93–94
reassigning
  cases, 238–239
  customers, 170–171
  leads, 170–171
  prospects, 170–171
receiving
  electronic payments, 105
  purchase orders, 126
reconciling accounts, 79–82
recording
  customer payments, 89–90
  deposits, 71–72
  opportunities, 183–185
  vendor bills, 100–102
records
  accessing information in, 43
  adding from list page, 44
  attaching events to, 50
  campaign, 142–143
  changing from list page, 44
  Create New toolbar, 42
  creating new, 41–42
  customer
    activities on, 192–193
    contacts on, 191–192
    files on, 194–195
    Marketing tab, 195–196
    messages on, 194
    overview, 191
    projects, 195
    subcustomers, 195
    time tracking, 195
    Upsell tab, 195–196
    user notes on, 193–194
  customizing, 31
  defined, 10
  finding, 397
  lead, 182–183
  locating using lists, 43–44
  overview, 40–41
  renaming, 24–25
  sorting, 405–406
redirects, 137, 323, 330–331

Referrer Reports, 335
registers
  account, 64–65
  bank, 78–79, 80–82
registration (shopper), 307–309
relating items, 283–284
Reminders, 53
removing
  Customer Center form fields, 243–245
  portlets, 54–55
renaming
  records, 24–25
  report layouts, 411
  transactions, 24–25
reorder point, 127
replenishing inventory, 127
Report Preview pane (reports), 402
report snapshots
  adding Report Snapshot portlet to
    dashboard, 387
  overview, 53, 386
  setting up Report Snapshot portlets,
    387–388
reporting
  on accounts payable, 104
  on accounts receivable, 94–96
  on inventory, 129–130
  overview, 18
  on reconciliation, 82
Reporting/Search settings, 29
reports
  accessing, 393
  analytics, 335
  A/R Aging Summary, 95
  A/R Payment History by Invoice, 96
  A/R Payment History by Payment, 96
  basic, 334
  Cart Abandonment, 334
  collapsing data in, 395
  customizing
    adding formula columns to reports,
      403–404
    editing columns, 401–403
    filtering data, 404–405
    overview, 400–401
    setting options, 407–408
    sorting records, 405–406
  detail, 394–395